Holistic Treatment

McFarland Health Topics

Holistic Treatment in Mental Health

A Handbook of Practitioners' Perspectives

Edited by CHERYL L. FRACASSO,
STANLEY KRIPPNER *and* HARRIS L. FRIEDMAN

Foreword by Kirwan Rockefeller

MCFARLAND HEALTH TOPICS
Series Editor Elaine A. Moore

McFarland & Company, Inc., Publishers
Jefferson, North Carolina

Advances in Parapsychological Research 10 (Edited by Stanley Krippner, Adam J. Rock, Harris L. Friedman and Nancy L. Zingrone, 2020)

Advances in Parapsychological Resarch 9 (Edited by Stanley Krippner, Adam J. Rock, Julie Beischel, Harris L. Friedman and Cheryl L. Fracasso, 2013)

Advances in Parapsychological Research 8 (Edited by Stanley Krippner. Managing editors Steven Hart and Elizabeth Schneck. Associate Editors Montague Ullman and Robert O. Becker, 1997)

Advances in Parapsychological Research 7 (Edited by Stanley Krippner, 1994)

Advances in Parapsychological Research 6 (Edited by Stanley Krippner, 1990)

Advances in Parapsychological Research 5 (Edited by Stanley Krippner, 1987)

Advances in Parapsychological Research 4 (Edited by Stanley Krippner, 1984)

LIBRARY OF CONGRESS CATALOGUING-IN-PUBLICATION DATA

Names: Fracasso, Cheryl L., editor. | Krippner, Stanley, 1932– editor. | Friedman, Harris L., editor. | Rockefeller, Kirwan, writer of foreword.
Title: Holistic treatment in mental health : a handbook of practitioner's perspectives / edited by Cheryl L. Fracasso, Stanley Krippner and Harris L. Friedman ; foreword by Kirwan Rockefeller.
Description: Jefferson, North Carolina : McFarland & Company, Inc., Publishers, 2020 | Series: McFarland health topics | Includes bibliographical references and index.
Identifiers: LCCN 2020033706 | ISBN 9781476669939 (paperback : acid free paper ∞)) ISBN 9781476640051 (ebook)
Subjects: LCSH: Holistic medicine. | Mind and body therapies. | Clinical psychology. | Mental illness—Alternative treatment.
Classification: LCC R733 .H648 2020 | DDC 610—dc23
LC record available at https://lccn.loc.gov/2020033706

BRITISH LIBRARY CATALOGUING DATA ARE AVAILABLE

ISBN (print) 978-1-4766-6993-9
ISBN (ebook) 978-1-4766-4005-1

Front cover image of holistic practitioner's hands © 2020 Shutterstock

Printed in the United States of America

McFarland & Company, Inc., Publishers
Box 611, Jefferson, North Carolina 28640
www.mcfarlandpub.com

We dedicate this book to Albert Ellis and his pioneering work in the field of psychotherapy. The essay written by his wife, Debbie Joffe Ellis, celebrates the memory of his many important contributions and their lasting impact on the field of psychotherapy and, more widely, holistic healing. Thank you, Debbie, for sharing your personal reflections on Al with our readers!

Acknowledgments

We thank all the authors who contributed essays to this book. A thank you is also in order to Kirwan Rockefeller who wrote its foreword, and to Debbie Joffe Ellis who wrote an essay in memory of Albert Ellis. Special thanks also are in order to Rosemary Coffey, Steve Hart, and Jessica Piller for their invaluable editorial assistance and tremendous attention to final details. The preparation of this book was supported by the Floraglades Foundation, the AUM Foundation, and a generous grant from Richard and Connie Adams, whom we all thank dearly.

Table of Contents

Foreword

KIRWAN ROCKEFELLER

It was a hot, very hot, humid summer day and it wasn't yet noon. This was the kind of day when I was bare-chested and barefoot as young boys often are, out and about exploring the neighborhood. I was five years old and my parents bought a new upright freezer. This was in the days when frequently a refrigerator and a freezer were separate items. The old, disconnected freezer was left at the back of the house to be picked up when the new one was delivered and installed. My next-door neighbor and best friend Buddy and I were playing Superman. There wasn't anything Superman couldn't do. In fact, Superman could run faster, jump higher, knock down solid doors and even burst through walls. I wanted to be like Superman, because best of all, he could fly. Buddy and I took turns swinging on the door of the old freezer, getting close inside, and just before the door closed, bursting out and for a brief moment flying through the air, yelling "Superman!"

After we played all morning, Buddy was called home to lunch. But I didn't want to stop playing. I continued swinging back and forth on the door, and for some reason, no doubt pretending I was Superman, I decided to climb into the freezer. In fact, into the lowest part, below one of the shelves. The door slammed shut and locked. When I tried to kick open the door with my Superman yell, it wouldn't budge. I was trapped inside.

The memories, visual images, and feelings are still crystal clear to my mind today, over sixty years later. It was pitch black inside. The shelf pressed against my back, legs, and sides, hard and unmoving. There wasn't any room for me to maneuver inside. I could feel the walls of the freezer closing in on me. I was crouched down inside on all fours. I screamed. I yelled. I cried. I lashed out, hitting the sides and anything I could with my fists and feet. I vomited, soiled myself and distinctly remember being backed into a corner and no matter how hard I fought, I couldn't get out. I passed out.

Then, as if by some sort of strange magic, I flew out of my body. Faster than I could comprehend, I felt myself shoot out the top of my head like a rocket, straight up into the sky. It was exhilarating. All I cared about was that suddenly, I was flying just like Superman. I remember briefly looking back at my body trapped in the freezer and thinking how odd it was. While it took many years for my adult mind to begin to understand and interpret what I was experiencing as a child, I distinctly remember funny people, dogs, cats and all kind of animals flying around with me. The sky was blue and cool, not a cloud in the sky. It was effortless, delightful, and I was soaring upward with each breath, zipping around. I was content to be out of the freezer and flying. After, what seemed to

1

be several minutes, I came to notice a bright light directly in front of me. I made a beeline directly to the light. This light was inviting, loving, warm, and glorious, and I paid no thought to the seemingly lifeless crumpled form whenever I turned to look back behind me. I had no time for that lifelessness because I was on an adventure.

As I soared upward, my adult mind recalls a voice saying abruptly to my child mind, "Nope. Not yet. Not your time. Go back."

As instantaneously as I had flown out of my body, I now came crashing back into the crumpled form with a thump. The next thing I remember is opening my eyes and being startled looking up into the beautiful, blue sky, not sure where I was, yet soiled, drenched from sweat, coughing, gasping, and disoriented. Somehow I was outside the freezer and lying on the grass. My sisters had been looking out for me that day, and since it was lunchtime they had gone around the neighborhood calling my name. As they walked back to the house, and as they describe to this day, for whatever reason they decided to open the freezer door. I rolled out, unconscious and blue. Not knowing what to do, and with both Mom and Dad away from home, they pulled my body out to the green grass. I was back.

Now, the point of this story is not so much in the actual occurrence, but how, well into my twenties and thirties, it played a significant and often unconscious role in my life, affecting my beliefs and behavior. I began to realize this childhood experience propelled me on a lifelong quest of discovery. Gradually, and by using many of the tools and techniques described in this book and with the help of qualified professionals, I realized that whenever I was metaphorically or symbolically backed into a corner or felt there was no way out, I would come out swinging with all my might, and when that didn't work, I would shut down emotionally. I didn't have the confidence to find my way out of tight or uncomfortable situations. When I wanted to explore the world, my thinking was, "Don't—you'll get boxed into a corner and you won't be able to get out." Along with this self-limiting belief, the image of a stark black monolith always appeared before me: unyielding, ominous, and literally taking my breath away. Consequently, when I had outgrown a situation such as a job or relationship, I frequently felt up against a hard wall and stuck. My belief was clearly, when in a tight spot, I felt I couldn't manage my way to safety or freedom.

As I grew older, instinctively, I began to explore more of the tools and techniques offered by the collaborators in this book, for an active-directive and multi-modal, holistic approach to navigating what this meant and who I was to become. I explored the expressive arts of dance/movement, art, soul collage, drama, holotropic breathwork, guided imagery, hypnosis, drumming, meditation, yoga, active imagination, a variety of bodywork modalities, and informal and formal spiritual practices, all in an attempt to make meaning of what I had experienced as a child and what increasingly came to feel as a "call to action" to move beyond limiting beliefs and make sense of what had transpired, and in doing so, to share my story with others. I also participated in a host of psychotherapeutic approaches, including cognitive-behavioral, existential, humanistic psychology, modern analytical, transpersonal, and object-relations modalities to help put a framework to my lived experience.

It was only in my late thirties, as my personal excursions began to closely intersect with my professional and academic evolution, did I come to recognize that my search for holistic modalities were those that soothed the body, calmed the mind, and lifted the spirit, and were a whole-person approach. As I explored, I sought to make sense out of something that had been essentially senseless at first, yet had a profound impact on my identity. Why did this happen to me? Why did I return? Why was I was on the planet? Was it part of a plan? Or, was it simply something to be forgotten?

I began to realize there was a deeper purpose to this experience as a young boy and there was nothing to be afraid of, as I shared my path with others who were navigating their own questions. My evolving academic research in the early 1990s on multiple loss, reoccurring bereavement, and survivor guilt within the AIDS epidemic demonstrated that humans have a thirst for expressing what they are experiencing. And as care providers, we seek ways to alleviate their suffering, reframe an experience, while integrating split aspects of our identities, ultimately lessening distress.

The editors of *Holistic Treatment in Mental Health*, Cheryl L. Fracasso, Stanley Krippner, and Harris L. Friedman are stellar, award-winning colleagues who provide roadmaps, tools, and techniques for clients and practitioners that are multimodal, multidisciplinary, and multifaceted for a whole-person approach to healing. "A whole-person approach to healing represents a paradigm shift from an illness, symptom-reduction, medical model to a growth, meaning-enhancing, integrative model. This approach incorporates intention, awareness, and mindfulness as the mediating variables between cognition and behavior" (Serlin, Krippner, & Rockefeller, 2019, p. 1).

As you read through this expert compilation, you will find various approaches to healing, evidence-based research on effectiveness, and a host of disorders that will benefit from the whole-person paradigm. While technology advances in ways beyond our wildest dreams, we must not lose sight of that which makes us most human. The need to draw, paint, dance, sing, tell our stories, share with community, be in nature to lift uncertainty, while allowing our hearts and spirits to marvel at the mysteries of life—to be whole and complete, here and now, to harvest better health, make and sustain lifestyle changes that support our resiliency and growth. A whole-person approach, as described in this book, includes significance and purposefulness, within an integrative model that embraces context, emotions, attitudes, perceptions, beliefs and a spiritual dimension that helps people answer the age-old questions, "Who am I? From whence have I come? Whither shall I go?"

REFERENCE

Serlin, I., Krippner, S., & Rockefeller, K. (2019). Integrated care of the traumatized: A whole-person approach. Landam, MD: Rowman & Littlefield.

Kirwan Rockefeller, Ph.D., serves as adjunct faculty at Saybrook University, College of Integrative Medicine and Health Sciences. He is the coeditor of Integrated Care for the Traumatized *(2019),* Spirituality and Healthcare, *volume 2 of the three-volume* Whole Person Healthcare *(2007), and the author of* Visualize Confidence: How to Use Guided Imagery to Overcome Self-Doubt *(2007).*

Introduction

CHERYL L. FRACASSO, STANLEY KRIPPNER
and HARRIS L. FRIEDMAN

The term "holistic" has attained considerable currency in mental health circles, and has become a code word for a set of shared perspectives and values that have guided humanistic psychology and related approaches to mental health care in its struggle to resist dehumanizing forces that reduce individuals to just being seen as a mechanical compilation of parts and their interactions. Holism takes a broad view, whether in psychology or other disciplines that employ that term (such as biology, philosophy, and sociology), as it rests on the notion that all of a system's properties cannot be reduced (i.e., determined by) to its components alone, as any system, including the human individual, must be taken as a whole to understand it. In this way, holism competes with what is often called "atomism," the view that the composite parts and relationship between them can adequately explain and even determine the behavior of a system. In contrast, holism views the whole system, however that might be demarcated, as essential, containing emergent properties that are greater than its mere parts by virtue of being a complete whole unto itself. Thus holism and atomism, as well as other forms of reductionism, offer competing worldviews with significant implications.

Holism argues for levels of being in which higher levels have emergent properties that cannot simply be reduced to lower levels. Reductionism, in contrast, argues that the simple parts themselves can adequately explain the higher levels. These provide quite different approaches for how to best understand and be of help to people in getting on with their lives. Holism can be seen in ecology where there is an equal emphasis on the forest, not just the trees, and in physics where a photon can be seen as only a particle from a reductionist vantage or as a "wavicle," which includes its wave-like properties from a holistic vantage. In the mental health arena, humanistic psychologists, and those from other disciplines who share humanistic values and assumptions, can be seen as most likely to focus on individuals as a whole, including transpersonal psychologists who see individuals as embedded in the most inclusive of wholes, the entire cosmos.

The term holistic was popularized in the modern English language by Jan Christiaan Smuts (1926), the noted South African statesman and philosopher. He referred to this term as representing the ultimate synthesis in which the whole is greater than the sum of its parts. For Smuts, holistic described entities that are self-regulating, self-organizing, and self-ordering. The term was also used by many others, however, such as Émile Durkheim, the sociologist; Alfred Adler, the psychotherapist; and Ludwig von Bertalanffy, the general-systems theorist. However, the word holism, which is derived from the Greek word "holos," which can be translated as "all" or "entire," as well as whole, was discussed at least as far back as in Aristotle's *Metaphysics*. In this regard, holism shares an emphasis on oneness and unity, resonating with many of the world's mystical traditions, as well as with more contemporary endeavors.

As applied to our book, we focus on "holistic healing," bringing together a diverse group of authors and their approaches who operate from a holistic vantage in promoting wellness and even optimum health. We note that the etymology of the word "healing" is literally "to make whole" (see https://www.etymonline.com/word/heal). The American Psychological Association, in its official dictionary, defines holistic healing as "a health care concept based on the premise that body, mind, and spirit function as a harmonium unit and that an adverse effect on one also adversely affects the others, requiring treatment of the whole to restore the harmonious balance" (VandenBos 2007, p. 443). Holistic health is a term that has achieved great currency in the United States; for example, Myers (2019) has used it to describe wellness as the integration of "mind, body, and spirit." He notes that wellness is not static, but constantly changes from day to day, echoing Smuts' emphasis on how the term suggests that self-organization is at work. In their book, *Wellness Counseling: A Holistic Approach to Prevention and Intervention,* Jonathon Ohrt, Philip Clarke, and Abigail Conley (2019) add "emotion" and "connection" to the triad of mind, body, and spirit.

At last count, there were about 600 psychotherapies, many of which claim to be holistic. Those making this claim often emphasize they have departed from the "medical model" of mental illness in favor of a "whole person" approach that emphasizes growth, meaning-enhancing, and integration (Serlin, Krippner, & Rockefeller, 2019). In the spirit of this movement, we decided to put out a call for proposals, asking prospective authors to describe holistic treatments: "interventions that take the whole person into account."

In an innovative mode, we asked authors to describe the minimum-educational requirements for their treatment, any licensing requirements that needed to be followed, sources of additional training, the populations and disorders for which the intervention is most effective, any evidence-based research that supports the effectiveness of the treatment, and the risks involved. We also required a step-by-step description of a sample clinical session. Some of these treatments lack back-up evidence, but it should be noted that a 2019 analysis of so-called "empirically-supported" treatments found half identified that way also woefully lacked such evidentiary support, and only about 20 percent had what was judged to be robust support (Sakaluk, Williams, Kilshaw, & Rhyner, 2019). In other words, the efficacy of all psychotherapies, even those that supposedly are the most solidly grounded in medical science, is still a frontier not yet adequately explored. In the face of real human suffering that requires helpful efforts, even if the data are not fully yet in, we offer this book as a preliminary map of a frontier.

Another purpose of this book is to provide guidelines for mental-health practitioners who are interested in integrating holistic interventions into their clinical practices, and information on training and licensure requirements necessary to practice these interventions legally and ethically. Practicing music, art, and dance-movement therapies, for example, requires specific training in these disciplines that are in addition to clinical training many practitioners may receive in graduate school. Knowing in advance what additional training is required to practice certain modalities and where to obtain that training, in our opinion, is much needed in the field, and we hope our book helps facilitate and share this valuable knowledge. One of the editors (Cheryl L. Fracasso) learned this early in her career when she first began working with the intellectually and developmentally disabled (IDD) population shortly after obtaining her Ph.D., and was humbled to find she was woefully unprepared in her clinical training that only taught "talk therapy," which was not an appropriate intervention for this population, many of whom were non-verbal clients. During that time Fracasso also observed clinicians claiming to practice "music therapy" or "art therapy," but who lacked proper education, training, and credentials to do so. We suspect many practitioners may be in this same boat, and it is our hope this book will provide a well-rounded source of information for clinicians interested in obtaining specialized training to practice some of these holistic disciplines.

We selected 21 of the submissions we received and are pleased to present them to our readers. With this shared, we reveal our biases, namely that we believe atomist approaches for helping humans to be quite limited. This is meant neither to devalue the medical model, and some of the real breakthroughs and advances discovered and promoted from that vantage, nor to devalue some of the more staid non-medical traditions for giving help that is less than holistic, but to instead emphasize the importance, and even necessity, of not missing the forest by focusing only on its trees and not missing seeing photons as "wavicles" by viewing them only as inert particles. Key aspects of the human being, such as autonomy, dignity, integrity, and so forth, can only be adequately included from a holistic approach, as reductionist approaches literally reduce people to nothing more than parts. In this spirit, we invite readers to delve into the many approaches to holistic healing shared by our book's contributors.

REFERENCES

Myers, K. (2019, August). A call to a more balanced life. *Counseling Today*, 14–16.

Ohrt, J.H., Clarke, P.B., & Conley, A.H. (2019). *Wellness counseling: A holistic approach to prevention and intervention*. Alexandria, VA: American Counseling Association.

Sakaluk, J.K., Williams, A.J., Kilshaw, R.E., & Rhyner, K.T. (2019). Evaluating the evidential value of empirically supported psychological treatments: A meta-scientific review. *Journal of Abnormal Psychology, 128*, 500–509.

Serlin, I.A., Krippner, S., & Rockefeller, K. (2019). The whole person approach to integrated health care. In I.A. Serlin, S. Krippner, & K. Rockefeller (Eds.), *Integrated care for the traumatized: A whole person approach* (pp. 1–10). Pittsburgh, PA: Rowman & Littlefield.

Smuts, J.C. (1926). *Holism and evolution*. New York, NY: Macmillan.

VandenBos, G.R. (Ed.). (2007). *APA dictionary of psychology*. Washington, D.C.: American Psychological Association.

PART 1

Psychotherapeutic Interventions

The Vigorous, Compassionate and Holistic Approach of Rational Emotive Behavior Therapy

Honoring the Work of Albert Ellis

Debbie Joffe Ellis

"You can't have one without the other…" is a lyric from a catchy song about love and marriage that was popular decades ago. That sentiment is not held by as many people in this day and age. But what I believe is irrefutable when it comes to understanding the underpinnings, mechanics, and nature of human life is that we are influenced by the inseparable interaction of mind, body, emotions, and behaviors. Indeed, one can't have one without the other!

We are biological creatures gifted with an ability—for those of us who choose to use it—not only to think, but also to think about our thinking. We are able to be aware of the thoughts we think, and to recognize that when we think in healthy ways we create healthy emotions. We are able to experience that, when we think in healthy ways and, as a consequence of doing so, create healthy and non-debilitating emotions, we are able to behave in productive ways at best, or—at the very least—in non-destructive ways. We can choose to make an effort to cherish the gift of life, and to think, feel, and act in ways that enhance that gift.

For those who want to experience greater joy in life, and minimize suffering, the qualities of courage, compassion, creativity, care—fueled by action—are, ideally, part of what many people might hope to attain and practice. Many people desire to feel that these ways of being are substantially and comfortably accessible and established within themselves, and seek help from effective therapeutic or philosophical approaches in making sure that is so.

I know of few other, perhaps no other, approaches that do so as thoroughly, and as deeply and substantially as the holistic approach of Albert Ellis's Rational Emotive Behavior Therapy (REBT) (Ellis & Ellis, 2019).

Some may think I have some bias, due to the fact that Albert Ellis and I were deeply connected soul-mates and husband and wife, and worked together in all aspects of our work throughout all of our years together. Some bias may be there—although I sincerely strive to be objective, and believe that in this instance I am being so! I was practicing and teaching REBT in Australia well before Al and I were a couple. And I was loving it, even before its creator made his way into my heart. In this essay, I will share with you the background and history of REBT, its main tenets, and its unique aspects, ending with a note of gratitude.

Background and History

Unlike many other therapeutic approaches, a large component of the formation and development of REBT was the creative and brilliant ability Albert Ellis displayed, starting at a remarkably young age, to find practical ways to cope with, and reduce, his own emotional suffering. He successfully applied ideas and actions that were to become part of REBT well before he could even imagine being a therapist.

From infancy and throughout his childhood, he experienced various illnesses including nephritis and stomach problems, often having to spend a stretch of months in a hospital. His family rarely visited him, and he felt deeply sad. He made the decision that he did not want to feel such sadness, so he read books from the children's hospital library, talked to fellow patients and their visitors, fell in love with his pretty nurses, used his imagination to think about what he would do when he grew up, and invented games that he and the other children in his ward could play after lights out. These actions helped him focus on things other than his sadness and neglect by his parents, a fine example of the effectiveness of *cognitive distraction*—which became, and is, an oft-used technique of REBT (Ellis, 1973, 2001, 2010; Ellis & Ellis, 2019).

When he was a teenage youth leader of a radical political group, he had a severe phobia about public speaking. In fact, he never dared to give a speech until he read of the early work of the psychologist John B. Watson (Watson, 1919; Wedding & Corsini, 2019) and the success of using in-vivo desensitization with young children to help them get over their intense fears of animals. Al forced himself, very uncomfortably, to speak often in public—and within weeks got over his phobia and discomfort to such a degree that he enjoyed public speaking greatly and proved to be most effective at it. He would often say, in workshops and lectures, when recalling that time: "I completely got over my phobia, and now you can't keep me away from the public speaking platform!"

He tackled his social anxiety and fear of talking to women, his other major paralyzing phobia, in a similar way, using in-vivo desensitization. He gave himself a homework assignment for the month of August of sitting next to at least 100 women on park benches in the Bronx Botanical Gardens and starting conversations with them. Although he only made one date, and she did not show up, he totally overcame his fear of approaching women! *In-vivo desensitization* became and remains one of the frequently used techniques of REBT (Ellis, 2010; Ellis & Ellis, 2019).

He read avidly, and elements of REBT can be recognized as having been influenced by some of the wise sages and philosophers he enjoyed. Unlike some contemporary theorists in our field, Albert Ellis regularly gave credit to those who influenced and inspired elements of his work, and he did not take credit for, or pretend to be inventing, any "wheels" that his predecessors had so ably created. It is a pity to observe that the contributions of Ellis, and some other inspiring pioneers and great thinkers who are no longer alive, are being neglected in the writings and teachings of some people who come up with new and appealing titles for their approaches, yet who are blatantly including elements of their predecessors' works without giving them due credit.

Some of the people, philosophies, and practices that Al acknowledged as being influential in his work included Gautama Buddha, Zen Buddhists, certain Hindu Yoga practices, even aspects of the ancient Hebrew and Christian philosophies—despite Al's position taken for most of his life as a "probabilistic atheist." He was particularly taken with Greek and Roman philosophers and Stoic philosophy, including the works of Epicurus, Epictetus, and Marcus Aurelius.

During the period in the early 1940s in which Al worked as a clinical sexologist, he followed the works of Havelock Ellis, W.F. Robie, and others who were physicians and practiced what could be called *cognitive behavior sex therapy*. Al was a contributing figure to the sexual revolution in America in the 20th century, writing and speaking about sexuality in the 1940s and throughout his life. He was one of very few to advocate vigorously for equal rights for gays, and for women's rights in the 1950s and onwards. He was a pioneering feminist who specifically taught women how they could choose to be assertive and not aggressive. He was a founder of the *Society for the Scientific Study of Sexuality*.

Al was inspired by writings of the general semanticist Alfred Korzybski, and those of such philosophers as Bertrand Russell, Paul Dubois, and Émile Coué (the latter two of whom used persuasive forms of psychotherapy). He enjoyed the works of Alexander Herzberg (who included homework assignments in his work) and the works of existential philosophers of his time such as Kierkegaard, Heidegger, Sartre, and Tillich.

When Al was trained in and practicing liberal psychoanalysis, he thought of himself as more of an existential analyst. Influences at that time included Erich Fromm, Karen Horney, Harry Stack Sullivan, and Alfred Adler.

Al increasingly found the psychoanalysis he was using with his clients to be too passive, inefficient, and lacking in educational and behavioral elements. He became more active-directive with his clients, abandoning psychoanalysis in 1953 and developing the approach now known as REBT. (It was first called Rational Therapy [RT], then Rational Emotive Therapy [RET] in the early 1960s, until in 1993 it became known as Rational Emotive Behavior Therapy.) Recognized as being an extremely humanistic approach, it brought profound changes to the practice of psychotherapy such as a greater emphasis on present issues, as opposed to past issues that might (or might not) have been pivotal in producing the presenting problem.

In his final decade of life in our work together, we began to present workshops on REBT and Buddhism. We would give much focus to, and emphasis on, the REBT tenets of Unconditional Acceptance—a part of REBT from its inception. In the climate of growing terrorism in that first decade of the new century, we focused more frequently upon these ideas than Al might have done at times in the past.

During his final years, some unanticipated and brutal events took place in our work life. The original mission statement for the Institute that he had created around 1959 had been changed without Al's knowledge; moreover, he was dismissed from duties, was no longer permitted to do any work or teaching within the Institute, and was ousted from the board of which he had been president. He did what he could in his fight for justice by filing two lawsuits, the outcome of one of which was that he was reinstated to the board. Yet after the reinstatement he had no practical power, and not long after that he succumbed to pneumonia. While he made exhausting efforts to regain health and strength during the 15 months that followed, despite his superhuman efforts, on July 24, 2007, he passed. He died before the second lawsuit could be pursued. His final years contained the saddest period in his life, as he felt shocked and deeply sad at what had happened in his Institute.

The Master was being tested, and he passed the test with distinction. He practiced what he preached until his end. Despite his disdain for the actions of the people involved, he hated what they *did*, but he did not hate them. He felt compassion for them. In consoling me one day, as my tears fell and I felt deeply sad following an action against him that I considered cruel and appalling, he said to me: "Debbie—you are forgetting to practice REBT now. You are such a good teacher and therapist—but now you are not applying it to yourself. Accept, accept, accept—they *have* to do what they are doing when they think the way that they are thinking. Accept."

He applied REBT attitude and action through practically every jolt and nasty situation during those times. Accepting, however, did not mean inaction. We did what we could to bring about change, and did not allow ourselves to curl into depressed, passive, and inert bundles of inactivity. We continued teaching and presenting in a very large rented room in the building next door.

Accepting what *is* does not mean not striving and acting to change it. But in accepting, there is the probability of feeling less rage, depression, and anxiety—and of experiencing, instead, a healthy concentrated, determined, and motivating drive to effect change, whilst also feeling disappointment, sadness, and concern—none of which debilitate, and may even motivate and facilitate the carrying out of productive actions.

In Al's final months, when it was clear that his health was rapidly declining and not likely to improve, and that it was unlikely that in his lifetime he would witness the justice that he sought, we continued to practice what he preached. Despite our deep sadness, ache, and disappointment (on top of which Al was in great physical pain much of the time), we focused on what was good in our lives. And that was our profound love. In so doing, we prevented ourselves from creating rage, or depression, or anxiety.

Each day we would hold and hug one another. If he was in too much pain for us to lie together in his hospital bed, I would stroke his head and hands. We felt deeply grateful that we had one another, that we were together, and that we shared a rare and profound love. Despite and including all the bitter circumstances we were facing and enduring, we focused on our love.

In the work I have done and continue to do since Al's passing in 2007, I give great emphasis in my teaching and writing to the importance and benefit of striving to experience and practice unconditional acceptance, gratitude, compassion, kindness, awe, and wonder in one's daily life. These are not new components of the REBT philosophy, but some of those on which I choose to focus and magnify during these times of increasing random and brutal violence and unrest (Ellis, 2015).

Basic Tenets of REBT

Rational Emotive Behavior Therapy (REBT) strives to help people to achieve lasting change, and, as part of that, educates them about the how-to's of doing so (Ellis & Ellis, 2019). In this way, REBT discourages clients from developing any unhealthy reliance on the therapist—it encourages self-effort and the resulting experience of greater empowerment, so that clients can rightly claim to create their own emotional destinies. It can be asserted that REBT can be more than simply an effective evidence-based therapeutic approach. For those who apply it, it is also a healthy philosophy and a positive way of life and living.

A basic goal of REBT is to help as many people as possible to suffer less emotional misery, and thereby to experience more joy in their lives. It asserts that it is not events or our circumstances that create our resultant emotional experiences and reaction, but **what we tell ourselves** about those events and circumstances. When we think in healthy and rational ways in response to adverse or unlikable circumstances, we create healthy and often life-enhancing emotions. When we think in irrational ways in response to adversity, we create debilitating and unhealthy emotions.

REBT takes a humanistic (Ellis, 1973) and holistic view of a person's life and tendencies (Ellis & Ellis, 2019). As noted earlier, it reminds us that our thoughts, feelings, and behaviors are interconnected. The more healthy our thinking, the more likely it is that our consequent emotions and resultant actions will enhance our experience of life (or, at the very least, not have a negative or destructive impact).

We humans are born and reared to think in both rational and irrational ways. While acknowledging the influence of biological and environmentally learned aspects in our lives, REBT strongly reminds us that, despite and including that fact, *with awareness we have choice.* In other words, we can choose to experience greater happiness and contentment, or to remain less happy and miserable. We can **choose** to think about our thinking, to recognize when we are thinking in irrational ways, and then to dispute and replace such beliefs.

REBT teaches the differences between rational and irrational thinking:

- **Rational Thinking.** Rational thinking is based on empirical reality; it creates appropriate and healthy emotions and behaviors; it includes preferences rather than demands; it encourages flexibility; it encourages healthy perspectives; it prescribes high frustration tolerance, unconditional acceptance, and the non-damning of self, others, and life; it encourages us to rate behaviors—not our essential selves; and it removes the tyranny of the "Shoulds" and "Musts."
- **Irrational Thinking.** Irrational thinking creates debilitating and unhealthy negative emotions and behaviors; it includes rigid and dogmatic demands; it leads to low frustration tolerance; it includes absolutistic attitudes and overgeneralizing; it exaggerates facts; and it involves "awfulizing" and "catastrophizing" (expressions created by Al); it creates low frustration tolerance and damnation of self/others and life when things do not go the way we have demanded that they **should** go; and it rates the *worth* of self/others/life.

Three core Irrational Beliefs that REBT has identified (Ellis & Ellis, 2019), from which countless others stem, are:

1. I must always do well and be loved and approved by others.
2. You must treat me well and act the way I think you should.
3. Life should be fair and just.

REBT clearly distinguishes between the Healthy and Unhealthy Negative Emotions (Ellis, 2015; Ellis & Ellis, 2019). (*Negative* in this context does not mean bad, but unpleasant, painful, or unenjoyable.)

REBT asserts that, when we think in irrational ways in response to not getting what we want, or to getting what we do not want, we are likely to create one or more of the self-defeating and unhealthy negative emotions, which include anxiety, depression, rage, guilt, shame, and jealousy. When we think in rational ways, in response to the same circumstances, we are likely to create healthy negative emotions (non-debilitating, and often motivating or enriching), such as concern, sadness and grief, healthy anger, and regret.

REBT offers "ABCDE" Self-Help Approach for Emotional Disturbance (Ellis & Ellis, 2019), which is simple to follow and apply. Through this approach one clarifies the connection between an activating event and its consequences by identifying the irrational beliefs involved. It then provides the means for replacing irrational beliefs with rational ones through disputation and the creation of effective new beliefs. People are encouraged to apply the "ABCDE" procedure by identifying the following:

A—Activating Event

C—Consequences: Emotions and/or Behaviors

B—Beliefs: Identify the Irrational Beliefs (yes, in this framework, B follows C!)

D—Disputing of the Irrational Beliefs, comprising: (i) Realistic Disputing—"Where is it written? Where is the evidence?" (ii) Logical Disputing—"Does it follow that…?" (iii) Pragmatic Disputing—"Where will it get me to maintain this irrational belief?"

E—Effective New Philosophies: These are healthy, functional and realistic beliefs that replace the former irrational ones as a consequence of thorough disputing; for lasting change, it is important to go over them often and regularly.

REBT reminds us that maintaining therapeutic and other gains requires ongoing work and practice, work and practice, work and practice! Homework is an essential part of REBT therapeutic practice (Ellis & Ellis, 2019). Techniques suggested by the therapist, or those selected for practice by an individual doing self-help, can be chosen from many, which include:

- **Cognitive**—The "ABCDE" Self-Help procedure, vigorous disputing, cost/benefit analysis, distraction activities, modeling, psycho-education, bibliotherapy, audio therapy, and video therapy (reading/hearing/viewing useful material).
- **Emotive**—Rational emotive imagery, shame-attacking exercises, creating and repeating strong coping statements, role play, *forcefully* disputing the irrational beliefs that one has recorded or written.
- **Behavioral**—Safe risk-taking, in-vivo desensitization, staying temporarily in a difficult situation (when safe to do so) to develop High Frustration Tolerance (HFT), skill training, relapse prevention, reinforcement, use of humor, and Rational Emotive Songs.

REBT strongly emphasizes the importance of the practices of three forms of Unconditional Acceptance, namely: (1) Unconditional Self-Acceptance (USA); (2) Unconditional Other Acceptance (UOA); and (3) Unconditional Life Acceptance (ULA).

Unconditional Other Acceptance (UOA) has for years been controversial, with some people arguing that it is foolish and unrealistic to expect people unconditionally to accept others who have acted in brutal and cruel ways toward them. Al and I continued to point out that unconditionally accepting that the person still has worth (despite and including their grave flaws and misdeeds) does not mean that we accept the rotten behavior. Certainly, REBT is all for seeking justice, but it asserts that it may be more aptly attained when coming from a place of emotional stability than from rage and the damnation of others. REBT invites us to think about the many people—some reported in the media, others whom we may know in our personal lives—who have succeeded in experiencing UOA and have genuinely applied forgiveness of the person or people who assaulted them, although not forgiving the bad deeds. REBT invites us to consider that, if we had had the backgrounds of those who act in despicable ways, and had their brain chemistry, and had been thinking the thoughts that they were thinking when doing their evil actions—then, in all probability, we might have acted in similar ways. This is commonly thought of as having empathy, and walking a mile in the other's shoes.

For those of us who are not cognitively impaired, and who recognize that we can choose our attitudes, it *is* possible to work to attain and experience UOA more of the time—and well worth it. REBT vigorously encourages us to do so. As a further demonstration of the holistic nature of REBT, much has been published that demonstrates the beneficial impact on one's physical health and fitness of adopting attitudes of empathy, compassion, forgiveness, and gratitude. When doing so, we strengthen our immune systems, experience greater cardiac health, and prevent high blood pressure and atherosclerosis, to name just a few physiological benefits.

REBT also encourages us to develop and maintain keen social interests. It urges us to apply care and kindness to one another, and to act in the interest of keeping the environment healthy, safe, and balanced.

In REBT, as in many other approaches, lasting change is attained through clients making an on-going effort (Ellis & Ellis, 2019). An initial part of the therapeutic process is the clarification of therapeutic goals. As described earlier, homework is a core part of the REBT therapeutic journey, as is encouraging clients to self-reflect, explore, and identify their beliefs and philosophy of life and living. REBT encourages clients to make an ongoing effort to challenge self-defeating ideas, dispute them, and replace them. REBT is not known for simply removing or placating symptoms, but aims to facilitate profound and lasting beneficial changes in the thinking, emotional, and active life of clients.

REBT takes into account the tendency that we can have to relapse into previous dysfunctional states, and so it has built-in relapse prevention methods. These include regular self-monitoring, vigorous application of the disputing methods which had been helpful in the past, and, perhaps most importantly, the practice of unconditional self-acceptance despite and including any relapses.

The effective REBT therapist ideally motivates clients to persist at making an effort to reduce their emotional misery and maximize their joy and tranquility. This may include inviting clients to consider the consequences with clear and direct honesty, and to avoid the arresting of efforts to change. It also may include helping clients to envision the fruits of continuing to make efforts and choices that enhance their lives. The effective REBT therapist models unconditional other acceptance when there are relapses, warmly acknowledges progress clients make on their therapeutic journeys, and encourages ongoing forward movement.

The therapist also makes an effort to develop rapport with clients. A gross misconception about REBT is that it asserts that rapport and the demonstration of empathy do not matter very much in the therapeutic process. This is a false distortion of REBT's encouragement for therapists to avoid allowing clients to depend predominantly on the therapist to "make them feel better." Instead, REBT assists clients to work on removing any excessive and inappropriate need to feel accepted by their therapist. REBT encourages clients to take responsibility for their emotions, and teaches the methods for doing so. However, that does not preclude the benefit of rapport and empathy from the therapist in assisting clients to learn the necessary tools and construct positive change.

A possible reason for the misconception referred to here was the judgment about the vigorous style and manner of Albert Ellis, when he conducted his demonstrations and sessions. His direct approach, his no-nonsense style, and his frequent use of colorful language led some people to infer incorrectly that his style was the only recommended REBT style. It also led to the inaccurate assumption that his manner prevented rapport and demonstrated an absence of empathy. There is no doubting that his manner was not "everyone's cup of tea," but he did not suggest that others copy it. Effective REBT practitioners apply the tenets, theory, methods, and philosophy of REBT—but in their unique ways and in their own unique style and manner. Al encouraged doing so when teaching in his supervision groups, which I co-led with him in his final years, and in his many trainings and workshops.

As for the assertion that his style and manner prevented rapport and empathy—for some clients that may have been true, but the massive number of letters and verbal feedback he received indicated the opposite. The letters and feedback from these people described their experience and sense of his truly understanding them, and their appreciation of his direct and honest communication. They felt that he genuinely cared about them and their well-being. It is just too hard to guess at or estimate the number of people who expressed such gratitude. A good number of prominent writers, teachers, and practitioners whose lives he helped, some of whom do not even practice REBT in their professional work, have also expressed such appreciation.

Effective REBT therapists listen well and educate themselves about aspects of the cultural, religious, or non-religious backgrounds of their clients. In so doing they can be better equipped to form rapport by understanding clients' unique cultural backgrounds and by choosing respectful ways of communicating that are less likely to be dismissed or misinterpreted by clients of different cultural backgrounds.

REBT is largely psycho-educational. In addition to print and video material on REBT that can be recommended to clients, the REBT therapist will also suggest materials derived from other approaches or philosophies if deemed helpful. Hence, REBT is truly multimodal in form. The effective therapist also stays abreast of current news—inspiring stories in particular—and popular books and movies that support themes being worked on in therapy that can be recommended to clients.

A strong part of any therapeutic change is the willingness of clients to be mindful, to reflect on their thinking, and to take appropriate actions. Awareness, a key element in change, is highlighted and encouraged. To that end, some clients are encouraged to learn and practice forms of meditation and relaxation. It is also beneficial when clients are motivated to keep making an effort towards healthy change, with realistic expectations—including the fact that change may not happen overnight or as quickly as they want. As a result, patience, high frustration tolerance, and endurance are encouraged.

REBT in the form of brief therapy is sufficient for some, but for those with deeper issues and disturbances longer-term REBT therapy is more helpful. Those requiring brief therapy can experience significant changes within 5 to 12 sessions (or even fewer). Achieving productive results through brief therapy depends on the ability and willingness of clients to take responsibility for constructing their emotional well-being, learning the tenets of REBT, and applying them on a frequent and regular basis.

Clients with severe emotional disturbances, greater endogenous disturbances, co-occurring conditions, or poor learning skills benefit from longer-term REBT therapy. Whilst a course of individual therapy is recommended, over time some clients may benefit from both individual and group therapy. As progress continues, they may solely attend group therapy as a means of beneficial reinforcement and the enhancement and maintenance of their therapeutic gains. Such clients are welcome to return for individual therapy if or when they may benefit from direct one-to-one refresher sessions, particularly if they have experienced any relapses.

A detailed description of the application of REBT to various and specific conditions, such as perfectionism, obsessive compulsive disorder, borderline personality disorders, addiction, the treatment of people with co-occurring problems, severe emotional disturbances and self-defeating behaviors, and other issues would turn into a book instead of an essay. Hence readers are strongly encouraged to read about such applications in one or many of the books by Albert Ellis, including *Overcoming Destructive Beliefs, Feelings and Emotions* (2001).

What is common in REBT treatment of the above-mentioned conditions is the setting of goals, the exploration of the beliefs contributing to debilitating emotions and unwanted behaviors, the ongoing encouragement and acknowledgment of any and all gains achieved by the clients, relapse prevention, the demonstration of tolerance, nonjudgment and acceptance if relapse does occur, the giving of homework activities to be done between sessions, and the teaching, reminding, and encouraging of clients to make on-going efforts to accept themselves, unconditionally, as worthwhile human beings. Such unconditional self-acceptance is of immense benefit to clients despite and including the challenges of any restrictive tendencies, biological conditions, difficulties in applying recommendations, or relapses.

There is a good amount of evidence-based research demonstrating the efficacy of REBT (Lyons & Woods, 1991). Specifically, hundreds of studies validate the major theoretical hypotheses of REBT (Ellis & Whitely, 1979). The vast body of CBT research also supports the premises and efficacy of the REBT approach, which is not surprising, since CBT has at its roots many of REBT's tenets. Many psychiatrists, licensed psychologists, mental health counselors, and coaches incorporate the REBT approach into their therapy practices. Sadly, it appears that a number of people who were trained by Ellis are now teaching a blend of CBT and REBT, which contributes to REBT being watered-down and marginalized. Others continue to teach REBT in its essential form, including this author. At present REBT workshops and CE programs are presented throughout the USA and in other countries. A full-semester REBT course is taught at Columbia University Teachers College (interestingly, this is the college from which Albert Ellis earned his MA and PhD). Other universities include REBT as part of other courses such as those titled "Comparative Psychotherapies" and "Cognitive Behavior Therapy." For non-professionals, the REBT approach is presented clearly and simply in the Ellis books and is successfully applied by great numbers of people in a self-help process.

Unique Aspects of REBT

There are a few aspects unique to REBT, described below. Although one or some of them may be seen or referred to, to some degree, in other approaches, it appears at this time that the others do not highlight them as much.

1. REBT emphasizes unconditional acceptance and addressing a person's philosophy of life and living. In 2003 Albert Ellis (2003) and, in a separate article, Aaron T. Beck and Christine A. Padesky (Padesky & Beck, 2003) compared Rational Emotive Behavior Therapy with Cognitive Therapy. In 2005 Ellis's article (2005) discussing those papers was published. In it he noted that, whilst in 2003 all three authors agreed that REBT is largely a philosophically-based psychotherapy and CT more empirically based, Ellis later saw that as only partly true. He believed that both approaches are philosophically *and* empirically based systems; however, he saw REBT as the more philosophical of the two.

2. REBT emphasizes the importance and benefit of vigorous, thorough, and substantial disputing of irrational ideas, prior to recognizing their rational counterparts. Many, if not most, therapeutic approaches would at some point discourage irrational thinking and encourage clients to replace unhelpful beliefs with healthy and realistic ones, however, no approaches of which this author is aware urge clients to apply such a systematic, forceful, energetic, and concentrated effort to dispute the irrational beliefs ("Zap them!"), as REBT does *before* replacing them with the new rational ones.

3. REBT offers three clear forms of disputation, as mentioned earlier: (1) Realistic Disputing, (2) Logical Disputing, and (3) Pragmatic Disputing.

4. While attending to cognition and behavior, REBT gives great attention to the *emotional* element of therapy and wellbeing (its "E"), which is additional evidence of its holistic nature. One of the false myths over the years has been that REBT neglects to do so. For many years, Ellis and Fritz Perls carried on a feud and debated strongly, following the accusation by Perls that REBT was too intellectual and ignored any emotional element. Other prominent psychologists and psychiatrists, including Aaron T. Beck and Martin E. Seligman, also credited Ellis for highlighting the cognitive element, and yet what many neglected, and still fail to recognize, is that he highlighted the emotive aspect equally. He clearly distinguished between what he called healthy and unhealthy negative emotions (referred to earlier in this essay). REBT encourages us to embrace the healthy negative emotions rather than to avoid or eliminate them, and actively teaches the difference between them and the debilitating unhealthy ones, as well as the process of creating the former.

5. REBT urges therapists to practice what they preach. Many REBT therapists may not do so, or may do so to a limited extent, yet may still be effective in helping clients due to REBT's clear structure, framework, theory, methods, and elegance. However, it asserts that therapists may be even more effective when practicing it in their own daily lives, because: (1) they may display an added component of greater authenticity, which can allow stronger empathy and rapport in the client-therapist relationship; (2) they act as credible models of the approach; and (3) they make ongoing efforts to keep themselves stable, steady, and un-upset during challenging

times in their own lives, which, in all probability, can enable them to remain focused and effective during sessions.

Conclusion

As I conclude here, I trust that you, my readers, have already noticed that implicit and explicit in the theory and philosophy of REBT are the attitudes of compassion and care, and the call to take productive and practical actions in order to effect beneficial change. I hope you recognize that REBT is more than simply an effective evidence-based theory and psychotherapeutic modality. It is also, indubitably, a most holistic approach and a way of life for those who use it as such. Its creator, Albert Ellis, dedicated his life to helping as many people as possible to realize that practically all of us create our own emotional destinies according to the way we think. His voluminous body of work is presented in ways understood and embraced by both academics and members of the general public. Many millions are grateful to him for formulating the approach that helped and, for many, saved their lives. REBT's beauty and elegance continue to benefit countless people who strive to embrace life, to cherish their moments, to minimize suffering, and to maximize joy. This happens when those of us who work professionally in roles that serve the health and well-being of people, and when others who also strive to contribute to those around them in positive and life-enhancing ways, not only talk about it—but also practice what we preach, with heartfelt gratitude for the opportunities to do so.

REFERENCES

Ellis, A. (1973). *Humanistic psychotherapy*. New York, NY: McGraw-Hill.
Ellis, A. (2001). *Overcoming destructive beliefs, feelings and emotions*. Amherst, NY: Prometheus Books.
Ellis, A. (2003). Similarities and differences between Rational Emotive Behavior Therapy and Cognitive Therapy. *Journal of Cognitive Psychotherapy: An International Quarterly, 17*(3), 225–240.
Ellis, A. (2005). Discussion of Christine A. Padesky & Aaron T. Beck, "Science and philosophy: Comparison of Cognitive Therapy and Rational Emotive Behavior Therapy." *Journal of Cognitive Psychotherapy: An International Quarterly, 19*(2), 181–189.
Ellis, A. (2010). *All out: An autobiography*. Amherst, NY: Prometheus Books.
Ellis, A., & Ellis, D.J. (2019). *Rational emotive behavior therapy* (2nd ed.). Washington, D.C.: American Psychological Association.
Ellis, A., & Whitely, J. (Eds.). (1979). *Theoretical and empirical foundations of rational emotive therapy*. Belmont, CA: Wadsworth.
Ellis, D.J. (2015). Reflections: The profound impact of gratitude in times of ease and times of challenge. *Journal of Spirituality in Clinical Practice, 2*(1), 96–100.
Lyons, L.C., & Woods, P.J. (1991). The efficacy of rational emotive therapy: A quantitative review of the outcome research. *Clinical Psychology Review, 11*, 357–369.
Padesky, C.A., & Beck, A.T. (2003). Science and philosophy: Comparison of cognitive therapy and rational emotive behavior therapy. *Journal of Cognitive Psychotherapy: An International Quarterly, 17*(3), 211–224.
Watson, J.B. (1919). *Psychology from the standpoint of a behaviorist*. Philadelphia: Lippincott.
Wedding, D., & Corsini, R.J. (2019). *Current psychotherapies* (11th ed.). Boston: Cengage Learning.

Time Perspective Therapy

An Evolutionary Therapy for PTSD

ROSEMARY SWORD *and* PHILIP ZIMBARDO

At some point in your life, there's a good chance you or people you know—perhaps clients—have experienced a trauma or series of traumatic events—events so devastating that they were life-altering. Although each of these experiences may be very different, there is one thing they have in common: A story emerged. The stories we tell ourselves are important keys in working through a catastrophic experience. In order to learn from and make sense of tragedy, our brain naturally formulates an account that describes what happened, how, and why. We are especially likely to develop stories—narratives—when an event is startling, troublesome, or violates our basic expectations. These narratives help us find meaning in our lives, and especially in our losses, which, in turn, can facilitate healing. Narratives play an important role in restoring a sense of well-being. And so, you might wonder why traditional psychology—which regularly uses life narratives in various ways—has had such a difficult time dealing with the increasing spread of posttraumatic stress disorder (PTSD) in many people. Maybe the reason is the tendency for traditional psychology to fight fire with fire. This is evidenced in the way the older treatment models focus on repetition, such as re-living the traumatic things that happened to the sufferers repetitively in an attempt to "desensitize" them to their long-term impact. *Time Perspective Therapy* (Zimbardo, Sword, & Sword, 2012) (TPT) has a significantly different focus from all previous models on the management of post-traumatic stress. Instead of replaying the trauma multiple times, TPT focuses on remembering the *positive* things of the past, rather than only the negatives, and then working in the present to create a brighter tomorrow. While TPT does not discount or gloss over traumatic memories (we clearly show respect for the origin of the trauma), we specifically avoid the trap of getting stuck in the traumatic negative past, which may increase its horrific effects via reliving it.

In TPT (Zimbardo, Sword, & Sword, 2012), we move forward rather than continually looking backward. We learn from the past and recall the client's wonderful memories—some good times that happened around the time of the traumatic event—on which we can build. This helps us all overcome the negative events of the past and motivate us to a brighter future.

This simple concept is reflected in the ordinary language that time perspective therapists use. Most people suffering from PTSD have already been labeled as anxious, depressed, or even "mentally ill." When they hear and identify with these words, the possibility of ever emerging from such a state may feel unattainable. We prefer to reframe their "illness" as a "mental injury," recasting their depression and anxiety as a "negative past" experience that they can replace with a "positive present" and with a "brighter future"—and ultimately with a balanced time perspective. This approach may seem overly simplistic, especially to those trained in psychotherapy. But to PTSD sufferers, the idea of having a forward-leaning framework in which to begin to understand and work with their therapist on their issues comes as an enormous relief and also a welcome ray of light in their previous darkness.

Time Perspective Therapy

We are all familiar with the three main time zones: the past, the present, and the future. In TPT (Zimbardo, Sword, & Sword, 2012), these time zones are divided into subsets: *past positive* and *past negative*, *present hedonism* and *present fatalism*, and *future positive* and *future negative*. When one of these time perspectives is too heavily weighted, we can lose out on what is really happening now and/or lose sight of what could be happening in our future, causing us to be unsteady, unbalanced, or temporally biased.

Being out of balance in this way shades the way we think as well as negatively impacting our daily decision-making process. For instance, if you are stuck in a past negative experience, you might think that, from now on, everything that happens to you will be negative, so why even bother planning for your future, because it's just going to continue to be same old bad stuff. Or if you are an extreme present hedonist adrenaline junky intent on spiking your adrenal glands, then you might engage in risky behaviors that unintentionally endanger yourself or others because you are living in the moment and not thinking about future consequences of today's actions. If you are out of balance in your future time perspective, constantly thinking and worrying about all the things you have to do or must do on your endless to-do list, you might forget or miss out on the everyday, wonderful things happening in your life and the lives of your loved ones in the here and now.

Six Main Time Perspectives in TPT

1. *Past positive* people focus on the good things that have happened.
2. *Past negative* people focus on all the things that went wrong in the past.
3. *Present hedonistic* people live in the moment, seeking pleasure, novelty, and sensation, and avoiding pain.
4. *Present fatalistic* people feel that planning for future decisions is not necessary because predetermined fate plays the guiding role in one's life.
5. *Future positive* people plan for the future and trust that their decisions will work out.
6. *Future negative* people feel that the future is fatalistic or apocalyptic, or have no future orientation.

Note: There is an additional subset of the future time-oriented people: **Transcendental future-oriented**. These people believe that, by leading a "good" life while on earth, they will be rewarded in the afterlife. As a significant percentage of our clients do not believe in an afterlife, the transcendental future-orientation is not used in our version of TPT, but, of course, it could be included in some treatments with specific clients.

Three Main TP Biases

1. *Past bias*: Good and bad things happen to everyone. But some of us view the world through rose-colored glasses (past positive), whereas others see the world through a darker lens (past negative). We have found that people who focus primarily on the past, value the old more than the new, the familiar over the novel, and the cautious, conservative approach over the daring, more liberal, or risky one.

2. *Present bias*: People who live in the present are far less—or not at all—influenced by either past experiences or future considerations. They focus only on the immediate present—what's happening *now* (present hedonism). Decisions are based on the immediate stimulus situation: internal hormonal signals, feelings, smells, sounds, the attractive qualities of the object of desire, and what others are urging them to do. Present-biased people who are influenced by past negative experiences are likely to feel stuck in the mire of the past *now* (present fatalism).

3. *Future bias*: No one is born thinking about how to plan for the future. A number of conditions—including living in a temperate zone (where it is necessary to anticipate seasonal change), living in a stable family or stable economic/political society (where they learn to trust promises made to them), and becoming educated—can create future positive-oriented people. In general, future-oriented people do very well in life. They are less aggressive, are less depressed, have more energy, take care of their health, have good impulse control, and have more self-esteem. But those stuck in the past, locked into negative memories, and feeling fatalistic about the present may have lost the ability even to conceive of a hopeful future (future negative).

Time Perspective Therapy Transforms the Past, Present and Future

Time perspective therapy (Zimbardo, Sword, & Sword, 2012) begins by respecting a traumatic experience for what it can teach us rather than dwelling on how it harmed us. TPT understands that we each have a unique time perspective narrative based on our personal experiences, and this perspective is the lens through which we view our lives. But our experiences do not define us. They do not need to lock us into a particular way of seeing the world and our place in it—particularly when that way of seeing things is destructive to ourselves and to those we love.

No matter what our experiences have been, the realization that we always have the choice to change how we view the times of our lives is essential. Over the course of TPT, PTSD sufferers move away from their traumatic past, pessimistic present, and negative thoughts of the future. Instead, they journey toward a *balanced time perspective* in which it once again seems possible to live a full and promising life in the present—learning to make time for what matters most—family, friends, fun, nature, hobbies, and constructive work.

Educational Requirement/Credentials/Licensing

To paraphrase TPT co-developer Richard Sword, our goal was to take TPT out of the ivory tower and place it squarely in the hands of the people. Following through with Rick's idea, we've determined that individuals with an undergraduate degree in psychology can practice TPT as they would CBT. As an aside, in presentations and workshops, we found that students and lay-people absorbed TPT concepts as quickly as, and in some instances more quickly than, those with multiple degrees. Richard thought that it was because they were not weighed down by years of accumulated knowledge.

Although TPT was developed for PTSD, it has proved effective for a wide-range of uses (Zimbardo & Sword, 2017) with some of the populations listed below. Aspects of TPT such as refocusing from past negatives to past positives and making plans for a brighter future positive, may be practical for a variety of occupations other than mental health. Here are some suggestions:

- Medical practitioners—as an addition to the bedside-manner routine for doctors, nurses, and aides; TPT instills hope by switching the focus from past and present negatives to a brighter future
- Physical/massage therapists—prior to, during, and post-sessions, TPT can instill a sense of control and hope for the future
- Alternative medicine practitioners—such as acupuncturists and chiropractors— pre- or post-session, TPT can be used to impart positivity and a sense of wellbeing
- School/university counselors—TPT can assist students through times of difficulty and adjustment, focusing on the future positive

Additional TPT Training

The Time Cure Therapist Guidebook (Zimbardo, Sword, & Sword, 2012) was created for therapists and those seeking self-help interested in the step-by-step TPT process. *The Guidebook* is the template for TPT workshops. Due to the simplicity of TPT, which complements an already established practice or can be the main therapy in a new practice, additional training is probably unnecessary. (If you are interested in receiving a free .pdf version of *The Guidebook*, contact us at timeperspectivetherapy.org.)

However, we are pleased to share an exciting opportunity that recently presented itself. Our book, *The Time Cure* (Zimbardo, Sword, & Sword, 2012), was published in the Polish language in 2015. Since then, TPT has quickly gained interest in Poland's growing field of psychology. In late 2016, Forum Media Polska (FMP), a Polish firm dedicated to education in the field of medicine, including mental health, contacted us. At its request, we presented TPT at the first psychological conference in Warsaw, Poland, in December 2016. TPT was so well received by the attendees that FMP asked us to conduct an online TPT nanodegree. We quickly agreed, and, since the spring of 2017, about 200 Polish mental health professionals have obtained a nanodegree in TPT through FMP. Our hope is to expand this program internationally in the near future.

Evidence-Based Research and Risks

Clinicians Richard and Rosemary Sword developed TPT based on Philip Zimbardo's time perspective theories as presented in *The Time Paradox* (Zimbardo & Boyd, 2010). In late 2008, the Swords commenced using TPT at their clinic on Maui with their clients, most of whom suffered from PTSD. The Swords contacted Zimbardo soon after to share their encouraging results. In June 2009, Phil dispatched San Francisco–based researchers Sarah Brunskill and Anthony Ferreras to Maui for two weeks to conduct research on the effectiveness of TPT in regards to a test-group of seasoned war veterans suffering from severe PTSD. Baseline data (2013) had been established at the beginning of therapy by administering a battery of psychological tests: The Burns Depression Checklist, the Burns Anxiety Inventory, the Post-trauma Checklist for the military, and later the Zimbardo Time Perspective Inventory.

To give you a little background on the significance of the percentage gains experienced by the TPT participants, a 30 percent improvement (Long, 2011) is typically considered significant in psychological research. Usually, there is about a 20 percent improvement due to the *halo effect* (Cherry & Fogoros, 2018)—which refers to the idea that global personality traits about a person influence judgments by others about that person's specific traits, or the *placebo effect* (Kaptchuk, 2012)—the subliminal expectation/belief of getting well (even if there is no medical basis for it)—that is, that 20 percent of the people will get better, regardless of whether or not they got the "real" treatment or merely believed that they did. In the TPT study (2013), we were able to document to a very high level of scientific confidence that the veterans found improvements far greater than the placebo or halo effects could account for. On average, positive treatment effects were found within only 6–8 therapy sessions (Zimbardo, Sword, & Sword, 2012). These were very encouraging results.

In the six-month period from January 2009 to June 2009, levels of depression improved 89 *percent*, levels of *anxiety improved 70 percent*, and levels of trauma improved 52 *percent*. The changes in depression and anxiety could be accounted for by chance only in less than one out of one thousand times. The changes in levels of trauma could be accounted for by chance only in fewer than one out of one hundred times. Clearly, TPT helped these veterans attain better levels on clinical assessments in comparison to their pre-therapy test levels. It also proved consistent with the researchers' direct clinical observations of these vet clients' behavior, as well as the qualitative assessment of them by the Swords and also by the clients' self-reports.

All thirty-two veterans were retested in June 2010 (Zimbardo, Sword, & Sword, 2012). The improvements endured, with slight improvements over the one-year period from June 2009 to June 2010. This is an important finding: *the significant improvement in symptoms demonstrated in the first phase of the study was maintained, and nearly two-thirds of the cases even improved over a one-year period.* In the June 2011 retest, two veterans were removed from the study, as they had relocated. But of the remaining thirty vets, their significant improvement in symptoms endured over a two-year period. Through follow-up interviews, the researchers discovered that a slight dip in trauma improvement from June 2010 to June 2011 was due to situational events that affect us all at some point in our lives, such as health issues and death of a loved one. However, despite these normal life problems, the veterans continued to experience relief from trauma symptoms.

With each re-test, symptoms' improvements endured. Overall, 87 percent of clients reported decreased trauma and PTSD symptoms, with an astonishing 100 percent decrease in their depression rating. This indicates that TPT is not a temporary fix; gains can be retained and even improved. In addition, during this four-year period, not a single veteran-client even attempted suicide—in dramatic contrast to the high percentage of their non-treated buddies who did commit suicide during that same time frame. There are no known risks in the implementation of TPT.

Populations TPT Is Effective in Treating

Time Perspective Therapy was originally developed to help those suffering from PTSD (Sword, Sword, Brunskill, & Zimbardo, 2014). As PTSD is comprised of a traumatic experience which leaves one depressed, anxious, and stressed, TPT can also be an effective treatment for depression, anxiety, and/or stress in non-veterans. It has also proven effective in individual, couples, and family counseling for a variety of social problems (Zimbardo, Sword, & Sword, 2012; Zimbardo, Sword & Sword, 2014). TPT works cross-culturally and cross-generationally (Zimbardo, Sword, & Sword, 2012). (Note: While TPT has been used with children and teenagers with some success, we found that they had difficulty grasping a far-future orientation due to an under-developed perspective on the future.)

An Example of TPT for PTSD in a Clinical Setting

We are happy to share our method of conducting TPT in a clinical setting; here it is in six sessions:

Session 1

The client is given an overview of what will occur in this and the following five sessions. (Note: Clients may want to discuss their trauma in detail. We suggest you ask your clients to share an abbreviated version and assure them that you will cover their trauma in detail during a later session. However, if your clients insist on reviewing their trauma in Session 1, be flexible. If their disclosure causes you to proceed out of sequence, you can easily resume in subsequent sessions.) In this session, you will introduce your clients to Zimbardo's Temporal Theory, the Zimbardo Time Perspective Inventory (ZTPI), and Time Perspective Therapy (TPT) itself as part of their new educational orientation.

1. PTSD—Start by explaining that PTSD consists of three components: Trauma, and its effects of depression and anxiety. Tell your clients you will administer psychological tests in the following session to determine whether or not they suffer from PTSD and, if so, to what degree—a little or a lot.
2. Zimbardo's Temporal Theory—Developed by Philip Zimbardo over three decades ago, Temporal Theory divides the three known time zones—Past, Present, and Future—into subcategories:
   - Past Negative—focus on went wrong in the past.
   - Past Positive—focus on the good things that happened.

- Present Hedonism—live in the moment, seeking pleasure, novelty, sensation, and avoiding pain; they may have an addictive personality.
- Present Fatalism—feel that decisions are moot because predetermined fate plays the guiding role in life. In the extreme, they believe that nothing good will ever happen.
- Future Negative (Fatalistic or No Future)—everything will be bad/won't turn out well.
- Future Positive—plan for the future and trust that their decisions will work out.

3. ZTPI—developed by Phil Zimbardo and John Boyd, (Zimbardo & Boyd, 2010), it is a 56-statement psychological test that gives you and your clients an idea of their different time perspectives scores. (Visit www.timeparadox.com to view the 56-statement ZTPI.) Also, Ryan T. Howell, Ph.D., developed the 15-statement ZTPI short form provided in Session 2, below. You will administer the 56-statement ZTPI, or the ZTPI short form, and the three tests mentioned in 1, above, in the next session.

Explain how people suffering from PTSD are generally normal people who have been through a trauma that changes nearly every aspect of their lives. Difficulty with situations that prior to the trauma would have been handled with ease is common in PTSD sufferers. The key is: Equal and Opposite Action for Reaction—in other words, to gain mental wellbeing, people must learn to counteract negativity with positivity.

Conclude the session by suggesting that the clients visit www.timeperspectivether apy.org and www.thetimeparadox.com for more information, and then also view the 20-minute *River of Time* video on Youtube.com, which was specially created to assist clients in the TPT process. Your clients' homework is to view *The River of Time* once a day until the next session. Explain that the video contains a breathing technique that is an important part of their TPT; they are to learn and practice this breathing technique. (Note: If you have practiced a specific breathing technique during previous therapy with your clients, there is no need to change to the suggested TPT technique.) If you have time, take your clients to the websites mentioned above to familiarize them in your presence.

Session 2

Confirm to the best of your ability that your clients suffer from PTSD. This is accomplished by administering the ZTPI as well as trauma, anxiety, and depression tests. We use the Post-trauma Checklist—Civilian, if working with a civilian client, or Post-trauma Checklist—Military, if working with a military service person or veteran, the Burns Anxiety Inventory, and the Burns Depression Checklist. We have found it most helpful to use paper copies of the ZTPI. (Contact us via the comment tab at www.timeperspectivetherapy.org for a .pdf of the 56-statement ZTPI and ZTPI graph.) This allows you to keep the copies in your clients' file for future reference. The 15-statement ZTPI short form is included on the following pages for your use in printing paper copies.

During this session. There are four main steps highlighted below:

1. Explain test scoring—since psychological tests may score differently, be sure to explain how each test is scaled. For example, some tests are scaled on 1–5 with 1 = "not at all" (no symptoms), 2 = "a little bit" (minimal symptoms), 3 =

"moderately" (moderate symptoms), 4 = "quite a bit" (severe symptoms), and 5 = "extremely" (extreme trauma symptoms). ZTPI scales are as follows: 1 = Very Untrue, 2 = Untrue, 3 = Neutral, 4 = True, 5 = Very True—about ME (the client).

2. Administer psychological tests and the ZTPI. Ask your clients each item on the trauma, depression, and anxiety tests and total the scores. When administering the ZTPI, your clients may get stuck in thoughts or feelings; note the areas you or your clients may wish to explore later and continue with the ZTPI until complete. If your clients have difficulty deciding on an answer, then mark #3 (neutral) and move on to the next item. If your clients want to take the psychological tests and ZTPI on their own, please allow them ample time (perhaps the entire session) to finish the tests.

3. Explain to your clients that you will review results next session. If you have additional time in Session 2, consider exploring one or more of the areas of concern you marked earlier in the ZTPI.

4. Review prior to next session—that is, prior to Session 3, review your clients' trauma, depression, and anxiety scores to determine the depth of their PTSD. If you have administered the ZTPI in paper form, go to the www.thetimeparadox.com website and input your clients' responses to each ZTPI statement. Print up your clients' scores, plot them on the graph (see Session 3, below), and staple the results to the front of your clients' hard copy ZTPI, noting which scores are highest and lowest. The graph is a visual blueprint for you to share with your clients; it shows what time perspectives you and your clients will work towards to gain an ideal time perspective.

Zimbardo Time Perspective Inventory (ZTPI) Short Form

Read each item and, as honestly as you can, answer the question: "How characteristic or true is this of me?" Please answer all of the following questions (Clinician—Use the scale below) from 1 (Very Untrue) to 5 (Very True)

1. I think about the bad things that have happened to me in the past.
2. Painful past experiences keep being replayed in my mind.
3. It's hard for me to forget unpleasant images of my youth.
4. Familiar childhood sights, sounds, smells often bring back a flood of wonderful memories.
5. Happy memories of good times spring readily to mind.
6. I enjoy stories about how things used to be in the "good old times."
7. Life today is too complicated; I would prefer the simpler life of the past.
8. Since whatever will be will be, it doesn't really matter what I do.
9. Often luck pays off better than hard work.
10. I make decisions on the spur of the moment.
11. Taking risks keeps my life from becoming boring. ·
12. It is important to put excitement in my life.
13. When I want to achieve something, I set goals and consider specific means for reaching those goals.

14. Meeting tomorrow's deadlines and doing other necessary work comes before tonight's play.

15. I complete projects on time by making steady progress.

Scale: Past negative: 1, 2, 3; Past positive: 4, 5, 6: Present fatalism: 7, 8, 9; Present hedonism: 10, 11, 12; Future: 13, 14, 15.

Session 3 (The Past)

1. Review—begin by lightly touching upon your clients' compliance with practicing the breathing technique on a daily basis. Ask if they have had the opportunity to employ it during times of stress and, if so, did they find it helpful. If not, discuss why. Reiterate the importance of continued practice in order to make it a part of their daily routine.

2. Test Results—share your clients' psychological (trauma, depression, and anxiety) test results. Explain their scores (minimal to no, minimal, moderate, severe, or extreme). If their scores are severe to extreme and this is upsetting to them, assuage their apprehension by telling them you will work together to improve their symptoms.

3. ZTPI—show your clients their ZTPI graph. PTSD survivors usually have high past negative scores, because their trauma keeps them stuck in their traumatic past. Their second highest score is generally present fatalistic or present hedonistic.

4. High Scores—explain the one or two highest scores. Past negative/present fatalistic, past negative/present hedonistic, past negative/future (negative/fatalistic)—these high score combinations are the hallmarks of trauma, depression, and/or anxiety.

5. Low Scores—explain the one or two lowest scores. Past positive/present hedonistic, past positive/future (positive)—these low score combinations are also the hallmarks of trauma, depression, and/or anxiety.

6. Comparison—compare and discuss your clients' scores with the suggested Ideal Time Perspective scores on the ZTPI graph (contact us at www.timeperspective.org for the graph).

7. Sharing—ask your clients to share with you a few past positive memories. If they have difficulty remembering anything positive, explain that they do, indeed, have past positive memories, but these have been overshadowed by their past negatives, which negate positive recollections. If your clients have undergone severe trauma, it's best to ask them to recall past positives prior to the trauma. If they still cannot recall a past positive, suggest they imagine, if they could have had a past positive experience, what would it have been like. These two suggestions will likely lead them to remembering an actual past positive, followed by additional positive memories. Ask about their best friends, best birthday, the best gift they ever received, and so forth, to pump the prime of good thoughts.

8. Explain—suggest to your clients that, whenever they have a past negative flashback or thought, they ought to immediately replace it with one of their past positive memories. Use specific individualized examples for your clients. For example, if your clients were in a motor vehicle accident and have flashbacks while driving, ask them to recall a positive experience while driving, such as singing along to

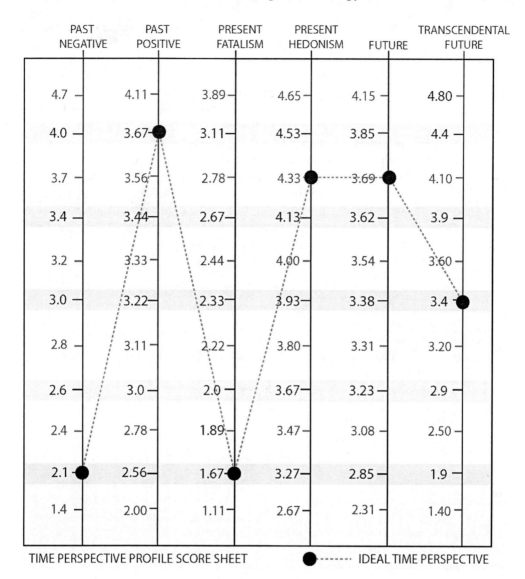

TIME PERSPECTIVE PROFILE SCORE SHEET   ●------- IDEAL TIME PERSPECTIVE

Table 1: Time Perspective Profile Score Sheet

a favorite song on the radio or enjoying the anticipation of reaching their destination, or which car they would like best to drive regardless of cost.

9. Practice—try replacing past negatives with past positives with your clients. If there is time remaining in the session, revisit one or more of the areas of concern you noted when your clients took the ZTPI.

Session 4 (The Present)

1. Review—begin by checking your clients' progress in replacing past negatives with past positives. If they have been having trouble, ask them to explain exactly what happens when this happens. If they find it impossible to replace a

severe traumatic flashback with a positive past experience, spend time reviewing past positive memories until they can easily recall them. Then ask them to practice recalling past positives throughout the day, so that, when a past negative occurs, they can more easily draw upon the past positive memories. Really, we want these practices to become habitual and not limited to treatment sessions.

2. Selected Present Hedonism—you and your client will employ *selected* present hedonism to offset *extreme* present hedonism or present fatalism. Also, prosocial behavior is an important aspect of TPT and is greatly encouraged. It offsets the tendency toward self-imposed isolation (anti-social behavior) experienced by many suffering from PTSD. Ask your clients what they enjoy doing. If they don't do anything other than work and/or isolate at home, ask them what they enjoyed doing prior to their trauma. Then suggest they take up that activity again. If they are unable to do so, for whatever reason—for example, an acquired disability—explore other feasible options.

Here are some suggestions to kick off prosocial present hedonistic behavior:

(a) Reconnecting via telephone or e-messaging with a family member or friend with whom your client has not felt like speaking since the trauma;
(b) Having a daily meal with family members or a friend instead of isolating in their room or at home;
(c) Participating in community or social functions that used to be of interest to your clients;
(d) Exploring the possibility of adopting a pet such as a small dog or cat;
(e) Growing a little, easy-to-tend garden; many herbs and plants can be grown indoors.
(f) Taking a leisurely walk outside, weather permitting, to a favorite place.
(g) Going to a local café for an afternoon coffee or tea.

3. Prosocial Behavior—if appropriate, you may wish to discuss with your clients the possibility of bringing a family member or members into subsequent sessions to assist them in the therapeutic process. During the family session(s), briefly explain TT and the TPT process so that family members understand what your clients are going through. On their own time, they might also take the ZTPI scale, so they become familiar with the terms of TPT.

4. Revisiting—if there is ample time remaining in the session, revisit one or more of the areas of concern you noted when your client took the ZTPI.

5. Session Conclusion—End the session on an up note by reinforcing that you are working together in the TPT process to help your clients learn simple and doable ways to improve their life in the present—more as teammates, than as client and therapist.

Session 5 (The Future)

1. Review—begin by checking your clients' progress:

(a) Replacing past negatives with past positives.
(b) Reviewing their selected present hedonism/new prosocial behaviors. Discuss what they have been doing in these areas to improve their lives. If they

are having difficulty, find out why and make appropriate suggestions; review Session 4, #5.

(c) Explaining how good memories lead to past positives, which are processed in the present. While in the present, your clients can create hopes and dreams and work toward a bright future positive.

2. Assist—help your clients make both short- and long-range plans for their brighter future. So that this is not an overwhelming task, start with their plans for the following day, followed by the week, the next two weeks, and so on. If they have difficulty with accomplishing daily activities due to lack of concentration and pace, suggest that they make a list of things they'd like to accomplish like organizing and paying bills, attending physician/therapist appointments, shopping or selected household chores, or spending time with important people in their lives. The list can be made and updated daily or weekly. Explain that there is no pass or fail—but that the goal in this process is to accomplish one or two of the items on their list each day, thereby proving to themselves that they are capable of planning for their future and following through with their plans. Areas to cover are occupational as well as social (family, friends, and acquaintances).

3. Revisit—if there is time remaining in the session, revisit one or more of the areas of concern you noted when your client took the ZTPI.

Session 6 (Balanced Time Perspectives Review)

1. Review—begin by checking your clients' progress. By this time, they should be practicing their breathing technique on a daily basis. They should also be able to replace all or most of their past negatives with past positives. However, if they are continuing to have difficulty, review Session 4., #1. Your clients should also be well on the way to practicing selected present hedonism/new prosocial behaviors. Discuss their progress. If they are having difficulty, discuss why and make appropriate suggestions. Review their future positive goals. Were they able to meet their short-term goals? If not, find out why.

2. Reinforce—emphasize that, previously, your clients' PTSD had kept them locked in their past negative trauma, but hopefully they have made good progress at reframing their past and are now equipped to plan for their brighter future positive while living in a more fulfilling present.

3. Revisit—if there are any areas of concern you noted when your clients took the ZTPI in Session 2, now is the time to address them. At this point in the TPT process, your clients may see that these are old issues that they have learned to deal with through TPT. If an issue is more deep-seated (such as abuse of any type—drug or alcohol, physical, sexual, or mental), then additional therapy may be necessary. Assure your clients that you will continue to work with them on such issues in future therapy.

4. Session Conclusion—during this, or a follow-up session, you may want to ask them to take the ZTPI once again. Scores may be reviewed and compared to their previous ZTPI scores administered in Session 2. You will know your clients understand and are implementing TPT in their lives if their scores have improved.

Be Flexible

Although we have used a logical progression in the development of each session, one of the beautiful things about TPT is the ability to move freely from one time perspective to another. We have found in our private clinical practice that some clients require additional time during one or more steps in the TPT process, or certain time perspectives may require immediate attention, superseding the suggested progression. The former usually occurs during Session 1, at which time the clients' need to review past negative trauma(s) replaces the therapy process we've just shared. As the clients' trauma is treated with great respect in TPT, you may have to spend two or more sessions reviewing their trauma and how it has affected their life. If this is the case, please do so. But by the fourth session, we suggest getting back on track with the TPT process as described. Another delay may occur when immediate present or future needs supplant the suggested TPT process. This is rare, but when it has been the case with our clients, we've been able to leap from Session 1 to Session 5, #2, then back to Sessions 2, 3, and 4 with a refresher Session 5, and concluding with Session 6—all with good results. So, feel free to improvise as needed.

We need to note, in conclusion, that there is now a large body of research and applications proving the many virtues of having a *balanced time perspective (BTP)*—high Past Positive, moderately high Positive Future, and moderate *selected* Present Hedonism, but low Past Negative and low Present Fatalism. That is the ideal time combination for all of us to achieve!

REFERENCES

Cherry, K., & Fogoros, R.N. (2018). The halo effect and how it affects you. Retrieved from https://www.verywellmind.com/what-is-the-halo-effect-2795906

Kaptchuck, T. (2012). Putting the placebo effect to work. Retrieved from https://www.health.harvard.edu/mind-and-mood/putting-the-placebo-effect-to-work

Long, P.W. (2011). Statistical/clinical significance. Retrieved from https://www.mentalhealth.com/dis-rs/rs-effect_size.html Sword, R.M., Sword, R.K.M., Brunskill, B., & Zimbardo, P. (2014). Time Perspective Therapy: A new time-based metaphor therapy for PTSD. *The Journal of Loss and Trauma: International Perspectives on Stress and Coping, 3*(19), 197–201.

Zimbardo, P., & Boyd, J. (2010). *The time paradox: The new psychology of time that will change your life.* New York, NY: Rider.

Zimbardo, P., & Sword, R.K.M. (2017). *Living & loving better with Time Perspective Therapy.* Jefferson, NC: McFarland.

Zimbardo, P., Sword, R.M., & Sword, R.K.M. (2012). *The time cure: Overcoming PTSD with the new psychology of Time Perspective Therapy.* San Francisco, CA: Wiley.

Zimbardo, P., Sword, R.M., & Sword, R.K.M. (2014). *The Time Cure Therapists Guide.* Available free of charge at www.timeperspectivetherapy.org

Transpersonal Psychotherapies

Harris L. Friedman

> A human being is a part of the whole called by us universe; a part limited
> in time and space. He experiences himself, his thoughts, and his feelings
> as something separate from the rest—a kind of optical delusion of con-
> sciousness.
>
> —Einstein (2010, p. 339)

Transpersonal psychology forms the basis for most transpersonal therapies, but there is little consensus as to the content, methods, and applications of this subfield of psychology. There are also people who would argue that transpersonal psychology is not a legitimate part of psychology, despite that its name includes "psychology," which is widely regarded as a science. In previous writings (e.g., Friedman, 2002, 2018), I have explored how mainstream psychology tends to reject transpersonal approaches as suffering from romanticism (i.e., by uncritically embracing pseudoscientific and unscientific approaches), as well how transpersonal psychology tends to reject mainstream approaches as suffering from scientism (e.g., by overcritically limiting what can be explored through ignoring or prematurely rejecting transpersonal phenomena). These concerns also apply to transpersonal therapies, and my approach to them is to try to reconcile both by finding a middle path via science (Friedman, 2015).

Defining Transpersonal Psychology

Despite many attempts to define the term "transpersonal psychology," its definition remains ambiguous. Ken Wilber (personal communication, 2002), a noted transpersonal philosopher, challenged efforts to adequately define the field, quipping "every year there is a contest to define *transpersonal*, and every year no one wins." Scholars, nevertheless, still attempt definitions, such as Hartelius, Caplan, and Rardin's (2007) based on three themes identified through their content analysis of previous definitions: (1) understanding self as beyond ego and interconnected with the cosmos as a whole; (2) including humans' spiritual and transcendent qualities beyond materialistic assumptions; and (3) emphasizing transformational growth processes. I also worked later with this paper's first author further refining a definition (Friedman & Hartelius, 2013; Hartelius & Friedman, 2010). In addition, I recently coedited *The Wiley-Blackwell Handbook of Transpersonal*

Psychology (Friedman & Hartelius, 2015/2013) in which its numerous chapters represent many varying approaches to transpersonal psychology, and I like to say, when pressed to define this diverse subfield, that this book—taken as a whole with its many contradictory viewpoints yet unreconciled, provides a good definitional starting place. However, in a recent interchange with Wilber (personal communication, 2019) when I wanted to claim the prize, he did not concede that I won the contest.

If pressed even more to share a definition, I usually sputter that the gist of transpersonal psychology for me rests on the recognition that the individual person is not some sort of isolated entity but, rather, is an interconnected web of relationships that can be seen as systems within systems within systems. In this sense, transpersonal psychology emphasizes that the fundamental nature of a person goes beyond (or "trans") the in"divid"ual (as in divided from the world as a separate and unitary entity). In other words, my holistic vision is to see persons as expansive, not limited to the boundary of their skin in the present time and place. I take from James's (1890) insight that people draw arbitrary distinctions between self and not-self, and I conclude that the person is not merely a biological organism, but an interconnected matrix that potentially includes all of the cosmos. I call my approach the "self-expansiveness" model, which I have been developing for many years (e.g., Friedman, 1983, 2018), and this serves as the basis for how I approach transpersonal therapies.

My model also rests on an unprovable value assumption, namely that the more expansive one's sense of self is, the more holistic one is, in a desirable way. If people see themselves in restricted ways (e.g., limited to just their biological organism in the "here and now"), they would act as but a small shadow of their larger potential selves. In contrast, if they see themselves as manifesting the cosmos (the largest imaginable whole), they would live more congruently with the insights of many of the world's great spiritual traditions, such as abiding in *grace* or in living in accord with the *tao*.

In this way, I consider seeking self-expansiveness as striving to go beyond a conventional-constricted view of the person toward holding a larger holistic vision that includes identifying with more of the world as being literally oneself. From this expansive perspective, the person no longer would remain alienated from the environment, both social and physical, that is the ground of their existence—and without which no individual human can exist. People require food, gravity, and oxygen—and the addition of interpersonal relationships, to develop and survive as persons. From this view, the notion of the isolated-individual human as an island unto itself is a destructive myth, which a transpersonal vision can supplant in a more sophisticated and beneficial way, including as understood through a scientific psychology.

This self-expansiveness model challenges some inherent aspects of the prevailing contemporary Western worldview, such as exists at the root of capitalism. Narrow self-interest is conventionally prioritized over altruistic concern for others and the environment within this economic worldview. As such, the selfish lack of an expansive vision leads to pathology that goes beyond mere psychopathology—as it results in a toxic-cultural malaise that puts all life on earth in peril. Transpersonal therapies can address this at the level of the individual, as in transpersonal psychotherapies, or at more comprehensive levels, as in using transpersonal therapies more broadly to heal larger systems. I note that the word "healing" derives etymologically from making whole, while the word "therapy" derives etymologically from divine healing. I also note that I use transpersonal "therapies" in this essay, rather than psychotherapies, as I see the former term to be more inclusive, allowing for interventions that are not limited to involving just the "psyche" at the personal level, as these therapies can focus in a more holistic way than restricted to individuals seen as apart from their contexts as, once more, humans can be seen as systems within systems within systems (Friedman, 2019).

The Scientific Basis of Transpersonal Psychology

Transpersonal psychology has pioneered the study of many areas that are now accepted, but were marginalized and even denigrated, by mainstream psychology until recently. Consciousness studies and meditation practices, for example, are now burgeoning scientific areas that, until recently, were dismissed as nonsense by psychology's mainstream. Such approaches that have long histories in many Eastern and indigenous cultures had previously been denigrated as "primitive," while transpersonal psychology explored these with a respect that anticipated the currently accepted multiculturalism. However, much of what is most interesting in transpersonal psychology has not yet been accepted within the mainstream. For example, transpersonal psychology challenges what is commonly viewed as proper scientific methods (Braud & Anderson, 1999) by advocating for alternatives, some of which are still too radical for mainstream acceptance, such as Tart's (1975) proposal for state-specific research. Using alternate states of consciousness, as Tart proposed, may be the best way to study some elusive transpersonal phenomena, such as related to exceptional experiences that may simply be incomprehensible within prevailing frameworks. For example, the typical Western study of meditation involves teaching beginners to meditate through short-term training. Contrast this to cumulative-cultural knowledge derived from spiritual traditions where practices to explore higher consciousness have been refined and tested over millennia within their cultural contexts by using meditators with a lifetime of experience as "researchers." These traditional ways of knowing result in empirical data, but from a different form of science than is customarily understood in the West. Consequently, alternate methods for studying extraordinary phenomena may be more appropriate than using conventional scientific approaches, which also applies to research on transpersonal therapies.

Transpersonal Therapies

There are many types of therapies that stem from, or seek to inculcate, a transpersonal vision, and broadly they can be called transpersonal, even though they differ considerably in their assumption and approaches. There are a number of books written on transpersonal therapies (e.g., Boorstein, 1996; Cortright, 1997), and I have also previously explored this topic (e.g., Friedman, 2012, 2014; Rodrigues & Friedman, 2015). A good example of an early psychotherapy that was explicitly called transpersonal is psychosynthesis (Assagioli, 1993). It starts with a conventional psychoanalysis but, once that personal work is accomplished, extends this by including a larger synthesis that incorporates many transpersonal components aiming to integrate the diverse aspects of a person into a more expansive-transpersonal whole. For example, psychosynthesis uses various exercises, such as visualizations, to bring people to a more integrated consciousness.

There are many other consciousness-altering methods, in addition to visualizations, that can help people grow beyond the delusion that they are isolated entities. One of these is holotropic breathwork (see Smirnova, this volume). By intentionally altering one's breathing, profound shifts in consciousness can occur that burst through the bubble in which people seem insularly separate toward a higher realization that the person is more than just what is bounded within the skin of an isolated individual. This consciousness shift can be attributed to simple physiological changes caused by voluntarily altering breathing patterns, which cause changes in blood-gas ratios, as well as due to set and setting (i.e., the internal and external context, respectively, in which change is expected), and this practice can be every bit as potent as ingesting psychedelic substances. The point is that it is difficult to wake-up from the prevailing cultural limitations that have literally entranced people to see themselves as but a fragment of their more holistic-transpersonal selves, so a practice that provides a profound alteration to so-called "normal" perception can offer a glimpse, given the proper set and setting, into a more expansive sense of self. Of course, a glimpse requires more to ensure a stable change from a fleeting state to an enduring trait, such as a regular spiritual practice or a long-term commitment to a transpersonal therapy.

I prefer not to privilege any one method for use in transpersonal therapies, but rather look toward waking up to the fact, not merely a belief, that the self is fundamentally more than personal—as it is profoundly transpersonal, and that this realization is healing in and of itself. If people see themselves as less that they could be, they are by definition diminished in their self-concept—and live their lives as smaller beings than they would if experiencing more self-expansiveness.

One transpersonal modality that is becoming quite acceptable these days involves using psychedelic medicines to heal. I recently was involved in a series of studies at some top U.S. medical schools using some of these substances to facilitate healing in patients suffering so-called "death anxiety" related to life-threatening cancers (e.g., Belser et al., 2017). The effects of these medicines in this context were shown to help people grow from anxiety to achieving a sense of peace with the inevitable they were facing. The use of these medicines that expand (rather than diminish, as is often the result of more conventional psychiatric drugs) one's experience is undergoing a renaissance after years of suppression within a culture that predominantly shuns recognizing that the belief in the self as being isolated is a fundamental delusion (Friedman, 2006). In my own experience, these medicines have been the most powerful tools for realizing an expansive sense of self.

However, the point is not that psychedelic medicines matter so much, as they are but one means of waking up to one's transpersonal nature. The waking is what is important, regardless of how that might be accomplished, and not the means by which one awakes. One can achieve this realization spontaneously, through something as simple as watching a sunset, feeling merged with a lover, meditating and praying, staring at a flickering light or listening to drumming, or through any number of other means, including through transpersonal therapies. Ways to intentionally alter consciousness exist in every culture, from the twirling of Sufi dervishes to the communally shared attention to dream states (including recognizing ordinary waking consciousness as possibly just being one among many dream states) in some Australian aboriginal group, so transpersonal therapies harness a cultural universal (Glover & Friedman, 2015), namely "psychotechnologies," to enter alternate (e.g., non-ordinary) states of consciousness, for healing purposes.

One example of this is "voice dialogue therapy" (Berchik, Rock, & Friedman, 2016).

This approach encourages clients to engage with their so-called "subpersonalities" through having internal conversations among different parts of the person. Clients engaging in this approach often report feeling in an alternate state, and often realize that their sense of self is not unitary but, instead, composed of parts that might be in competition or even conflict, rather than in harmony, with each other. This illustrates how the usual-unitary sense of self is limited, and seeing the self as a system composed of many subordinate systems that, in turn, composes many superordinate systems is a better depiction.

Using any one of the many consciousness-altering modalities to heal in a larger way than just for symptom removal is common in transpersonal therapies, but their use is not necessary to constitute a transpersonal therapy in my view. If a therapist embraces a transpersonal view when working with a client, then I would accede transpersonal status to whatever therapeutic modality is used. I would extend this to including doing even the most basic behavioral conditioning, if used by therapists who recognize themselves, as well as their clients, in a transpersonal way.

Transpersonal therapies can be particularly useful for concerns that are not well understood, or respected, by mainstream approaches. To treat someone as being psychotic when they are only temporarily unhinged during a transition to a higher state is a potentially grave mistake, but something not uncommon in mainstream practice. Near-death experiences, for example, often lead to people embracing more spiritual lives, but are often very disruptive initially, as people might choose to leave unfulfilling careers and relationships after having such an awakening (Fracasso, Greyson, & Friedman, 2015). For people with such extraordinary experiences, mainstream approaches might even be iatrogenic, and transpersonal therapies especially helpful.

Making Sense of Diverse Transpersonal Modalities

The following are four categories, not exhaustive, that can be used to make further sense of transpersonal modalities. This categorization is based on techniques emphasized, along with examples of therapies.

Attentional: Attention-modifying strategies, such as hypnosis, meditation, and neurofeedback (Evans, 2006), to name just a few, can be used to explore higher states of consciousness for therapeutic ends.

Depth psychological. Mostly from a psychoanalytic tradition, depth psychotherapies can be extrapolated to a transpersonal level. Jungian therapy (Jung, 1970; Levy, 1983), as just one, works with deep layers of collective unconscious, unconscious, and conscious material, which are often transpersonal.

Somatic. Various somatic (using the body) approaches, such as holotropic breathwork, can facilitate deep consciousness alterations. Similarly, working with the body in other ways (e.g., bioenergetics; Glazer & Friedman, 2009), as well as by using traditional body-based practices (e.g., yogic postures, repetitive movements like Sufic twirling, evocative music from shamanic drumming, and photic stimulation from staring into a flame) can achieve alternate consciousness states. Various medicines, especially those called psychedelics, can also be used for such exploration, as can alternative healing practices (e.g., acupuncture and many variants of so-called energy medicine).

There are also some commonalities that can be generalized about many transpersonal therapies. Focus on immediate experience, not just conceptualizations about experience, is typical to many transpersonal therapies. Seeing these experiences as "sacred," although not necessarily in any religious sense of this term, is also common. In addition, therapeutic goals are not usually limited to treating dysfunctions, but instead often are growth oriented. Last, the therapeutic relationship is tantamount, as transpersonal psychotherapists tend to relate to their clients in a way that allow greater exchanges of potential information, such by acknowledging profound interconnectedness, as well as the sacredness of both the therapist and client—and their relationship.

As a transpersonal therapist, despite whatever modalities I might use, I still work from a transpersonal orientation. Even if I am just applying simple behavioral techniques, I would be mindful that my client is not merely a pigeon or rat being operantly conditioned, but a person who is a biopsychosocial-spiritual whole human being. With that stated, I also have access to a wide-range of modalities that can bring people into transpersonal places, in addition to the usual therapeutic tools.

Concerns About Transpersonal Therapies

It is important to raise the concern about whether any therapy can actually be transpersonal based on the vexing question, does the personal matter from a transpersonal vantage? Many spiritual traditions minimize working through psychological issues by seeing these as attachments to let go rather than to resolve. From this vantage, any therapy dealing with the mundane world could simply be seen as a distraction from the "real" spiritual work needed to attain so-called "enlightenment." Some gurus and spiritual guides might suggest that, instead of working on personal and interpersonal concerns, one should instead meditate or pray harder. From this perspective, all therapies may be seen as unworthy of the transpersonal label. However, I disagree, as there are a myriad of spiritual traps (e.g., spiritual bypass, spiritual materialism, etc.) showing the need for personal healing, despite focus of therapy might be placed on the transpersonal. Even an enlightened teacher, not just a novice on a spiritual path, could commit atrocities due to unresolved psychological issues, and such abuses are rampant among spiritual practitioner in all traditions. In this regard, I want to mention that I often have been approached by potential clients seeking transpersonal therapy who seemed to me to need personal therapy instead. One of the important skills for a transpersonal therapist is to know when to say "no." I am thinking of a client, a trance medium who had troubling dissociative episodes that frequently placed her in dangerous circumstances. I told her she did not need transpersonal therapy at that point in her life (as her transpersonal experiences seemed to exceed my own) but needed, instead, to work on her personal issues causing her fugues. Of course, as a transpersonal therapist, I respected her transpersonal experiences, but I chose to focus elsewhere for helping her.

There are also many other pitfalls for transpersonal therapists to avoid. In a situation fraught with ambiguity, such as in trying to discern whether a reported spiritual experience is genuine or something else (e.g., a psychotic experience) is quite challenging. Great harm can be done in either underestimating or overestimating levels of psychopathology.

It is also especially difficult in this area of practice to remain humble, as transpersonal therapists often receive adulation from their clients. This could even lead to cults forming around their work, turning a transpersonal therapy into a New Age religion, and for such aggrandizement to seduce a transpersonal therapist into assuming a "guru" role, rather than one vested in healing grounded in science, which could be a tragic mistake.

It is also imperative for transpersonal therapists to recognize that practices that can heal can also harm. Transpersonal modalities are powerful and can be, in certain circumstances, iatrogenic. For example, even something that seems as innocuous as meditation can cause great damage to some (Schlosser, Sparby, Voros, Jones, & Marchant, 2019).

Mentioning these pitfalls is neither meant to dissuade practitioners from engaging in transpersonal therapies, nor clients from seeking these services. After all, conventional therapies suffer from their comparable pitfalls, such as the damage often done by mislabeling people with genuine transpersonal concerns in denigrating ways that lead to bad outcomes, especially when people are vulnerable while on the cusp of transformative changes, such as during spiritual emergence.

One last concern involves the lack of much systematic evidence for the effectiveness of transpersonal therapies. There are many unique challenges in doing research evidencing their effectiveness, including with any attempts to standardize techniques and measure relevant variables. Especially problematic is finding adequate funding to do such research well, as transpersonal therapies are marginalized by the mainstream, so funding is rarely available. Consequently, most studies in this area have only been done with small sample sizes and lacked adequate controls, and often the researchers involved had a vested interest in the outcome for their "pet" therapies. However, there are many robust studies on some modalities that are implicitly, if not explicitly, transpersonal, such as mindfulness-based techniques that have been associated with positive outcomes in the treatment of various psychopathologies, but this literature also suffers from many flaws, such as tending to ignore possible iatrogenic effects. In general, transpersonal therapies should be seen as not yet established as effective when using conventional standards to judge effectiveness. That, however, does not mean these are to be avoided, as they are often the only approaches that will deal with client's transpersonal concerns. In general, I would place transpersonal therapies in the same evaluative position as humanistic therapies, and conclude that, although much work is still needed, they are amply enough supported by scientific research to be used with caution (Friedman, 2016b).

Who Is Qualified to Practice Transpersonal Therapy?

There is no singular path to become qualified to do transpersonal therapy, just as there is no singular transpersonal therapy. However, there are training programs in various modalities that are called transpersonal, as well as in therapies that explicitly use this term. For example, one can attend individual workshops, get certified by professional associations, and even get accredited-graduate degrees in psychosynthesis from some schools. There are also burgeoning areas, such as numerous training programs in mindfulness approaches, that can be seen as transpersonal, even if not called by that name. One area in particular that seems on the upswing is in using psychedelics within therapy, as there are several programs recently started (e.g., at the California Institute for Integral Studies' Center for Psychedelic Therapies and Research). There are also a few training programs in "generic" transpersonal therapies that do not emphasize any specific modality (e.g., those accredited by the European Society of Transpersonal Psychotherapy).

In my opinion, it is best to first become a trained professional in one or more conventional types of therapy before embarking on becoming a transpersonal therapist. After working from such a vantage, expanding into other areas can be done with formal training or simply by growing as a professional through readings, taking workshops, seeking supervision, and following a personal practice. My own path included receiving a conventional doctoral degree and licensure in clinical psychology, as well as completing, at a postdoctoral level, training as a bioenergetic and gestalt, as well as hypno-, therapist. I also explored many other modalities through seeking out therapeutic experiences and various workshops. Insofar as transpersonal therapy is a holistic endeavor, one who dares to present themselves as a transpersonal therapist needs not only deep and broad training, including for working with personal concerns from mainstream perspectives, but also transpersonal experiences that are uniquely suited for helping clients delve into their transpersonal concerns.

In seeking out a transpersonal therapist, I caution potential clients to look at certain indicators that could mean trouble. If a therapist dogmatically pushes a particular worldview, or seems arrogant rather than humble, I would avoid that person. I suggest seeking a therapist who possesses solid mainstream credentials—and is respected by the mainstream, as in being appropriately licensed, belonging to recognized professional associations, having affiliations with institutions such as universities or hospitals, and so forth, yet has gone beyond these to embrace transpersonal perspectives. My opinion is that working with therapists holding themselves to be transpersonal in orientation is a somewhat risky endeavor, but one is likely to find some of the best healers, as well as the worst abusers, in that lot.

The Process of Doing Transpersonal Therapy

Transpersonal therapies should ideally start with some sort of assessment that respectfully considers transpersonal concerns. One common concern involves differential diagnosis of the emergence of higher consciousness from psychosis, as these often share common religious and spiritual themes (Johnson & Friedman, 2008). There are a number of transpersonal assessment strategies, including various tests useful in such assessments (see Friedman & MacDonald, 1997; MacDonald & Friedman, 2002, 2015). I want to mention the Self-Expansive Level Form (SELF; Friedman, 1983, 2018), which I find useful for this purpose. From there, various transpersonal interventions, including psychotherapies, can be used. The following brief case study shows one way I proceeded to work with a client through an explicitly transpersonal approach.

An attractive young woman sought psychotherapy with me because she felt like her life had no meaning. She literally described herself as feeling like an ant, small and insignificant. Although she was bright and artistically talented, she had worked mostly menial jobs, including some occasional sex work, and had not pursued higher education. Her relationships were emotionally shallow, and she had never been with a partner very long. She often engaged in what could be called "hook-up" culture that involved superficial sex rather than forming deeper interpersonal connections. She disparaged conventional religious beliefs and denigrated mainstream lifestyles as boring and pointless. Yet she recognized that something was missing in her life, and she had enough motivation to explore a psychotherapeutic solution to her problems. As part of my clinical assessment,

I administered the SELF to her and, as expected, she showed a pattern of disidentifying with everything on that measure. Her sense of self was very constricted, as reflected both on that measure and during her clinical interview. She was not only disconnected to her here-and-now personal self, but she felt nowhere (a reversal of here-now to now-here but dropping the hyphen) in all aspects of her life.

After assessing her and her situation, I engaged her initially with a series of bioenergetic exercises (Friedman & Glazer, 2010). I had her hit a pillow while encouraging her to voice her despair by shouting louder and louder variants of "life sucks!" This was her perceived reality, and she chose the specific words. She quickly got into the feeling of rage, accompanied by angry tears. Then there was a breakthrough, a softening accompanied by a longing for something deeper in her life, so I asked her to reach out to the world by putting forth her hands and voicing "I want more—give it to me!" She oscillated between feelings of anger and longing, and I encouraged her to express these physically in an alternating pattern, like rocking a car back and forth to free it from being stuck in mud. Processing her experience after these enactments led to discussions about purpose in life, including not only about deeper connections with people but also, over time in later sessions, to transpersonal connections in her life.

I worked with this woman for several years, usually weekly but sometimes taking long breaks. I typically started work with physical exercises to bypass her sense of being stuck by getting her moving and voicing her emotions. Then the focus tended to shift toward the end of her sessions to processing what arose from her experiences in therapy, including deeper and deeper transpersonal reflections. Her physical and vocal expressions of things such as "why is life so unfair?" led to her becoming more connected to not only her feelings in the here-and-now but, also, to a larger sense of social justice—and her wanting to make the world a more meaningful place for all. I note that the physical exercises resulted in significant alterations of consciousness states and enabled her to expand her sense of self experientially, not just cognitively. As therapy came toward termination, I had her once more take the SELF as a measure of her changes, and she identified with many aspects of the world with which she had formerly rejected as being related to herself, including all personal and many of the transpersonal items on that measure. She returned to school to study in the helping professions and, last that I heard from her, she was working internationally with a nonprofit helping children in refugee camps in war-torn areas.

Conclusion

I prefer using the term transpersonal therapies to the term transpersonal psychotherapies because I see the former as more inclusive of a variety of levels of intervention. In my own work these days, I am gravitating toward doing "transpersonal coaching," working in ways unfettered by antiquated and restrictive regulations that limit what a psychologist can do as a healer. I am also working more these days within organizational settings, including international contexts, with issues such as resolving conflicts that affect many, rather than a few, individuals (e.g., Glover & Friedman, 2015; Friedman, 2016a). The skillset is the same, but the scope of applications is larger.

I like to imagine a world where a wider acceptance of transpersonal therapies could lead. Could programs dealing with criminal offenders focus on developing transpersonal self-expansiveness that could increase empathy for victims and facilitate more acceptance of altruistic, rather than predatory, social roles? Could corporate leaders be encouraged to develop transpersonal perspectives that increase their commitment to environmental preservation and social justice? Could politicians be expected to show genuine deep empathy toward their constituents in order to be elected, and their performance measured not by material growth but, instead, by willingness to share resources more equitably in order to achieve a healthier and more balanced world? Being able to explore these types of concerns from a transpersonal perspective that scrupulously avoids metaphysical (e.g., religious and spiritual) language and is scientifically accessible could be better received than using parochial approaches based on divisive nonscientific traditions.

Therapists practicing from a scientific transpersonal framework could conduct outcome studies to ensure that their clinical interventions are worthwhile and, I am confident, that such studies could generate results favorable when compared to other therapeutic approaches. By embracing transpersonal perspectives, therapists could also avoid both romantic and scientistic limitations and, instead, have a vision that is based on science, but a science that is more expansive than what the mainstream currently offers. Transpersonal therapists could operate under the most inclusive perspectives to heal individuals and larger systems through ways that are secular, yet facilitating the optimum development of the further reaches of human potential.

Transpersonal therapies are likely to become more important through the resurgence of psychedelic therapeutic applications, as well as through the many significant advances happening in neurobiology providing various technologies for altering consciousness (Krippner & Friedman, 2010). Finally, transpersonal psychology is forging a role in social change and other larger systems applications (Friedman, 2016a). I believe that the transpersonal perspective provides the most inclusive framework for holistic applications in an increasingly fragmented world, and is uniquely suited to heal divides that threaten not just humanity's sanity but very existence.

References

Assagioli, R. (1993). *Psychosynthesis*. London: Thorsons.

Belser, A.B., Agin-Liebes, G., Swift, T.C., Pilgreen, S., Devenot, N., Friedman, H.L., … Ross, S. (2017). Psilocybin as a treatment for anxiety in cancer patients: An interpretative phenomenological analysis. *Journal of Humanistic Psychology*, 57(4), 354–388.

Berchik, Z., Rock, A., & Friedman, H. (2016). Allow me to introduce my selves: An introduction to and phenomenological study of Voice Dialogue therapy.

Boorstein, S. (Ed.) (1996). *Transpersonal Psychotherapy* (2nd ed.). Albany, NY: State University of New York Press.

Braud, W., & Anderson, R. (1999). *Transpersonal research methods for the social sciences: Honoring human experience*. Thousand Oaks, CA: Sage.

Cortright, B. (1997). *Psychotherapy and spirit: Theory and practice in transpersonal psychotherapy*. Albany, NY: State University of New York Press.

Einstein, A. (2010). *The ultimate quotable Einstein*. Princeton, NJ: Princeton University Press.

Evans, J. (2006). *Handbook of neurofeedback: Dynamics and clinical applications*. London. UK: Haworth.

Fracasso, C., Greyson, B., & Friedman, H. (2015/2013). Near-death experiences and transpersonal psychology: Focus on helping near-death experiencers. In H. Friedman & G. Hartelius (Eds.). *The Wiley-Blackwell handbook of transpersonal psychology* (pp. 367–380). Oxford, UK: Wiley-Blackwell.

Friedman, H. (1983). The Self-Expansiveness Level Form: A conceptualization and measurement of a transpersonal construct. *The Journal of Transpersonal Psychology, 15*, 37–50.

Friedman, H. (2002). Transpersonal psychology as a scientific field. *International Journal of Transpersonal Studies, 21*, 175–187.

Friedman, H. (2006). The renewal of psychedelic research: Implications for humanistic and transpersonal psychology. *The Humanistic Psychologist, 34*(1), 39–58.

Friedman, H. (2012). Transpersonal psychotherapies: An approach critical to mainstream assumptions and practices. *Journal of Critical Psychology, Counselling and Psychotherapy, 12*(4), 199–209.

Friedman, H. (2014). Finding meaning through transpersonal approaches in clinical psychology: Assessments and psychotherapies. *International Journal of Existential Psychology and Psychotherapy, V,* 45–49.

Friedman, H. (2015). Further developing transpersonal psychology as a science: Building and testing middle-range transpersonal theories. *International Journal of Transpersonal Studies, 34*(1–2), 175–184.

Friedman, H. (2016a). Using transpersonal and transcultural psychological concepts for reconciling conflict: Focus on Aikido and related martial arts, such as Hapkido. *Neuroquantology, 14*(2), 213–225.

Friedman, H. (2016b). Humanistic psychotherapies are amply supported by scientific research. *PsycCRITIQUES, 61*(26), n.p. (Article 6).

Friedman, H. (2018). Transpersonal psychology as a heterodox approach to psychological science: Focus on the construct of self-expansiveness and its measure. *Archives of Scientific Psychology, 6*(1), 230–242.

Friedman, H. (2019). Transpersonal healing. In P. Dunn (ed.), *Holistic healing: Theories, research and practices* (pp. 198–213). Toronto, Canada: Canadian Scholars.

Friedman, H., & Glazer, R. (2010). Bioenergetic therapy. In I.B. Weiner & W.E. Craighead, *Corsini encyclopedia of psychology* (4th ed., pp. 234–235). Hoboken, NJ: Wiley.

Friedman, H., & Hartelius, G. (2013). Transpersonal psychology. In T. Teo (Ed.), *Encyclopedia of critical psychology* (pp. 2036–2040), New York, NY: Springer Verlag.

Friedman, H., & Hartelius, G. (Eds.). (2015/2013). *The Wiley-Blackwell handbook of transpersonal Psychology.* Oxford, UK: Wiley-Blackwell.

Friedman, H., & MacDonald, D. (1997). Towards a working definition of transpersonal assessment. *Journal of Transpersonal Psychology, 29,* 105–122.

Glover, J., & Friedman, H. (2015). *Transcultural competence: Navigating cultural differences in the global community.* Washington, D.C.: American Psychological Association.

Hartelius, G., Caplan, M., & Rardin, M. (2007). *Transpersonal psychology: Defining the past, divining the future.* The Humanistic Psychologist, 35*(2), 1–26.

Hartelius, G., & Friedman, H. (2010). Transpersonal psychology. In I.B. Weiner & W.E. Craighead (Eds.), *Corsini encyclopedia of psychology* (4th ed., pp. 1800–1802). Hoboken, NJ: Wiley.

James, W. (1950/1890). *The principles of psychology.* New York, NY: Dover.

Johnson, C., & Friedman, H. (2008). Enlightened or delusional? Differentiating religious, spiritual, and transpersonal experience from psychopathology. *Journal of Humanistic Psychology, 48*(4), 505–527.

Jung, C. (1970). *Collected Works.* London, UK: Routledge.

Krippner, S., & Friedman, H. (Eds.). (2010). *Mysterious minds: The neurobiology of psychics mediums, and other extraordinary people.* Santa Barbara, CA: Praeger.

Levy, J. (1983). Transpersonal psychology and Jungian psychology. *Journal of Humanistic Psychology, 23*(2), 42–52.

MacDonald, D., & Friedman, H. (2002). Assessment of humanistic, transpersonal and spiritual constructs: State of the science. *Journal of Humanistic Psychology, 42,* 102–125.

MacDonald, D., & Friedman, H. (2015/2013). Quantitative assessment of transpersonal and spiritual constructs. In H. Friedman & G. Hartelius (Eds.). *The Wiley-Blackwell handbook of transpersonal psychology* (pp. 281–299). Oxford, UK: Wiley-Blackwell.

Rodrigues, V., & Friedman, H. (2015/2013). Transpersonal psychotherapies. In H. Friedman & G. Hartelius (Eds.). *The Wiley-Blackwell handbook of transpersonal psychology* (pp. 580–594). Oxford, UK: Wiley-Blackwell.

Schlosser, M., Sparby, T.,Voros, S., Jones, R., & Marchant, N. (2019)Unpleasant meditation-related experiences in regular meditators: Prevalence, predictors, and conceptual considerations. *PLoSONE 14*(5): e0216643. https://doi.org/10.1371/journal.pone.0216643

Smirnova, M. (this volume). Holotropic breathwork in a clinical setting.

Tart, C. (1975). *States of consciousness.* New York, NY: E.P. Dutton.

PART 2

Creative and Expressive Arts Interventions

Natalie Rogers's Person-Centered Expressive Arts Therapy

Sue Ann Herron

Who was Natalie Rogers (1928–2015)? She was the daughter of Helen Rogers, an artist and designer, and Carl Ransom Rogers, a distinguished and renowned American psychologist who was, along with Abraham Maslow, among the founders of the humanistic approach to psychology. Both men had an early influence on the evolution of N. Rogers's fundamental understanding of humanistic psychology, as she incorporated their philosophy in the development of her work with expressive arts as a psychotherapist. She called her unique multimodal, client-centered approach to expressive arts therapy, *person-centered expressive arts therapy* (Herron, 2010).

Natalie Rogers met Lawrence Fuchs in 1949 while they were both working at the United World Federalists in New York City. In 1950, Fuchs and Rogers married. While Fuchs was a professor at Brandeis University, he and Rogers were introduced to Abraham Maslow, who had founded the Psychology Department at Brandeis and taught there from 1951 to 1969 (Burrows, 2013). During a faculty gathering at the Fuchs's home, Maslow urged Rogers to enroll in Brandeis University to further her professional goals, informing her that tuition was free for spouses of faculty members. Delighted, Rogers took Maslow's advice to heart, enrolled, and completed her master's degree under Maslow's supervision in 1960. Her master's thesis was titled, *A Play Therapist's Approach to the Creative Art Experience* (Rogers, 1960). This was the genesis of Rogers's interest in creativity and art therapy (Herron, 2010).

In 1961 she began her career as a psychotherapist and continued to do psychotherapy in the Boston area for the next 12 years (Herron, 2010). During that time Rogers also "immersed herself in more social activism, self-empowerment, and encounter group work at Greenhouse training program in Boston" (p. 28). After completing her training there, she "was ready to take her newly acquired feminism and group skills to the West Coast" (p. 28). In 1970, after 20 years of marriage and raising three children, Rogers divorced, and in 1974 she moved to the San Francisco Bay Area to start a new life. There she opened a practice in psychotherapy and studied movement and embodied creativity with Anna Halprin in her Dancers' Workshop in San Francisco (Herron, 2008). From the late 1930s on, Halprin has been "creating revolutionary directions for dance, inspiring artists in all fields" ("Anna Halprin: Biography," para. 1). Rogers described how her training with Anna, and later with Daria Halprin, "brought me to full awareness of the unerring wisdom of the body and its language" (Rogers, 2011, p. 13).

Rogers also spent time studying Gestalt art therapy with Janie Rhyne, who wrote *The Gestalt Art Experience* (Rhyne, 1973). Rhyne studied with Fritz Perls at the Gestalt Institute of San Francisco from 1965 to 1967, and received her doctoral degree in psychology from the University of California, Santa Cruz, in 1979 (Lusebrink, 2013).

After immersing herself in embodied creativity and Gestalt art therapy, Rogers was primed with new skills in her psychotherapeutic repertoire, going on to create the Person-Centered Expressive Therapy Institute (PCETI), a nonprofit institute, with her daughter Frances, where Rogers developed and first offered her intensive training program called person-centered expressive arts therapy (Herron, 2010). Rogers learned about the client-centered or person-centered philosophy initially through osmosis and then through working together as a colleague with her father in six workshops on the Person-Centered Approach (PCA) (Herron, 2010, pp. 79–108). In a 1942 article, C. Rogers defined his client-centered or person-centered philosophy as follows:

> Client-centered therapy operates primarily upon one central and basic hypothesis which has undergone relatively little change with the years. This hypothesis is that the client has within himself the capacity, latent if not evident, to understand those aspects of his life and of himself which are causing him pain, and the capacity and the tendency to reorganize himself and his relationship to life in the direction of self-actualization and maturity in such a way as to bring a greater degree of internal comfort. The function of the therapist is to create such a psychological atmosphere as will permit this capacity and this strength to become effective rather than latent or potential [Rogers, 1950, p. 23].

Although Natalie Rogers was close to her father, it was also important to her to be recognized for her own distinctive work apart from his. Early on in the Person-Centered Approach (PCA) workshops with C. Rogers, she struggled to be recognized as a colleague. Chilton (2006) wrote about a significant personal event that happened to Natalie during the 1974 PCA workshop. A handwritten note in the archives reads, "Carl noted her anger at having recently left one situation where she was the 'wife of' and now found herself in a situation where she was seen as the 'daughter of' … would like to be my colleague but not my secy-helper[*sic*]" (Rogers, 1975, p. 12).

In Herron's (2010) dissertation, *Natalie Rogers: An Experiential Psychology of Self-Realization Beyond Abraham Maslow and Carl Rogers*, analysis of data gathered from 25 interviews with N. Rogers uncovered four of her ultimate goals:

(a) to be her own person, someone who is recognized and valued for her own work rather than being recognized and valued for being Carl Rogers's daughter;

(b) to have her work with person-centered expressive arts therapy (PCEAT) viewed as her own unique contribution to and enhancement of Carl Rogers's person-centered approach and legacy;

(c) to empower others, especially women, through her person-centered expressive arts therapy work;

(d) to promote conflict resolution and world peace through the use of expressive arts work internationally [pp. 12–13].

By the time Rogers died in 2015 at age 87, she had fulfilled all four of her ultimate goals.

Rogers was a pioneer in the field of expressive arts therapy and the founder of person-centered expressive arts therapy. She helped organize the International Expressive Art Therapy Association, believing in the greater merits of an inclusive, cross-cultural, worldwide organization. In 1998, she received a Shining Star Award from the International

Expressive Art Therapy Association, a lifetime achievement award for "being a pioneer in the field of integrative arts therapy, education, and consultation" (Herron, 2010, p. 216). Rogers also received the Carl Rogers Heritage Award for "outstanding contribution to the theory and practice of humanistic psychology" ("Carl Rogers Award," n.d.). She authored three books, *Emerging Woman: A Decade of Midlife Transitions* (1980), *The Creative Connection: Expressive Arts as Healing* (1993), and *The Creative Connection for Groups: Person-Centered Expressive Arts for Healing and Social Change* (2011), and numerous articles. She lectured at and facilitated workshops worldwide, in Russia, Latin America, Japan, South Korea, and across Europe. Rogers's 2-year PCEAT training program continues under the leadership of Sue Ann Herron through the Person-Centered Expressive Arts Institute (www.person-centeredexpressivearts.com), offered in collaboration with Meridian University.

Person-Centered Expressive Arts Therapy

What is Person-Centered Expressive Arts Therapy? Rogers (1993) described it this way:

Expressive arts therapy uses various arts—movement, drawing, painting, sculpting, music, writing, sound, and improvisation—in a supportive setting to facilitate growth and healing. It is a process of discovering ourselves through any art form that comes from an emotional depth. It is *not* creating a "pretty" picture. It is *not* a dance ready for stage. It is *not* a poem written and rewritten to perfection.... *Expressive* art refers to using the emotional, intuitive aspects of ourselves in various media.... Going into our inner realms to discover feelings and to express them through visual art, movement, sound, writing, or drama.... Humanistic expressive arts therapy differs from the analytic or medical model of art therapy, in which art is used to diagnose, analyze, or "treat" people [pp. 1–2].

The most important component of PCEAT is engagement in the *process*, which includes the ability to tap into our deep emotions and expressing them freely in a safe, supportive, non-judgmental environment:

The creative experience itself, and not the *products* of the process, is critical to PCEAT. The PCEAT art products are never judged or evaluated by Natalie, her co-facilitators, or others in the cohort group. Individuals are engaged in unearthing their own meaning from their art or movement. However, other group members may be invited to comment on how the art, dance, story, and so on, *made them feel*—as opposed to their interpretation of what the art means to the artist [Herron, 2010, pp. 145–146].

By engaging in PCEAT, "People become immersed in the creative process reflecting on what their creative products meant to *them* and surface with a new self-insight and self-understanding.... The meaningfulness of each piece of artwork is sought only through the eyes of its creator" (Herron, 2004, p. 14).

What Is Person-Centered?

There have been many accounts written about what Carl Rogers meant by *person-centered*. PCEAT is grounded in C. Rogers's person-centered approach. This is how Natalie Rogers (1993) described the person-centered approach as it relates to her work in expressive arts therapy:

The person-centered aspect of expressive arts therapy describes the basic philosophy underlying my work. The *client-centered* or *person-centered* approach developed by my father, Carl Rogers, emphasizes the therapist's role as being empathic, open, honest, congruent, and caring as she listens in depth and facilitates the growth of an individual or a group. This philosophy incorporates the belief that each individual has worth, dignity, and the capacity for self-direction. Carl Rogers's philosophy is based on a trust in an inherent impulse toward growth in every individual. I base my approach to expressive arts therapy on this very deep faith in the innate capacity of each person to reach toward her full potential.

Carl's research into the psychotherapeutic process revealed that when a client felt accepted and understood, healing occurred. It is a rare experience to feel accepted and understood when you are feeling fear, rage, grief, or jealousy. Yet it is this very acceptance and understanding that heals. As friends and therapists, we frequently think we must have an answer or give advice. However, this overlooks a very basic truth. By genuinely hearing the depth of the emotional pain and respecting the individual's ability to find her own answer, we are giving her the greatest gift. Empathy and acceptance give the individual an opportunity to empower herself and discover her unique potential. This atmosphere of understanding and acceptance also allows you, your friends, or your clients to feel safe enough to try expressive arts as a path to becoming whole [pp. 3–4].

The Creative Connection Process

What is the Creative Connection process? N. Rogers discovered the Creative Connection process "whereby the experience of several different expressive arts activities in various sequences greatly enhances the depth of the client's work" (Herron, 2010, p. 146). PCEAT includes dance therapy, art therapy, and music therapy, as well as therapy through journal writing, poetry, imagery, meditation, and improvisational drama; these expressive arts activities are used in the Creative Connections process to deepen the work with clients.

Natalie Rogers's Creative Connection process is, next to the person-centered philosophy, the most important element of her PCEAT work. N. Rogers (2011) described how the Creative Connection works:

> One expressive art form awakens the creative energy of another. Movement enhances writing and painting; using color, collage, and clay supports insight and new ideas, sounding and singing open the heart and bring forth images to paint, draw, or sculpt, thus opening us to new discovery in group work [p. 6].

Using the Creative Connection sequences helps "clients experience themselves on the kinesthetic, symbolic, mythological, and spiritual level, bringing the unconscious or unknown into awareness" (N. Rogers, 1993, p. 129). It not only uncovers feelings like fear, anger, and grief, it may also bring forth feelings of joy and love.

N. Rogers (1993) developed her own creed as a psychotherapist, as "the credo I have developed over the years summarizes, in a very personal way, my adaptation of the person-centered philosophy" (p. 103), and shares her value system as a psychotherapist, which is "important [for clients] to be aware of when using the Creative Connection® process" (p. 103):

> My Credo
> I am aware that going on one's inner journey can be a frightening, exhilarating, exhausting adventure.
> I will be present for you but not intrusive.
> I have faith that you know how to take care of yourself. I won't be responsible for you or take away your power.

I will not abandon you.

I will respect you and your decisions for yourself. I have faith in your ability.

I will support you and encourage you on your inner journey.

I may challenge you and your belief system, at times, but I will always respect you and your truth.

I will encourage you to try new things, to take risks into the unknown of your inner world, but I will never push you.

I will offer you expressive arts media to help you open to your innate creativity and discover your inner essence. You are free not to use these media.

At times, I will give you my opinions and feedback, but will always check it out to see if it is meaningful to you.

I will honor my own boundaries and yours to the best of my ability.

I will share my value system and beliefs with you so that you know why I am saying and doing what I say and do.

I am open to learning from you at all times.

I make mistakes, do things I'm not pleased with, and am misguided at times. In such instances I will say so. I am able to say, "I'm sorry" [N. Rogers, 1993, p. 103].

Rogers also thought it was important to specify clearly the humanistic principles that embody her work and lists them in her book, *The Creative Connection* (1993):

Humanistic Principles

All people have an innate ability to be creative.

The creative process is healing. The expressive product supplies important messages to the individual. However, it is the process of creation that is profoundly transformative.

Personal growth and higher states of consciousness are achieved through self-awareness, self-understanding, and insight.

Self-awareness, understanding, and insight are achieved by delving into our emotions. The feelings of grief, anger, pain, fear, joy, and ecstasy are the tunnel through which we must pass to get to the other side: to self-awareness, understanding, and wholeness.

Our feelings and emotions are an energy source. That energy can be channeled into the expressive arts to be released and transformed.

The expressive arts—including movement, art, writing, sound, music, meditation, and imagery—lead us into the unconscious. This often allows us to express previously unknown facets of ourselves, thus bringing to light new information and awareness.

Art modes interrelate in what I call the creative connection. When we move, it affects how we write or paint. When we write or paint, it affects how we feel and think. During the creative connection process, one art form stimulates and nurtures the other, bringing us to an inner core or essence which is our life energy.

A connection exists between our life-force—our inner core, or soul—and the essence of all beings.

Therefore, as we journey inward to discover our essence or wholeness, we discover our relatedness to the outer world. The inner and outer become one [N. Rogers, 1993, pp. 7–8].

Using Expressive Arts with Clients

In *The Handbook of Person-Centered Psychotherapy and Counselling* (Cooper, O'Hara, Schmid, & Bohart, 2013), Rogers observed that using expressive arts enhances the therapeutic relationship in many ways. It helps the client:

- Identify and be in touch with feelings
- Release and transform energy
- Explore unconscious material
- Gain insight

- Solve problems
- Discover spiritual aspects of self [p. 239]

Rogers believed that art is a universal language and that using expressive arts enables clients to access deep inner material more quickly than verbal therapy alone: "When the client shares her personal art, she is opening a window to her soul to me as a therapist. I am in awe as I view the strong images of self-expression that help me comprehend the client's inner world" (Cooper et al., 2013, p. 239). One of Rogers's clients remarked, "It is much easier for me to deal with some heavy emotions through expressive play than through thinking and talking about it," and another client reported, "I discovered in exploring my feelings that I could break through inner barriers/structures that I set for myself by moving and dancing the emotions. To draw that feeling after the movement continued the process of unfolding" (Rogers, 1993, p. 5). In therapy, Rogers introduced the possibility of using expressive arts sometime during the first three sessions. She might start by saying:

> I may offer you the opportunity to use movement or art to help you explore your thoughts and feelings. This may give you new information about yourself. I don't use art to diagnose or interpret you. The art and movement processes are available to you as another avenue of self-exploration and healing.
>
> Some people are eager to use the art materials. Others say, "I can't draw, or I'm not a creative person," or "I've got two left feet and can't dance." Briefly, I reassure them that it is not a test of their creativity or drawing or dancing ability, but a method of self-discovery. I might say, "I will make suggestions and encourage you, but the decision is up to you. I will respect that." One might ask, "Is offering expressive arts a distraction from the purpose of therapy?" Rather than being a distraction, using the arts helps both the client and the therapist to focus on the emotional or feeling aspect that has been occurring in the verbal dialogue [Cooper et al., 2013, pp. 240–241].

To demonstrate a few practical applications of PCEAT, several examples of counseling sessions from therapists are discussed next.

PCEAT with Clients

Example 1

The following case demonstrates a therapist using the PCEAT with an elder who resides in an eldercare residence. The therapist used music, singing, movement, and art to achieve the following therapeutic goals: develop trust, decrease anxiety, facilitate communication of her needs to care providers, and increase socialization.

Lian is a 93-year-old second-generation Chinese woman who has lived in a long-term eldercare facility for over 10 years. Lian has been diagnosed with dementia and anxiety. She is no longer able to ambulate and spends most of her time in a wheelchair in the milieu. She has difficulty with short-term and long-term memory but enjoys sharing a variety of episodic memories with the therapist. Client has a sweet disposition and is well liked by both staff and residents at the eldercare facility. Client is always happy to see the therapist and is animated and quite verbal in discussing her immediate needs, concerns, and memories both in English and Mandarin.

Therapist's early focus with client was on building trust. This was done using person-centered listening as client shared her episodic memories of childhood, family, childrearing, religion, and cooking. During these sessions, therapist uncovered client's love for Chinese opera and afterward downloaded some classic Chinese operas on therapist's smartphone. Therapist asked client if she would enjoy hearing some Chinese opera music. Client said yes. As therapist played the operas for client, client began to sing along. Therapist noticed client was moving her hands slightly to the music and invited her to "dance with her hands." Client and therapist danced with their hands together to the music. Client was smiling, singing, and initiating more verbal interactions with therapist. Client frequently remarked, "I miss you" and "you are my friend" during counseling sessions. Trust was established. Therapist continued to play opera music at client's request. Therapist then offered colorful scarves to client inviting her to use them while dancing with her hands. Client was immediately attracted to the brightly colored scarves and chose the colors she liked. Client and therapist danced with scarves to the music.

In following sessions, therapist offered a variety of art materials to client, including colored paper, pictures from magazines, colored markers, soft, non-toxic modeling clay, and colorful feathers. Client liked the bright colored paper, so therapist invited her to choose colors, shapes, and pictures she liked to make a collage. Therapist would assist client in gluing the items onto her paper canvas. Client also liked the soft tactile feeling of the clay and liked making sea creatures, farm animals, and birds in particular, because she liked decorating them with colorful feathers. Client became more decisive about what shapes and colors she used as the session continued. Client felt proud of her artwork and clay sculptures and asked therapist to share them with her friends at the residence. Therapist and client showed her art to other residents and they responded with positive comments. Some of the residents expressed a desire to make art, so therapist started a successful PCEAT group for elders at the residence.

Assessment. PCEAT and the Creative Connection approach enabled the client to meet her therapeutic goals. Trust was developed through person-centered listening to and validation of the client's important meaningful events in her life. Anxiety was decreased through the use of music, singing, and movement. Client was more effective in initiating requests to get her needs met, which substantially decreased her anxiety. Client's experience of making art received positive reactions from other residents. Hearing other residents respond positively to her art both increased the client's self-esteem and opened up more social interactions with peers.

Example 2

Jenny is a 65-year-old woman whose husband died 1 year ago. She was married for 30 years and had no children. Client entered counseling for grief because she was not "getting over" the loss of her husband, and she was gaining weight, was unable to sleep in their bedroom, and had begun drinking a bottle of wine a day. She also stopped visiting her friends and rarely left the house.

Session 1. Therapist discussed client's feelings of grief, depression, and drinking, which started when her husband died.

Session 4. Jenny reported she had stopped drinking and removed all alcohol from her house. However, she was still "feeling very fat." Client felt really heavy, "like I am weighted down, like I am wearing an extra body or something."

Therapist: "Would you like to explore this heavy feeling using art materials and perhaps some soft music in the background?" Client said yes.

Therapist rolled out 2 large pieces of paper on the floor, put soft music on, offered client a variety of markers, pastels, and color crayons. Therapist asked client if she would like to move to the music before doing art. Client said yes. Therapist asked client if she would like therapist to join her in movement. Client said yes. Jenny began to move, and therapist mirrored her movement. After moving for a few minutes, client sat on the floor and began to write a variety of words related to grief and loss with a black marker. When client finished, therapist asked if client would like to wear her grief. Client said yes and then wrapped the paper around her waist, inviting the therapist to do the same. Client requested help taping the grief skirt around her waist. Therapist did so and client did the same for the therapist. Client began to move to the music and, as her movements became larger, her "grief skirt" ripped a little. Client began to vigorously rip grief skirt and therapist mirrored the ripping. Client began to cry, sat down on the floor, and continued to rip the grief skirt into smaller pieces. Client gathered all the torn pieces into a pile. In silence, client placed the torn pieces in a box and taped it shut. Client hugged the therapist and left. Client left the box at the therapist's office for three more sessions and then requested to take it home.

Assessment. Two months later, Jenny reported she had stopped drinking and was proactively working through her feelings of grief, loss, and depression. She was feeling less depressed, better about her weight, and more energetic. Jenny started engaging in more social activities. She joined an exercise class with a group of women, resulting in weight loss, had her hair cut, colored, and styled differently, reported she was sleeping in her bedroom and had begun to paint the rooms in her house bright spring colors. Sessions ended after 4 months.

Example 3: PCEAT with a Group

For the last 40 years, Rogers has facilitated and participated in countless person-centered groups, including 6 years with her father at the PCA workshops. She noticed the following difference between expressive arts groups and verbal groups:

> I experience verbal groups as oppressive in many ways. Words are important of course; however my experience in verbal groups is that people really don't listen to each other because they are busy thinking of what they will say when it is their turn to speak. And the fear of revealing oneself in a large group looms large. Furthermore, as each person shares her personal life, those who are listening are stirred to remember similar experiences or have reactions to what is being said. These memories, thoughts, feelings don't have anywhere to go—they get stored in the mind and body of the listener as she waits her turn to speak.... However, in a person-centered expressive arts group, after an hour in a large circle there are ways for all the participants to express and release their emotions through art—all at the same time! It is not necessary for each person to be seen and heard by the whole group; yet, eventually each participant does have an opportunity to be known by all others [Rogers, 2011, p. 51].

The following example illustrates the use of PCEAT and the Creative Connection using meditation, movement, and a closing ritual with a group of male inmates in a correctional facility, ranging in age from 20 to 60 years old. The therapist has been working with this group of inmates, many of whom are addicts, once a week for over a year. This is the second session of a two-part series with the group. In part one, inmates wrote a goodbye letter to something, someone, or an attitude that is holding them back. Part two is the session where inmates "let go" of what they identified as holding them back in part one. Below is a discussion of part two.

Hearts-on-a-String: Letting go of something or someone that is unhealthy and unproductive in our lives through the use of meditation, somatic exercises, and a closing ritual.

Therapist provided supplies for center of the room: Bowl/Rocks/Aromatherapy/Paper Hearts on a string that contain a positive word on both sides, such as hope, dream, and rest.

Therapist introduces the topic of saying goodbye and letting go. The therapist offers a guided meditation, somatic movement via stretching, simple yoga exercises and poses representing holding on and letting go, and a closing ritual exercise.

Therapist: "Sometimes saying goodbye to something or someone in our lives is difficult. Rituals can be a good way to help us to solidify the closure, like reading the last page of a book and putting it away. Once we say goodbye, your thing may come back; if so, keep letting it go. Awareness is the key. If it returns, I invite you to just acknowledge and observe it nonjudgmentally—oh, there you are again—pride, anger, craving, whatever it is, and let it go again."

Therapist: "I would like to invite you to use yoga and movement as part of your goodbye ritual. This thing that we are giving up has possibly served us or benefited us in some way. Consider if or how your actions and emotions may have served as coping skills or protection in the past. Perhaps ask whether or not these emotions or actions still work for you as you move toward a healthier lifestyle. As you begin to incorporate more positive emotions or coping skills, reflect on how that makes you feel. Do you feel gratitude or some other feeling? Is anyone willing to talk about what the person, place, thing, or emotion taught them that they are grateful for?" Group share.

"I invite you to take a few moments to think about whether you are open to saying goodbye to the old and open to visualizing something new and better in its place. We might all be in different stages of willingness to change and wherever you are in that process is fine. Your goodbye letters are a way of letting go of what is holding you back and embracing the positive change your heart on a string represents for you. Your hearts on a string are an invitation to change and to notice the change when it happens."

Yoga: Invite group to follow therapist's movements, or move in any way they choose that symbolizes holding on and letting go.

Therapist:

- Says: "First, set your intention. Think about the person, place, or thing that you are saying goodbye to…"
- Demonstrates the prayer position.
- Says: "Turn to the right. Second, we give gratitude to that which it has taught us…" (2nd step in sun salutation, warrior one position, hands in prayer, look up)
- "Third, facing backward, we feel how it has kept us bound up" (warrior two—look at the past, humble warrior)
- "Fourth, turn to the left, we open ourselves up to the change, whatever stage we are in" (warrior two, triangle)
- "Finally, we realize we must let it go" (bow position, hold, hold, hold until you can't hold anymore, then release, superman position, hold, hold, hold until you can't hold anymore, then release)
- Relaxation pose

Therapist invites clients to join her in a guided meditation using imagery about releasing a heavy weight that binds the heart and floating free or to quietly meditate in their own way, if they choose. After meditation is complete, therapist asks: "Would anyone be willing to read your goodbye letter or share something from it?" Inmates were then invited to do any movement or pose they wanted, or react to their letter by stomping on it, or shredding it and leave it behind in the bowl in the center of the room. "Choose any heart-on-a-string that you wish, cut the string, and keep it to represent positive change in our life."

After everyone shared who wanted to share and chose their heart-on-a-string:

"Now that there is an empty spot where the thing you let go of once was; what will you fill it with? If you feel the need to fill it, I encourage you to notice it and be aware of what you might be wanting to fill it with—food, another negative emotion or feeling, gambling, finding fault in others … or something good—friendship, caring for others, laughter, spirituality, you choose."

Therapist: Passes the singing bowl and invites each client to comment on their experience, if they wish.

Assessment. Correctional officers have reported a reduction in the level of aggression and the number of grievances in the group. Therapist has received reports from inmates that they keep their heart where it is visible as a daily reminder for them to "let go" and embrace "positive change." One inmate reported how powerful this group session was because it allowed him to say goodbye and that he had never been able to do that before. This session allowed him to choose what he wanted to say goodbye to and let it go on his own terms, and that was deeply meaningful to him.

Research and Applications

PCEAT has been used in a variety of settings including, hospitals, mental health clinics, counseling services, social services, addiction treatment centers, schools, hospices, prisons, and elder care residential facilities. It can also be used in individual and group settings and in inpatient and outpatient programs. Research has shown that PCEAT has been effective in treating a wide range of client populations cross-culturally, including children, adolescents, adults, and elders.

As discussed in Chapter 10 of Rogers's book *The Creative Connection for Groups* (2011), the therapeutic use of person-centered expressive arts has been an effective intervention for treating depression, anxiety, PTSD, sexual abuse, addiction, grief and loss, anger, stress reduction, eating disorders, Alzheimer's, domestic violence, child stutters, aiding cancer patients and the developmentally disabled, encouraging self-care for therapists, and promoting self-empowerment, creativity, growth, and development.

Natalie Rogers (2011) wrote, "Having research that validates (or not) the powerful healing aspects of person-centered expressive arts therapy is crucial" (p. 439). Current and continued research validates the effectiveness of Person-Centered Expressive Arts Therapy, evidenced by 34 research studies conducted between 1982 and 2014 (Person Centered Arts Research, n.d.). There is more research being conducted on PCEAT. This author is currently serving as a committee member on three dissertations whose topics involve research in person-centered expressive arts.

Professional Registration and Licensing Requirements

After having completed Rogers's 2-year PCEAT training program, many licensed therapists have successfully incorporated PCEAT into their practices and no additional training is required. They abide by their own professional standards and codes of ethics. Rogers's PCEAT Training Program fulfills the educational requirement of the International Expressive Arts Therapy Association's Registered Expressive Arts Therapists (REAT) standard and requirements. Graduates who wish to become Registered Expressive Arts Therapists may apply to the International Expressive Arts Therapy Association (IEATA), a non-profit organization founded in 1994 "to encourage the creative spirit" whose "inclusive, culturally diverse organization supports expressive arts therapists, artists, educators, consultants and others using integrative, multimodal arts processes for personal and community growth and transformation" (International Expressive Arts Association, n.d.-b). Their key mission is to:

Promote professional excellence and standards of practice for practitioners and consumers. To that end, we established the titles of Registered Expressive Arts Therapist (REAT) and Registered Expressive Arts Consultant/Educator (REACE), and developed screening and registration processes to certify qualified members. All REATs and REACEs agree to abide by a code of ethics, an expression of values and goals that help us define our behavior as a professional community [International Expressive Arts Association, n.d.-a, para. 1].

To apply, one must have training in Expressive Arts Therapy and one of the following degrees:

- Master's Degree in Expressive Arts Therapy
- Master's Degree in Psychology or Related Counseling Discipline
- Master's Degree in Fine Arts plus training in Therapeutic Process
- Doctoral Degree in Expressive Arts Therapy
- Exceptional Category with Master's Degree or higher in Expressive Arts, Psychology or Fine Arts.

Person-Centered Expressive Arts Training

Rogers's PCEAT graduate training program is held in the United States and is offered in collaboration with Meridian University. There are also training programs available in Japan, Argentina, South Korea, Hong Kong, and the United Kingdom (Rogers, 2011, pp. 415–417). Links to the websites are listed below. Rogers's unique PCEAT certificate program combines experiential learning, theory, and practice in the person-centered philosophy of Carl Rogers and the expressive arts: Movement, sound, visual arts, creative writing, and drama. The program consists of six week-long Residential Intensives over 2 years. Participants come to California from around the world wishing to use the expressive arts in counseling, teaching, mediation, healthcare, social action, and group facilitation, and/or to awaken personal growth and creativity. The training program *Expressive Arts for Healing and Social Change: A Person-Centered Approach* has been taught at Saybrook University and Sofia University, and is now offered in collaboration with Meridian University. The comprehensive in-depth PCEAT training program began when Natalie Rogers first integrated the expressive arts with the person-centered philosophy of her father into a training program in 1985, and she refined it over the last 28 years. Hundreds of graduates have reported that the PCEAT training program has been personally transformative and they are applying person-centered expressive arts in their life and work with clients. Person-Centered Expressive Arts practitioners can be therapists, social workers, educators, creativity coaches, consultants, pastoral counselors, healthcare professionals, or individuals working in both nonprofit and for-profit organizations.

Participants come from around the globe to learn how to use the expressive arts. People of all ages and disciplines from England, Russia, Canada, Latin America, Japan, Hong Kong, Austria, Greece, and South Korea have participated in the training. Cross-cultural work is emphasized. For more information about Rogers's PCEAT training program go to: www.personcenteredexpressivearts.com

Contact information for additional training programs is as follows:

Argentina: http://www.pcetiargentina.com.ar
Hong Kong: http://cbh.hku.hk

Japan: http://hyogen-art.com
South Korea: http://www.misul75.net
United Kingdom: tess_sturrock@hotmailwww

REFERENCES

Anna Halprin: Biography. (n.d.). Retrieved from https://www.annahalprin.org/biography

Burrows, L. (2013). Memory of Abraham Maslow faded, not forgotten. Retrieved from http://www.brandeis.edu/now/2013/may/maslow.html

Carl Rogers Award. (n.d.). Retrieved from http://www.apadivisions.org/division-32/awards/carl-rogers.aspx?tab=4

Chilton, J. (2006). *Natalie Rogers: The person-centered approach workshops, 1974–1979.* Unpublished manuscript. San Francisco, CA: Saybrook Graduate School and Research Center.

Cooper, M., O'Hara, M., Schmid, P., & Bohart, A. (Eds.). (2013). *The Handbook of person-centered psychotherapy & counselling.* New York, NY: Palgrave Macmillan.

Herron, S.A. (2004). *Person-centered expressive arts therapy workshop.* Unpublished journal notes. Sonoma, CA: Sue Ann Herron's Personal Archives.

Herron, S.A. (2008). *Transcript of audiotaped interview on April 8, 2008, with Natalie Rogers.* Unpublished document. Sonoma, CA: S.A. Herron's Personal Archives.

Herron, S.A. (2010). *Natalie Rogers: An experiential psychology of self-realization beyond Abraham Maslow and Carl Rogers* (Doctoral dissertation). Retrieved from ProQuest Dissertations and Theses database (UMI No. 3428084).

International Expressive Arts Association. (n.d.-a). Professional registration for REAT and REACE. Retrieved from http://www.ieata.org/profesional-registration.html

International Expressive Arts Association. (n.d.-b). Who we are. Retrieved from http://www.ieata.org/who-we-are.html

Lusebrink, V.E. (2013). A tribute to Janie Rhyne. *Journal of the American Art Therapy Association, 12*(2), 95–97.

Person-Centered Expressive Arts Research. (n.d.). Retrieved from http://www.personcenteredexpressivearts.com/natalie-rogers-1928-2015/pcea-research/

Professional Registration for REAT and REACE. (n.d.). Retrieved from http://www.ieata.org/profesional-registration.html

Rhyne, J. (1973). *The Gestalt art experience.* Monterey, CA: Brooks/Cole.

Rogers, C. R. (1950). A current formulation of client-centered therapy. *Social Services Review, 24,* 443.

Rogers, C. (1975). *Memo from phone conversation with Natalie Rogers, August 25* [Transcription of audiotape]. Washington, D.C.: Library of Congress, Carl R. Rogers Papers (Carton 3, Folder 1).

Rogers, N. (1960). *A play therapist's approach to the creative art experience.* Unpublished Master's thesis. Waltham, MA: Brandeis University, Department of Psychology.

Rogers, N. (1980). *Emerging woman: A decade of midlife transitions.* Santa Rosa, CA: Personal Press.

Rogers, N. (1993). *The creative connection: Expressive arts as healing.* Palo Alto, CA: Science & Behavior Books.

Rogers, N. (2011). *The creative connection for groups: Person-centered expressive arts for healing and social change.* Palo Alto, CA: Science and Behavior Books.

Dance/Movement
as a Holistic Treatment

*Using Creative, Imaginal and Embodied Expression
in Healing, Growth and Therapy*

Ilene A. Serlin *and* J. Ryan Kennedy

"Movement, to be experienced has to be found in the body, not put on like a dress or coat. There is that in us which has moved from the very beginning; it is that which can liberate us."
—Mary Starks Whitehouse (1999, p. 53)

Physical expression, ritualized movement, and choreographed folk dance have been a significant and ongoing aspect of community healing practices for as long as recorded time (Serlin, 1993; Wosien, 1974). This is because movement and dance are often experienced as integrative processes that help individuals organize and make meaning out of unpredictable, and emotion-laden life experiences (Siegel, 1984, 1995). These practices also help communities transmit or communicate important values and historical narratives across time and between generations, as well as celebrate and remember the important events and transitions in the lives of their members (Adler, 1992; Chodorow, 1991; Lewis Bernstein, 1979). The ancient capacity for dance and expressive movement to support self-growth, strengthen connections, and facilitate communication continues to be present today, and is at the heart of what defines dance/movement therapy. In today's world of disembodiment, fragmentation, dislocation, and isolation, the enlivening, integrating, and connecting energy of dance therapy can be a powerful path to healing.

The American Dance Therapy Association (ADTA) defines the practice of *dance/ movement therapy* as "the psychotherapeutic use of movement to promote emotional, social, cognitive, and physical integration of the individual" (ADTA Website, 2017). Dance/movement therapy educator Penny Lewis (1996) noted that:

The concept of dance in the context of dance therapy is a wider one perhaps than its usual definition would reveal. It includes, of course, all forms of traditional and nontraditional performance art, ethnographic ritual dance, folk, and social dance. But it also includes the dance of everyday gesture and the pas de deux of all relationships: the dyadic dances of couples, care givers, and their children, family dances, organizational dances, and those of other groups [p. 97].

Currently, there are about 1169 dance/movement therapists credentialed by the ADTA, with most located in the United States. Additionally, in recent years several other countries around the world have begun developing and/or expanding upon their own professional associations and their credentialing and approval processes (American Dance Therapy Association, 2017).

As a profession, dance/movement therapy is relatively new, but it is one of the few modalities offering practitioners such a complete vehicle for bringing body-based, movement-oriented assessment and intervention tools directly into their psychotherapeutic work. Though other modalities may include the body and/or movement as elements of what they have to contribute, these somatic therapies are usually limited to separate bodies. Dance/movement therapy, on the other hand, works with the nonverbal language of movement between people and across space. It is especially designed to integrate creative process work with attuned, relational, and engaged support for those on a healing journey (Schmais & White, 1986; Schoop & Mitchell, 1974). This is because it is steeped in the creative, imaginal, embodied, intuitive, and artistic practice of understanding the meaning of movement from the inside out (Aposhyan, 1999; Cohen, 1993; Serlin, 1996). In this way, dance/movement therapy is truly a holistic, integrative, and experientially transformative approach.

This essay further explores the psychotherapeutic practice of dance/movement therapy as a holistic therapy by first taking a brief look into the early background and more recent history of the field. Next, several career-based topics are discussed, including the minimum education requirements to enter the field, the programs that offer training in dance/movement therapy, evidence-based research on the effectiveness of the modality, and its applicability to various demographic populations and psychiatric diagnoses. The essay ends with an overview of some of the key features of a typical session, including dance/movement therapy specific assessment tools, and dance/movement therapy effectiveness measures.

Background and History

The roots of dance/movement therapy extend back centuries and are deeply connected to forms of individual and community healing rituals associated with many indigenous cultures (Canner, 1992; Sandel, Chaiklin, & Lohn, 1993; Stanton-Jones, 1992). As a profession, it arose primarily out of modern dance in the middle part of the 20th century, and therefore has a strong connection to the emancipatory practices associated with that dance form in particular (Mettler, 1990; Roskin Berger, 1992). Other forms of dance and expressive movement, such as authentic movement, also have their place in the history of the profession (Levy, 1995; Lewis, 1979, 1984). As the field has matured into a profession in more recent years, dance/movement therapy has additionally been adopted as a specialization within the larger disciplines of counseling and psychology. In this way it retains a fundamental connection to its early inspirations and foundations in indigenous healing practices as well as in modern and other types of dance, while also drawing upon contemporary research and innovations in psychology, philosophy, neuroscience, and beyond (Bruno, 1990; Chaiklin, 1997; Levy, 2005; Schmais & White, 1996).

From a psychotherapeutic perspective, though the use of movement and dance were historically known to have a healing or therapeutic effect, their overt use as agents of change and transformation had become obscured and even lost with the advent of the modern industrial world, modern medical practices, and the introduction of classical psychoanalytic techniques (Payne, 1992; Schmais & White, 1986; Siegel, 1984, 1995). In philosophy and science, mind and body were understood as separate, and the body was understood as an object, something functional rather than expressive. In other words, it had been reduced to a "Mute Body" (Serlin, 1996). Psychotherapy was still primarily verbal, and those practicing it were psychoanalytic, behavioral, or cognitive in their approach. Expressive movement and creative expression were only rediscovered as a contemporary psychotherapeutic modality in the 1940s, parallel to the field of humanistic psychology, when, quite by accident, various teachers of modern dance began to notice that their dance classes had an uplifting effect on class participants and that psychiatrists were remarking on the surprising beneficial effect that movement had on their patients (Espenak, 1981; Lefco, 1974; Levy, 2005; Sandel, Chaiklin, & Lohn, 1993).

One of the early pioneers and innovators on the east coast of the United States was Marian Chace at St. Elizabeth's Hospital and Chestnut Lodge in Washington, D.C. Others located in New York City, included Blanche Evan and her "dance as creative transformation," Liljan Espenak and her "psychomotor therapy" at the Alfred Adler Institute, and Irmgard Bartenieff and her "Effort/Shape work" at the Dance Notation Bureau (now the Laban Institute of Movement Studies, or LIMS). On the west coast, primarily in California, were Mary Starks Whitehouse at the C.G. Jung Institute, Trudi Schoop at Camarillo State Hospital, and Alma Hawkins at the University of California in Los Angeles (Hawkins, 1988, 1991; Levy, 2005).

Today dance/movement therapists come from many diverse theoretical orientations and personal backgrounds, but all of them focus on both subtle and expansive movements as they are expressed in the therapeutic relationship and understand these behaviors as both communicative and adaptive strategies used to meet important personal, developmental, and relational needs (Loman, 1992; Naess Lewin, 1998; Schmais & White, 1996). Dance/movement therapists are trained to meet this implicit language of movement with skill, care, and trained curiosity (North, 1995; Schoop & Mitchell, 1974; Serlin, 2006). Indeed, they are specifically taught to access and activate the transformative power of creative process, experiential work, expressive movement, and embodied practices to support psychological health and mind/body integration (Dosamantes Beaudry, 1997; Goodill, 2005; Lewis, 1996).

Because dance/movement therapy draws so directly on the creative process and concomitantly on the practitioners' own ability to access, adapt, and utilize that process through their own artistic development, it belongs squarely to the family of other expressive and creative arts therapies such as art therapy, music therapy, drama therapy, and poetry therapy. Likewise, because it invites deep exploration and understanding of sensation and subtle internal processes, it also belongs to the family of somatically based psychotherapies such as bioenergetics, core energetics, Gestalt therapy, Sensorimotor Psychotherapy*, Somatic Experiencing*, Body-Mind Centering*, and many more (Caldwell, 1997; Hartley, 1995). This point was illustrated by Payne (2006) in her integrative article published in the inaugural issue of the international journal, *Body, Movement, and Dance in Psychotherapy*, that outlined the intersection between the two fields of dance/movement therapy and body psychotherapy. In the article, she clearly laid out that:

Much is recognizable to both body psychotherapy and dance/movement therapy; they connect through several bridges. There is a shared attention to aspects of theory and practice such as holism in psyche and soma, the powerful connection between emotion and the body, therapist involvement-in-action, embodied relationship, spontaneous non-verbal cues in the "here and now," and the importance of reclaiming the often dissociated body/movement in counseling/psychotherapy (with their limitations of the dominant left brain) is central in both disciplines [p. 11].

Because of this implicit recognition and understanding of subtle, internal, sensate processes along with clearly visible, external expressive dynamics, dance/movement therapists have much to offer the larger field of psychotherapy (Hanna, 2006; La Barre, 2001; Levy, 1988, 2005; Lewis & Loman, 1990; Musicant, 1994; North, 1972).

Professional and Educational Requirements

The American Dance Therapy Association (ADTA) is the national professional association that promotes, supports, regulates, and advocates for the field of dance/movement therapy in the United States. The ADTA was established in 1966, with Marian Chace as its first president, and is currently based in Columbia, Maryland. The purpose of the ADTA, according to its website, is to "establish, maintain, and support the highest standards of professional identity and competence among dance/movement therapists by promoting education, training, practice, and research" (2017). ADTA also encourages dialogue between dance/movement therapists and those in affiliated disciplines, and is engaged in promoting dance/movement therapy to the public through social media campaigns and other types of outreach.

According to ADTA requirements, a master's degree is the entry level for the practice of professional dance/movement therapy. The ADTA has established two levels of credentialing for professionals within the field, corresponding to similar types of credentialing for art and music therapists, thereby helping to secure its place among the older art therapies. The first level of practice is the Registered Dance/Movement Therapist (R-DMT), which allows a practitioner to work clinically as a dance/movement therapist under supervision. The second level of practice is the Board Certified Dance/Movement Therapist (BC-DMT), which allows a practitioner to work independently, supervise other dance/movement therapists, teach dance/movement therapy–specific courses, and sit on dance/movement therapy–specific thesis committees. The Dance/Movement Therapy Certification Board, Inc. (DMTCB), an independent affiliate of the ADTA, reviews and approves applications for the two levels of credentialing provided by the ADTA. The DMTCB is comprised of professional members of the ADTA, who are elected by credentialed members of the organization to serve in this capacity (ADTA, 2017).

In order to attain the R-DMT or entry-level credential, there are three possible pathways available. The first is to complete an ADTA-approved graduate program in dance/movement therapy. Graduates from such programs are immediately eligible to apply for the R-DMT credential without specific review of their individual coursework. The second pathway is to complete a graduate program in dance/movement therapy that is not approved by the ADTA. In such instances, applicants would need to provide detailed paperwork substantiating that they had met the education and training requirements set forth by the ADTA for the R-DMT credential. The last option, known as the alternate route, typically involves completing a master's degree in a mental health-related discipline and then pursuing a self-directed course of study in dance/movement therapy from individually approved BC-DMT trainers or educators, including a dance/movement therapy-specific internship. These courses can be arranged privately or taken as part of several established alternate route training programs scattered throughout the USA. Applicants interested in pursuing the R-DMT credential through the alternate route are well advised to contact the ADTA before beginning the process, to ensure that they are following the appropriate steps, in the correct order, with officially approved ADTA trainers and educators. To learn more about the R-DMT credential and how to apply for it, please visit this weblink: http://adta.org/r-dmt/

The advanced practice credential, or BC-DMT, has only one pathway. Earning a BC-DMT requires first attaining and maintaining the R-DMT credential, completing 3,640 hours of paid employment over a minimum of 24 months doing dance/movement therapy, receiving 48 hours of clinical supervision from a BC-DMT, and submitting two separate but related essays to the Dance/Movement Therapy Certification Board. The first essay needs to articulate the candidate's theoretical orientation as a dance/movement therapist, and the second essay should demonstrate that orientation in action through a detailed session analysis. To learn more about the BC-DMT credential and how to apply for it, please visit this weblink: http://adta.org/bc-dmt/

Training Programs

Currently, there are six graduate-level training programs in the United States that have been approved by the ADTA. They are, in alphabetical order: (1) Antioch University, New England, in Keene, New Hampshire; (2) Columbia College in Chicago, Illinois; (3) Lesley University in Cambridge, Massachusetts; (4) Naropa University in Boulder, Colorado; (5) Pratt Institute in Brooklyn, New York; and (6) Sarah Lawrence College in Bronxville, New York. See the section on Additional Dance/Movement Therapy Resources below for more details, or visit this weblink: https://adta.org/approved-graduate-programs/

Finding a Dance/Movement Therapist

Finding a dance/movement therapist who is credentialed through the ADTA is a fairly quick and easy process. By simply going to the ADTA website, it is possible to search an online database by state and country. The database subsequently identifies all practitioners within that particular region. Once the list has been generated, it is then possible to determine which level of credential the practitioner holds: R-DMT for the entry-level, and BC-DMT for the advanced practice level. To access and view the practitioner database, please visit this weblink: http://adta.org/find-a-dancemovement-therapist/

Applicable Populations and Psychiatric Diagnoses

Dance/movement therapists are fully trained psychotherapists. Though they come into their dance/movement therapy training with specific experience in creative and expressive movement, and also gain more skills in this area as part of their graduate training, all R-DMTs and BC-DMTs receive rigorous clinical training through their coursework, clinical fieldwork and internship placements, and post-graduate supervised hours. In other words, dance/movement therapists are fully trained counselors and psychotherapists with an additional set of body-centered, movement-oriented, clinically relevant skills (Loman & Merman, 1996; Payne, 1992). Because of this, dance/movement therapists are well positioned to work with clients from a diverse array of demographics and populations, with a variety of psychiatric diagnoses and presenting problems, and across the continuum of care (Dosamantes Beaudry, 1997; Goodill, 2005; Levy, 1995, 2005; Serlin, 2010).

On one end of the continuum of care, dance/movement therapists are working in a highly structured manner with groups and individual patients in inpatient psychiatric, residential, and institutional settings. On the other end, they are facilitating deep personal growth work with individual clients in private practices or as wellness or executive coaches. In the middle are dance/movement therapists working in schools, universities, businesses, and not-for-profit organizations. Some work as medical dance/movement therapists in traditional medical settings on issues such as oncology and gerontology and at the bedside (Goodill, 2005), and others work as educators, researchers, and entrepreneurs (Levy, 1988, 1995, 2005; Lewis, 1979, 1984; Stanton-Jones, 1992). Dance/movement therapists are also working within the field of alternative and complementary medicine (Serlin, 2006). In all of these roles and contexts, dance/movement therapists are bringing an understanding of the body and its inherent capacity to access and utilize creative and expressive movement as a force for healing, connection, and change into the work they do (ADTA, 2017).

Like most therapies, dance/movement therapy can be adapted to almost any situation to meet a client's emergent clinical concerns and developmental needs. For example, it can be used effectively with clients who have anxiety problems, attention and concentration issues, depressive symptoms, existential and identity confusion, body image disturbances, attachment and relational concerns, and much more (Levy, 1995, 2005; Lewis, 1979, 1984; Payne, 1992). Typically, if a client lacks internal psychological structure, the dance/movement therapist would provide that structure externally through interventions like rhythm, tempo, clear spatial boundaries, synchronized movement, guided imagery, and supported phrasing (Bartenieff & Lewis, 1980; Lefco, 1974; Schmais, 1985; Siegel, 1995; Stanton-Jones, 1992). By contrast, if a client is able to maintain internal structure, the dance/movement therapist might invite the client to explore a diverse range of somatic themes and physical expressions without much specific guidance or direction (Chodorow, 1991; Musicant, 1994; Sandel, Chaiklin, & Lohn, 1993).

For clients referred into dance/movement therapy by a primary therapist, the dance/movement therapist and referral source would engage collaboratively with one another to identify the client's presenting problems and treatment goals, and communicate about the course of therapy. It should be noted, however, that, although dance/movement therapists often work in conjunction with other clinicians across the continuum of care and within the range of mental health disciplines, they are also quite prepared to practice independently, if they are appropriately licensed by the state in which they practice. In that case, a client can work with a dance/movement therapist as a primary therapist without needing a referral or auxiliary practitioner (ADTA, 2017; Dosamantes Beaudry, 1997; White, 1994).

Overview of a Session

Dance/movement therapy sessions look as different as the various types of clients whom dance/movement therapists see. Each session is tailored to the specific needs and presenting issues that are associated with the particular individual, couple, family, or group with which the dance/movement therapist is working on a particular day. Because most dance/movement therapists work from a deeply experiential, phenomenological, theoretical orientation that takes into account the importance of establishing kinesthetic empathy (Sandel, Chaiklin, & Lohn, 1993) or a state of attuned, somatic resonance with their clients, dance/movement therapy tends to endorse many of the same qualities in a session as other psychotherapeutic approaches located within the humanistic/existential psychotherapy tradition (Behar-Horenstein & Ganet-Sigel, 1999; Serlin, 2012). Even though dance/movement therapists may come from a variety of theoretical orientations, in general dance/movement therapy does not lend itself to manualized treatment, linear protocols, or one-size-fits-all strategies.

That being said, one quite common session structure adopted by many dance/movement therapists is that developed by dance/movement therapy pioneer and first ADTA president Marian Chace. Essentially, there are three parts to this approach: (1) warm-up; (2) theme development; and (3) integration and closure (Levy, 2005). The warm-up phase consists of first creating a safe space. Some therapists will use an archetypal format like a circle, while others encourage individuals to explore the room and their own bodies independently. During this phase, the clients begin to connect with themselves and each other through body-centered and movement-oriented mirroring exercises. The purpose is to get a pulse on what is vital and alive for the client or clients at that particular time. This could include activities like using rhythmic movement to vitalize the body, initiating body part exploration through progressive movement, using the breath to wake up the body, grounding into or connecting with the floor as a base of support, and playing with polarities in the body to experience physical and emotional contrasts (Johnson & Sandel, 1977; Lefco, 1974; Levy, 1995; Naess Lewin, 1998).

Perhaps the primary point of this first warm-up phase is for the dance/movement therapist to identify thematic material that can then be deepened during the second part of the dance/movement therapy session, which is the theme development phase. Identifying and developing a theme can be accomplished through engaging both implicit and explicit channels; dance/movement therapists are specifically trained for this (Levy, 2005; Payne, 1992). Their training in counseling helps them track verbal content that emerges overtly as potential thematic material (Caldwell, 1996, 1997; La Barre, 2001; Serlin, 2010). In addition, their theoretical, observational, and embodied knowledge of movement patterns and expressive possibilities helps them detect subtle thematic cues of which the client may not be aware (Hackney, 2002; Naess Lewin, 1998; Stanton-Jones, 1992). These include standard body/movement assessment elements such as the ways in which clients relate to posture, gesture, developmental movement patterning, facial expressivity, dynamic expression, the shapes the body inhabits and how shape changes occur, spatial pathways and use of space, personal kinesphere, and interpersonal space (Bartenieff & Lewis, 1980; Espenak, 1981; Kestenberg Amighi, Loman, Lewis, & Sossin, 1999; Laban, 1960, 1974; Laban & Lawrence, 1974; Moore & Yamamoto, 1988; North, 1972). From these cues, and also from the therapist's own kinesthetic counter-transference, the therapist may help clients become more aware of what their bodies are telling them.

The therapist works with the client or group at this point to explore and amplify the kinesthetic images (Serlin, Rockefeller, & Fox, 2007). Some think of this part as if it were working with a dream image. Movements can be repeated or intensified, sounds amplified, and expressions made bigger in space … until the "aha!" moment when the group or individual has a felt sense of rightness. The dance/movement therapist might then act as mirror, coach, partner, or witness, but would not interpret the image, instead inviting the client to discover personal meaning through the imagery. Sometimes the therapist might encourage the client to amplify the images through drawing, poetry, or a different modality. Healing happens in this act of objectifying the psyche rather than overidentifying with it. Instead of being hijacked by the emotion or energy of the image, clients can begin to develop their observing ego or inner witness. What is healing is the act of symbolizing, the process of finding one's authentic voice, of being grounded in one's embodied truth, such that there is congruence between verbal and nonverbal expressions (Wallock & Eckstein, 1983). Telling one's story through movement and nonverbal behaviors, and being in the flow state where the transcendent function between the conscious and unconscious mind can arise more deftly, act as tools of the dance/movement therapy (Jung, 1966; Serlin, 2007).

The final element of this common dance/movement therapy structure is the closure and integration component. This is the time when the dance/movement therapist helps the client consolidate what was experienced and explored during the session into a meaningful and coherent personal narrative that can be returned to later as a point of reference, as a new skill, or potentially as a novel way to view or define the self (Sandel, Chaiklin, & Lohn, 1993). Reflection comes from making the explicit movements smaller and smaller, until they become implicit traces in the muscle memory. These are experienced as kinesthetic images (Serlin, Rockefeller, & Fox, 2007), which, like dream images, resonate with personal and universal meaning. As they tell a story, the therapy becomes similar to narrative therapy. Serlin calls this process, "Action Hermeneutics," because the movement itself, as it finds its authentic form, is a meaning-making process. Meaning is not separated from movement. Indeed, as meaning is discovered, both verbally and nonverbally, words and action become integrated. Because one of the primary objectives of dance/movement therapy is to help individuals expand their movement repertoires and have greater access to, as well as choices within, their expressive styles, this final phase of a common dance/movement therapy session frequently highlights and affirms such objectives. That is to say that this final integrative phase of a dance/movement therapy session supports clients to feel greater alignment between what they are experiencing internally with what they are doing externally (Lewis, 1996; Payne, 1992; Schmais, 1981, 1998, 1999; Schmais & White, 1986)—that is, greater integration of body, speech and mind.

Through the heightened consciousness of their movements, clients learn to own the aspects of themselves that emerge in the movement, and then find constructive ways of bringing these new patterns into their daily lives. The product is less important than the process of discovery, and, even as early dance therapists emphasized, the inherent healing power of creativity is itself what encourages this healing. The creative process involves novelty, learning, being in the flow state, and the reduction of stress. Clearly, it can promote mental wellbeing (Evans, 2007; Hanna, 2006). From this perspective, the experience of dance/movement therapy is one in which "each individual has the opportunity to enjoy and benefit from that which is rightfully his [sic] possession—the power to create" (Hawkins, 1988, p. 8).

Dance/Movement Therapy Assessments

When it comes to assessments in dance/movement therapy, there are not a great many objective measurements, and very few of them have been standardized using any type of psychometrically robust principles to ensure validity of the content being assessed and/or reliability of the measurement's accuracy (Johnson, Sandel, & Eicher, 1983; Kestenberg Amighi, Loman, Lewis, & Sossin, 1999; Leedy & Ormrod, 2014). This is largely because the goals and objectives of dance/movement therapy are usually quite subjective. While most dance/movement therapists proceed from the assumptions that a full and balanced movement repertoire is better than an unbalanced or incomplete repertoire, and grounded is more desirable than ungrounded (Lewis, 1979, 1984), there is not one set of movement patterns or expressive capacities that has been identified as ideal (Hackney, 2002; Moore & Yamamoto, 1988).

Because movement is fluid and dynamic, the field of dance/movement therapy has traditionally gravitated toward adopting a more or less value-free system of body/movement observation and assessment that uses a set of descriptive words to convey an individual's movement signature (Bartenieff & Lewis, 1980). This notation system, which is known as Laban Movement Analysis, or LMA, originated from the work of German choreographer and movement educator Rudolf von Laban in the early part of the 20th century. In the United States and Great Britain, his colleagues Warren Lamb, Marion North, and Irmgard Bartenieff further developed it, and there were several others in Europe who contributed as well (Bradley, 2009; Levy, 2005). The system, as it is practiced in the United States, conceptualizes all of human movement as being composed of the following aspects: Body Organization, Effort or Energy, Shape/Modes of Shape Change, and Space/ Space Harmony, otherwise known as BESS (Dell, 1970; Dell, Crow, & Bartenieff, 1977; Hackney, 2002).

In brief, *body organization* has to do with things like how breath supports the body, how core muscles support stability so that peripheral muscles can be more expressive, how movement initiates and sequences, how alignment facilitates movement, and how early developmental patterns underpin and support more complex patterns (Hackney, 2002). *Effort* focuses on dynamic expression, addressing the ways in which a person relates to the polarities among the four qualitative elements of free and bound Flow, indirect and direct Space, light and strong Weight, and sustained and quick Time (Laban & Lawrence, 1974). *Shape* emphasizes the actual morphology of the body, or the qualities of general expansion and contraction that organize the body, as well as how the body relates to itself and the environment (Bartenieff & Lewis, 1980). Finally, the category of *Space and Space Harmony* takes into account the amount of physical space that is occupied by the body, the zones and levels in which it occurs, the pathways or traceforms that are left behind as the body moves through space, the tensions and countertensions that are created as the body engages with space, and the crystalline forms that can be used to explore various movement themes such as stability/mobility, exertion/recuperation, inner/outer, and expression/function (Bradley, 2009; Dell, 1970; Dell, Crow, & Bartenieff, 1977; Laban, 1960, 1974; Laban & Lawrence, 1974; Loman, 1992).

A close cousin to Laban Movement Analysis (LMA) is the Kestenberg Movement Profile, or KMP. Whereas the LMA system remains fairly descriptive in its approach and thus has applications well beyond dance/movement therapy, the KMP was specifically designed as a psychological assessment tool. Developed by child psychiatrist Judith

Kestenberg, MD, in the mid- to late 1960s with the Sands Point Movement Study Group in Long Island, New York (Kestenberg Amighi, Loman, Lewis, & Sossin, 1999; Loman, 1992), the KMP combines LMA with the psychodynamic theories of object relations and self-psychology. The KMP essentially views the Effort category of LMA as a system for understanding the expression of individual temperamental styles, and the Shape category of LMA as a system for making sense of how the self is supported in relationship. The two systems are placed within developmental trajectories that reflect levels of psychological and interpersonal maturity that develop in relation to one another and within the context of the human lifespan (Loman & Merman, 1996).

Both LMA and KMP are complicated systems of movement observation and assessment that take a certain degree of concentrated attention to learn and master and are, therefore, beyond the scope of in-depth explanation here. Combined or separately, they are systems of movement observation and assessment that most dance/movement therapists learn in school; thus, they are two of the most common assessment tools available across the field. Because of that, they provide an instantly accessible and imminently useful language for dance/movement therapists to use when communicating assessment, diagnostic, and/or treatment data to one another. They can also be used when communicating to people from other mental health disciplines, but typically the terms and concepts would need to be translated into more pedestrian terminology, given that they are quite detailed and specific to the field of body/movement observation and assessment.

Though LMA and KMP are two of the most common assessment tools used in the practice of Dance/Movement Therapy, it should be noted that they are not the only tools available, are not used by all dance/movement therapists, and are not exclusive to the field of Dance/Movement Therapy. Because dance/movement therapists can align with a variety of other theoretical orientations, they can also draw from the assessment tools associated with those additional approaches.

Dance/Movement Therapy Effectiveness Measures

Because the field of dance/movement therapy is relatively new, focuses on training practitioners rather than researchers, and has a small professional association and quite limited resources, research into its effectiveness has been mostly anecdotal for the first part of its history (Chaiklin, 1997; Cruz & Berrol, 2012). Because the field of psychology was itself trying to be more scientific during the nascent period of dance/movement therapy as a profession, the experimental method was established as the gold standard for all psychologically oriented studies; thus, outcome research has focused on symptom reduction as measurable through quantitative methods rather than qualitative or even mixed methods (Cruz & Berrol, 2012; Kestenberg Amighi, Loman, Lewis, & Sossin, 1999). This did not align well with the clinical and anecdotal findings dance/movement therapists were discovering, which fit more congruently with phenomenological approaches, holistic theories, qualitative research methods, and process-based ways of working psychologically (Levy, 2005; Payne, 1992). In other words, the kind of knowledge being generated by practicing dance/movement therapists in the early years of the profession was not valued within the traditional medical model, which made it difficult to complete any outcome studies substantiating the efficacy of dance/movement therapy as an effective treatment. As a result, funding to investigate further the therapeutic power of dance and expressive movement was not readily available, so practitioners focused primarily on their clinical work and less on research.

Over the last two decades, however, the field of dance/movement therapy has stepped more fully into its place as a specialization within the counseling discipline. In so doing, it has demanded more qualitative and quantitative research to substantiate its efficacy as a therapeutic modality (Cruz & Berrol, 2012). Moreover, the broader field of somatic psychology has also burgeoned during this time, bringing with it significant research from neuroscience, interpersonal neurobiology, and developmental psychology that corroborates many of the theories, methods, and approaches introduced by the founding mothers of dance/movement therapy (Aposhyan, 2004; Caldwell, 1997; Leedy & Ormrod, 2014). This has led to a greater respect in recent years for the role of research within the profession of dance/movement therapy, and a greater understanding of how practitioners and researchers can better collaborate with one another in service of the profession, individual practitioners, and, ultimately, the clients they serve.

Conclusion

Movement is healing and transformative. It can unlock primitive feelings and experiences that are stored in the body, restoring one's connection with the body and the earth. As a psychotherapeutic modality, dance/movement therapy first emerged in the middle part of the 20th century, though its historical roots are actually quite ancient and ubiquitous among indigenous cultures and communities throughout the ages. Early dance/movement therapists drew from their extensive personal experience in modern, ballet, and other forms of dance and expressive movement, integrating that experience with direct observations they were gathering from their groups and classes, along with various psychological and developmental theories. Out of that integration was born the field of dance/movement therapy, a therapeutic approach that encompasses elements from the expressive and creative arts therapies as well as the somatically oriented psychotherapies.

This essay reviewed key aspects of the history of dance/movement therapy as a profession, emphasizing how it accesses and uses creative, imaginal, and embodied forms of expression as fundamental to healing, growth, and therapy. A definition of *dance/movement therapy* was provided, as well as information about its professional association in the USA. The ways in which new professionals might access training and credentialing within the field were outlined, and information about how credentialed practitioners could be contacted was supplied. The effectiveness of this approach was reviewed, along with a brief summary of how it could be adapted to support people from diverse demographic groups and psychiatric diagnoses. A summary of elements often included in a typical dance/movement therapy session was shared, as well as common tools employed by dance/movement therapists for conducting assessments, making diagnoses, and crafting treatment plans or interventions. The role of an embodied, creative process that draws on expressive movement and personal expression was emphasized throughout the essay as an intrinsic and necessary element of any dance/movement therapy experience.

Additional Dance/Movement Therapy Resources

Dance/Movement Therapy
Professional Associations (Non-Exhaustive)

- American Dance Therapy Association (ADTA): http://www.adta.org/
- Association for Dance Movement Psychotherapy United Kingdom (ADMP-UK): http://admp.org.uk/
- Dance Movement Therapy Association in Canada (DMTAC): http://dmtac.org/
- Dance Movement Therapy Association of Australasia (DTAA): http://dtaa.org.au/
- European Association Dance Movement Therapy (EADMT): http://www.eadmt.com/

Dance/Movement Therapy Scholarly Journals

- American Journal of Dance Therapy (AJDT): https://link.springer.com/journal/10465
- Body, Movement, and Dance in Psychotherapy (BMDP): http://www.tandfonline.com/loi/tbmd20
- The Arts in Psychotherapy (TAP): http://www.journals.elsevier.com/the-arts-in-psychotherapy/

ADTA Approved Dance/Movement
Therapy Graduate Programs in the USA

- Antioch University, New England; Keene NH; Website: http://www.antiochne.edu/applied-psychology/dance-movement-therapy/
- Columbia College; Chicago IL: Website: http://www.colum.edu/academics/fine-and-performing-arts/creative-arts-therapies/index.html
- Lesley University, Cambridge MA: Website: http://www.lesley.edu/master-of-arts/expressive-therapies/dance-therapy/mental-health-counseling/
- Naropa University, Boulder CO: Website: http://www.naropa.edu/academics/masters/clinical-mental-health-counseling/somatic-counseling/dance-movement-therapy/index.php
- Pratt Institute, Brooklyn NY: Website: https://www.pratt.edu/academics/school-of-art/graduate-school-of-art/creative-arts-therapy/creative-arts-therapy-degrees/dance-movement-therapy-ms/
- Sarah Lawrence College, Bronxville NY: Website: https://www.sarahlawrence.edu/dance-movement-therapy/#.TxnU6bNnV6c.email

Dance/Movement Therapy Programs
Outside the USA (Non-Exhaustive)

- International Dance/Movement Therapy Programs: https://adta.org/international-programs/

REFERENCES

Adler, J. (1992). Body and soul. *American Journal of Dance Therapy, 14*(2), 73–94.

American Dance Therapy Association. (2017). ADTA general questions website. Retrieved from https://adta. org/faqs/

Aposhyan, S. (1999). *Natural intelligence: Body-mind integration and human development.* Baltimore, MD: Williams and Wilkens.

Aposhyan, S. (2004). *Body-mind psychotherapy: Principles, techniques, and practical applications.* New York, NY: W.W. Norton and Company.

Bartenieff, I., & Lewis, D. (1980). *Body movement: Coping with the environment.* New York, NY: Gordon and Breach, Science Publishers.

Behar-Horenstein, L.S., & Ganet-Sigel, J. (1999). *The art and practice of dance/movement therapy.* Upper Saddle River, NJ: Pearson Education.

Bradley, K.K. (2009). *Rudolf Laban.* New York, NY: Routledge.

Bruno, C. (1990). Maintaining a concept of the dance in dance/movement therapy. *American Journal of Dance Therapy, 12*(2), 101–113.

Caldwell, C. (1996). *Getting our bodies back: Recovery, healing, and transformation through body-centered psychotherapy.* Boston, MA: Shambhala Publications.

Caldwell, C. (1997). *Getting in touch: The guide to new body-centered psychotherapies.* Wheaton, IL: Quest Books.

Canner, N.G. (1992). At home on earth. *American Journal of Dance Therapy, 14*(2), 125–131.

Chaiklin, H. (1997). Research and the development of a profession revisited. *American Journal of Dance Therapy, 19*(2), 93–103.

Chodorow, J. (1991). *Dance therapy and depth psychology: The moving imagination.* New York, NY: Routledge.

Cohen, B.B. (1993). *Sensing, feeling, and action: The experiential anatomy of Body-Mind Centering.* Northampton, MA: Contact Editions.

Cruz, R.F., & Berrol, C.F. (Eds.). (2012). *Dance/movement therapists in action: A working guide to research options* (2nd ed.). Springfield, IL: Charles C. Thomas, Publisher.

Dell, C. (1970). *A primer for movement description: Using Effort-Shape and supplementary concepts* (rev. ed.). New York, NY: Dance Notation Bureau Press.

Dell, C., Crow, A., & Bartenieff, I. (1977). *Space Harmony: Basic terms.* New York, NY: Dance Notation Bureau Press.

Dosamantes Beaudry, I. (1997). Reenvisioning dance/movement therapy. *American Journal of Dance Therapy, 19*(1), 15–23.

Espenak, L. (1981). *Dance therapy: Theory and application.* Springfield, IL: Charles C. Thomas.

Evans, J.E. (2007). The science of creativity and health. In I. Serlin (Ed.), *Whole person healthcare* (pp. 87–105). Westport, CT: Praeger.

Goodill, S.W. (2005). *An introduction to medical dance/movement therapy.* Philadelphia: Jessica Kingsley Publishers.

Hackney, P. (2002). *Making connections: Total body integration through Bartenieff Fundamentals.* New York, NY: Routledge.

Hanna, J.L. (2006). *Dancing for health: Conquering and preventing stress.* New York, NY: Rowman & Littlefield Publishers.

Hartley, L. (1995). *Wisdom of the body moving: An introduction to body-mind centering.* Berkeley, CA: North Atlantic Books.

Hawkins, A. (1988). *Creating through dance.* Pennington, NJ: Princeton Book Company.

Hawkins, A. (1991). Marian Chace Annual Lecture—The intuitive process as a force in change. *American Journal of Dance Therapy, 13*(2), 105–116.

Johnson, D., & Sandel, S. (1977). Structural analysis of group movement sessions: Preliminary research. *American Journal of Dance Therapy,* Fall/Winter, 32–36.

Johnson, D.R., Sandel, S.L., & Eicher, V. (1983). Structural aspects of group leadership styles. *American Journal of Dance Therapy, 6*, 17–30.

Jung, C.G. (1966). On the relation of analytical psychology to poetry. In *The spirit in man, art, and literature* (pp. 65–83). Princeton, NJ: Princeton University Press.

Kestenberg Amighi, J., Loman, S., Lewis, P., & Sossin, K.M. (1999). *The meaning of movement: Developmental and clinical perspectives of the Kestenberg Movement Profile.* Amsterdam, The Netherlands: Gordon and Breach Publishers.

Laban, R. (1960). *The mastery of movement.* Boston, MA: Plays.

Laban, R. (1974). *The language of movement: A guidebook to choreutics* (2nd ed.). Boston, MA: Plays.

Laban, R., & Lawrence, F.C. (1974). *Effort: Economy of body movement.* Boston, MA: Plays.

La Barre, F. (2001). *On moving and being moved: Nonverbal behavior in clinical practice.* Hillsdale, NJ: The Analytic Press.

Lefco, H. (1974). *Dance therapy: Narrative case histories of therapy sessions with six patients.* Chicago, IL: Nelson-Hall Company.

Leedy, P.D., & Ormrod, J.E. (2014). *Practical research: Planning and design* (10th ed.). Upper Essex, UK: Pearson Education Limited.

Levy, F.J. (1988). *Dance movement therapy: A healing art*. Reston, VA: The American Alliance for Health, Physical Education, Recreation, and Dance.

Levy, F.J. (1995). *Dance and other expressive arts therapies: When words are not enough*. New York, NY: Routledge.

Levy, F.J. (2005). *Dance movement therapy: A healing art* (2nd rev. ed.). Reston, VA: The American Alliance for Health, Physical Education, Recreation, and Dance.

Lewis Bernstein, P. (Ed.) (1979). *Eight theoretical approaches in dance/movement therapy*. Dubuque, IA: Kendall/Hunt Publishing Company.

Lewis, P. (1979). *Theoretical approaches in dance/movement therapy,* Vol. I. Dubuque, IA: Kendall/Hunt Publishing Company.

Lewis, P. (1984). *Theoretical approaches in dance/movement therapy,* Vol. II. Dubuque, IA: Kendall/Hunt Publishing Company.

Lewis, P. (1996). Depth psychotherapy in dance/movement therapy. *American Journal of Dance Therapy, 18*(2), 95–114.

Lewis, P., & Loman, S. (1990). *The Kestenberg Movement Profile: Its past, present applications, and future directions*. Keene, NH: Antioch New England Graduate School.

Loman, S. (1992). *The body-mind connection in human movement analysis*. Keene, NH: Antioch New England Graduate School.

Loman, S., & Merman, H. (1996). The KMP: A tool for dance/movement therapy. *American Journal of Dance Therapy, 18*(1), 29–52.

Mettler, B. (1990). Creative dance—Art or therapy? *American Journal of Dance Therapy, 12*(2), 95–100.

Moore, C., & Yamamoto, K. (1988). *Beyond words: Movement observation and analysis*. New York, NY: Gordon and Breach Sciences Publishers.

Musicant, S. (1994). Authentic movement and dance therapy. *American Journal of Dance Therapy, 16*(2), 91–106.

Naess Lewin, Joan L. (1998). *The dance therapy notebook*. Columbia, MD: Marian Chace Memorial Fund of the American Dance Therapy Association.

North, M. (1972). *Personality assessment through movement*. Boston, MA: Plays.

North, M. (1995). Marian Chace Annual Lecture—Catch the pattern. *American Journal of Dance Therapy, 17*(1), 5–14.

Payne, H. (Ed.). (1992). *Dance movement therapy: Theory and practice*. New York, NY: Routledge.

Payne, H. (2006). Tracking the web of interconnectivity. *Body, Movement, and Dance in Psychotherapy, 1*(1), 7–15.

Rockefeller, K., Serlin, I.A., & Fox, J. (2007). Multimodal imagery and healthcare. In I.A. Serlin, K. Rockefeller, & S.S. Brown (Eds.), *Praeger perspectives. Whole person healthcare Vol. 2. Psychology, spirituality, and health* (pp. 63–81). Westport, CT: Praeger Publishers.

Roskin Berger, M. (1992). Isadora Duncan and the creative source of dance therapy. *American Journal of Dance Therapy, 14*(2), 95–110.

Sandel, S.J., Chaiklin, S., & Lohn, A. (Eds.). (1993). *Foundations of dance/movement therapy: The life and work of Marian Chace*. Columbia, MD: Marian Chace Memorial Fund, American Dance Therapy Association.

Schmais, C. (1981). Group development and group formation in dance therapy. *The Arts in Psychotherapy, 8*, 103–107.

Schmais, C. (1985). Healing processes in group dance therapy. *American Journal of Dance Therapy, 8*, 17–36.

Schmais, C. (1998). Understanding the dance/movement therapy group. *American Journal of Dance Therapy, 20*(1), 23–35.

Schmais, C. (1999). Marian Chace Annual Lecture-Groups: A door to awareness. *American Journal of Dance Therapy, 21*(1), 5–18.

Schmais, C., & White, E. Q. (1986). Introduction to dance therapy. *American Journal of Dance Therapy, 9*, 23–30.

Schmais, C., & White, E.Q. (1996). Opening Keynote Address, 30th Annual Conference—ADTA: Where, when and how it all began. *American Journal of Dance Therapy, 18*(1), 5–20.

Schoop, T., & Mitchell, P. (1974). *Won't you join the dance?: A dancer's essay into the treatment of psychosis*. New York, NY: Mayfield Publishing Company.

Serlin, I. (1993). Root images of healing in dance therapy. *American Journal of Dance Therapy, 15*(2), 65–76.

Serlin, I.A. (1996). Kinesthetic imagining. *Journal of Humanistic Psychology, 36*(2), 25–33.

Serlin, I.A. (2006). Expressive therapies. In M. S. Micozzi (Ed.), *Complementary and integrative medicine in cancer care and prevention* (pp. 81–94). New York, NY: Spring Publishing Company.

Serlin, I.A. (2007). *Arts and health* (Vol. III). San Francisco, CA: Union Street Health Associates.

Serlin, I. (2010). Dance/Movement Therapy. In *The Corsini Encyclopedia of Psychology* (4th ed.) (pp. 459–460). Hoboken, NJ: John Wiley & Sons.

Serlin, I.A. (2012). *The courage to move*. In S. Schwartz, V. Marcow Speiser, P. Speiser, & M. Kossak (Eds.),

The arts and social change: The Lesley University experience in Israel (pp. 117–125). Zur Yigal, Israel: Porat Books.

Siegel, E.V. (1984). *Dance-movement therapy: Mirror of our selves—The psychoanalytic approach*. New York, NY: Human Sciences Press.

Siegel, E.V. (1995). Psychoanalytic dance therapy: The bridge between psyche and soma. *American Journal of Dance Therapy, 17*(2), 115–128.

Stanton-Jones, K. (1992). *An introduction to dance movement therapy in psychiatry*. New York, NY: Routledge.

Wallock, S.F., & Eckstein, D.G. (1983). Dance/movement therapy: A primer for group facilitators. *The 1993 Annual for Facilitators, Trainers, and Consultants* (pp. 195–202).

White, E.Q. (1994). Marian Chace Annual Lecture—Dance/movement therapy: Always a showcase, never a star. *American Journal of Dance Therapy, 16*(1), 5–12.

Whitehouse, M.S. (1999). Physical movement and personality. In P. Pallaro (Ed.), *Authentic Movement: Essays by Mary Starks Whitehouse, Janet Adler, and Joan Chodorow* (Vol. 1, pp. 51–57). Philadelphia, PA: Jessica Kingsley Publishers.

Wosien, M.G. (1974). *Sacred dance: Encounter with the gods*. New York, NY: Avon Books.

Drama Therapy

Integral Healing Through Imagination and Action

GARY RAUCHER, RENÉE EMUNAH *and* DOUG RONNING

Drama therapy is one of the creative arts therapies, along with its siblings—art, music, dance/movement, and poetry therapy. Drama therapy may be defined as the intentional application of techniques and processes from the dramatic arts to achieve therapeutic goals (North American Drama Therapy Association, 2017). Drama therapy processes include therapeutically adapted forms of improvisation, role-play, theater games, performance, creative drama, and mask and puppet work. Clients do not need prior theater/drama experience to engage in or benefit from such processes.

While the link between drama and healing has been recognized across many world cultures since antiquity (Grainger, 1990), the field first emerged as a distinct discipline within the U.S. in 1979 with the founding of what is now the North American Drama Therapy Association (NADTA). The field is also established or developing in many other countries, including England, the Netherlands, Israel, Japan, India, Taiwan, and Hong Kong.

Drama therapy processes are used in a variety of clinical, educational, and human services settings, and may be adapted to work with individuals, couples, families, and groups. The setting, presenting issues, and client configuration (individual, group, family, etc.) shape the nature of the drama therapy work done.

Scope of This Essay

In this essay, we will offer a concise discussion of the following topics:

- Approaches to drama therapy
- Drama therapy as a holistic practice
- Benefits and cautions
- Training and credentialing
- Applications with populations across the lifespan
- Case examples illustrating process
- Research regarding efficacy
- Resources for further information

Approaches to Drama Therapy

As a field, drama therapy has evolved to encompass several distinct but interrelated approaches, each highlighting a particular theoretical perspective or mode of practice. For example, three approaches taught and practiced commonly in North America (very briefly described) are:

1. *The Integrative Five Phase Model* (Emunah, 2009, 2020). A flexible and pragmatic framework for helping clients advance gently through a drama therapeutic treatment, using both fictional and psychodramatic aspects of the dramatic medium in a paced progression, focusing on emotion, perspective, and relationship.

2. *Role Method* (Landy, 1993, 1994, 2009). A methodology based on social role theory that uses a performance metaphor of life and pursues healing through the discovery and integration of roles identified by clients as pertinent to their issues and goals.

3. *Developmental Transformations* (commonly known as DvT) (Johnson, 2009). An approach rooted in improvisational play between practitioners and clients, often seen as a form of free association in action. The therapeutic focus of DvT is helping clients to overcome rigid defensive patterns based on fear of change and the instability of being.

Most drama therapy practice involves process work done within the confidential confines of therapy spaces. However, when clinically indicated (or appropriate to particular goals in non-clinical settings), it may involve the generation and presentation of performances that are typically offered to invited audiences. Two examples of performance-based drama therapy are:

1. *Therapeutic theatre performance* (Snow, 2009), in which clients dealing with a common challenge present a devised theatre piece. The performance might (but would not necessarily) include metaphoric or realistic enactments pertaining to shared issues.

2. *Self-revelatory performance* (Emunah, 2015, 2016), a form in which a performer crafts a theatre piece drawn from current life challenges, using drama therapy processes both in developing and performing the piece. There is a clear intention to deepen perspective and reach for healing.

While drama therapy is a distinct field, it shares some characteristics with other action-oriented, experiential approaches to psychotherapy, such as play therapy and psychodrama. Aspects of drama therapy are likewise similar to community building processes such as sociodrama (Sternberg & Garcia, 1989, 2009) and Theatre of the Oppressed (Boal, 1992; Sajnani, 2009). However, these are distinct practices with their own objectives and should not be confused with clinically applied drama therapy.

Drama Therapy as Holistic Practice

Holistic wellness refers to healthy and integrated functioning within and between individuals in their physical, emotional, mental, and spiritual aspects. This necessarily extends to sound relationships with other individuals within community, and ecologically to the larger natural world (Milton, 2009). Holistic healing modalities acknowledge these multiple dimensions, and address them inclusively in therapy in accordance with their impact and relevance to clients' issues.

As in humanistic psychology, holism emphasizes health rather than pathology. Accordingly, all creative arts therapies share a core holistic value: they regard a person's creativity, in whatever form it takes, as a fundamental aspect of underlying health and *wholeness*—regardless of the life challenges a person may face (Emunah, 1994). Drama therapy is integrative as well as holistic. It is rooted in theater, the most synthetic of the arts, incorporating language, movement, music, and the visual arts. And because the expressive medium for exploration and working through in drama therapy is the client's embodied self rather than an external project or artifact, this modality works with the immediacy of lived here-and-now experience. Clients engage in powerful, creative, and immersive whole-person explorations of issues and challenges they are facing, and the healing opportunities that arise through the process.

Benefits and Cautions in the Use of Drama Therapy

While holism recognizes personhood across the spiritual-psycho-social-physiological spectrum, the focal point of much contemporary psychotherapy is a person's *emotional* life. Psychological health, or its lack, manifests most directly as disturbances of affect and mood. Affect and body awareness are closely linked, and drama therapy, as an embodied and imaginative modality, helps people to recognize ties between outer and inner states of awareness, a significant step in mastering emotional regulation. Although drama therapy is direct and immersive, it allows for titration in the intensity of a client's emotional experience through intentional and modulated use of fictive distance. This is one of drama therapy's most dynamically beneficial features, and is notable when working with trauma. Significant wounding can be most productively (and compassionately) worked with and healed through interventions that progress artfully over time from indirect suggestion to more direct depictions of real life circumstances linked to wounding. The skilled facilitation of experiential enactments modified by distancing through aesthetic representation enables clients to process core emotional content (including instances of trauma) within a productive zone that bypasses the extremes of numbing and flooding (Hudgins, 2002). This allows for regulated cathartic releases where needed, accompanied by the cognitive distance necessary to allow insights into the memories and situations being explored. The balance of cognition and affect—sometimes called *aesthetic distance* (Landy, 1994; Scheff, 1981)—is a core construct in drama therapy, and can be leveraged in trauma work to decouple traumatic triggering from associated but non-traumatic stimuli. Drama therapy is thus an effective method for implementing the healing potentials of exposure and desensitization therapy (Johnson, 2014; Pitre, Sajnani, & Johnson, 2015).

Drama therapy is useful for clients struggling with cognitive, perceptual, or behavioral challenges. In drama therapy, clients can rehearse pro-social behaviors, receiving constructive feedback in contained, low-stakes role-plays. Thus, clients suffering from a range of difficulties, including treatable degrees of psychosis or addiction can benefit from drama therapy in developing behavioral and emotional regulation skills even as they participate in complementary treatment from other disciplines (such as psychiatry).

Like all potentially powerful tools, drama therapy must be applied ethically with knowledge, care, and experience to avoid possible misuses and harmful unintended consequences such as traumatic re-experiencing. The following section addresses the training and credentialing requirements for such safe and ethical practice.

The Training and Credentialing of Drama Therapy Practitioners

The ethical practice of drama therapy in North America is regulated by the North American Drama Therapy Association (NADTA), which awards the RDT credential (Registered Drama Therapist) to qualifying Master's level practitioners. NADTA serves to uphold standards of professional competence and ethics, develops criteria for training and education, reviews and accredits educational institutions offering drama therapy programs, administers registry requirements, reviews applications for RDT registry, promotes the field, and sponsors conferences and publications. Additionally, Registered Drama Therapists with the requisite experience may attain an advanced credential from NADTA, that of Board Certified Trainer (of drama therapists), or BCT. Drama therapists with the BCT credential constitute the core training faculty of NADTA.

The RDT is specific to the practice of drama therapy. However, most drama therapists are dual-credentialed, holding a state mental health license such as the LMFT (Licensed Marriage, Family Therapist) or LPC (Licensed Professional Counselor) and the RDT. Government licensure (such as LMFT, LPC, or LCSW) in most of the U.S. allows drama therapists to offer other forms of psychotherapy in which they are trained, to take third party payments, and to refer to themselves as psychotherapists (in addition to drama therapists). State licensure specifically for creative arts therapists is rare at this time; New York is the exception, with its LCAT license (Licensed Creative Arts Therapist). NADTA and its sister creative arts therapies associations actively advocate for direct state licensure for trained and qualified clinicians among their members. The NADTA website maintains a useful and periodically updated FAQ page on credentialing issues related to drama therapy.

Educational Requirements for RDTs

RDT credentialing requires a combination of education and experience in both theater/drama and, typically, a Master's degree in drama therapy. The theater training background required of an RDT may involve acting, directing, improvisation, or other forms of theater education and performance experience. While the minimum requirement is 500 hours, most drama therapists exceed this, combining, for example, a BA or BFA in Theatre (or Theatre/Psychology majors/minors) with some form of professional or community experience in theater or as a teaching artist. Most RDTs acquire Master's level training at one of the NADTA-accredited drama therapy programs in North America. Accreditation means that these programs are contracted to provide the specific educational requirements that NADTA mandates for RDT credentialing, including specific drama therapy related curriculum, clinical study, law and ethics, and at least 800 hours in a supervised fieldwork practicum. Additionally, RDTs are required to log 1,000 hours of professional post–Master's experience before applying for the RDT, and to then maintain their RDTs through documented continuing education.

As of June 2019 (at the projected time of this publication) NADTA accredited Master's-level drama therapy programs included:

- California Institute of Integral Studies (CIIS) in San Francisco (MA in Counseling Psychology—Concentration in Drama Therapy). The authors of this essay are affiliated with this program
- New York University (MA in Drama Therapy)
- Concordia University in Montreal (MA in Creative Arts Therapy—Option in Drama Therapy)
- Lesley University in Boston (MA in Mental Health Counseling—Specialization in Drama Therapy)
- Antioch University Seattle, (MA in Clinical Mental Health Counseling or Couple and Family Therapy with Concentration in Drama Therapy)
- Kansas State University, Manhattan KS (MA in Theatre—Concentration in Drama Therapy)

The CIIS and NYU programs are the longest-standing programs; both began in the early 1980s. The foundational vision of CIIS is the integration of mind, body, and spirit. The Drama Therapy Program at CIIS embraces the holistic core of drama therapy, which over time has increasingly encompassed applications of drama therapy in social justice work. The roots of the NYU Drama Therapy Program are embedded in Educational Theatre, role theory, and arts/performance-based research. Each of the five accredited programs brings its own particular perspective to the theory and practice of drama therapy.

For people who have already earned (or are close to completing) a relevant and applicable Master's degree in a field other than drama therapy, it is possible to pursue RDT credentialing through NADTA's Alternative Track Training option. Qualifying Master's degrees include theater, psychology, counseling, education, or variants of these. The Alternative Track route involves the mentorship of a BCT (Board Certified Trainer) contracted to customize a curriculum that fills in gaps between the candidate's particular degree requirements and those established by NADTA for drama therapists. This supplemental training typically includes courses at academic institutions, workshops and trainings offered by BCTs, independent study, and supervised practicums. Additional information may be found on the NADTA website.

Limited Use of Drama Therapy Techniques by Other Clinicians

Licensed clinicians interested in incorporating dramatic and action-oriented methods with their verbally or somatically focused practices can often find workshop and training opportunities. Action methods can serve as catalysts or "ice-breakers" in group therapy, or as a way to introduce play, elicit perspective, provide behavioral practice, or evoke emotion in individual therapy. It is totally acceptable for clinicians to use such techniques judiciously on occasion (typically without elaboration, and without sustaining—or intervening within—the drama therapeutic mode); however, brief trainings or workshops do not confer on practitioners proficiency or eligibility to practice drama therapy, nor can they ethically refer to themselves as drama therapists. Clinicians who believe that particular clients might benefit from a sustained use of drama therapy should refer these clients to Registered Drama Therapists. The NADTA website includes listings by states of practicing RDTs.

Sample Drama Therapy Applications Across the Lifespan

Drama therapists have found manifold ways to adapt their work to varied settings, populations, and configurations of clients. In this section, we offer brief examples of how drama therapy is applied with sample populations across the lifespan in a variety of settings. Drama therapists are trained to be highly flexible and to adapt to the needs of diverse clients, taking into consideration their abilities, goals, proclivities, and cultural expectations.

Children

Children of all ages respond naturally to opportunities to engage in dramatic play; indeed it is their way of mediating and expressing their inner experience (Cattanach, 1996; Emunah, 2020). Drama therapy can be highly effective for treating individual children dealing with a variety of struggles, including those affected by trauma. For such children, age-appropriate fictive structures provide both distancing and a symbolic container (Onoe, 2014) in which children can explore the narratives, feelings, and aftermath of difficult or traumatic experience. Projective objects, such as puppets, masks, or action figures, can help modulate distance. Skillful use of role play and selective use of reenactment can help therapists understand more of a child's lived experience, and help the child to express and contain multiple emotions, and develop internal resources and strengths in coping with pain. As specific examples, drama therapy has been used to help children to recover from sexual abuse (Cattanach, 1996; James, Forrester, & Kim, 2005), process exposure to severe domestic violence (Weber, 2005), and forge reparative attachments in foster placements. (Onoe, 2014; Pitre, 2014).

Many applications of drama therapy with children address the building of socialization skills, and numerous schools count drama therapists among their counseling staff. Some school districts contract with drama therapy providers to bring in programming to address particular needs such as anti-bullying campaigns (No Bully, 2017) or the cultivation of social-emotional intelligence in classrooms (Feldman, Jones, & Ward, 2009). Drama therapy has proven effective with socialization of children with attention deficit hyperactivity disorder (ADHD) (Guli, Semrud-Clikeman, Lerner, & Britton, 2013) and on the Autism Spectrum (D'Amico, LaLonde, & Snow, 2015; Feldman et al., 2009). One innovative program called ALIVE (Sajnani Jewers-Dailley, Brillant, Puglisi, & Johnson, 2014) in the New Haven, Connecticut Public School System weaves drama therapy into various strands of a comprehensive approach to supporting student wellbeing, educational goals, and overall school climate. Their services range from contributing dramatic enactments to enliven curriculum to brief individual drama therapy sessions that reduce symptoms of traumatic stress through relational play.

Adolescents

Adolescents can be resistant to any form of treatment, as they desire the privileges of adulthood while exhibiting an often developmentally appropriate degree of rebelliousness (Emunah, 2020). It is also a time when peer relationships come to the fore, making drama therapy groups with teens a useful social laboratory once their resistance has been adequately tamed. Drama therapists at times start by playing with teen resistance (Emunah, 1985), inviting and amplifying it through embodiment, sound, and movement and then transforming it. Teens will often come "on board" once an activity "passes muster" as being in-line with their concerns. Drama therapy is employed in school settings for psychoeducation, skill building, and emotional support related to the transitions of adolescent life. New York–based ENACT (Feldman et al., 2009) and STOP-GAP (Laffoon & Kenny, 2009) in Southern California have been conducting drama therapy workshops in schools since the 1980s. Both use a progression of warm-ups, enactments, and facilitated dialogue to explore student issues and concerns. Drama therapy has also been employed for groups with specialized needs, such as teens living with HIV (Meyer, 2010), or teen trauma survivors needing support to contain revenge fantasies (Haen & Weber, 2009).

Adults

Though the socialization of adults in our culture marginalizes the value of imaginal or "as-if" play, drama therapy empowers adults in treatment to reconnect to this innate and generative capacity that many have lost with their childhood. Drama therapy with adults takes many shapes. Fictional improvisational scene work has proven effective with adults in in-patient psychiatric therapy (Emunah & Johnson, 1983; Emunah, 2020), couples work (Wiener, 2010), and in parent training (Zuver & Grigsby, 2007), among others. On the other hand, playing with real-life scenarios at variable degrees of realism or circumstantial accuracy enables adults to safely attempt alternative ways of conducting themselves and relating to partners, families, workplace colleagues, and community peers. For example, a parent skills training group has parents role-play multiple strategies to engage an emotionally activated child, then consult with one another on best practices and outcomes (Zuver & Grigsby, 2007). Drama therapists often use processes adopted from psychodrama (Emunah, 1997), a related form of therapy used primarily with groups and focusing on a single protagonist, that help explore real life situations, past events, or parts of self. These adapted processes range in form from exploratory sculpts of conflictual intrapsychic states to interpersonal enactments of desired future scenarios. Clients can attain cathartic release of toxic emotions and gain new perspectives on personal narratives of wounding or unfinished business.

Other types of dramatic processes, including the use of metaphor, story-making, and improvisational free play, have been used in settings treating survivors of trauma and crisis, for example: to assist refugee women in attenuating past trauma during resettlement (Landis, 2014), to mitigate post-traumatic stress in veterans (Ali & Wolfert, 2016; James & Johnson, 1997) and to reform prison cultures by working with staff and offenders to forge therapeutic communities (Bergman, 2009).

Geriatric Adults

Drama therapy is used in a variety of residential and day-treatment settings that serve seniors to address issues of that life-stage, such as isolation, depression, dementia, and existential anxieties associated with declining health and mortality. The objective of such treatment is to enhance quality of life rather than to reverse symptoms inherent to the aging process. For example, Johnson (1986) and Wilder (2007) describe conducting drama therapy groups to reduce loneliness and social isolation, while nurturing empathy and support among participants through the sharing of life stories. The use of gentle embodied techniques can tap into sense memories that liberate previously forgotten stories or stimulate shared fantasies of new adventures. Drama therapy has been shown to lift affect and improve quality of life for people with various forms of dementia (Jaaniste, Linnell, Ollerton, & Slewa-Younan, 2015) and improvisational play has been demonstrated to be an effective way of exploring and processing the frequently masked existential anxieties of this life stage, such as fears surrounding loss, declining abilities, and mortality (Parkinson, 2008; Smith, 2000).

Case Examples Illustrating Drama Therapy Process

This section aims to offer a "taste" of drama therapy in action by providing a brief glimpse into the flow of sample processes within a session and over a series of sessions, using case examples from individual and group practice. The disguised scenarios used are particular to the cases on which they are based, and, naturally, do not represent the field as a whole. Among the diverse approaches to drama therapy, a basic three-part structure marks the beginning, middle, and end of sessions, whether they involve individuals, couples, family units, or groups. In simple terms, the three parts are (1) warm-up, (2) main phase, and (3) closure.

Warm-up activities help clients transfer their focus from external concerns into being present with the therapeutic work at hand. Drama therapy warm-ups tend to involve some degree of physical activation, as appropriate to the needs and capacities of a given population. One example of a frequently used drama therapy warm-up for groups is a "sound and movement check-in." Participants in turn briefly convey their current feeling states through an expressive gesture accompanied by a sound, word, or short phrase. The group then mirrors this back to each participant as a form of acknowledgment and rapport. Whatever forms they take, warm-ups are foundational to preparing for the second or middle phase of work, which is where the main therapeutic thrust of the session is pursued. Main phase interventions vary widely according to the needs of clients and the phase of therapy. Finally, the recap and closure phase is frequently ritualistic in form; it helps clients review and consolidate gains from the main phase, and aids in the transition back to their outside lives.

On a broader, multi-session level, the same principles apply over the course of a continuing drama therapy series. There is a warm-up or "getting-to-know-you" sequence of sessions in which trust and cohesion are cultivated as a foundation for the main or "working-through" sessions, concluded by more ritualized sessions marking closure and termination. Emunah's Integrative Five Phase Model of drama therapy (2009, 2020) is a nuanced elaboration of these principles.

Example of a Single Session
in Individual Therapy

The following is a brief description of a single session in the lead author's (GR) treatment of a partnered 29-year-old working class man who pursued drama therapy to address compulsive behaviors, the primary objective being a reduction of alcohol abuse. The session described was several months into treatment, and was focused on conscious pattern disruption after a stress-related relapse of excessive social drinking on the eve of an important job interview.

During our session's verbal check-in, "Nathan" characteristically demonstrated both insight and motivation to discontinue behaviors he recognized as self-sabotaging. After verbally deconstructing the events of the problematic evening, we collaboratively agreed that the relapse was due in part to Nathan's not recognizing a series of triggers. We used drama therapy to revisit the triggering circumstances, but only after first establishing and externalizing two important sobriety-related resources—his AA sponsor and a close friend. Nathan set up chairs with colored pillows to represent these two resources, and I had him step into role as each of them (standing behind and touching each chair) to offer (to himself) heartfelt words of encouragement. We then concretized and walked through a detailed timeline of the evening in question, marking specific micro events on the floor with colored scarves, rating each in terms of triggering impact by stopping to notice somatic shifts at each station, which I then asked him to embody through a drama therapy process called "Self-sculpting" (Emunah, 2020). When Nathan felt flooded or overwhelmed, I had him step over to one of his resource chairs to reconnect with its associated support until he felt ready to return to reviewing the timeline. We concluded with a facilitated three-way conversation between Nathan, his friend, and his sponsor (portrayed by him with prompts from me). By this means, he identified stress-related triggers that he had not recognized before, and on my recommendation followed through as homework by writing letters to those parts of himself that he had discovered were susceptible. The upshot was that he was subsequently able to redirect his behavior preventing further relapses.

In this example, the embodied and experiential dimensions of drama therapy treatment served the client's progress in a way that a verbal discussion about his stressors and triggers in prior therapies and 12-step meetings had not. The imaginal enactment helped him to recognize stressors and triggers through somaticized and imaginal evocation of time and place, a form of state-dependent learning (Hudgins, 2002). Drama therapy's access to somatic and imaginal dimensions of experience make it a potent catalyst in such change.

Examples from a Group Process

Drama therapy is common in hospitals, schools, mental health clinics, recovery centers, and settings where garnering peer support and serving multiple clients economically are important. Group drama therapy can be effective for all ages. Group size can vary from a few to a few dozen depending on the setting and circumstance; larger groups benefit from the use of co-facilitators. Optimal group size for clinical purposes ranges from six to ten, though more can be accommodated in workshop settings.

As an example of a group process within a series, the following describes two sessions from a drama therapy group for adolescents with behavioral and substance use issues conducted by one of the authors (DR). The group met for three hours weekly over twelve weeks as part of an intensive outpatient program that also incorporated other forms of family, group, and individual therapy. Each week, all treatment centered around a particular recovery-related theme.

Each drama therapy session began with a review of group guidelines followed by a warm-up pertinent to the week's theme. For example, for a grief themed week, each client was asked to write a letter to someone (or something) associated to a loss they had experienced. The letters addressed grandparents, pets, friends, lost childhood toys, and in some cases, a former substance of choice. Clients read their offerings aloud, emulating a memorial service with music and candles. The teens were then invited to explore their feelings nonverbally through gesture, sound, and movement, leading to group sculptures that were further clustered into dioramas by individual clients depicting their experiences of loss. Peers not involved in a given sculpt served as empathic witnesses. The group ended with a weekly closing ritual in which clients, seated in a circle, shared something they would take away from the session, followed with the passing of a hand squeeze in a wave-like motion around the circle.

For the session focused on anger, the group began with clients listening to songs that expressed or evoked anger, such as "St. Anger" by Metallica and "Angry Chair" by Alice in Chains, while creating anger masks on three-dimensional plastic mask forms using paint and collage materials to represent their internal experience of anger. Clients introduced their anger mask to the group and spoke briefly about the design. Then, peers donned their masks and matched it with a sound and movement to amplify (but through the safety of the mask) their expression of anger. Finally, an "angry chair" was set up and one-by-one volunteers placed their masks on the chair and had a conversation with it. Facilitated role reversal was used to help clients enter into an externalized dialog with their anger, cultivating their observing egos and insight.

Research on the Efficacy of Drama Therapy

Research into the efficacy of drama therapy has evolved considerably since the field's inception. Many inquiries from the early years of drama therapy's emergence were single-case vignette studies authored by practitioner-investigators, which offered a narrative of clinical change through the lens of a particular approach to practice (Aldridge, 1994). An obvious limitation of this model is that it is difficult to estimate the validity of the practice outside of the sample cases or practitioner's experience.

Over time, voices within the field advocated for more rigor in evaluating drama therapy's effectiveness with different populations (Johnson, Emunah, & Lewis, 2009; Jones, 2015; Landy, 2006). An analysis of efficacy research in the field undertaken by British drama therapist Phil Jones (2015) between 2009 and 2013 found that 76 percent of published articles employed a qualitative methodology, 13 percent used quantitative measures, and 11 percent used mixed methods. Jones and others argued that, while qualitative case studies do provide one type of useful data for evaluating efficacy over the course of treatment, additional emphasis on quantitative and mixed methods research is necessary for drama therapy to grow in acceptance (Landy, 2006).

In the early 2000s, the North American Drama Therapy Association (NADTA) and its UK counterpart, The British Association for Drama Therapists (BADth), set out to promote and expand forms of research in the field of drama therapy. In 2014, NADTA added a Research Chair position to its Board of Directors. Both associations publish peer-reviewed journals: the NADTA began publishing *Drama Therapy Review* in 2015 which includes, "but is not limited to qualitative and quantitative studies, literature reviews, arts-based research, and context-specific case vignettes," (NADTA, 2015). BADth publishes the *Dramatherapy Journal*, which released its 37th volume in 2015 (Taylor & Francis Online, n.d.).

One systematic examination of existing English language case studies (Cassidy, Turnbull, & Gumley, 2014) used grounded theory analysis to examine meta-processes in drama therapy as they correlate to change patterns in the client's experience. Among the meta-processes that appeared to influence clients' perceptions of change were working in the "here and now" with the drama therapist attuning to present moment experiences; "working alongside," with the drama therapist taking on roles to support the encounter; "establishing safety" and using drama therapy "techniques as a container" to help clients modulate affect and feel safe; "avoiding interpretation," "being actively involved" with "timely choice of techniques," and offering clients "choice and control" to keep them engaged.

Empirically measuring the efficacy of the experiential nature of drama therapy has been further explored in studies of emotional arousal in core processes of drama therapy (Armstrong et al., 2015) and linking experiencing in core processes to client change (Armstrong et al., 2016). Both of these studies focused on two core processes found in all forms of drama therapy (Jones, 2008), dramatic projection and dramatic embodiment. The data set used in both comprised video and transcripts from a documentary that depict three sessions of drama therapy with a single client (Landy, 2005). To measure emotional arousal, the Client Emotional Arousal Scale—III (CEAS) (Warwar & Greenberg, 1999) was used. To measure the client's level of experiencing the observer-rated Experiencing Scale (EXP) (Klein Mathieu-Coughlan, & Keisler, 1986) was employed. The findings, while limited due to the small data set, do demonstrate that it is possible to distinguish and measure processes taking place within drama therapy sessions.

Another project set out to measure the efficacy of utilizing drama therapy interventions to teach social skills to children with Autism Spectrum Disorders (D'Amico et al., 2015). It used pre and post data collection from the Parent and Student Forms of the Social Skills Improvement System-Rating Scales (SSIS-RS) (Gresham & Elliott, 2008). Though the sample size of this study was limited (six children, 10–12 years old), within this sample "the SSIS-RS results showed statistically significant improvements in engagement, coupled with decreased externalizing, hyperactivity, inattention and Autism Spectrum behaviors at the end of the project" (D'Amico et al., 2015, p.32).

These studies, in combination with the growing interest in making research a priority within the American and British drama therapy associations, represent a maturation within the field. Drama therapists are increasingly acknowledging the importance of bringing quantitative and empirical modes of inquiry on efficacy into their arts-based interventions. While it remains impossible to identify and measure all the variables within a holistic, arts-based approach to healing, it is important to recognize when and how such research does improve practice and demonstrate drama therapy's efficacy to the many who can benefit from it.

Conclusion

Drama therapy, when used skillfully and ethically, offers both a playful and powerful means to help people express and master emotion, expand role and behavioral repertoire, heighten perspective, deepen self-awareness, and heal from psychological wounds. The distance afforded by the fictional mode can facilitate the gradual exposing and tackling of clinically sensitive issues through a progressively unfolding process. The imaginary realms can also be liberating, and afford participants a respite from real life struggles. Integrating body, mind, spirit, and creativity, drama therapy is a holistic form of treatment that can bypass the limitations of language (or the potential restrictions in having only verbal options to communicate a range of experience).

Drama therapy is currently used with a wide variety of populations, age groups, formats (group, individual, couple, family, and communities, and in both brief and long-term treatment), as well as within both clinical and non-clinical settings. It is our hope that the unique field of drama therapy—which integrates the art form of theater and the art and science of psychotherapy—will continue to add to the wealth of holistic therapeutic options that can address the vast range of human struggles, needs, and hopes.

SELECT RESOURCES FOR FURTHER INFORMATION

The following resources are suggested as a quick start list. Please also refer to this essay's reference list for further resources.

Emunah, R. (2020). Acting for real: Drama therapy process, technique, and performance (2nd ed.). New York and London: Routledge/Taylor and Francis.

Johnson, D.R., & Emunah, R. (2009). Current approaches in drama therapy (2nd ed.). Springfield, IL: Charles Thomas.

Landy, R. (1993). Persona and performance: The meaning of role in drama therapy and everyday life. New York, NY: Guilford Press.

North American Drama Therapy Association Website: www.nadta.org

REFERENCES

Aldridge, D. (1994). Single-case research designs for the creative art therapist. *The Arts in Psychotherapy, 21*(5), 333–342.

Ali, A., & Wolfert, S. (2016). Theatre as a treatment for post-traumatic stress in military veterans: Exploring the psychotherapeutic potential of mimetic induction. *The Arts in Psychotherapy, 50,* 58–65.

Armstrong, C.R., Rozenberg, M., Powell, M.A., Honce, J., Bronstein, L., Gingras, G., & Han, E. (2016). A step toward empirical evidence: Operationalizing and uncovering drama therapy change processes. *The Arts in Psychotherapy, 49,* 27–33.

Armstrong, C.R., Tanaka, S., Reoch, L., Bronstein, L., Honce, J., Rosenberg, M., & Powell, M.A. (2015). Emotional arousal in two drama therapy core processes: Dramatic embodiment and dramatic projection. *Drama Therapy Review, 1*(2), 147–160.

Bergman, J. (2009). The Bergman drama therapy approach: Creating therapeutic communities in prisons. In D. R. Johnson & R. Emunah (Eds.), *Current approaches in drama therapy* (2nd ed.) (pp. 330–354). Springfield, IL: Charles Thomas.

Boal, A. (1992). *Games for actors and non-actors* (A. Jackson, Trans.). London, UK: Routledge.

Cassidy, S., Turnbull, S., & Gumley, A. (2014). Exploring core processes facilitating therapeutic change in dramatherapy: A grounded theory analysis of published case studies. *The Arts in Psychotherapy, 41*(4), 353–365.

Cattanach, A. (1996). The use of dramatherapy and play therapy to help de-brief children after the trauma of sexual abuse. In A. Gersie (Ed.), *Dramatic approaches to brief therapy* (pp. 177–187). Bristol, PA: Jessica Kingsley Publishers.

D'Amico, M., LaLonde, C., & Snow, S. (2015). Evaluating the efficacy of drama therapy in teaching social skills to children with autism spectrum disorders. *Drama Therapy Review, 1*(1), 21–39.

Emunah, R. (1985). Drama therapy and adolescent resistance. *The Arts in Psychotherapy, 12*(2), 71–79.

Emunah, R. (1997). Drama therapy and psychodrama: An integrated model. *The International Journal of Action Methods, 50*(3), 108–134.

Emunah, R. (2009). The integrative five phase model of drama therapy. In D.R. Johnson & R. Emunah (Eds.), *Current approaches in drama therapy* (2nd ed.) (pp. 37–64). Springfield, IL: Charles Thomas.

Emunah, R. (2015). Self-revelatory performance: A form of drama therapy and theatre. *Drama Therapy Review 1*(1), 71–85.

Emunah, R. (2016). From behind the scenes to facing an audience in self-revelatory performance. In S. Pendzik, R. Emunah, & D.R. Johnson (Eds.), *The self in performance: Autobiographical, self-revelatory, and autoethnographic forms of therapeutic theatre* (pp. 37–52). New York, NY: Palgrave MacMillan.

Emunah, R. (2020). *Acting for real: Drama therapy process, technique, and performance* (2nd ed.). New York and London: Routledge/Taylor and Francis.

Emunah, R., & Johnson, D. R. (1983). The impact of theatrical performance on the self-images of psychiatric patients. *The Arts in Psychotherapy, 10*(4), 233–239. Retrieved from https://doi.org/10.1016/0197-4556 (83)90024-2

Feldman, D., Sussman Jones, F., & Ward, E. (2009). The ENACT method of employing drama therapy in schools. In D. R. Johnson & R. Emunah (Eds.), *Current approaches in drama therapy* (2nd ed.) (pp. 284–307). Springfield, IL: Charles Thomas.

Grainger, R. (1990). *Drama therapy and ritual. From drama and healing—The roots of drama therapy*. Bristol, PA: Jessica Kingsley Publishers.

Gresham, F.M., & Elliott, S.N. (2008). *Social skills improvement system-rating scales (SSIS-RS)*. Bloomington, MN: Pearson Assessments.

Guli, L.A., Semrud-Clikeman, M., Lerner, M.D., & Britton, N. (2013). Social competence intervention program (SCIP): A pilot study of a creative program for youth with social difficulties. *The Arts in Psychotherapy, 40*(1), 37–44.

Haen, C., & Weber, A.M. (2009). Beyond retribution: Working through revenge fantasies with traumatized young people. *The Arts in Psychotherapy, 36*(2), 84–93.

Hudgins, M.K. (2002). *Experiential treatment for PTSD: The therapeutic spiral model*. New York, NY: Springer.

Jaaniste, J., Linnell, S., Ollerton, R.L., & Slewa-Younan, S. (2015). Drama therapy with older people with dementia: Does it improve quality of life? *The Arts in Psychotherapy, 43*, 40–48.

James, M., Forrester, A., & Kim, K. (2005). Developmental transformations in the treatment of sexually abused children. In A. Weber & C. Haen (Eds.), *Clinical applications of drama therapy in child and adolescent treatment* (pp. 67–86). New York, NY: Brunner/Routledge.

James, M., & Johnson, D.R. (1997). Drama therapy in the treatment of combat-related post-traumatic stress disorder. *The Arts in Psychotherapy, 23*(5), 383–395.

Johnson, D.R. (1986). The developmental method in drama therapy: Group treatment with the elderly. *Arts in Psychotherapy, 13*, 17–34.

Johnson, D.R. (2009). Developmental transformations: Towards the body as presence. In D.R. Johnson & R. Emunah (Eds.), *Current approaches in drama therapy* (2nd ed.) (pp. 89–116). Springfield IL: Charles Thomas.

Johnson, D.R., Emunah, R., & Lewis, P. (2009). The development of theory and methods in drama therapy. In D.R. Johnson & R. Emunah (Eds.), *Current approaches in drama therapy* (2nd ed.) (pp. 16–23). Springfield IL: Charles Thomas.

Johnson, D.R. (2014). Trauma-centered developmental transformations. In N. Sajnani & D.R. Johnson (Eds.), *Trauma-informed drama therapy: Transforming clinics, classrooms, and communities* (pp. 68–92). Springfield, IL: Charles Thomas.

Jones, P. (2008). Research into the core processes of drama therapy: Vignettes and conversations. *The Arts in Psychotherapy, 35*(4), 271–279.

Jones, P. (2010). *Drama as therapy* (Vol. 2). *Clinical work and research into practice*. New York, NY: Routledge.

Jones, P. (2015). Three challenges for drama therapy research: Keynote NADTA conference, Montreal, 2013, Part 1. *Drama Therapy Review, 1*(1), 87–99.

Klein, M.H., Mathieu-Coughlan, P., & Kiesler, D.J. (1986). The experiencing scales. In L.S. Greenberg & W.M. Pinsof (Eds.), *Guilford clinical psychology and psychotherapy series. The psychotherapeutic process: A research handbook* (pp. 21–71). New York, NY: Guilford Press.

Laffoon, D., & Kenny, F. (2009). The STOP-GAP approach to drama therapy. In D.R. Johnson & R. Emunah (Eds.), *Current approaches in drama therapy* (2nd ed. (pp. 284–307). Springfield, IL: Charles Thomas.

Landis, H. (2014). Drama therapy with newly-arrived refugee women. In N. Sajnani & D.R. Johnson (Eds.), *Trauma-informed drama therapy: Transforming clinics, classrooms, and communities* (pp. 287–305). Springfield, IL: Charles Thomas.

Landy, R.J. (1993). *Persona and performance: The meaning of role in drama, therapy, and everyday life*. New York, NY: Guilford Press.

Landy, R.J. (1994), *Drama therapy, concepts, theories and practices*. Springfield, IL: Charles Thomas.

Landy, R.J. (2005). *Three approaches to drama therapy*. New York, NY: New York University. [Documentary film].

Landy, R.J. (2006). The future of drama therapy. *The Arts in Psychotherapy, 33*(2), 135–142.

Landy, R.J. (2009). Role theory and role method of drama therapy. In D.R. Johnson & R. Emunah (Eds.), *Current approaches in drama therapy* (2nd ed.) (pp. 65–88). Springfield, IL: Charles Thomas.

Meyer, K. (2010). Dramatherapy with adolescents living with HIV: Story making drama and body mapping. In P. Jones (Ed.), *Drama as therapy* (Vol. 2): *Clinical work and research into practice* (pp. 126–151). New York, NY: Routledge.

Milton, M. (2009). Waking up to nature: Exploring a new direction for psychological practice. *Ecopsychology, 1*(1), 8–13

NADTA. (2015). Drama Therapy Review (DTR). Retrieved from http://www.nadta.org/about-nadta/drama_therapy_review.html

NADTA. (2017). What is drama therapy? Retrieved from http://www.nadta.org/index.html

No Bully. (2017). Retrieved from https://www.nobully.org/

Onoe, A. (2014). The healing and growth of little monsters hurt within: Drama therapy at a foster home in Japan. In N. Sajnani & D.R. Johnson (Eds.), *Trauma-informed drama therapy: Transforming clinics, classrooms, and communities* (pp. 329–347). Springfield, IL: Charles Thomas.

Parkinson, E. (2008). Developmental transformations with Alzheimer's patients in a residential care facility. *The Arts in Psychotherapy, 35*, 209–216.

Pitre, R. (2014). Extracting the perpetrator: Fostering parent/child attachment with developmental transformations. In N. Sajnani & D.R. Johnson (Eds.), *Trauma-informed drama therapy: Transforming clinics, classrooms, and communities* (pp. 243–269). Springfield, IL: Charles Thomas.

Pitre, R., Sajnani, N., & Johnson, D.R. (2015). Trauma-centered developmental transformations as exposure treatment for young children. *Drama Therapy Review, 1*(1), 41–54.

Sajnani, N. (2009). *Theatre of the oppressed: Drama therapy as cultural dialogue.* In D.R. Johnson and R. Emunah (Eds.), *Current approaches in drama therapy* (2nd ed.) (pp. 445–460). Springfield, IL: Charles Thomas.

Sajnani, N., Jewers-Dailley, K., Brillante, A., Puglisi, J., & Johnson, D.R. (2014). Animating learning by integrating and validating experience. In N. Sajnani & D.R. Johnson (Eds.), *Trauma-informed drama therapy: Transforming clinics, classrooms, and communities* (pp. 206–240). Springfield, IL: Charles Thomas.

Scheff, T. (1981). The distancing of emotion in psychotherapy. *Psychotherapy: Theory, Research and Practice, 18*, 46–53.

Smith, A. (2000). Exploring death anxiety with older adults through developmental transformations. *The Arts in Psychotherapy, 22*(5), 321–334.

Snow, S. (2009). Ritual/theatre/therapy. In D.R. Johnson and R. Emunah (Eds.), *Current approaches in drama therapy* (2nd ed.) (pp. 117–144). Springfield, IL: Charles Thomas.

Sternberg, P., & Garcia, A. (1989). *Sociodrama: Who's in your shoes?* Westport, CT: Praeger.

Sternberg, P., & Garcia, A. (2009). Sociodrama. In D.R. Johnson & R. Emunah (Eds.), *Current approaches in drama therapy* (2nd ed.) (pp. 424–444). Springfield, IL: Charles Thomas.

Taylor & Francis Online. (n.d.). *Dramatherapy Journal Publication History.* Retrieved from http://www.tandfonline.com/loi/rdrt20

Warwar, S.H., & Greenberg, L.S. (1999). *Client Emotional Arousal Scale—III.* (Unpublished manuscript). Toronto, Canada: York University.

Weber, A. (2005). Don't hurt my mommy: Drama therapy for children who have witnessed severe domestic violence. In A. Weber & C. Haen (Eds.), *Clinical applications of drama therapy in child and adolescent treatment.* New York, NY: Brunner-Routledge.

Wiener, D.J. (2010). Rehearsals for growth: Drama therapy with couples. In D.R. Johnson & R. Emunah (Eds.), *Current approaches in drama therapy* (2nd ed.) (pp. 355–373). Springfield, IL: Charles Thomas.

Wilder, R. (2007). Lifedrama with elders. In A. Blatner & D.J. Wiener (Eds.), *Interactive and improvisational drama: Varieties of applied theatre and performance* (pp. 23–33). New York, NY: iUniverse, Inc.

Zuver, D.J., & Grigsby, M.K. (2007). Learning to parent apart: Drama in parent skills training. In A. Blatner & D.J. Wiener (Eds.), *Interactive and improvisational drama: Varieties of applied theatre and performance* (pp. 196–204). Lincoln, NE: iUniverse.

Music Therapy as a Holistic Treatment for Mental Health

LILLIAN EYRE

> And harmony, which has motions akin to the revolutions of the Soul within us, was given by the Muses to him ... as an auxiliary to the revolutions of the Soul, when it has lost its harmony, to assist in restoring it to order and concord within itself.
>
> —Plato, *Timaeus,* 49d

> (Music therapy) can make the difference between withdrawal and awareness, between isolation and interaction, between chronic pain and comfort—between demoralization and dignity.
>
> —Barbara Crowe, Past President of the American Music Therapy Association (AMTA, 2017a)

History of the Development of the Music Therapy Profession

From antiquity to the present, music has been an integral part of human existence. As a precursor of speech, music served as a means of emotional communication and bonding (Perlovsky, 2008; Tomlinson, 2015). As a vital component of the psyche, the musical brain was the prime motivator in creating the development of art and language, which owe their existence to the evolution of a common brain structure (Levitan, 2008). The ontology of the human psyche positions music at the center of our essential human nature (Levitan, 2008; Perlovsky, 2008; Tomlinson, 2015). It is not surprising, then, that the vast majority of human beings across cultures use music collectively to connect to others, to serve as a ritual to signify important events, and to establish and reinforce a multiplicity of cultural identities. On a personal level, individuals use music spontaneously to alter mood, to increase motivation, and to experience, communicate, and express emotions, whether these be feelings of loss and grief or joy and celebration. Thus, music is naturally suited to meet the therapeutic needs of clients in a mental health setting who are experiencing difficulties with thoughts, feelings, and perceptions. In fact, many health professionals, particularly nurses, are drawn to the use of music with their clients, principally to help clients to alter their mood positively (Murrock & Higgins, 2009).

This essay will introduce the development of the modern profession of music therapy in mental health and provide information on music therapy training and processes, give examples of how music therapy sessions address therapeutic goals for persons with serious mental illness (SMI), and provide references and resources. While music therapy can only be practiced by an accredited and, in some states, licensed music therapist, musical interventions that can be used by mental health professionals will be discussed.

Early History of the Therapeutic Use of Music

Music has been used therapeutically to address emotional and mental health throughout antiquity. Preliterate cultures used drums, rattles, and chants as an integral part of the healing ceremony (Sigerist, 1970), while in Egypt priests healed ailments with chant (Abdel-Salhen, 2005), as did First Nations medicine men (Dufrene & Coleman, 1994). The Greeks valued music as a cure for emotional instability (Feder & Feder, 1981). Plato prescribed listening to particular musical modes to build one's character or to alter mood, while Aristotle believed music to be a powerful force in achieving the cathartic release of difficult emotions (Feder & Feder) and Hippocrates played music for his patients who had mental illness (Hippocrates, 1849 trans.). References to the therapeutic use of music can be found throughout modern history. Burton (1651/1869) noted the powerful effect of music on melancholy, a concept that can be traced through various European and American writings (Heller, 1987; Horden, 2000). The concept of music as healer is later found in two 19th-century medical dissertations, Atlee (1804) and Mathews (1806) (AMTA, 2017b). The importance of these literary, philosophical, and scientific works lies in the fact that the concept of exploiting music as a valuable alternative treatment for persons with severe physical and emotional problems was recognized and promoted throughout history and across every culture. These are the roots of modern music therapy practice.

The Development of the Profession of Music Therapy

While music therapy in current practice is used for myriad populations with a variety of physical, cognitive, and emotional conditions, it is the use of music specifically as a treatment for mental health issues that played a pivotal role in the development of modern music therapy practice, education, and research (AMTA, 2017b). The early 20th century saw the return of veterans from both World Wars who had intractable mental health issues, most probably related to Post Traumatic Stress Disorder (PTSD). Anecdotal observations indicated that music was a powerful means of helping these veterans with physical and emotional problems to positively alter their mood, begin to engage with others, and motivate them to invest in their recovery (Taylor, 1981). Based on the therapeutic success of using music with veterans, doctors and nurses began to request the hiring of musicians to provide therapy for their hospitalized patients (AMTA, 2017b). As a result of this positive, and sometimes dramatic, experience using music therapeutically to improve mental health, a number of musician-healers began to establish music therapy as a profession in the early 20th century (Davis, Gfeller, & Thaut, 2008). In 1938, Altshuler established a program of music therapy for hospitalized persons with mental illness (Davis, 2003), and in 1944 van de Wall was appointed to oversee the establishment and development of music therapy programs in psychiatric hospitals (Davis et al., 2008). In the 1940s,

E. Thayer Gaston established the first internship training site for music therapy in the inpatient units of the influential Menninger Clinic (Davis et al., 2008), and the first music therapy training programs were created at Michigan State in 1944 (AMTA). Today there are over 75 music therapy educational and training programs offering degrees at the bachelor's, master's, and doctoral levels (Music Therapy Source Website, 2017).

Professional Organizations, Accreditation and Licensing Bodies

The AMTA: Professional Music Therapy Organization

Following the establishment of educational programs for the profession of music therapy, in 1950 the National Association for Music Therapy (NAMT) was founded to develop standards for education, clinical training, ethical guidelines, and certification, as well as to promote research through the publication of music therapy journals and conferences (AMTA, 2017b). The American Association for Music Therapy (AAMT), which had a more holistic philosophy than the NAMT, was established as an alternate association in 1971. In 1998, the two associations merged to create the current American Music Therapy Association, with a mission to educate and advocate for the music therapy profession (AMTA). The AMTA oversees educational standards for all university programs, publishes two research journals, educational texts, research bibliographies, podcasts, and newsletters, and promotes music therapy through state and federal advocacy and social media streams (AMTA). The AMTA is the largest music therapy association in the world and includes members from over 30 countries.

The Certification Board for Music Therapists: Accreditation

The Certification Board for Music Therapists (CBMT; 2017a) was incorporated in 1983 as a separate organization independent from the AMTA and has been fully-accredited by the National Commission for Certifying Agencies (NCCA) since 1986 (CBMT, 2017b). The CBMT assures the competency of accredited music therapists through their accreditation exam and continuing education reaccreditation requirements, thereby strengthening the credibility of the profession and ensuring a "standard of excellence in the development, implementation, and promotion of an accredited certification program for safe and competent music therapy practice" (CBMT). The CBMT and AMTA jointly developed the 2015 Scope of Music Therapy Practice (CBMT, 2017c, 2017d), while the CBMT has developed exam certification domains based on current clinical practice (CBMT). There are over 7,000 members of the CBMT who hold the accreditation credential Music Therapist, Board Certified (MT-BC). It is important to note that, while many musicians claim to practice music therapy or to be music therapists, only those persons who possess the MT-BC credential have completed the educational and clinical requirements to be accredited music therapists.

State Licensure for Music Therapy

In addition to the MT-BC credential, some states require a license to practice music therapy. These states are: Connecticut, Georgia, New York State, Nevada, North Dakota, Oklahoma, Oregon, Rhode Island, Utah, and Wisconsin (CBMT, 2017e). State licensure is an important step in the development of the profession for two primary reasons:

1. It protects clients or patients from potential harm or misrepresentation from individuals that are not board-certified music therapists and are not practicing under the CBMT Scope of Practice (i.e., non-music therapy musicians in healthcare)

2. It allows patients or clients and their families to access services provided by a board-certified music therapist (CBMT, 2017c).

Because of the importance of protecting consumers, increasing access to reimbursable music therapy services, and developing the profession, music therapists in many other states are advocating through state legislatures to establish licensure (CBMT, 2017e).

Counseling License

In addition to the MT-BC credential, and in the absence of state licensure, many music therapists with master's and doctorate degrees, particularly those who work in the field of mental health, have opted to complete the requirements for Licensed Professional Counselors. Each state has different requirements for inclusion, and not all AMTA-approved music therapy programs meet educational eligibility requirements. These requirements generally include 60 credits in a master's degree in counseling (some states include therapeutic creative arts as a related field), completion of credits in specified content areas, and additional hours of clinical supervision beyond the master's degree.

Training of the Music Therapist

Entry Level Music Therapy Training

To be accredited as a music therapist, the training must be completed in a university program approved by the AMTA. Currently, the entry level for a music therapist is a bachelor's degree, but this may change to a Master's Level Entry (MLE) in the future, as AMTA committees have been studying the impact of such a move for the last few years and are set to make a decision in the near future (AMTA, 2017c). The bachelor's education consists of 4.5 years of clinical training and academic studies in programs that address competencies in core music subjects (theory, harmony, conducting, aural skills, instrumental playing, ensembles, counterpoint, history, and world music), psychology courses (developmental, abnormal, personality, statistics, therapeutic approaches, and psychology of music), and music therapy (foundational concepts; working with diverse populations; methods, models and techniques used with various populations including developmental, medical, rehabilitation, and mental health; research methods; ethics; and clinical music skills), as well as other subjects in liberal arts and sciences (e.g., human biology) (AMTA, 2017d). In addition, the music therapy trainee must complete 200 hours of clinical practice with a minimum of three different populations during the bachelor's degree, followed by 1,000 hours of internship in a clinical site supervised by an accredited music therapist (AMTA, 2017d). Following the completion of all academic and clinical requirements, the trainee must pass the accreditation exam administered by the CBMT to earn the accreditation of Music Therapist, Board Certified (MT-BC).

Graduate Music Therapy Training

Although the MT-BC credential is currently the entry level for the field, many institutions, particularly those whose mandate is hospice and mental health care, require a master's degree in addition to the MT-BC credential for their music therapy positions. This is understandable, given the level of maturity and advanced skills needed to work effectively with these populations. At the master's level, a music therapist develops a comprehensive understanding of theories and practices in assessment, treatment, evaluation, and termination, and can be expected to take on an independent role in working with the multidisciplinary team to integrate music into client treatment plans (AMTA, 2017a).

A master's degree in music therapy is achievable in two ways: (1) after the completion of the bachelor's degree for those holding the MT-BC credential, and (2) as a combined accelerated bachelor's and master's degree for those who have completed an undergraduate degree in music or a related field such as psychology or social work; this is often called an "equivalency" degree (AMTA, 2017a). Students electing the equivalency path will complete all the academic and clinical requirements of the bachelor's degree leading to the MT-BC, followed by the advanced skills requirements of the master's degree at one of the 30 AMTA-approved master's programs (AMTA, 2017a). Students entering the master's degree with an MT-BC will complete the advanced skills courses of the master's degree. At the master's level, universities offer specialized degree programs with different foci on "issues relevant to the clinical, professional, and academic preparation of music therapists, usually in combination with established methods of research inquiry" (AMTA, 2017a).

The doctoral degree is offered in music therapy or a related discipline at a few universities in the USA. Typically, these degrees have unique curricula and focus on advanced competencies related to research, theory, clinical practice, university teaching, clinical administration, or a combination thereof (AMTA, 2017a).

Specialized Music Therapy Training

Nordoff-Robbins Music Therapy. Following the establishment of music therapy college programs in the 1950s, clinicians began to develop specialized models of music therapy practice to work with specific client populations. One of the first of these was *Creative Music Therapy*, now known as *Nordoff Robbins Music Therapy* (Hadley, 2003a). In 1966, Paul Nordoff and Clive Robbins began a training program based on clinical improvisation to work with children with developmental delays and severe disabilities (Hadley, 2003a). Based on theories developed from the anthroposophical teachings of Rudolf Steiner, Nordoff and Robbins believed in the therapeutic use of music to influence and develop the child's abilities through a profound respect for the child's unique inner life (Guerrero, Marcus, & Turry, 2015). Principles of reciprocity and communication through music and the use of clinical improvisatory techniques stemming from this model have been employed with other populations, in particular adults with medical conditions such as coma, HIV, Parkinson's, dementias, cancer, and stroke (Guerrero et al., 2015). Training in the Nordoff Robbins model in the USA is offered at the graduate level at New York University, Steinhardt School (Steinhardt, NYU) and Molloy College (Molloy College Website, 2017). The credential associated with this specialized training is *Nordoff-Robbins Music Therapist.*

Guided Imagery and Music (GIM). Two other music therapy models were also established during the 1970s. In the USA, Helen Bonny developed Guided Imagery and Music (BMGIM) as an approach to self-exploration, psychotherapy, and spiritual growth (Ventre & McKinney, 2015). Utilizing the capacity of classical music to evoke biographic and symbolic imagery when the psyche is in a relaxed, altered state of consciousness, BMGIM employs the receptive method of music therapy. Clients address therapeutic issues by listening to programmed excerpts of classical music while engaging in a dialogue with the therapist related to the imagery, sensations, and feelings evoked by the music (Ventre & McKinney, 2015). BMGIM is typically used with healthy adults with strong ego boundaries and nonpsychotic mental health conditions such as mood disorders and anxiety (Körlin & Wrangsjö, 2002; McKinney, Antoni, Kumar, & Kumar, 1995), as well as recovery from addiction, trauma, and medical conditions (Ventre & McKinney, 2015). While the original model of BMGIM would not normally be appropriate for a psychiatric setting where clients have poor ego boundaries and may be experiencing psychosis (Summer, 2002), modifications of the method that include elements of imagery and music listening while in a relaxed state have been used successfully and safely with clients with SMI (Goldberg, 1989; Moe, 2002; Moe, Roesen, & Raben, 2000; Muller, 2014).

Training for BMGIM is offered for certified music therapists at the graduate level through various training institutions in eight countries around the world (Association for Music and Imagery [AMI], Resources, 2017). Trainings are endorsed by the AMI and require a minimum of three years of postgraduate study to complete, culminating in the credential of Fellow of the Association for Music and Imagery (FAMI; AMI, 2017).

Analytical Music Therapy (AMT). In the 1970s, Mary Priestley, Peter Wright, and Marjorie Wardle established the Analytical Music Therapy (AMT) model in Britain. Working with clients in a psychiatric hospital and in private practice, Priestley integrated psychoanalytic principles with clinical music improvisation, drawing on the theories of Sigmund Freud, Melanie Klein, and Carl Jung (Scheiby, 2015). AMT draws upon symbolic psychic material of unconscious and conscious processes similar to BMGIM, but the major difference is that the client participates actively in the therapeutic sessions by creating improvisations with the therapist (Priestley, 1994). Improvisations are processed with the client verbally and through subsequent improvisations to help clients connect to feelings, body states, and symbols that emerge from the psyche, and to increase insight into interpersonal relationships (Priestley, 1994). Priestley also developed techniques that are particularly helpful for clients with SMI, including *reality rehearsal* and *exploring relationships.* AMT and improvisation techniques based on AMT have been used extensively with clients with SMI in both individual and group sessions (Eyre, 2007, 2013b; Hunt, 2013; Pedersen, 2003) as well as in medical practice and rehabilitation (Scheiby, 2002a, 2002b, 2010), issues of cultural adjustment (Kim, 2013), for caregivers (Stewart et al., 2005), and in private practice as a depth psychoanalytic orientation and in supervisory training (Priestley, 1994). Training for analytical music therapy occurs at the postgraduate level and is offered in the USA by Benedikte B. Scheiby at the Institute in Analytical Music Therapy in New York City.

Vocal psychotherapy. Based on 25 years of clinical practice, Diane Austin integrated theories of depth psychology with vocal music psychotherapy practices to develop the vocal psychotherapy model. This model uses breath, natural sounds, vocal improvisation, songs and dialogue within a client and therapist relationship to facilitate intrapsychic and interpersonal change and growth (Austin, 2017). While many of the techniques in this model were developed for persons with strong ego boundaries, they are often adapted for safe use with persons with SMI. This postgraduate certificate training takes two years to complete and is offered at the Music Psychotherapy Center (Austin, 2017).

Neurologic Music Therapy (NMT). Michael Thaut presented this model in 1999 (Hurt-Thaut & Johnson, 2015). Founded upon evidence-based research related to neurological responses to music, NMT addresses domains of sensorimotor, speech and language, and cognitive abilities. It is primarily used for persons with stroke to address cognitive, communication, and movement deficits, and is also used with clients with traumatic brain injury (TBI), degenerative neurological diseases, and developmental conditions affecting communication such as autism (van Bruggen-Rufi, 2013). NMT is used with persons with dual diagnoses of mental health problems attenuated by TBI and is therefore commonly used with veterans with TBI (Thaut et al., 2009). Training in NMT is offered in the form of a 36-hour workshop followed by clinical supervision (International Training Institutes in NMT, 2017).

Conclusion. In mental health settings, music therapy addresses a variety of client goals in both individual and group sessions. These goals include cognition, interpersonal relationships, behavior, intrapersonal insight, and affect. Most often, music therapists in mental health settings hold a master's degree and may have additional training. Music therapists are most effective when they are members of an interdisciplinary team working with other health professionals.

Music Therapy in Clinical Treatment

The complexity of music as a neurological phenomenon is such that the whole brain is activated in order to process it, whether one is listening receptively or participating actively (Alluri et al., 2012; Mannes, 2011). Music therapists exploit this whole-brain experience to meet each client's treatment needs in the cognitive, motor, physiological, affective, communicative, behavioral, and/or spiritual domains of human functioning. Thus, music therapy is integrated into the treatment of many conditions for children, adolescents, adults, and older adults, serving myriad populations with varying problems such as learning differences and developmental delays (Hintz, 2013), pediatric medical care (Bradt, 2013), adult medical care (Allen, 2013), and mental health (Eyre, 2013b).

Types of Music Therapy Experiences

When people hear about music therapy, most naturally imagine the powerful therapeutic effect of listening to music. This is the receptive method, but there are four additional distinctive kinds of music experiences commonly used by music therapists to assess, treat, and evaluate client treatment goals (Bruscia, 2014). These music experiences, or methods, are: receptive (or listening), improvisation, re-creative (or performance), and composition. Each of these involves different sensorimotor behaviors, requires different perceptual and cognitive skills, evokes different kinds of emotions, and engages a different interpersonal process. Thus, each method has unique therapeutic potentials and applications (Bruscia, 2014).

In receptive music therapy, the therapist engages the client in listening to music, either through a recording or live music created by the therapist. In addition, the experience may focus on imagery, drawing, movement, or perceptual tasks. Improvisation involves the client in spontaneously making up music and/or lyrics using voice or body sounds and/or instruments, or it may involve the client conducting and cuing in one or more improvisers to create spontaneous song or music. The re-creative method involves the client in learning, singing, playing, or performing precomposed music and/or song. Composition involves the client in writing songs, lyrics, instrumental pieces, or any kind of musical product such as videos or compilations. The client can participate in all of these methods either in an individual session with the therapist or in a group (Bruscia, 2014).

How the Music Therapist Helps the Client

Through an assessment process and, where appropriate, in conjunction with the treatment team, the therapist develops a treatment plan for the client and prepares music experiences that will best engage the client in meeting the treatment goals. Bruscia (2014) described various ways that the therapist helps the client to achieve this through music experiences, the interpersonal relationship with the client, and the group dynamics where applicable. For example the therapist helps the client by understanding the client's strengths, resources, and needs, and appropriately providing validation, affirmation, presence, and empathy. The therapist helps the client to give voice and express oneself, communicates with the client, contains and supports the intensity of the client's struggle, provides opportunities to the client for self-reflection and to explore alternative choices and behaviors, helps the client reconnect to oneself and to others, guides where necessary, and motivates the client to create and take ownership of personal therapeutic goals and work towards achieving them.

In the following sections, the use of music experiences to assess, treat, and evaluate the outcomes for particular mental health problems will be discussed, followed by a description of a typical session for a group of clients in an inpatient mental health facility.

Clinical Treatment of Clients with Mental Health Disorders

In 2013, Barcelona Publishers released a four-volume set of edited books outlining clinical guidelines for practice in various populations, one of which is mental health (Eyre, 2013b). Each chapter describes assessments, client goals, and protocols using each of the music methods, as well as outcomes, contraindications, and related research. The mental health volume addresses the following populations: schizophrenia and psychotic disorders; inpatient groups; persons with SMI in recovery model settings; children and adolescents in inpatient psychiatric settings; foster care youth; adjudicated adolescents; juvenile male sex offenders; male and female adults, adolescents and children who are survivors of developmental trauma, abuse and neglect, PTSD, and catastrophic event trauma; adults with depression, disorders such as borderline personality, eating disorders, and substance use (adults and adolescents); persons in correctional and forensic facilities; and older adults in nursing facilities and with dementias and diseases of aging. Music therapy in mental health also addresses such areas of concern as professional burnout, stress reduction and wellness, and spiritual practices. Thus, a certified music therapist can utilize a number of music methods and techniques with a wide range of populations and treatment settings to meet a variety of outcomes.

Assessments

The opportunity and need for individual music therapy assessments varies with the setting in which the music therapist is practicing. In an individual session, the therapist begins with an assessment, either by using a validated (non-music therapy) measurement tool for a specific outcome or population, or an unvalidated tool found in the music therapy literature. It is also common for music therapists to create original assessment protocols based on their specific population, knowledge, experience, and philosophical orientation. Some music therapy-specific assessments used in the mental health setting are the following: *A Music Interaction Rating Scale for Schizophrenia* (MIR[S]) to assess the level of autonomy and music interaction (Pavlicevic & Trevarthen, 1989); *Girard Medical Center Rehabilitative Creative Arts Therapy Service Group Assessment* to identify level of functioning and placement in specific groups (in Hunt, 2013); *Music Therapy Assessment for Children and Adolescents in an Inpatient Psychiatric Setting* (Doak, 2013); *Improvisation Assessment Profiles* to assess a range of personality characteristics (Bruscia, 1987); *13 Areas of Inquiry* for music psychotherapy (Loewy, 2000); *An Individual Music Therapy Assessment Procedure for Emotionally Disturbed Young Adolescents* (Wells, 1998); and *Geriatric Music Therapy Clinical Assessment* to assess music skills and related behaviors (Hintz, 2000).

In settings where there is no formal music therapy assessment, which often occurs when the main delivery format is group therapy, much of the assessment is developed through direct observation of the client in the group, communication with team members, and documentation in the client's medical chart. Areas of observation for assessment are specific to the setting and population. In general, when working with persons with SMI, music therapists observe the client's music preferences, level of functioning, affect, motivation and engagement, and self-image, as well as the client's ability to attend to a task, listen to and follow instructions, relate to others in the group, and express oneself verbally and non-verbally. Other domains of assessment may include suicide risk, environment and family support, stressors, external interests, and substance and drug use (Doak, 2013; Eyre, 2013a; Murphy, 2013; Zanders, 2013).

Example of an Inpatient Group Session

A music therapy group will differ according to the institutional mandate and the clients' needs, levels of functioning, diagnoses, state of recovery, and the treatment team goals. Music therapists are trained in the skillful use of all four music therapy methods and use a variety of techniques within these methods. However, individual music therapists have particular philosophies based on psychological approaches, and each therapist has unique musical skills that are integrated into their sessions to achieve therapeutic outcomes. For example, some therapists use primarily song choice, interactive live song singing, and song composition in their groups. Others may use more improvisation, drumming, and imagery techniques, or any combination thereof. Thus, while a description of a typical music therapy session is an impossible task, it is possible to describe the essential elements of a particular kind of session. For the purpose of this essay, the inpatient group music therapy session will be described based on Eyre's (2013a) description of methods used with this population.

Each group begins with a check-in. In many instances, the therapist arrives at the group with little previous knowledge of the majority of participants. It is, therefore, important that s/he assess the individuals in the group as well as the group dynamics to ascertain their functioning level, affect, motivation, potential to function together as a group, musical preferences, various cultures present in the group demographic, and therapeutic issues that the group members share. To assess this, the therapist begins with music experiences that require little interaction among group members, such as an opening song in which clients are invited to participate musically and verbally, short movement experiences using imagery, or instrumental experiences using short, repetitive, call and response rhythms. Following these check-in experiences, the therapist will better understand each client's psychological disposition, level of motivation, and engagement, and have a sense of the group dynamics in order to determine the kinds of therapeutic processes, methods, and techniques that are most appropriate for individuals and for the group as a whole.

The first couple of music experiences also provide the therapist with some ideas of therapeutic themes that can be developed to deepen the therapeutic process. For example, if a theme of loss or sadness emerged in the check-in experiences, the therapist might choose a song that reflects this theme, inviting the clients to engage physically by playing untuned percussion instruments and singing, while the therapist sings and plays the song on guitar or piano. A discussion among clients is facilitated as the therapist finds commonalities among group members and helps individuals to support one another. This might be followed by a suggestion to choose another song that reflects the group's feelings to sing together. In the discussion, the therapist encourages clients to find meaning in the lyrics, often drawing their attention to positive aspects of the lyrics and asking clients how they relate to these. When the therapist observes that the group has been able to shift its negative internal experience to something more positive, s/he may suggest that the group re-write parts or all of a particular song to personalize it, so that it has greater meaning for each client's particular situation, and sing this new version together.

Another method used in the inpatient setting is improvisation. In this case, the therapist might begin with simple percussion improvisation, where clients choose an instrument and engage in a rhythmic call and response, or are assigned a role such as "Begin after you listen to the person beside you and play your instrument in a way so that your sound blends with his or hers." Once the members of the group are able to listen to each other and have developed some familiarity with the timbres and manipulation of the tuned and untuned percussion instruments at their disposal, the therapist may continue with a referential improvisation, in which the clients spontaneously make up music that refers to an external theme or metaphor, or paints a picture such as *Finding my feet,* or *Dancing in chains*, or simply playing music that matches a picture of a nature scene. The role of the therapist is to help the clients connect their inner experience and feelings to the image or metaphor, to find an instrument with a timbre that evokes that feeling, and find ways to sound their feelings on that instrument. The therapist works with each member individually to achieve this, and s/he and the group decide on the dynamics and structure of the improvisation to integrate the various ideas and sounds. For example, if the group is creating a thunderstorm followed by calm, the therapist will provide guidelines for signaling when the storm changes to calm. The therapist also provides a musical foundation rhythmically, harmonically, and dynamically, using piano or guitar and voice, or another major instrument to the extent needed by the group to ensure a positive, non-chaotic, cohesive music experience for clients in the inpatient setting. The improvisation is followed by a discussion based on personal responses, including feelings during the music, physical sensations, interactions with other members, sense of self, thoughts, and imagery that was evoked. The therapist frames the discussion to address therapeutic needs with a focus on client strengths and contributions.

A vital part of the group session is the closure, where the clients are invited to identify what they will take with them from the group. This can be done in a number of ways. If the clients have re-written lyrics of the song, the therapist may sing this again, with the members all supporting each other's personal lyrics, or the group may repeat a chorus from a song with a positive message that they related to during the group. Alternatively, the therapist may choose a chant from his or her repertoire and have the group play a rhythmic heartbeat, while repeating the chant to internalize the positive message. The therapist may also close the group with an original song with improvised lyrics, in which s/he notes the contribution of each group member and thanks each one for their unique participation.

Individual Music Therapy Sessions

Individual sessions are implemented with clients to meet specific treatment goals, using a variety of approaches and techniques based on the client's therapeutic needs, motivation, musical and creative interests, and institutional mandate, and the therapist's advanced training. Case studies with music therapy approaches for all populations, including persons with mental health issues, can be found in two edited case study books: Meadows (2011) and Bruscia (1995). In addition, a psychodynamic approach is found in Hadley (2003), and an approach using rap and hip-hop music is found in Hadley and Yancy (2011).

Research

There is a strong body of research literature related to music therapy with mental health, developmental delays, and medical problems. Each chapter in the *Guidelines for Music Therapy Practice* (Allen, 2013; Bradt, 2013; Hintz, 2013, & Eyre, 2013b) cites the most relevant research for each population. A number of studies have been conducted with persons with SMI both with psychotic and non-psychotic symptoms. Silverman (2003) found in his meta-analysis that music therapy was effective in reducing symptoms of psychosis. These findings were upheld by a Cochrane systematic review that found that music therapy helps people with psychotic and non-psychotic severe mental disorders to improve global state, negative symptoms, and social functioning (Mössler, Chen, Heldal, & Gold, 2011). However, Gold, Solli, Krüger, and Lie (2009) found that more frequent sessions are needed to achieve more substantial benefits. Carr, Odell-Miller, and Priebe (2013) also found that, in addition to the number of sessions, the use of active music therapy methods where the clients were involved in making music had an impact on the effectiveness of music therapy. Studies on depression have suggested that people with depression are open to receiving music therapy and had a reduction in symptoms compared to standard care (Maratos, Gold, Wang, & Crawford, 2008). A Cochrane Review by Ueda, Suzukamo, Sato, and Izumi (2013) found that music therapy is effective for the management of behavioral and psychological symptoms of dementia; in particular, studies that lasted three months or more revealed a large effect size on anxiety.

A meta-analysis of music therapy with children and adolescents with pathology revealed that music therapy had a medium-to-large positive effect that is statistically highly significant and homogeneous on clinically relevant outcomes; interestingly, effects tended to be greater for behavioral and developmental disorders than for emotional disorders (Gold, Voracek, & Wigram, 2004). A Cochrane Review was also conducted on children with autism. Gold, Wigram, and Elefant (2006) examined the effect of daily sessions over one week for autistic children, finding that music therapy was effective in improving verbal and gestural communicative skills.

The music therapy literature is convincing in its breadth. However, the challenge at this time in the field of music therapy is to create randomized studies that are designed as pure research, rather than small N studies where the clinical music therapist designs the study, administers the treatment, and collects and analyzes the data. Partnerships with other healthcare professionals are needed to advance research in the field.

Conclusion

Healthcare professionals who would like to use music in their work with clients can use their professional expertise to encourage clients to listen to music that they prefer and that is appropriate for their treatment phase. Listening to a client's speech and sounds while NOT attending to the *content* can provide clues to the client's internal experience at that moment; often, a calming musical speaking tone can help to ease clients who are sad or agitated. Healthcare professionals who enjoy singing can also hum or sing to clients when they are agitated, helping them to access their own internal resources of positive experiences. Clients can be encouraged to sing, draw, move, and listen to music to provide a non-verbal means of expression.

Music therapy is an effective and attractive treatment for clients of all ages with mental health, medical, or developmental problems. Music is naturally engaging, appealing at once to emotions and personal associations as well as to joint attention and social affiliation. Used appropriately, it has a positive effect on cognition, motivation, and behavior. It helps one to find meaning and strengthen one's internal resources. Music is meant to be created in harmony with others, and thus has a natural impact on social behavior and interpersonal connection. Music is a transcultural phenomenon, providing the therapist with a means to bridge the gulf that exists across diverse languages, cultures, and identities. In the hands of a trained therapist, music provides a way of expressing empathy, thereby allowing the therapist to enter into the client's world, whether the client is a child with autism, an adolescent with depression, an adult with schizophrenia, or an older adult with dementia. Music is an inherent aspect of being human and, used correctly, fosters the development of positive internal resources, social affiliation, and healing. It is, therefore, a natural resource suited to therapeutic work.

References

Abdel-Salhen, E. (2005). Music therapy in Egypt. *Voices Resources*. Retrieved from http://testvoices.uib.no/community/?q=country-of-the-month/2005-music-therapy-egypt.

Allen, J. (Ed.). (2013). *Guidelines for music therapy practice in adult medical care*. Gilsum, NH: Barcelona Publishers.

Alluri, V., Toiviainen, P., Jääskeläinen, I.P., Glerean, E., Sams, M., & Brattico, E. (2012). Large-scale brain networks emerge from dynamic processing of musical timbre, key and rhythm. *Neuroimage, 59*(4), 3677–3689.

AMTA. (2017a). Career in music therapy. Retrieved from http://www.musictherapy.org/careers/employment/

AMTA. (2017b). History of music therapy. Retrieved from http://www.musictherapy.org/about/history/

AMTA. (2017c). Master's level entry: Moving forward. Retrieved from www.musictherapy.org/assets/1/7/Masters_Entry-Moving_Forward.pdf

AMTA. (2017d). Standards for education and clinical training. Retrieved from http://www. musictherapy.org/members/edctstan/

Association for Music and Imagery (AMI). (2017). Resources. Retrieved from https://ami-bonnymethod.org/find-a-training/institutes

Austin, D. (2017). *Vocal psychotherapy*. Retrieved from http://dianeaustin.com/music/

Bradt, J. (Ed.). (2013) *Guidelines for music therapy practice in pediatric care*. Gilsum, NH: Barcelona Publishers.

Bruscia, K.E. (1987a). Improvisation assessment profiles. Unit nine. In K. Bruscia, *Improvisational models of music therapy* (pp. 401–496). Springfield, IL: Charles C Thomas Publishers.

Bruscia, K.E. (1987b). *Improvisational models of music therapy*. Springfield, IL: Charles C Thomas Publishers.

Bruscia, K.E. (2014). *Defining music therapy* (3rd ed.). University Park, IL: Barcelona Publishers.

Burton, R. (1651/1869). *The Anatomy of melancholy*. Philadelphia, PA: J.B. Lippincott & Co.

Carr, C., Odell-Miller, H., & Priebe, S. (2013). A systematic review of music therapy practice and outcomes with acute adult psychiatric in-patients. *PloS one, 8*(8), e70252.

CBMT. (2017a). Retrieved from http://www.cbmt.org

CBMT. (2017b). About CBMT. Retrieved from http://www.cbmt.org/about-cbmt/

CBMT. (2017c). Advocacy. Retrieved from http://www.cbmt.org/advocacy/state-recognition/

CBMT. (2017d). Home. Retrieved from http://www.cbmt.org

CBMT. (2017e). State Licensure. Retrieved from http://www.cbmt.org/examination/state-licensure/

Crowe, B. (2017). *Definition and quotes*. Retrieved from http://www.musictherapy. org/about/quotes/

Davis, W. (2003). Ira Maximillian Altshuler: Psychiatrist and pioneer music therapist. *Journal of Music Therapy, 43*(3), 247–263.

Davis, W., Gfeller, K., & Thaut, M. (2008). *An introduction to music therapy theory and practice* (2nd ed.). Silver Spring, MD: American Music Therapy Association.

Doak, B. (2013). Children and adolescents in an inpatient psychiatric setting. In L. Eyre (Ed.), *Guidelines for music therapy practice in mental health* (pp. 168–204). Gilsum, NH: Barcelona Publishers.

Dufrene, P.M., & Coleman, V.D. (1994). Art and healing for native American Indians. *Journal of Multicultural Counseling and Development, 22*(3), 145–152.

Eyre, L. (2007). Changes in images, life events and music in analytical music therapy: A reconstruction of Mary Priestley's case study of "Curtis." *Qualitative Inquiries into Music Therapy, 3*, 1–31.

Eyre, L. (2013a). Adult groups in an inpatient setting. In L. Eyre (Ed.), *Guidelines for music therapy practice in mental health* (pp. 71–114). Gilsum, NH: Barcelona Publishers.

Eyre, L. (Ed.). (2013b). *Guidelines for music therapy practice in mental health*. Gilsum, NH: Barcelona Publishers.

Feder, E., & Feder, B. (1981). *The expressive arts therapies*. Engelwood Cliffs, NJ: Prentice Hall.

Gold, C., Solli, H.P., Krüger, V., & Lie, S.A. (2009). Dose-response relationship in music therapy for people with serious mental disorders: Systematic review and meta-analysis. *Clinical Psychology Review, 29*(3), 193–207.

Gold, C., Voracek, M., & Wigram, T. (2004). Effects of music therapy for children and adolescents with psychopathology: A meta-analysis. *Journal of Child Psychology and Psychiatry, 45*(6), 1054–1063.

Gold, C., Wigram, T., & Elefant, C. (2006). *Music therapy for autistic spectrum disorder*. Hoboken, NJ: John Wiley & Sons.

Goldberg, F.S. (1989). Music psychotherapy in acute psychiatric inpatient and private practice settings. *Music Therapy Perspectives, 6*(1), 40–43.

Guerrero, N., Marcus, D., & Turry, A. (2015). Nordoff-Robbins Music Therapy. In B. Wheeler (Ed.), *Music therapy handbook* (pp. 183–195). New York, NY: Guilford Press.

Hadley, S. (Ed.). (2003a). *Psychodynamic music therapy: Case studies*. Gilsum, NH: Barcelona Publishers.

Hadley, S. (2003b). Meaning making through narrative inquiry: Exploring the life of Clive Robbins. *Nordic Journal of Music Therapy, 12*(1), 33–53.

Hadley, S., & Yancy, G. (Eds.). (2011). *Therapeutic uses of rap and hip-hop*. New York, NY: Routledge.

Heller, G.N. (1987). Ideas, initiatives, and implementations: Music therapy in America, 1789–1848. *Journal of Music Therapy, 24,* 35–46.

Hintz, M.R. (2000). Geriatric music therapy clinical assessment: Assessment of music skills and related behaviors. *Music Therapy Perspectives, 18*(1), 31–40.

Hintz, M. (Ed.). (2013). *Guidelines for music therapy practice in developmental health*. Gilsum, NH: Barcelona Publishers.

Hippocrates. (1849). *The genuine works of Hippocrates*. (F. Adams, Trans.). London, UK: Sydenham Society.

Horden, P. (2000). *Music as medicine: The history of music therapy since antiquity*. Aldershot, UK: Ashgate.

Hunt, A. (2013). Adults with schizophrenia and psychotic disorders. In L. Eyre (Ed.), *Guidelines for music therapy practice in mental health* (pp. 21–70). Gilsum, NH: Barcelona Publishers.

Hurt-Thaut, C.P., & Johnson, S. (2015). Neurologic music therapy. In B. Wheeler (Ed.), *Music therapy handbook* (pp. 220–232). New York, NY: Guilford Press.

International Training Institute in NMT. (2017). Retrieved from https://nmtacademy.co/training-opportunities/nmt-training-institute/

Kim, S.A. (2013). Re-discovering voice: Korean immigrant women in group music therapy. *The Arts in Psychotherapy, 40,* 428–435.

Körlin, D., & Wrangsjö, B. (2002). Treatment effects in GIM. *Nordic Journal of Music Therapy, 11*(2), 3–12.

Levitan, D. (2008). *The world in six songs: How the musical brain created human nature*. London, UK: Dutton.

Loewy, J. (2000). Music psychotherapy assessment. *Music Therapy Perspectives, 18*(1), 47–58.

Mannes, E. (2011). *The power of music: Pioneering discoveries in the new science of song*. New York, NY: Bloomsbury Publishing.

Maratos, A., Gold, C., Wang, X., & Crawford, M. (2008). Music therapy for depression. Hoboken, NJ: John Wiley & Sons Ltd.

McKinney, C., Antoni, M., Kumar, A., & Kumar, M. (1995). The effects of guided imagery and music on depression and beta-endorphin levels. *Journal of the Association for Music and Imagery, 4,* 67–78.

Meadows, A. (Ed.). (2011). *Developments in music therapy practice: Case study perspectives*. Gilsum, NH: Barcelona Publishers.

Moe, T. (2002). Restitutional factors in receptive group music therapy inspired by GIM: The relationship between self–objects, psychological defence maneouvres and restitutional factors: Towards a theory. *Nordic Journal of Music Therapy, 11*(2), 152–166.

Moe, T., Roesen, A., & Raben, H. (2000). Restitutional factors in group music therapy with psychiatric patients based on a modification of guided imagery and music (GIM). *Nordisk Tidsskrift for Musikkterapi, 9*(2), 36–50.

Molloy College. (2017). Retrieved from https://www.molloy.edu/academics/graduate-programs/graduate-music-therapy/nordoff-robbins-training

Mössler, K., Chen, X., Heldal, T.O., & Gold, C. (2011). *Music therapy for people with schizophrenia and schizophrenia-like disorders*. Hoboken, NJ: John Wiley & Sons.

Muller, B. (2014). *Variations in guided imagery and music: Taking a closer look*. University Park, IL: Barcelona Publishers.

Murphy, K. (2013). Adults with substance use disorders. In L. Eyre (Ed.), *Guidelines for music therapy practice in mental health* (pp. 449–501). University Park, IL: Barcelona Publishers.

Murrock, C.J., & Higgins, P.A. (2009). The theory of music, mood and movement to improve health outcomes. *Journal of Advanced Nursing, 65*(10), 2249–2257.

Music Therapy Source. (2017). Retrieved from http://musictherapysource.com/students/musictherapyschools/

Pavlicevic, M., & Trevarthen, C. (1989). A musical assessment of psychiatric states in adults. *Psychopathology, 22,* 325–344.

Pedersen, I.N. (2003). The revival of the frozen sea urchin: Music therapy with a psychiatric patient. In S. Hadley (Ed.), *Psychodynamic music therapy: Case studies* (pp. 375–388). Gilsum, NH: Barcelona Publishers.

Perlovsky, L. (2008). Music and consciousness. *Leonardo, 41*(4), 420–421.

Plato. (n.d.). *Timaeus*, Section 47d. Retrieved from http://www.perseus.tufts.edu/hopper/text?doc=Perseus:text:1999.01.0180:text=Tim.:section=47d&highlight=music%2Crestoring%2Csoul

Priestley, M. (1994). *Essays on analytical music therapy*. Gilsum, NH: Barcelona Publishers.

Scheiby, B. (2002a). *Caring for the caregiver: The use of music and music therapy in grief and trauma*. Silver˙ Spring, MD: American Music Therapy Association.

Scheiby, B. (2002b). Improvisation as a musical healing tool and life approach: Theoretical and clinical applications of analytical music therapy improvisation in a short- and long-term rehabilitation facility. In T. Eschen (Ed.), *Analytical music therapy* (pp. 115–153). London, UK: Jessica Kingsley.

Scheiby, B. (2015). Analytical music therapy. In B. Wheeler (Ed.), *Music therapy handbook* (pp. 206–219). New York, NY: Guilford Press.

Sigerist, H.E. (1970). *Civilization and disease* (3rd ed.). Chicago, IL: University of Chicago Press.

Silverman, M.J. (2003). The influence of music on the symptoms of psychosis: A meta-analysis. *Journal of Music Therapy, 40*(1), 27–40.

Steinhardt, NYU. (2017). Nordoff-Robbins Center for Music Therapy. Retrieved from http://steinhardt.nyu.edu/music/nordoff/about/

Stewart, K., Silberman, J., Loewy, J., Schneider, S., Scheiby, B., Bobo, A., ... & Salmon, D. (2005). The role of music therapy in care for the caregivers of the terminally ill. In C. Dileo & J. Loewy (Eds.), *Music therapy at the end of life* (pp. 239–250). Cherry Hill, NJ: Jeffrey Books.

Summer, L. (2002). Group music and imagery therapy: Emergent receptive techniques in music therapy practice. In K. Bruscia & D. Grocke (Eds.), *The Bonny method of GIM and beyond* (pp. 297–306). Gilsum, NH: Barcelona Publishers.

Taylor, D.B. (1981). Music in general hospital treatment from 1900 to 1950. *Journal of Music Therapy, 18,* 62–73.

Thaut, M.H., Gardiner, J.C., Holmberg, D., Horwitz, J., Kent, L., Andrews, G., ... & McIntosh, G.R. (2009). Neurologic music therapy improves executive function and emotional adjustment in traumatic brain injury rehabilitation. *Annals of the New York Academy of Sciences, 1169*(1), 406–416.

Tomlinson, G. (2015). *A million years of music: The emergence of human modernity*. Cambridge, MA: MIT Press.

Ueda, T., Suzukamo, Y., Sato, M., & Izumi, S.I. (2013). Effects of music therapy on behavioral and psychological symptoms of dementia: A systematic review and meta-analysis. *Ageing research reviews, 12*(2), 628–641.

van Bruggen-Rufi, M. (2013). Neurological music therapy (NMT). In K. Kirkland (Ed.), *International dictionary of music therapy* (p. 92). New York, NY: Routledge.

Ventre, M., & McKinney, C. (2015). The Bonny method of Guided Imagery and Music. In B. Wheeler (Ed.), *Music therapy handbook* (pp. 196–205). New York, NY: Guilford Press.

Wells, N.F. (1998). An individual music therapy assessment procedure for emotionally disturbed young adolescents. *The Arts in Psychotherapy, 15*(1), 47–54.

Zanders, M. (2013). Foster care youth. In L. Eyre (Ed.), *Guidelines for music therapy practice in mental health* (pp. 205–236). Gilsum, NH: Barcelona Publishers.

Art Therapy

An Existential Perspective

Joseph Madigan

> All art that comes from an emotional depth provides a process of self-discovery and insight. We express inner feelings by creating outer forms. When we express these feelings in visible forms, we are using art as a language to communicate our inner truths.
>
> —Rogers, 2001, p. 163

As a social species, humans have been making art throughout our history and have historically used images and symbols to communicate and record ideas. Some of the oldest archeological sites discovered contain evidence of well-developed art making. This "primitive" art often contains images depicting the same concerns of existence (such as life, meaning, freedom, community, and productivity) with which we are confronted in today's society. The process referred to by Rogers (2001), above, involves nonverbal and/or metaphorical expression, and this use of metaphor serves as an associative link that leads to the illumination of specific images or memories that relate to inner experience. Because these images and memories are specific to each individual, they may provide a unique framework for self-identity.

The practice of using art in therapy traces its historical lineage to the evolution of ideas that took place in psychology and the arts during the last two centuries. This synthesis arose in response to overly narrow, reductive methods of viewing human experience, and is the result of a lengthy evolution in the treatment of mental disorders (MacGregor, 1989). By including art in the therapeutic process, we are employing a modality to consider qualitative aspects of the person that are not readily measured by quantitative, laboratory-based methods, although there is a large and growing body of evidence for its effectiveness.

What Is Art Therapy?

Traditional forms of psychotherapy have limited effectiveness for many people. For example, talk therapy may not be effective with those who are less articulate, or who, for emotional or neurological reasons, are not able to use language to access feelings and ideas. For optimal health, we need to be able to connect feelings and ideas (both right and left hemispheres of the brain), to link past and present, to make sense of the now, and to plan for the future. For those who have particular difficulty expressing themselves verbally, the arts offer a way to make contact, connect, and begin a meaningful dialogue.

Art therapists are trained and credentialed professionals who use specific art-based approaches with individuals of all ages, groups, and families, to develop physical, emotional and cognitive functioning, interpersonal skills, and quality of life (Malchiodi, 2012). It is the therapeutic use of art-making, within a professional relationship, by people who experience illness, trauma, or challenges in living, and by people who seek personal development (Malchiodi, 2012).

Art therapy is not a single, unitary form of therapy. The field is an eclectic undertaking that embraces (but is not limited to) aspects of psychoanalytic, Jungian, Gestalt, phenomenological, humanistic, and cognitive psychotherapies (Rubin, 2001). Since art therapy relies on symbolic communication rather than language, it lends itself to treatment in multicultural settings, where it may promote a richer therapeutic relationship than occurs when the methods of treatment are based solely on language.

What Is Existential Art Therapy?

Partly as a consequence of the increasing acceptance of a rationalistic, reductive outlook, modern Western psychotherapy has attempted to ignore or marginalize the irrational and subjective aspects of our psyche in favor of a "scientific" view of psychology. However, those conditions that are termed illnesses or pathologies also are creative processes (Diamond, 1996; MacGregor, 1989). This natural science view of the individual that is part of traditional psychoanalytic and cognitive behavioral theory also fails to account adequately for art, creativity, religion, love, and other human endeavors.

Rollo May (1991) examined the failed promise of the ascendency of rationalism in psychology that took place during the 20th century. It was May's position that this new form of "enlightenment" has led Western society to attempt to medicalize and pathologize conditions such as depression and anxiety, when, in fact, they may be creative existential reactions to our existence. May contended that, by employing the freedom of artistic expression, the "daimonic" (overpowering) aspects of the artist's personality could be exposed and confronted through physical interaction with art media (May 1969). These negative qualities can be transformed into creative activity (Diamond, 1996), allowing the artist to acknowledge, contain, and integrate them.

The "psychology" of this form of art therapy is concerned with how artists negotiate the choices they confront, what values inform those decisions, their experience in making them, and what place these decisions take in the wider context of the artists' lives. In this existential use of art in treatment, artists use everyday experience to infuse their art with cognitive, emotional, and tactile meaning (Madigan, 2014). When actively engaged with the art, the artists' central concerns are making choices and confronting limitations. Since a significant challenge typically facing individuals in treatment for almost any disorder is how to be both free, and responsible, art-making appears to be an excellent training ground for learning these skills.

In my practice, I have found that this existential-humanistic vision of art therapy is not used as a method of diagnosis or treatment per se. Instead, this method starts with the belief that individuals are capable of personal growth and of finding self-direction.

The art-making process is used as a means by which to explore inner feelings and to give them a physical form. The art-making is done without concern for the appearance of the finished product, as it emphasizes imagination and the intuitive process as opposed to logical and linear thought.

If we adopt this existential approach to art therapy, some guidelines emerge. The first is that existential art therapy is not a comprehensive psychotherapeutic system, but a frame of reference. It is primarily an experiential rather than a cognitive or experimental approach. Since it embodies a philosophical approach rather than a firm theoretical model, as a consequence it employs few formal techniques. Existential art therapy considers the individual's subjective experience of existential isolation, freedom, and the awareness of death, and stresses an attempt at a deep subjective understanding of the individual's life situation. Indeed, the creative process is an attempt to help the individual deal with such questions and crises as how we use our freedoms that arise in the course of life. The emotional intensity of these existential concerns parallels the experience of anxiety and freedom when making art.

Despite presenting a surface appearance of being anti-scientific, this psychotherapeutic form actually appears as an attempt to be more scientific by advocating for the acceptance of a greater breadth of scientific epistemologies and methodologies. In many cases, individuals who are seeking relief from a serious condition are attempting to create an identity that is totally new to them and that often has little to do with their previous behaviors, thoughts, and feelings. They are not attempting to "recover" in the original, medical sense of the term. Recovery implies that they are trying to regain some earlier state of being, but it was while in that state of being that their problems arose. So, in reality, they are *creating*, as their success depends upon their willingness and ability to find and integrate new ways of being in the world, much the same way an artist creates new images and realities. It could be said that these individuals are not in recovery but in "creation."

Educational Requirements for Practicing Art Therapy

While art therapy is practiced worldwide, in the United States the governing organizations for the practice of art therapy are the American Art Therapy Association (AATA) and the Art Therapy Credentialing Board (ATCB). The educational requirements to practice art therapy typically consist of a master's degree in art therapy from a program approved by AATA. The course content of these programs includes the following: history and theories of art therapy; human and creative development; assessment and evaluation; counseling and psychotherapy, ethics; individual, group, and family art therapy techniques; studio art; multicultural issues; and standards of practice. These programs also require a research component (in the form of a thesis or project), and include 100 hours of supervised practicum in preparation for 600 hours of supervised internship in clinical, community, or other settings.

The ATCB is the organization that is responsible for credentialing and for ensuring that educational and professional standards of education and ethical conduct are maintained. There are three levels of credentialing:

1. The Registered Art Therapist (ATR) is the credential held by practitioners who have completed the necessary graduate-level education in art therapy, 1000 hours post-master's art therapy experience, and 100 hours of supervision.

2. The Board Certified Art Therapist (ATR-BC) is the credential held by registered art therapists who have passed a comprehensive national examination testing their knowledge of the theories and clinical skills used by art therapists.

3. The Art Therapy Certified Supervisor (ATCS) is a practitioner who has acquired specific training in clinical supervision.

All credential holders must abide by the ATCB Code of Ethics.

Individual states have their own regulations that address art therapy practice and licensing. Many states also have local art therapy associations, which provide databases of credentialed professionals as a resource for referrals to other health professionals. The ATCB also maintains a national database of over 5000 credentialed art therapists.

Art Therapy as an Evidence Based Practice

Humans have commonly used the creative process as an aid in the treatment of illness, and there is a growing body of published research that points to its efficacy. Stuckley and Nobel (2010) reviewed the literature on engagement with the creative arts and health outcomes from 1995 through 2007, concluding that such engagement had positive effects on health in the form of improved medical outcomes and reductions in stress and anxiety. A review of the published literature from January of 1999 through December of 2007 by Slayton, Archer, and Kaplan (2010) found 30 studies reporting the efficacy of art therapy, including 7 qualitative studies, 13 pre/posttest studies, 4 studies with control group and no random assignment, and 11 clinical trials with random assignments.

There is also research indicating the efficacy of art therapy in allied health and mind-body medicine. When Wood, Molassiotis, and Payne (2010) reviewed 12 studies of cancer patients, they found that art therapy can lead to improved adjustment to pain, loss, and the uncertainty of living with cancer. Their review also suggested that art therapy helped with meaning-making through the physical act of making art. Several studies have demonstrated that art therapy enhances the psychosocial treatment of cancer, including decreased symptoms of distress, improved quality of life, increased perceptions of body image, reduction of pain perception, and general physical and psychological health (Monti et al., 2006; Nainis, Paice, & Ratner, 2002; Svensk et al., 2009). Studies have indicated a reduction of depression and fatigue levels in cancer patients on chemotherapy who participated in art therapy (Bar-Sela, Atid, Danos, & Epelbaum, 2007). Art therapy has been found to strengthen positive feelings, alleviate distress, and help individuals to clarify existential questions for adult bone marrow transplant patients (Gabriel, Bromberg, Vandenbovenkamp, Kornblith, & Luzzato, 2001). Research with children with cancer has indicated that engaging in drawing and painting is an effective method for dealing with pain and other disturbing symptoms of illness and treatment (Rollins, 2005).

Research on art therapy with children with asthma has shown that it reduces anxiety, improves feelings of quality of life, and strengthens self-concept (Beebe, Gelfand, & Bender, 2010). Evidence indicates that art therapy and other creative arts therapies stimulate cognitive function in older adults who have dementia or related disorders (Levine-Madori, 2009) and may reduce depression in those with Parkinson's disease (Elkis-Abuhoff, Goldblatt, Gaydos, & Corrato, 2008). Art-making may also reduce anxiety and stress reactions among family caregivers of patients with cancer, as measured by salivary cortisol samples taken before and after art therapy sessions (Walsh, Radcliffe, Castillo, Kumar, & Broschard, 2007).

Other Populations Where Art Therapy Has Been Effectively Used

Art Therapy has been successfully used with all age groups and with an extremely wide variety of populations and disorders. Populations that have benefited from art therapy include those with major psychiatric disorders (schizophrenia, bi-polar disorder), anxiety, depression, personality disorders, developmental disorders, autism, and traumatic brain injury; moreover, art therapy has been effectively used in both in-patient and community-based settings (Haeyen, van Hooren, & Hutschemaekers, 2015; Levine, 2009; Metzl, 2009; Slayton Archer, & Kaplan, 2010). Additionally, Epp (2008) reported on the efficacy of using art therapy to improve the social skills of adolescents with autistic spectrum disorder.

Art therapy has provided an alternative mode of expression for dementia patients (Cowl *& Gaugler,* 2014) and can reduce stress and depression while improving social functioning (Ehresman, 2014). Art therapy has also been used in the treatment of dyslexia (Ree, 1998). Other populations where art therapy has been used successfully include: those in addiction recovery, incarcerated inmates, and ex-offenders (Erickson & Young, 2010).

A Typical Session with an Existential Art Therapist

Existential art therapy is essentially a collaborative experience between two people. This is not a "top-down" therapeutic approach where the therapist provides "answers," nor is it an art class. The art therapist does not direct the process, as occurs in many other forms of therapy that are often intentionally directive, such as many solution-focused therapies. While we may consider artistic decisions on a technical level (materials, colors, and line structure, for example), on a deeper level we are collaborating in the artists' visual expression of self-exploration and their search for meaning. All art materials have limitations that force artists to confront the limitations of their own abilities and learn new ways of confronting these challenges. As tangible objects, the art materials provide a means of bringing existential challenges within physical reach, where they can be confronted and overcome.

As stated above, an art therapy session is not an art class. Working with personal symbols is different from working with language, and there is no wrong way to do it. It is not about fine art or artistic talent. The intent is to create a safe space where individuals can confront the existential challenges that they face; furthermore, the primary concern is what the artists think of the art that they create. Below is a description of a typical session employing existentially informed art therapy.

Assessment

Prior to the first session the art therapist will want to examine the clients' case history, if it is available. This would include a study of all the facts available regarding the individuals and the nature of the condition that brings them to treatment. The purpose is to obtain general information about the people with whom they will be meeting, not a diagnosis or prognosis. One of the primary questions concerns the attitudes of the individuals toward being in treatment. Are they resistant and coming to the session to avoid some consequence? Are they motivated toward insight and self-exploration? The answers to these questions often have a direct impact on the outcome. This is, in sum, an active treatment modality. To be most effective, the artists are actively receptive to the freedom of choice and responsibility implied by the object (i.e., the art).

Individuals seen in treatment will often have a diagnosis or some form of objective, measured assessment. While this is a fact of life for mental health practitioners, equally important is an individual's self-assessment, which can be a much more reliable indicator of the success of treatment. On meeting the individual, the art therapist will want to attempt to assess the issue presented for treatment, its degree of severity, and the individual's response to it. This will hopefully facilitate establishing rapport in an attempt to create an empathic relationship based upon an understanding of the individual. This develops through increased and meaningful contact between the therapist and the client or "artist."

General Guidelines for Facilitating a Session

Based on their assessment, the art therapists now must decide what art-based interventions they are going to introduce to the therapeutic space. Some of the questions to consider are:

1. How has their assessment led them to choose a particular form of art making?
2. What do they hope to accomplish in the session?
3. Why have they chosen the materials they are using?

By considering these questions, the therapists will be better able to ensure that the session is taken seriously by their clients. It should be clear that Artwork is Art Work. What the therapists and clients do together does not have to be solemn and lifeless, but there should be a clear therapeutic rationale behind the intervention and materials that are used in the session.

Materials and Safety

Allow the clients to drive the art as much as possible, particularly in selecting what materials they will be using. While there may be limitations placed on materials due to the nature of the facility or economic constraints, it is almost always possible to have at least two types of art-making materials present during the session. It may be as simple as offering pastels and markers or different sizes of paper. The idea is to offer the individuals the opportunity to make decisions freely about the materials they will be using. Allowing them to select what materials they will be using helps to encourage them to embrace the concept of freedom within the context of the session, and can be used as a means to encourage them to embrace freedom in other areas of their lives. Attempt to balance this freedom of choice of materials with the idea of their responsible use, much in the same way that our personal freedoms are limited by our responsibilities in the world.

All materials have limitations that force artists to confront the weaknesses of their own abilities and to learn new ways to confront these challenges. Different materials have different properties that can be adapted to the mutual goals of treatment. For example, individuals who suffer from anxiety can often benefit from experimenting with looser, more fluid media, such as paint or watercolors. Chalk or oil pastels can be offered if anxiety precludes liquid materials. Within a supportive relationship with the therapist, individuals can learn to tolerate the anxiety and frustration that often accompany the sometimes unpredictable outcomes inherent in these materials; moreover, clients may begin to generalize these experiences to other areas of their life.

The properties of some materials can also create adverse reactions. Caution is recommended, particularly with tactile, regressive materials such as clay, finger paints, and watercolors. Consult with someone trained in art therapy, if you are not confident about the materials that you are considering using.

If you feel that your clients are having difficulty with the session, stop and process with them. These can be very important moments in treatment.

Almost any types of materials will lend themselves to this process. However, the safety of your clients is the first priority, so the media should be matched to what you and they are trying to achieve in treatment. As with any other form of treatment (and art), you are limited only by your imagination. The simplest visual materials are paper and pencils, markers, pastels, and watercolors, and the list goes on almost infinitely from there. People who are uncomfortable drawing may be more comfortable using tactile, three-dimensional techniques such as assemblage or sculpture. Typically, the art form to which your clients naturally gravitate will be more effective, and there may be a period of experimentation (if you are seeing these persons regularly), where a variety of forms and materials get used.

Greeting and Check-in

Establish and keep a routine. The therapist and the art area should evoke a feeling of comfort, trust, and safety. Ideally, clients should not have to deal with unusual environmental problems, although in institutional settings this is not always possible. Attempt to create an atmosphere where the clients will feel it is safe to experiment with materials and not be concerned with the appearance of the finished art. Familiarity and routine create a feeling of safety for clients who are seen regularly, even if they initially felt anxious about making art. Make your clients as comfortable as possible; considering the lighting in the area, playing music that the clients enjoy, or offering food or beverages if it is appropriate to do so in your clinical setting.

The Session

You might consider engaging the clients in some stretching or warm-up exercises before they start creating art. If appropriate, acquaint your clients with the art medium. Introduce new materials and art forms in a manner that expands your therapeutic relationship. Any stimulus that is introduced is based upon the therapist's assessment and is intended to address mutually agreed-upon treatment goals. This helps to develop and deepen the therapeutic relationship and evokes a sense of relation and motivation. Encourage "structured" art-making in an open-ended format. Be aware that structure and intervention are to be minimal, and the outcomes will be different for each individual. The art becomes the space where the artist and therapist meet each other. In this view, the appearance of the art object (which may or may not be aesthetically pleasing) is secondary. In some cases, the therapist and client may collaborate on the art and use it as a metaphorical dialogue that employs symbols rather than language.

Do not end the art-making period abruptly, but alert clients when there is approximately 5–10 minutes of art-making time remaining. The art does not have to be "finished," and can be stored to be continued during another session. It is often helpful for people to take their art with them and to continue working on it after the session. The art can be then viewed and processed during the next session, or new art can be introduced.

Processing the Session (Outcome)

One of the problems that therapists often encounter when using art in therapy is that the intensity or content of the images often causes them to overlook what actually occurred in the session. The simplest way for therapists to process the session is to consider what they observed. What did they see during the session? How did the artists behave? How did they respond to any stimulus that was suggested? How did they respond to the materials that were suggested? What was their affect while making art? How much support did they require to complete the session (if they were able to do so)? What did they say while making art? What was their body language? What did they say about the art itself? After these questions are considered, then it is time to ask, "What is the expressive content of the art?"

Here are some open-ended areas of discussion that you may want to examine with clients after the art-making period of the session. These ideas can be adapted to different forms of art, depending on the client and the situation:

- Tell me the story of this (art tells stories, so take the time to allow the narrative to develop).
- Did you experience any physical sensations while making the art?
- Do you wish anything was different about the _____?
- Can you imagine how those differences could come about?
- What happens next?
- How did it make you feel?
- How do you feel now?
- Do you feel safe?
- Are you afraid of anything right now?

This is by no means an exhaustive list of areas that might be discussed. Ideally, the artists will also lead the discussion in the same way that they lead the art-making, but this may not be the case. They may require some time to reflect upon the art, and it may be more productive to discuss it during the next session. Time-management skills also become critical, as making the art may take up the majority of the time allotted for the session.

It is imperative that the therapist be confident that the clients are able to tolerate the emotional effects of any images that they have created during the session and that they will be safe after the session has ended.

The emotional interaction between the artist and the developing art object changes both of them. The object acquires new meaning as it is dyed with the color of the artist's emotional response, and the artist is similarly changed through embodying his or her emotion in the material. (Sullivan & McCarthy, 2009, p. 183)

Discuss any independent art and ideas (goals) for the following session.

The outcome of the session now becomes part of an ongoing assessment process that leads to subsequent interventions. It provides a continuously updated source of information about the therapeutic relationship and the efficacy of the treatment being provided. The art becomes part of a visual treatment record (HIPPA standards apply), and can be used to assess how effective the ongoing therapy is. Since this process is dynamic, it allows for flexibility in planning successive sessions

The benefit lies in the artists' doing (introspection), not in the technical skills or the finished product. You may be tempted to consider artistic decisions on a technical level (e.g., materials, colors, line structure, and style), but, as interesting as these aspects of the art may be, on a deeper level, the art reflects an expression of the artists' self-exploration and search for meaning. Therefore, it is important to avoid categorizing or pathologizing the art. Existential art therapy is focused on how artists negotiate the choices they confront. In the anxiety and ambiguity of these encounters, as well as in the need to find the meanings within them, the artists may make subjective decisions that begin to define the kind of person they are attempting to become (Bakhtin, 1990). The goal is the eventual, gradual removal of the therapist from the individual's creative process. This is not termination of the therapy, but a point where the clients are able to create art independently.

Expressive Arts and Considerations for Cultural Competency

Using art in treatment may permit clients to use cultural symbolism in a unique way to enrich the therapeutic relationship. Since it is less oriented to language, using art in treatment may be less culture-bound than verbal psychotherapy (Hocoy, 2002). Like any other form of treatment, the use of art in therapy does not take place in isolation from cultural influences. As with other forms of therapy, therapists will benefit from a rigorous examination of their own cultural competency.

However, cultures have their own ways of categorizing phenomena and experiences, and using art in treatment cannot be assumed to be universally accepted. An understanding of the communities in which the clients live, their resources (e.g., religious organizations), and the impinging issues (e.g., interpersonal violence, social problems, etc.) is critical for effective and appropriate art-based interventions (Douglas, 1993). An investigation of the community and how art is utilized as a means of psychological healing in a client's culture of origin is invaluable. However, avoid stereotypical generalizations and maintain openness to individual variations.

Conclusion

All art forms present challenges that force artists to confront the limitations of their own abilities and learn new ways of confronting those challenges. As tangible objects, the art provides a means of bringing personal challenges within physical reach, where they can be examined and confronted. In the anxiety and ambiguity of making artistic decisions, and in the need to find the meanings within them, the artists may be presented with the opportunity to make subjective decisions that begin to define the kind of person they are attempting to become.

REFERENCES

American Art Therapy Association. (2017). See http://arttherapy.org/

Bakhtin, M.M. (1990). *Art and answerability: Early philosophical essays by M.M. Bakhtin.* (Edited by M. Holquist and translated by V. Liapunov). Austin, TX: University of Texas Press.

Bar-Sela, G., Atid, L., Danos, S., & Epelbaum, R. (2007). Art therapy improved depression and influenced fatigue levels in cancer patients on chemotherapy. *Psych-oncology, 16*(11), 980–984.

Beebe, A., Gelfand, E.W., & Bender, B. (2010). A randomized trial to test the effectiveness of art therapy for children with asthma. *Journal of Allergy and Clinical Immunology, 126*(2), 263–266.

Cowl, A.L., & Gaugler, J.E. (2014). Efficacy of creative arts therapy in treatment of Alzheimer's disease and dementia: A systematic literature review. *Activities, Adaptation and Aging, 38*(4), 281–330.

Diamond, S.A. (1996). *Anger, madness and the daimonic: The psychological genesis of violence, evil and creativity.* Albany, NY: State University of New York Press.

Douglas, B. C. (1993). *Psychotherapy with troubled African American adolescent males: Stereotypes, treatment amenability, and clinical issues.* Paper presented at the Annual Meeting of the American Psychological Association, Toronto, Ontario, Canada.

Ehresman, C. (2014). From rendering to remembering: Art therapy for people with Alzheimer's disease. *International Journal of Art Therapy, 19*, 43–51.

Elkis-Abuhoff, D.L., Goldblatt, R.B., Gaydos, M., & Corrato, S. (2008). Effects of clay manipulation on somatic dysfunction and emotional distress in patients with Parkinson's disease. *Art Therapy, 25*(3), 122–128.

Epp, K.M. (2008). Outcome-based evaluation of a social skills program using art therapy and group therapy for children on the autism spectrum. *National Association of Social Worker, 30*(1), 27–36.

Erickson, B.J., & Young, M.E. (2010). Group art therapy with incarcerated women. *Journal of Addictions and Offender Counseling, 31*(1), 38–51.

Gabriel, B., Bromberg, E., Vandenbovenkamp, J., Kornblith, A., & Luzzato, P. (2001). Art therapy with adult bone marrow transplant patients in isolation: A pilot study. *Psycho-Oncology, 10*, 114–123.

Haeyen, S., van Hooren, S., & Hutschemaekers, G. (2015). Perceived effects of art therapy in the treatment of personality disorders, cluster B/C: A qualitative study. *The Arts in Psychotherapy, 45*, 1–10.

Hocoy, D. (2002). Cross-cultural issues in art therapy. *Journal of the American Art Therapy Association, 19*(4), 141–145.

Levine M. L. (2009). Using the TTAP method for cognitive and psychosocial wellbeing. *American Journal of Therapeutic Recreation, 8*(1), 25–31.

MacGregor, J.M. (1989). *The discovery of the art of the insane.* Princeton: NJ: Oxford Press.

Madigan, J. (2014). *An application of the concepts of existential psychotherapy to art therapy* (Doctoral dissertation). Retrieved from ProQuest Dissertations Publishing Database (Order no.3628237).

Malchiodi, C. (2012, April 2). *Defining art therapy in the 21st century.* Retrieved from https://www.psychology today.com/blog/arts-and-health/201304/defining-art-therapy-in-the-21st-century

May, R. (1969). *Love and will.* New York, NY: W.W. Norton.

May, R. (1991). *The cry for myth.* New York, NY: W.W. Norton.

Metzl, E. S. (2009). The role of creative thinking in resilience after Hurricane Katrina. *Psychotherapy of Aesthetics, Creativity and the Arts, 3*(2), 112–123.

Monti, D.A., Peterson, C., Kunkel, E.J., Hauck, W.W., Pequinot, E., Rhodes, L., & Brainers, G.C. (2006). A randomized, controlled trial of mindfulness-based art therapy (MBAT) for women with cancer. *Psycho-Oncology, 15*(5), 363–373.

Nainis, N., Paice, J., & Ratner, J. (2006). Relieving symptoms in cancer: Innovative use of art therapy. *Journal of Pain and Symptom Management, 31*(2), 162–169.

Ree, M. (1998). *Drawing on difference: Art therapy with people who have learning difficulties.* Abingdon, UK: Routledge.

Rogers, N. (2001). Person-centered expressive arts therapy. In J. Rubin (Ed.), *Approaches to art therapy: Theory and technique* (2nd ed., pp.163–178). Ann Arbor, MI: Sheridan Books.

Rollins, J. (2005). Tell me about it: Drawing as a communication tool for children with cancer. *Journal of Pediatric Oncology Nursing, 22*(4), 203–221.

Rubin, J.A. (2001). *Approaches to art therapy: Theory and technique* (2nd ed). Philadelphia, PA: Brunner-Routledge.

Slayton, S., Archer, J., & Kaplan, F. (2010): Outcome studies on the efficacy of art therapy: A review of findings. *Journal of the American Art Therapy Association, 27*(3), 108–118.

Stuckley, H.L., & Nobel, J. (2010). The connection between art, healing, and public health: A review of current literature. *American Journal of Public Health, 9*, 254–263.

Sullivan, P., & McCarthy, J. (2009). An experiential account of the psychology of art. *Psychology of Aesthetics, Creativity, and the Arts, 3*(3), 181–187.

Svensk, A., Oster, I., Thyme, K., Magnusson, E., Sjodin, M., Eismanm, A.S., & Lindh, J. (2009). Art therapy improves experienced quality of life among women undergoing treatment for breast cancer: A randomized controlled study. European Journal of Cancer Care, 18(1), 69–77.

Walsh, S.M., Radcliffe, S., Castillo, L.C., Kumar, A.M., & Broschard, D.M. (2007). A pilot study to test the effects of art-making classes for family caregivers of patients with cancer. *Oncology Nursing Forum, 34*(1), 9–16.

Wood, M.J., Molassiotis, A., & Payne, S. (2011). What research evidence is there for the use of art therapy in the management of symptoms in adults with cancer? A systematic review. *Psycho-Oncology, 20*(2), 135–145.

PART 3

Mind/Body and Energy Medicine Interventions

Holistic Benefits
of Clinical Hypnosis

MARINA A. SMIRNOVA

A Brief Overview of Hypnosis and Clinical Hypnosis

Since the time of Franz Anton Mesmer, hypnosis has been igniting powerful fascination, galvanizing evocative reactions and responses, and inspiring disciplined theoretical, practical, and research inquiries and pursuits. "Hypnosis can reasonably be considered the original 'positive psychology'" (Yapko, 2008, p. 564) because those who apply it do so "with a firm belief that people have more resources than they consciously realize, and that hypnosis can help bring these resources to the fore" (p. 564). Paradoxically and unsurprisingly, until this very day, mental health and medical professionals, practitioners, and researchers continue to investigate, to unearth, to gain insight into, and to imbue with meaning the various layers comprising, arising out of, and surrounding hypnosis and multifaceted hypnotic phenomena. Being effectively "caught" and/or, in some ways, invited or summoned by the field of clinical or therapeutic hypnosis, propels the clinicians, practitioners, and researchers toward meaningful advances and pathways toward facilitating healing, health, and wholeness. Such pathways continue to honor the individual's fullness of being (mind-body-psyche-spirit), highlighting embodied, wholeness-oriented avenues toward health.

At the very beginning of this essay about hypnosis, it is of essence to invite the reader to contemplate perceived and also factual differences between (a) stage hypnosis and stage/lay hypnotists (who, with some degree of proximity, are familiar to many) and (b) clinical hypnosis and licensed mental health/medical professionals, who hold respective professional degrees and also certification in clinical hypnosis. The sole purpose of stage hypnosis is amusement and/or entertainment, often at the expense of the hypnotic subject who agrees to participate in the stage hypnosis exercise. Unfortunately, (a) "there are very few restrictions placed on who can legally practice hypnosis" (Yapko, 2012, p. 219) and (b) "there are many nonprofessional programs that accept anyone who can afford the tuition as the sole entry criterion, and they provide their students with credentials and titles proclaiming their expertise" (p. 219). In contrast and by design, clinical hypnosis is facilitated by a licensed mental health/medical professional (who holds a graduate degree and is bound by the professional code of ethics) and serves solely therapeutic, healing aims (within therapeutic and/or medical settings and contexts, such as

119

clinical settings, hospitals, surgery rooms, outpatient clinics, rehabilitation centers, dental offices, and the like). Thus, by identifying, acknowledging, and intentionally attending to individual misperceptions about hypnosis in general and about clinical hypnosis in particular, one opens up a door and discovers a path toward a deeper understanding of the healing properties of clinical hypnosis that inevitably reveal themselves through the individual's phenomenologically-valid, experience-based encounters with clinical hypnosis and its therapeutic means.

Trance, Hypnosis and Clinical Hypnosis: Accentuating a Neurobiological Perspective and the Golden-Standard Training in Clinical Hypnosis

Hypnosis and hypnotic phenomena have been examined from a wide variety of conceptual models and scientific frameworks and lenses that include, yet are not limited to (a) dissociation theories of hypnosis (Woody & Sandler, 2008); (b) social cognitive theories of hypnosis (Lynn, Kirsch, & Hallquist, 2008); (c) new cognitive theories of hypnotic responding (Barnier, Dienes, & Mitchell, 2008); (d) a psychoanalytic theory of hypnosis (Nash, 2008); (e) state- and non-state theoretical debates (that have been examining hypnosis as an altered, heightened, or expanded state of consciousness and/or non-state) (Jamieson, 2007); (f) the empathic involvement theory (Wickramasekera, 2015); (g) a cognitive neuroscience framework (Jamieson, 2007); and (h) a neurobiologically-grounded theoretical framework (Hope & Sugarman, 2015). "It seems an oversimplification to attribute all hypnotic behavior to the unitary variables many theorists have posited as responsible for hypnosis" (Hammond, 2015, p. 440). Nevertheless, following a new conceptualization of trance, of hypnosis, and of clinical hypnosis proposed by Hope and Sugarman (2015), for the purpose of this essay (that primarily highlights the utilitarian function and the inherent potentials of clinical hypnosis), *clinical hypnosis* is defined as a set of particular, context-specific, therapeutic skills.

While offering a neurobiologically-grounded framework for conceptualizing the nature of hypnosis and its clinical applications, Hope and Sugarman (2015) described "trance as a naturally occurring opportunity for psychophysiological plasticity … the process of developing plasticity … [and] something that happens" (pp. 213–214). Hypnosis may be viewed as merely "a *skill set* that (a) utilizes trance to influence the direction of that plasticity" (Hope & Sugarman, 2015, p. 213); (b) makes use of "innate biological abilities for changing cognition, emotion, perception, neural networks, and physiology" (p. 214); and (c) "perturbs or influences the entranced system in a given direction" (p. 214). Furthermore, the hypnosis skill set may be viewed to be inherently *neutral*, with multidimensional contextual applications that vary in intentionality, morality, and social influence (Hope & Sugarman, 2015).

"The skill set of *clinical* hypnosis then becomes the set of communication skills that a clinician uses to help a client utilize his or her own adaptive resources for the purpose of *therapeutic* change. Self-hypnosis becomes a term that represents the set of skills used by a person to direct his or her own psychophysiological plasticity" (Hope & Sugarman, 2015, p. 214). Thus, the clinical hypnosis skill set can be best understood and utilized not as a stand-alone therapeutic intervention, but rather as a supportive, adjunctive orientation-modality for a variety of therapeutic approaches in working with clients.

Professional Degree and Licensure Requirements and Clinical Hypnosis Certification

It is of essence to note that it is incumbent upon clinicians and medical professionals to make use of the clinical hypnosis skill set in ways that are highly consistent with their respective graduate-level professional training, licensure and certifications (including a professional certification in clinical hypnosis), specializations, and scope of practice. In the United States, two professional organizations provide licensed mental health and licensed medical professionals with graduate-level education (as well as graduate students in the mental health and medical fields) with the golden-standard training, supervision, and certification in clinical hypnosis. These two clinical hypnosis legacy organizations are American Society of Clinical Hypnosis (ASCH) and Society for Clinical and Experimental Hypnosis (SCEH). ASCH offers a member referral search for individuals who are seeking to identify licensed mental health/medical professionals ASCH-certified in clinical hypnosis.

Clinical Hypnosis Presuppositions and Emerging Core Principles and Key Communication Skills

During the long decades of biomedical approach to health care, the field of clinical hypnosis has positioned itself to utilize, skillfully and with discernment, the allopathic diagnose-and-treat model toward alleviating human suffering (Hammond, 1990; Rossi & Cheek, 1988). While supporting and also helping to lead the continuous shift from the reductionistic biomedical to a biopsychosocial-spiritual paradigm of health care, with increased intensity, vigor, and dedication, the field of clinical hypnosis continues to infuse its theoretical and clinical practice domains with deeply humanistic, grounded-in-the-phenomenological-perspective, and also transpersonal frameworks, pathways, practices, and considerations (Appel, 2014; Ewin & Eimer, 2006; Hunter & Eimer, 2014; Leskowitz, 2000; Rossi, 1993, 2002, 2007).

Alter and Sugarman (2017) articulated six emerging core principles of contemporary clinical hypnosis that capitalize upon and honor an expanded understanding of human nature, will continue to influence the practice and research in the field of clinical hypnosis, and can be summarized as follows:

1. Individuals are self-organizing and also self-reorganizing organisms that are blueprinted to adapt, adjust, and evolve in the presence of internal and external stressors.

2. Novelty and uncertainty of life (within and outside of the clinical hypnosis communication) galvanize disorientation and also reorientation—central neurobiological patterns that access and harness inner resources toward the organism's adaptive reorganization.

3. Individuals are resourceful, and their internal resources abide as potentials. Clinical hypnosis becomes a pathway toward mobilizing the client's potentials in a manner that is context-specific.

4. The clinician's close attention and attunement to the client's internal quest for sound solutions to his or her life's circumstances affords the most effective utilization of the client's internal resources.

5. When the clinician's orientation is grounded in a sense of curiosity and wonder toward the client's creative process of adjustment, adaptation, and problem-solving, it shifts away from the diagnosis-and treatment model of allopathic care, tending to the uniqueness of the client as an individual.

6. The clinician's attention moves away from *"what should be done to what can emerge.* Such a shift is rooted in evolutionary experimentation ... that looks at each life as a unique living expression from among infinite possible expressions of meeting that individual's life circumstances"* [Alter & Sugarman, 2017, p. 243].

While a number of clinical hypnosis inter- and intrapersonal communication skills may be useful, three essential groups of such skills are recognized as fundamental and reflect intentional attitudes and resources of the clinicians: (1) sensitivity and responsivity to evidence of autonomic shift (that naturally occurs in trance), (2) rearousal of childhood plasticity, and (3) being evocative (Hope & Sugarman, 2015). Sensitivity and responsivity to evidence of autonomic shift, which takes place in a state of trance, is exemplified by a superlatively observant therapist/professional who supports the client in creating change by helping to amplify the client's experiences of novelty, rapport, wonder, and spontaneity (Hope & Sugarman, 2015). Both groups of skills—rearousal of childhood plasticity and being evocative—encourage the client in accessing and utilizing his or her inner resources within intentionally-interactive therapeutic environment facilitated by the clinician (Hope & Sugarman, 2015). Rearousal of childhood plasticity skills allows the clinician to evoke "implicitly, within the safe confines of rapport, experiences of childhood wonder" (Hope & Sugarman, 2015, p. 222) and also childhood plasticity. In turn, being evocative may galvanize the client's capacity to access his or her inner resources.

Clinical Hypnosis Interactions and Sessions in Clinical Settings

Historically and practically, the continuum (or the landscape) of interpersonal communication in hypnosis stretches between the two poles, namely, (1) *prescriptive*, in which hypnotic interactions are directed by the clinician, and (2) *naturalistic*, which is characterized by the clinician's responsiveness to the client's phenomenological, intrapersonal experiences in the creative process of trance that entirely belong to the client (Alter & Sugarman, 2017). Prescriptive or highly-structured, highly-directive hypnotic interactions offer effective solution-oriented and context-specific outcomes for some clients. Engaging the naturalistic end of the pole and placing it at the heart of interpersonal communication in hypnosis is likely to foster collaborative, highly-individualized, client-empowering, and thus meaningful pathways toward healing, health, and wholeness.

Formal hypnotic interactions typically incorporate the following general stages or phases: (1) thorough preparation for the hypnotic experience (including informed consent and psychoeducation about clinical hypnosis); (2) rapport building; (3) attentional absorption (a focused concentration that is typically directed inward); (4) hypnotic induction (formal and/or conversational, naturalistic); (5) deepening (intensification of the experience of trance); (6) building a response set (increasing the client's responsiveness); (7) hypnotic utilization (focused therapeutic work); (8) posthypnotic suggestion; (9) re-alerting (re-orienting the client toward external realities and external world); and (10) initial integration of the hypnotic experience, closure, and disengagement (Yapko, 2012). In addition to formal, highly-structured, and technique-oriented hypnotic interactions, hypnosis offers conversational (naturalistic, Ericksonian, flexible) strategies that allow the clinician to "elicit responses by employing hypnotic patterns of communication that capture client's attention and focus them on experiences that will be personally and therapeutically significant" (Yapko, 2012, p. 320).

Standardized instruments for formal, initial assessment of hypnotic responsiveness (or hypnotizability) include the Stanford Hypnotic Susceptibility Scales (SHSS), Harvard Group Scale of Hypnotic Susceptibility (HGSHS), and the Hypnosis Induction Profile (HIP). Because a substantial difference exists between the individual's hypnotic responsiveness scores (from standardized instruments) and his or her capacity or potential for such responsiveness, standardized assessment scores may not be useful in predicting actual clinical responsiveness and clinical outcomes (Barber, as cited in Yapko, 2012).

For this and other important reasons, a majority of clinicians prefer to make use of informal, more individualized assessments of the client's hypnotic responsiveness. Yapko (2012) clearly stated:

> Instead of attempting to discover if my clients are suggestible, I find it a much more practical use of my mental energy to discover how I can best structure my suggestions to increase the likelihood of their getting accepted based on their response style, attentional style, cognitive style, and other such self-organizing patterns of subjective experience. For the clinician who does not share this perspective or who may not feel subjective assessments are reliable or adequate, formal suggestibility tests may be a useful tool [Yapko, 2012, p. 246].

Notably, the Hypnotic State Assessment Questionnaire (HSAQ) highlights the value of data-gathering during individual hypnosis sessions and equips the clinician with the means to assess and document the effectiveness of hypnotic interventions and the client's progress. Additionally, each clinician conducts ongoing assessment of the effectiveness of clinical hypnosis interventions for each client, incorporating his or her clinical observations and also the client's lived hypnotic experiences and the meaning arising within and out of them.

Evidence-Based Research in Clinical Hypnosis, Population and Conditions Treated and Potential Risks

Clinical hypnosis has been utilized to assist children, adolescents, and adults with alleviating a variety of biopsychosocial-spiritual conditions. Evidence-based research in clinical hypnosis demonstrated the effectiveness of clinical hypnosis in the treatment of many biopsychosocial-spiritual conditions and considerations, including, yet not limited, to the following:

(a) cognitive control processes (Egner & Raz, 2007);

(b) pain and acute and chronic pain disorders and associated symptoms—sleep disturbance, depression, and anxiety (Boly, Faymonville, Vogt, Maquet, & Laureys, 2007; Jensen & Patterson, 2008; Miltner & Weiss, 2007; Moore & Tasso, 2008);

    (c) anxiety and anxiety disorders (Bryant, 2008);

    (d) depression (Yapko, 2008);

    (e) health-compromising behaviors (Elkins & Perfect, 2008; Moore & Tasso, 2008);

    (f) immune functioning, medical illness, and medical conditions and procedures (Covino, 2008; Moore & Tasso, 2008);

    (g) conversion and somatization disorders (Moene & Roelofs, 2008);

    (h) trauma-related disorders and dissociation (Bayne, 2007; Peebles, 2008); and

    (i) sport-related considerations (Morgan & Stegner, 2008).

Regardless of the client's diagnoses and even of his or her measured or perceived responsiveness to clinical hypnosis (or hypnotizability), the goal of the clinician facilitating clinical hypnosis is to capitalize upon the client's strength and account for limitations, "to go beyond client labels, to build genuinely therapeutic relationships that foster responsiveness, and there by discover the unique resources of each person that can be amplified and mobilized in the service of the therapeutic goals" (Yapko, 2012, pp. 178–179). Furthermore, Yapko (2012) advised, "there is no individual in treatment with whom you [the clinician] need to avoid either doing hypnosis or, at least, being hypnotic. But certain disorders are considerably more challenging to treat" (p. 174). Such conditions, for instance, include psychosis (particularly drug-induced and aging-related psychosis), bipolar (in manic phase), senility (degree-dependent) (Yapko, 2012). Importantly,

> There is no evidence whatsoever that hypnosis causes psychosis, precipitates suicide, triggers panic, strips people of their psychological defenses, or otherwise harms people. There is a high level of consensus after all these years among hypnosis researchers and practitioners that hypnosis holds no inherent dangers when used appropriately by a well-trained clinician [Yapko, 2012, p. 218].

Potential risks associated with clinical hypnosis interventions include: unintended interpretations of offered suggestions, spontaneous regressions and abreactions, symptom substitution and unenduring results, confabulations, and failure to remove suggestions (Barabasz & Watkins; Weitzenhoffer; as cited in Yapko, 2012, p. 219).

Concluding Thoughts

As a thoroughly-researched and widely-utilized embodied approach to healing, health, and wholeness, clinical hypnosis serves as an effective adjunctive orientation-modality that helps to alleviate human suffering. Clinical hypnosis is offered within a therapeutic context by a licensed mental health/medical professional who has earned a Master's degree (or higher level of education) in his or her respective field and has also obtained proper training, supervision, and certification in the field of clinical hypnosis. While the benefits of utilizing clinical hypnoses are many, including, (a) heightened biopsychosocial-spiritual functioning and self-regulation; (b) enhanced sense of agency and empowerment; and (c) opportunities to access one's inner resources—associated potential risks are few. All things considered, clinical hypnosis approaches continue to invite individuals—through the inward space and one journey at a time—into the richness of the highest human potentials. May the journeys taken be deeply rewarding, individually and also collectively.

REFERENCES

Alter, D.S., & Sugarman, L.I. (2017). Reorienting hypnosis education. *American Journal of Clinical Hypnosis, 59*(3), 235–259.

Appel, P.R. (2014). A transpersonal model for hypnotically mediated psychotherapy. *American Journal of Clinical Hypnosis, 56*(3), 249–268.

Barnier, A.J., Dienes, Z., & Mitchell, C.J. (2008). How hypnosis happens: New cognitive theories of hypnotic responding. In M.R. Nash & A.J. Barnier (Eds.), *The Oxford handbook of hypnosis: Theory, research, and practice* (pp. 141–178). New York, NY: Oxford University Press.

Bayne, T. (2007). Hypnosis and the unity of consciousness. In G.A. Jamieson (Ed.), *Hypnosis and conscious states: The cognitive neuroscience perspective* (pp. 93–109). New York, NY: Oxford University Press.

Boly, M., Faymonville, M.-E., Vogt, B.A., Maquet, P., & Laureys, S. (2007). Hypnotic regulation of consciousness and the pain neuromatrix. In G.A. Jamieson (Ed.), *Hypnosis and conscious states: The cognitive neuroscience perspective* (pp. 15–27). New York, NY: Oxford University Press.

Bryant, R.A. (2008). Hypnosis and anxiety: Early interventions. In M.R. Nash & A.J. Barnier (Eds.), *The Oxford handbook of hypnosis: Theory, research, and practice* (pp. 535–547). New York, NY: Oxford University Press.

Covino, N.A. (2008). Medical illness, conditions, and procedures. In M.R. Nash & A.J. Barnier (Eds.), *The Oxford handbook of hypnosis: Theory, research, and practice* (pp. 611–624). New York, NY: Oxford University Press.

Egner, T., & Raz, A. (2007). Cognitive control processes and hypnosis. In G.A. Jamieson (Ed.), *Hypnosis and conscious states: The cognitive neuroscience perspective* (pp. 29–50). New York, NY: Oxford University Press.

Elkins, G., & Perfect, M. (2008). Hypnosis for health-compromising behaviors. In M.R. Nash & A.J. Barnier (Eds.), *The Oxford handbook of hypnosis: Theory, research, and practice* (pp. 569–592). New York, NY: Oxford University Press.

Ewin, D.M., & Eimer, B.N. (2006). *Ideomotor signals for rapid hypnoanalysis: A how-to manual.* Springfield, IL: Charles C. Thomas.

Hope, A.E., & Sugarman, L.I. (2015). Orienting hypnosis. *American Journal of Clinical Hypnosis, 57*(3), 212–229.

Hammond, D.C. (Ed.). (1990). *Handbook of hypnotic suggestions and metaphors.* New York, NY: Norton.

Hammond, D.C. (2015). Defining hypnosis: An integrative, multi-factor conceptualization. *American Journal of Clinical Hypnosis, 57*(4), 439–444.

Hunter, C.R., & Eimer, B.N. (2014). *The art of hypnotic regression therapy: A clinical guide.* Bethel, CT: Crown House.

Jamieson, G.A. (Ed.). (2007). *Hypnosis and conscious states: The cognitive neuroscience perspective.* New York, NY: Oxford University Press.

Jamieson, G.A. (2007). Previews and prospects for the cognitive neuroscience of hypnosis and conscious states. In G.A. Jamieson (Ed.), *Hypnosis and conscious states: The cognitive neuroscience perspective* (pp. 1–11). New York, NY: Oxford University Press.

Jensen, M.P., & Patterson, D.R. (2008). Hypnosis in the relief of pain and pain disorders. In M.R. Nash & A.J. Barnier (Eds.), *The Oxford handbook of hypnosis: Theory, research, and practice* (pp. 503–533). New York, NY: Oxford University Press.

Leskowitz, E.D. (Ed.). (2000). *Transpersonal hypnotherapy: Gateway to body, mind, and spirit.* Kill Devil Hills, NC: Transpersonal Publishing.

Lynn, S.J., Kirsch, I., & Hallquist, M.N. (2008). Social cognitive theories of hypnosis. In M.R. Nash & A.J. Barnier (Eds.), *The Oxford handbook of hypnosis: Theory, research, and practice* (pp. 111–140). New York, NY: Oxford University Press.

Miltner, W.H.R., & Weiss, T. (2007). Cortical mechanisms of hypnotic pain control. In G.A. Jamieson (Ed.), *Hypnosis and conscious states: The cognitive neuroscience perspective* (pp. 51–66). New York, NY: Oxford University Press.

Moene, F.C., & Roelofs, K. (2008). Hypnosis in the treatment of conversion and somatization disorders. In M.R. Nash & A.J. Barnier (Eds.), *The Oxford handbook of hypnosis: Theory, research, and practice* (pp. 625–645). New York, NY: Oxford University Press.

Moore, M., & Tasso, A.F. (2008). In M.R. Nash & A.J. Barnier (Eds.), *The Oxford handbook of hypnosis: Theory, research, and practice* (pp. 697–725). New York, NY: Oxford University Press.

Morgan, W.P., & Stegner, A.J. (2008). Hypnosis in sport: Cases, techniques, and issues. In M.R. Nash & A.J. Barnier (Eds.), *The Oxford handbook of hypnosis: Theory, research, and practice* (pp. 681–696). New York, NY: Oxford University Press.

Nash, M.R. (2008). A psychoanalytic theory of hypnosis: A clinically informed approach. In M.R. Nash & A. J. Barnier (Eds.), *The Oxford handbook of hypnosis: Theory, research, and practice* (pp. 201–222). New York, NY: Oxford University Press.

Peebles, M.J. (2008). Trauma-related disorders and dissociation. In M.R. Nash & A.J. Barnier (Eds.), *The Oxford handbook of hypnosis: Theory, research, and practice* (pp. 647–679). New York, NY: Oxford University Press.

Rossi, E.L. (1993). *The psychobiology of mind-body healing: New concepts of therapeutic hypnosis.* New York, NY: Norton.

Rossi, E.L. (2002). *The psychobiology of gene expression: Neuroscience and neurogenesis in hypnosis and the healing arts.* New York, NY: Norton.

Rossi, E.L. (2007). *The breakout heuristic: The new neuroscience of mirror neurons, consciousness, and creativity in human relationships.* Phoenix, AZ: Milton H. Erickson Foundation Press.

Rossi, E.L., & Cheek, D.B. (1988). Mind-body therapy: Ideodynamic healing in hypnosis. New York, NY: Norton.

Wickramasekera, I.E. (2015). Mysteries of hypnosis and the self are revealed by the psychology and neuroscience of empathy. *American Journal of Clinical Hypnosis, 57*(3), 330–348.

Woody, E.Z., & Sandler, P. (2008). Dissociation theories of hypnosis. In M.R. Nash & A.J. Barnier (Eds.), *The Oxford handbook of hypnosis: Theory, research, and practice* (pp. 81–110). New York, NY: Oxford University Press.

Yapko, M. (2008). Hypnotic approach to treating depression. In M.R. Nash & A.J. Barnier (Eds.), *The Oxford handbook of hypnosis: Theory, research, and practice* (pp. 549–567). New York, NY: Oxford University Press.

Yapko, M. (2012). *Trancework: An introduction to the practice of clinical hypnosis* (4th ed.). New York, NY: Routledge.

Holotropic Breathwork
in a Clinical Setting

Marina A. Smirnova

Holotropic Breathwork is an experiential, deeply embodied biopsychosocial-spiritual approach to self-exploration, to psychospiritual growth and development, and to psychotherapy. It capitalizes upon, trusts, and engages the individuals' inner healing intelligence using a proper set, setting, and supportive context and container. To support the individuals' inner journey, Holotropic Breathwork makes use of circular, accelerated breathing of 124 evocative music; of focused body work that supports energetic and psycho-emotional release; and of creative expression (Grof & Grof, 2010). It is designed to harness and to galvanize the potentials of a particular sub-group of non-ordinary states of consciousness that can be described as *holotropic states*—states that offer support to individuals in their journeys towards healing, health, wellness, individuation, and wholeness (Grof & Grof, 2010). Holotropic Breathwork may be used by individuals who have some and/or extensive experience in navigating expanded states of consciousness, as well as by those who are new to the exploratory work that engages expanded states of consciousness.

Hylotropic and Holotropic States of Consciousness

While Holotropic Breathwork shares some features with experiential approaches and therapies of humanistic psychology, the practice of Holotropic Breathwork cultivates holotropic states of consciousness—states of consciousness that differ qualitatively and may be distinguished from non-ordinary states of consciousness (Grof & Grof, 2010). *Holotropic* "literally translates as aiming for totality or moving toward wholeness (from the Greek *holos* = whole and *trepein* = moving in the direction of)" (Grof, 1988, p. 239). In contrast, *hylotropic consciousness* or matter-oriented consciousness, a state of mind, or a mode that is encountered as everyday consciousness and that allows individuals "to experience only the present moment and the present location ('here and now') in the phenomenal world of consensual reality" (Grof, 1988, p. 240). This is the mode of consciousness that Western psychology and psychiatry traditionally deems normal, proper, and permissible (Grof, 1988). Most importantly, however, "in contrast to the narrow and restricted hylotropic mode, the *holotropic variety* involves the experience of oneself as a

127

potentially unlimited field of consciousness that has access to all aspects of reality without the mediation of senses" (Grof, 1988, p. 239).

Both, hylotropic and holotropic states of consciousness appear to be in a lively interplay and competing for the individuals' attention (Grof, 1988). Consequently, "the understanding of the nature of psychopathology as interference of the holotropic and hylotropic modes of consciousness then suggests new therapeutic strategy" (Grof, 1988, p. 242). Holotropic Breathwork technique, practice, or approach becomes a therapeutic strategy that offers a pathway to holotropic states of consciousness for the purpose of gaining an expanded perspective on the individual's life journey, lived experiences, symptoms, and potential solutions and helpful strategies. In Holotropic Breathwork sessions and their integration process, the individual's experiences and symptoms often spontaneously emerge as holotropic themes and/or holotropic gestalt that incorporate not only the recollective-biographical, but also perinatal (related to biological birth) and transpersonal material and relevance (Grof, 1988).

The Expanded Cartography of the Psyche, the Inner Healer and COEX

While traditional psychology and psychiatry favor a cartography of the human psyche that is limited to postnatal recollective-biographical/biographical or postnatal level and individual unconscious, the expanded cartography of the psyche incorporates two transbiographical domains—perinatal and transpersonal (Grof, 1988; Grof & Grof, 2010). The biographical domain is experientially familiar to many individuals and contains biographical material that may be fully or partially available to the individual's consciousness and/or unconsciously present. The perinatal domain captures experiences and experiential territories associated with, and circumstances surrounding, one's biological birth process and suggests a pattern of psychospiritual death-rebirth cycles throughout one's lifetime, in one's journey toward wholeness.

The transpersonal domain houses the experiences and the experiential realms and territories that go above and beyond, yet through the personal, as the meaning of prefix "trans" in the term "trans-personal" suggests. Grof's (2000) transpersonal domain of the psyche is quite opulent and incorporates three large experiential categories: (1) experiential extension within space-time and consensus reality; (2) experiential extension beyond space-time and consensus reality; and (3) transpersonal experiences of psychoid nature (Grof, 2000). For instance, while identification with other individuals and/or with ancestral experiences belong to the first experiential category of the transpersonal experiences/domain, the individual's experiences with the Supracosmic and Metacosmic Void fall into the second experiential category (Grof, 2000). Additionally, one's lived experiences of synchronicities and/or of spiritistic phenomena and physical mediumship are recognized as transpersonal experiences of psychoid nature and belong to the third experiential category (Grof, 2000).

Though holotropic states afford access to direct experiences of and/or experiential identification with a wide variety of potentially-innumerable aspects of the universe and cosmos (Grof, 2000), it is acknowledged that each individual's inner intelligence, also referred to as the Inner Radar and/or the Inner Healer, is the guiding force in the process of self-exploration and/or therapy in Holotropic Breathwork (Grof, 2000; Grof & Grof,

2010). As a function of holotropic states of consciousness, the Inner Healer "automatically brings into consciousness the contents from the unconscious that have the strongest emotional charge, are most psychodynamically relevant at the time, and most available for conscious processing; this represents a great advantage in comparison with verbal psychotherapy" (Grof, 2000, p. 28) and allows the therapist an opportunity to fully support the breather's internalized experiences. According to Grof (2000), the contents of the individual's unconscious, are stored as "complex dynamic constellations ... COEX systems, which is short for 'systems of condensed experience'" (p. 22).

"As general organizing principles of the human psyche" (Grof, 2000, p. 23), COEX systems or constellations bear resemblance to Jungian complexes, seem to be rooted in various transpersonal phenomena, and appear to be "superimposed over and anchored in a particular aspect of the trauma of birth" (Grof, 2000, p. 23). Every COEX system or constellation has a unifying element—a theme or emotion, for instance—that runs through the individual's personal, perinatal, and transpersonal experiences and attracts and links together the individual's emotionally-relevant lived experiences (Grof, 2000). Each individual's COEX systems may be classified and experienced as positive and negative; however, compared with positive COEX systems, negative COEX constellations seem to come in abundant supply and variety (Grof, 2000). Thus, a Holotropic Breathwork approach to self-exploration, therapy, and healing offers an opportunity to encounter, to engage, to explore, to process, and to integrate embodied experiences that belong to biographical, perinatal, and transpersonal domains of the psyche and to various COEX systems or constellations within the individual's psyche. Because COEX constellations dynamically interact with and are influenced by internal and external environmental factors, creating a proper set and setting for a rewarding Holotropic Breathwork experience is of paramount importance (Grof, 2000).

About Holotropic Breathwork Sessions

Holotropic Breathwork technique, practice, or approach harnesses the power of the following essential components of this work: holotropic states of consciousness; the healing, therapeutic potential of the breath, of the music, and of the releasing bodywork; and safe, supportive, and nourishing physical presence and contact (Grof & Grof, 2010). Holotropic Breathwork practice can be experienced in individual, small group, and large group sessions. It calls for a skillfully-selected setting (ideally, a retreat or retreat-like setting or other supportive space, like a therapist's office or a private room) that is conducive to deep, embodied inner work and its processing, as well as its effective integration. Moreover, selecting a room for Holotropic Breathwork that is in close proximity with restrooms is necessary. This allows all participants of Holotropic Breathwork to stay with the unfolding process while easily accommodating basic human needs.

Ideally, in individual sessions with a client or with several clients, the therapist fulfills the role of the trained and certified facilitator; this scenario requires the presence of one sitter for each breather. However, if the therapist offers a one-on-one sessions with a client, and a sitter is unavailable, the therapist will function as both—the facilitator and the sitter. In this case, the absence of the sitter inevitably limits the supportive physical contact and body work the therapist-facilitator may offer to the breather (Grof & Grof, 2010). The length of the individual sessions varies. While therapists may prefer to offer individual Holotropic Breathwork sessions at the end of their therapeutic workday (Grof & Grof, 2010), it is not uncommon for the therapists to dedicate a day (and, in some cases, two days) to facilitating individual or group Holotropic Breathwork sessions in a resort or other residential facility. It is essential, however, that the Holotropic Breathwork facilitators plan to and remain with the breathers until the breathers' experience is concluded for the day (Grof & Grof, 2010).

While a typical Holotropic Breathwork session itself is 2.5–3 hours or longer, each Holotropic Breathwork experience consists of three critical parts: (1) preparation, (2) experience (Holotropic Breathwork session itself), and (3) processing and integration. As a part of the preparation process, well in advance of the Holotropic Breathwork experience, all potential Holotropic Breathwork participants are closely screened (via a medical questionnaire) for physical and emotional contraindications (Grof & Grof, 2010). It is important to insure that Holotropic Breathwork practice is the right practice for each of the potential participants, given their (a) current physical, psychiatric, psychological, and emotional health and history thereof and (b) reasonably-developed capacity to recognize their inner experiences as internal events and to own them, thus avoiding engaging in external projections.

The process of preparation for Holotropic Breathwork experience also includes holding a meeting that offers a proper theoretical and practical orientation to the participants. Such orientation helps the participants to build a sound framework for the Holotropic Breathwork experience and its preparation, as well as for its processing and integration. While the orientation allows the participants to navigate the entire Holotropic Breathwork process in general and every step of the process in particular, it also informs them about (a) the qualitative shift in consciousness experienced during the Holotropic Breathwork process, (b) the three stages in the work—preparation, experience, and processing and integration; (c) the essence of holotropic states and their transformative and healing potential; (d) the expanded cartography of the psyche and its territories; (e) the importance of surrendering to the process and of following the innate healing intelligence— the Inner Healer; (f) the guidelines of engagement as breathers, sitters, and facilitators; (g) the necessity of trusting, owning one's inner process while refraining from projecting it externally; and (h) "the importance of staying in the present moment, focusing on emotions and physical feelings, and refraining from intellectual analysis" (Grof & Grof, 2010, p. 55). Additionally, the process of preparation allows the participants to form Holotropic Breathwork dyads (and to discuss in dyads the participants' needs and preferences), to ask questions that may arise, and to clarify understanding. Thus, a sense of support, safety, and respect is purposively cultivated and exemplified throughout the process of Holotropic Breathwork and remains a sound foundation of and a container for the Holotropic Breathwork modality.

Whether Holotropic Breathwork sessions take place individually (the therapist works one-on-one with the client-breather, with the support of the sitter) or in small or large groups, where the participants work in dyads, the Holotropic Breathwork sessions are always facilitated by certified Holotropic Breathwork facilitators, whose work, at times, may be supported by Holotropic Breathwork apprentices—advanced Holotropic Breathwork students. Each dyad consists of a breather and a sitter. While the breather is the one who is directly engaging the Holotropic Breathwork technique, the holotropic state of consciousness, and the guidance of the Inner Healer, the sitter is the one who supports the breather's process by being fully present and by honoring the breather's needs and preferences during the process.

How a Session Would Unfold in a Clinical Setting

Before the Holotropic Breathwork experience begins, the facilitators, the breathers, and sitters arrange a soft-surface breathing mattresses or mats (a pillow and a yoga mat, a sleeping bag, or similar surfaces) for each breather, insuring that a couple of a few additional pillows are available (if needed) and also a light blanket or a sheet, a box of Kleenex, and a plastic bag. To maximize the use of the room/space for groups, the facilitators often arrange "the mattresses parallel to each other in long lines, leaving a sufficient gap between them for participants to be able to walk in and out of the room if they need to and for facilitators to do their work" (Grof & Grof, 2010, p. 63). The breathers lie down face-up on their mats; cover their eyes with a scarf, bandanna, or an eye-shade; and prepare for their journey. The sitters position themselves close by and give their undivided attention and support to their respective breathers. The Holotropic Breathwork facilitators support the entire process and assist individual breathers and sitters as needed.

Once all of the participants are prepared and in the room, a Holotropic Breathwork session begins. A typical Holotropic Breathwork session opens with a brief facilitator-led introduction to the experience and is followed by a progressive muscle relaxation exercise. Moreover, the breathers receive an invitation to connect with their higher source of inspiration and with their Inner Healers and to surrender to the experience. Then the breathers are invited to begin breathing a little bit deeper and a little bit faster (connecting their in-breath and their out-breath), and Holotropic Breathwork music (a set of music specifically prepared for a Holotropic Breathwork session) begins. Each Holotropic Breathwork music set follows a particular trajectory. It is carefully and thoughtfully designed to evoke holotropic states of consciousness, to support the breathers' process of self-exploration and self-discovery, and to optimize an opportunity for breathers to experience a breakthrough and/or a successful resolution of their experience "on the mat." During the Holotropic Breathwork session, breathers and sitters may invite the facilitators to assist in the process. Additionally, facilitators offer their support throughout the process, as needed.

Several significant premises that inform Holotropic Breathwork influence its practice. Firstly, as Holotropic-states research suggested, the individual's symptoms "represent the manifestation of a self-healing impulse of the organism that is trying to free itself from traumatic memories and other disturbing material from the biographical, perinatal, and transpersonal domains of the unconscious" (Grof & Grof, 2010, pp. 88–89) and, therefore, "should be encouraged to emerge and brought to full expression rather than suppressed" (p. 89). Secondly, "the holotropic state of consciousness functions as a universal homeopathic remedy" (Grof & Grof, 2010, p. 89) that "tends to intensify all pre-existing symptoms (which are functional or psychogenic and not organic in origin).... It also brings into manifestation previously latent symptoms and makes them available for processing" (p. 89).

The ideal attitude of the breather to the experience is to focus his or her full attention on the process as it unfolds from one moment to another, rather than on any specific goal or outcome. The breathers ideally maintain the faster breathing rhythm irrespective of the form the experience takes—buildup of physical tensions, surfacing of intense emotions, emergence of specific memories, or progressive relaxation.... The facilitators walk around, monitoring the situation in the room, looking for instances where some special assistance might be needed. They might be asked to step in and sit with a breather while the sitter visits the restroom. Occasionally, they also might offer emotional support to the sitter who responds to the situation with intense emotions.... Much of the active work with trained facilitators is done in the termination period of the sessions with breathers whose experience has not reached an adequate closure and who are experiencing some residual symptoms. This is the time for releasing bodywork and subsequent ... nourishing physical contact [Grof & Grof, 2010, pp. 66–67].

When the Holotropic Breathwork session comes to a conclusion, before leaving the Holotropic Breathwork room, breathers are required to check-in with one of the facilitators. This safety measure is built into each Holotropic Breathwork session to insure that each breather's Holotropic Breathwork experience is complete for the day, so that he or she can proceed to the next steps—drawing a mandala, reflecting upon and integrating the Holotropic Breathwork experience, and processing the experience in groups. While many breathers, by the end of the session, will feel that their work is complete and that their emotions, mind, and body are clear, some breathers may have emotional or otherwise residual tension, which can be addressed by means of bodywork. "The large array of the interventions Holotropic Breathwork facilitators are using thus has one common denominator; it is the effort to intensify the existing symptoms and bring the material underlying them to full expression" (Grof & Grof, 2010, p. 89).

Once the work "on the mat," has been concluded, the sitter leads his or her breather to the mandala room, which offers a meditative environment and a variety of art supplies for breathers (and also for sitters, if sitters are interested) to reflect upon their experiences. Mandala drawing allows the breathers to express the essence of their experience, capturing a right-brain perspective on the experience. There are assessments to administer to measure the effectiveness of a Holotropic Breathwork session. After mandala drawing, when group processing of the Holotropic Breathwork experience takes place, verbal, non-verbal (mandala), and, when useful, psychodramatic means are utilized to continue the process of integration of the lived experience using support of the group (Grof & Grof, 2010). "A loving, supportive, and nourishing attitude of the peers expressed in words, touch, and hugs can go far in providing a corrective experience for breathers who are wide open as a result of their breathwork sessions" (Grof & Grof, 2010, p. 95). It is valuable to note that Holotropic Breathwork facilitators who lead the group processing refrain from interpreting the breathers' and the sitters' experiences and insure that the nascent meaning of the participants' experiences continue to unfold of their own accord, without purposeful and/or incidental impositions of others. "The group member who, being the experiencer, is the ultimate expert as far as his or her experience is concerned" (Grof & Grof, 2010, p. 95). Thus, safety-, support-, and respect-in-action continue to inform the entire Holotropic Breathwork practice and process.

At the closing circle of each Holotropic Breathwork event or workshop, the participants are informed how best to transition from their Holotropic Breathwork experiences to the demands of the everyday life. They are reminded to exercise proper, nurturing self-care and to postpone making radical changes in their lives based on their lived Holotropic Breathwork experience. Additionally, they are encouraged to continue to integrate their Holotropic Breathwork experience with the help of their Holotropic Breathwork partners, therapists, friends, and trusted others. A special emphasis and importance are placed upon the continuous processes of meaning making and of integrating the participants' Holotropic Breathwork experiences. Finally, highlighted are the necessities of daily psychospiritual practices and the power of staying connected with the Holotropic Breathwork community.

Minimum Certification Requirements for Facilitating Holotropic Breathwork

Although many certified Holotropic Breathwork facilitators who facilitate Holotropic Breathwork sessions for others are licensed, experienced, and practicing mental health professional, there is no degree and no licensure requirements currently for those individuals who are interested in exploring Holotropic Breathwork practice and earning Holotropic Breathwork training and certification. Grof Transpersonal Training, Inc. (GTT) remains the only organization that offers Holotropic Breathwork workshops/training and Holotropic Breathwork certification in the U.S. and world-wide. Individuals interested in obtaining Holotropic Breathwork certification pursue GTT training in transpersonal psychology and Holotropic Breathwork over a period of at least two years (or longer). Two certification tracks are available for those who desire to become certified in Holotropic Breathwork—*Educational* track and *Practitioner* track (Grof Transpersonal Training, n.d.). Successful completion of (a) seven six-day modules (four required modules and three elective modules), (b) ten Holotropic Breathwork workshops; (c) ten hours of consultation with GT certified Holotropic Breathwork facilitators; and (d) a 10-day certification intensive is necessary to meet the GTT certification requirements for both certification tracks (Grof Transpersonal Training, n.d.).

It is important to note that, according to GTT requirements (Grof Transpersonal Training, n.d.), only those Holotropic Breathwork facilitators who certified under the *Practitioner* track and who have apprenticed four times (with certified Holotropic Breathwork facilitators during Holotropic Breathwork workshops and/or modules) can offer independently-held Holotropic Breathwork experiential sessions and/or workshops to others. To retain GTT Holotropic Breathwork certification, the recently-certified persons are obligated to adhere to continuous professional development requirements by partaking in two Holotropic Breathwork sessions a year. Such sessions must be facilitated by GTT-certified Holotropic Breathwork facilitators. If a mental health practitioner is not certified in Holotropic Breathwork, he or she cannot offer Holotropic Breathwork sessions to clients independently and should refer his or her clients to a GTT-certified Holotropic Breathwork facilitator who completed a *Practitioner* track. Importantly, regardless of his or her Holotropic Breathwork certification-related status, a mental health practitioner can continue to be of support to clients who engage Holotropic Breathwork technique and are interested in the process of integration.

Brief Overview of Evidence-Based Research on the Effectiveness of HB

Since the mid–1970s, conclusions about the effectiveness of Holotropic Breathwork as a modality for self-exploration, for psychospiritual growth, and for therapy have been reached based on the lived experiences reported and documented by Holotropic Breathwork breathers. According to Rhinewine and Williams (2007), "few studies have examined empirically the therapeutic potential of HB" (p. 773). Furthermore, "only three studies appear to meet commonly accepted minimum criteria of methodological sophistication to be considered as constituting reliable empirical evidence … and only one of these has been published in a peer-reviewed journal" (Holmes, Morris, Clance, & Putney, 1996; Rhinewine & Williams, 2007, p. 773). This quasi-experimental study (Holmes, Morris, Clance, & Putney, 1996) suggested that "therapeutic improvement in death anxiety and self-esteem was stronger with a combination of Holotropic Breathwork and experientially oriented verbal psychotherapy than with experientially oriented verbal psychotherapy alone" (p. 119) and that "the combination of Holotropic Breathwork and experientially oriented verbal psychotherapy may be a useful therapeutic modality" (p. 119).

The findings of a qualitative dissertation study by Cervelli (2009) suggested that Holotropic Breathwork technique "positively impacts the process of self-actualization and self-healing" (p. iii) and that "the Holotropic Breathwork™ technique and the integral mandala artwork may be effective for some individuals for spiritual development, personal-growth workshops, or as an adjunct or compliment to conventional individual, group psychotherapy or spiritual guidance and direction" (p. iii). In a qualitative dissertation study, Smirnova (2013) concluded that Holotropic Breathwork may promote and support the breathers' experiential process of reconciliation with and integration of the subjectively-experienced "fragmented and alienated experiential realities imbued with pain, judgment, stigma, or taboo" (p. 165). Notably, the meaning of this process is linked with the breathers' "phenomenologically experienced sense of psychospiritual healing, transformation, and conscious wholeness" (Smirnova, 2013, p. iv).

A quasi-experimental study by Miller and Nielsen (2015) emphasized that Holotropic Breathwork "can induce very beneficial temperament changes, which can have positive effects on development of character, measured as an increase in self-awareness" (p. 796). Moreover, "the four HB sessions significantly reduced the whole group's (n = 20) scores with regard to persistence, hostility, and interpersonal problems, including overly accommodating problems and intrusive/needy problems" (Miller & Nielsen, 2015, p. 803). Additionally, Miller and Nielsen (2015) concluded that "HB practice can provide a more organized character development measured as progression in the development of self-awareness" (p. 803).

Physical and Emotional Contraindications; Recommended Populations; and Associated Risks

As an embodied approach to clearing unhelpful biopsychosocial-spiritual imprints, energetic blockages, and/or traumatic events, Holotropic Breathwork is typically utilized by young and mature adult populations. While Holotropic Breathwork is a fairly safe approach to embodied exploration, to psychospiritual growth, and to psychotherapy, risks in Holotropic Breathwork are typically associated with several physical, emotional, and/or psychiatric conditions. Because in Holotropic Breathwork sessions the breathers may encounter temporary significant emotional, psychological, or physical activation and distress, the following conditions are general contraindications. They present various degrees of risk and require a thorough consultation with an appropriate medical professional in advance of Holotropic Breathwork sessions: (a) "serious cardiovascular disorders—high blood pressure, aneurysms, a history of heart attacks, brain hemorrhage, myocarditis, atrial fibrillation, or other similar problems" (Grof & Grof, 2010, pp. 55–56); (b) pregnancy; (c) "history of convulsive disorders, particularly grand mal epilepsy" (p. 57); (d) recent physical injuries and/or operations such as "bone fractures, herniated disks, dislocated shoulders or knees, incompletely healed surgical wounds, and similar afflictions" (p. 57); (e) some contagious conditions; (f) asthma and/or debilitating conditions; and (g) history of serious psychiatric problems. Grof and Grof (2010) noted that "Holotropic Breathwork can actually be used in the therapy of a wide range of emotional and psychosomatic disorders, including spiritual emergencies, if we have the appropriate facility and support system" (p. 60). Nevertheless, "until the theory and practice of psychiatry is revolutionized and centers based on the new paradigm readily available, a history of psychiatric treatment will represent a contraindication for participation in short Holotropic Breathwork workshops" (pp. 60–61).

REFERENCES

Cervelli, R.L. (2009). *An intuitive inquiry into experiences arising out of the Holotropic Breathwork technique and its integral mandala artwork: The potential for self-actualization* (Doctoral dissertation). Retrieved from ProQuest Dissertations and Theses database (UMI No. 3380360).

Grof, S. (1988). *The adventure of self-discovery: Dimensions of consciousness and new perspectives in psychotherapy and inner exploration.* Albany, NY: State University of New York Press.

Grof, S. (2000). *Psychology of the future.* Albany, NY: State University of New York Press.

Grof, S., & Grof, C. (2010). *Holotropic Breathwork: A new approach to self-exploration and therapy.* Albany, NY: State University of New York Press.

Grof Transpersonal Training, Inc. (n.d.). Grof Transpersonal Training: Application Pack. Retrieved from http://www.holotropic.com/pdf_docs/GTT%20Training%20pack%202017.pdf

Holmes, S.W., Morris, R., Clance, P.R., & Putney, R.T. (1996). Holotropic Breathwork: An experiential approach to psychotherapy. *Psychotherapy, 33*(1), 114–120.

Miller, T., & Nielsen, L. (2015). Measure of significance of Holotropic Breathwork in the development of self-awareness. *The Journal of Alternative and Complementary Medicine, 21*(12), 796–803.

Rhinewine, J.P., & Williams, O.J. (2007). Holotropic Breathwork: The potential role of a prolonged, voluntary hyperventilation procedure as an adjunct to psychotherapy. *The Journal of Alternative and Complementary Medicine, 13*(7), 771–776.

Smirnova, M.A. (2013). *Atonement with the dreadful manifestations of the sacred in Holotropic Breathwork: Interpretive phenomenological analysis of the breather's embodied experience and the meaning arising within and out of it* (Doctoral dissertation). Retrieved from ProQuest Dissertations and Theses database (UMI No. 3557624).

Emotional Freedom Techniques for Psychological Symptoms and Disorders

PETA STAPLETON

Emotional Freedom Techniques (EFT) is a brief intervention combining elements of exposure, cognitive therapy, and somatic stimulation. It is often referred to as "tapping," as it uses a two-finger tapping process with a cognitive acceptance statement. EFT has been researched in more than 10 countries, by more than 60 investigators, whose results have been published in more than 130 different journal articles (Church, 2013). These clinical trials have shown that EFT is able to rapidly reduce the emotional impact of memories and incidents that trigger emotional distress. This essay represents a summary of the major research supporting the use of EFT for disorders and symptoms such as depression, anxiety, and Post-Traumatic Stress Disorder (PTSD).

An Overview of Clinical EFT

Clinical EFT, which represents the version of EFT tested in clinical trials, has been manualized since its inception (Church, 2013; Craig & Fowlie, 1995). Participants typically identify a concern or issue they wish to address with the technique, and rate their level of distress on a Likert scale out of 10 (10 is the maximum amount of distress, while 0 represents the minimum or a neutral state). Called a Subjective Unit of Distress (SUDS) scale, it has long been used as a subjective measure of a participant's discomfort in therapy (Wolpe, 1973). Participants then state their concern in a "Setup Statement," which assists them in tuning into their level of distress. This is typically stated in this format: "Even though I have this problem (e.g., anger), I deeply and completely accept myself." The aim of the setup is two-fold: to expose the participants to their problem, and to emphasize self-acceptance. Participants then engage in the somatic tapping process on acupoints on the body, while they repeat a shortened phrase to stay engaged (e.g., "feel angry"). This is called the "Reminder Phrase." The tapping sequence, which uses eight acupoints on the face and upper body (see Figure 1), is normally repeated until the SUDS rating becomes very low (one or zero).

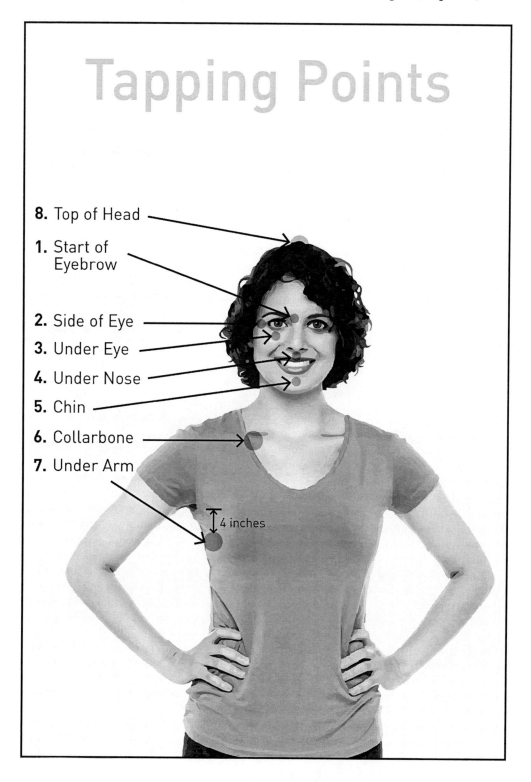

Figure 1: EFT Tapping Points

Minimum Education Requirements and Credentials to Practice EFT

EFT is a treatment emerging with strong evidence in the psychological therapeutic field. Three main organizations (EFT Universe, The Association for Comprehensive Energy Psychology, and EFT International, previously known as the Association for the Advancement of Meridian Energy Therapies) offer these trainings worldwide; when registered EFT practitioners and trainers have their qualifications validated, they agree to work to Codes of Conduct and Ethics. There is no minimum education requirement to train as an EFT practitioner; however, these organizations offer training schedules that include face-to-face training, completion of case studies and session notes, mentoring by a qualified trainer, and exams to complete the certification process.

Evidence-Based Research for EFT

Populations and Disorders

EFT has been extensively studied for a wide range of disorders and populations. The following list represents a very small sample.

POPULATIONS
- College students (Church, De Asis, & Brooks, 2012; Stapleton et al., 2017)
- Veterans (Church et al., 2013; Church, Stern, Boath, Stewart, Feinstein, & Clond, 2017; Geronilla, McWilliams, & Clond, 2014)
- Pain patients (Bougea et al., 2013; Church & Nelms, 2016; Stapleton et al., 2017)
- Overweight adults (Stapleton, Bannatyne, Porter, Urzi, & Sheldon, 2016; Stapleton, Church, Sheldon, Porter, & Carlopio, 2013; Stapleton, Sheldon, & Porter, 2012)
- Hospital patients (Karatzias et al., 2011)
- Athletes (Church, 2009b; Llewellyn-Edwards & Llewellyn-Edwards, 2012)
- Healthcare workers (Church & Brooks, 2010)
- Gifted students (Gaesser & Orv, 2016; Stapleton et al., 2017)
- Chemotherapy patients (Baker & Hoffman, 2014), and
- Phobia sufferers (Baker & Siegel, 2010; Salas, Brooks, & Rowe, 2011; Wells, Polglase, Andrews, Carrington, & Baker, 2013).

DISORDERS/CONDITIONS
- General anxiety (Andrade & Feinstein, 2004; Temple & Mollon, 2011, for dental anxiety)
- Test anxiety (Benor, Ledger, Toussaint, Hett, & Zaccaro, 2009; Boath, Stewart, & Carryer, 2013; Jain & Rubino, 2012; Jones, Thornton, & Andrews, 2011; Sezgin, Ozcan, & Church, 2009; Stapleton et al., 2017)
- Phobias (Baker & Siegel, 2010; Wells et al., 2003)
- Obsessive compulsive disorder (Moritz et al., 2011)
- PTSD (Burk, 2010; Church, 2009a; Church & Brooks, 2013, 2014; Church, Geronilla, & Dinter, 2009; Church et al., 2013; Church, Pina, Reategui, &

Brooks, 2011; Gurret, Caufour, Palmer-Hoffman, & Church, 2012; Hartung & Stein, 2012; Karatzias et al., 2011; Stein & Brooks, 2011; Zhang, Feng, Xie, Xu, & Chen, 2011)

- General trauma (Kober et al., 2002; Lubin & Schneider, 2009; Swingle, Pulos, & Swingle, 2005)
- Stress (Bougea et al., 2013; Church & Brooks, 2010; Church, Yount, & Brooks, 2011; Rowe, 2005)
- Depression (Chatwin, Stapleton, Porter, Devine, & Sheldon, 2016; Church, De Asis, & Brooks, 2012; Stapleton, Church, Sheldon, Porter, & Carolopio, 2013; Stapleton, Devine, Chatwin, Porter, & Sheldon, 2014)
- Addiction (Church & Brooks, 2013; Palmer-Hoffman & Brooks, 2011)
- Obesity/emotional eating/food cravings (Stapleton, Sheldon, Porter, & Whitty, 2011; Stapleton, Sheldon, & Porter, 2012a, 2012b; Stapleton, Church, Sheldon, Porter, & Carlopio, 2013; Stapleton, Bannatyne, Porter, Urzi, & Sheldon, 2016; Stapleton et al., 2016a, 2016b)
- Pain/fibromyalgia/tension headaches (Bougea et al., 2013; Brattberg, 2008; Church, 2008; Ortner, Palmer-Hoffman, & Clond, 2014; Stapleton, Chatwin, Sheppard, & McSwan, 2016c)
- Frozen shoulder (Church & Nelms, 2016)
- Psoriasis (Hodge & Jurgens, 2011)
- Insomnia (Lee, Chung, & Kim, 2015)
- Seizure disorders (Swingle, 2010)
- Sporting/athletic performance (Church, 2009b; Church & Downs, 2012; Llewellyn-Edwards & Llewellyn-Edwards, 2012; Rotheram, Maynard, Thomas, Bawden, & Francis 2012)
- Learning disabilities/educational issues (McCallion, 2012; Stapleton et al., 2017)
- Epigenetic and physiological functioning (Church, Yount, Rachlin, & Nelms, 2016; Maharaj, 2016)
- General psychological functioning (Church, 2008; Stewart, Boath, Carryer, Walton, & Hill, 2011).

EFT has been found to be an "evidence-based" practice for anxiety, depression, phobias, and PTSD when measured against the standards of the American Psychological Association's Division 12 Task Force on Empirically Validated Treatments (Feinstein, 2012; Church, 2013a). Thought Field Therapy (Callahan & Trubo, 2002), a precursor to EFT, has been rated by the Registry of Evidence-based Programs and Practices as being effective for personal resilience/self-concept, self-regulation, and trauma and stressor-related disorders, and "promising" for depression; general functioning and well-being; phobia, panic and generalized anxiety; and "unspecified" and other mental health disorders.

Anxiety

EFT has been extensively investigated for anxiety. In one of the first large-scale studies of 5,000 patients seeking treatment for anxiety in 11 clinics over a 5½-year period, patients were allocated to traditional psychological treatment (Cognitive Behavioral Therapy, CBT) that included medication if needed, or acupoint treatment (the precursor

TFT) with no medication (Andrade & Feinstein, 2004). Ninety percent of acupoint patients improved in an average of three sessions, compared to 63 percent of CBT patients in an average of 15 sessions. One year later, 78 percent of the acupoint group maintained their improvements, compared to 69 percent of the CBT group.

Treatment with EFT of anxiety in students has also been studied. In a comparison of EFT with progressive muscular relaxation (PMR), Sezgin, Ozcan, and Church (2009) found that 70 students out of 312 were identified as having a high level of test-related anxiety. They were randomly assigned to a control group, which received PMR or EFT treatment. Both groups experienced a significant decrease in student anxiety; however, a significantly greater decrease was observed for students who received EFT. Both groups scored higher on test examinations following the treatment, although greater performance was observed for the EFT group (even though the difference was not statistically significant). In another student investigation, following a 15-minute EFT workshop and 15-minute lecture on EFT, 46 students suffering from public speaking anxiety experienced a significant reduction in subjective units of distress and anxiety (Boath, Stewart, & Carryer, 2013).

A study of 216 healthcare workers who self-applied two hours of EFT at various professional conferences (five, in total), resulted in significant improvements for pain, depression, emotional distress, and cravings (Church & Brooks, 2010). Greater subsequent use of EFT was also associated with a significant decrease in psychological symptoms, although not in how many symptoms participants had (in terms of range or breadth).

Finally, a meta-analysis of 14 randomized controlled trials of EFT for anxiety disorders (n = 658) found a very large treatment effect of d = 1.23 (95 percent CI: 0.82–1.64, p < 0.001), while the effect size for combined controls was 0.41 (0.17–0.67, p = 0.001). Even when accounting for the effect size of control treatment, EFT treatment was associated with a significant decrease in anxiety scores (Clond, 2016).

Depression

A meta-analysis of EFT for depression examined 20 studies (Nelms & Castel, 2016), which included outcome studies (n = 446) as well as randomized clinical trials (n = 653; 306 EFT and 347 control). EFT demonstrated a very large effect size (Cohen's d across all studies was 1.31) in the treatment of depression. Effect sizes at post-test, less than 90 days, 90 days, and greater than 90 days, were 0.63, 0.17, and 0.43, respectively. EFT was more efficacious than Diaphragmatic Breathing as well as psychological interventions such as supportive interviews. EFT was also superior to standard treatments, and efficacious in treatment time frames ranging from one to 10 sessions. The mean of symptom reductions across all studies was –41 percent (Nelms, & Castel, 2016).

A feasibility study of EFT to treat Major Depressive Disorder (MDD) in 11 adults in a group setting found that an 8-week (16 hours) program resulted in a change in diagnosis in each of the participants, with data indicating an overall improvement for the treatment group. Two of the participants no longer met MDD as a major diagnosis, and all the other participants no longer met their secondary diagnoses (e.g., generalized anxiety disorder). These improvements were maintained at 3-months follow-up (Stapleton, Devine, Chatwin, Porter, & Sheldon, 2014). Further research evaluated the effectiveness of CBT versus EFT in the treatment of depression and comorbid anxiety. Participants were randomly assigned to an 8-week (16 hours) CBT or EFT treatment program. Findings indicated that both treatment approaches produced significant reductions in depressive symptoms, with the CBT group reporting a significant reduction post-intervention, which was, however, not maintained with time. The EFT group reported a delayed treatment effect indicating a significant reduction in symptoms at the 3- and 6-months follow-up points (Chatwin, Stapleton, & Sheldon, 2016).

Following six sessions of EFT, delivered over the course of one week, seven veterans with PTSD experienced a significant decrease in the severity of PTSD symptoms (up to 40 percent), depression (decreased by 49 percent), and anxiety (decreased by 46 percent; Church, Geronilla, & Dinter, 2009). Improvements were maintained after 90 days. Church and Brooks (2014) also investigated 59 veterans with clinical levels of PTSD; findings revealed significant reductions in depression, anxiety, and the severity and range of psychological symptoms/distress, following six sessions of EFT coaching (supplementary to primary care).

Finally, Church, De Asis, and Brooks (2012) investigated 18 college students who received EFT for depression. First-year students received either EFT or no treatment; those who received EFT were found to have significantly less depression, with an average depression score in the "non-depressed range" following treatment, compared to the control group, whose members demonstrated no change in depressive symptoms.

PTSD

EFT has been extensively examined with veterans, to the point where PTSD and clinical guidelines have now been published (Church et al., 2018). In one study of veterans meeting the clinical criteria for PTSD on the PTSD Checklist–Military (PCL-M; National Center for PTSD, 2008) who were randomly assigned to EFT treatment (30 in total) or standard care (29 in total), those participants who received the 6-hour EFT intervention were found to have significant reductions in psychological distress and PTSD symptoms following EFT treatment (Church et al., 2013). All participants completed the PCL-M and the Symptom Assessment-45 (a short form of the Symptom Checklist; Davison et al., 1997; Maruish, 1999) at baseline, during the intervention after three sessions, and at the end of the intervention after six sessions. Follow-up assessments were obtained at 3 and 6 months. Following both the EFT treatment and standard care treatment, 90 percent of those who received EFT no longer met criteria for PTSD, compared to only 4 percent in a wait-list standard care group (i.e., 96 percent of the standard care group continued to meet the clinical criteria for PTSD following standard care). Three months later, 86 percent of those who received the EFT intervention remained in remission, whilst 80 percent were still in remission at six-months.

Investigation of EFT and other energy psychology techniques for PTSD symptoms in veterans and their spouses has also demonstrated a substantial symptom reduction for spouses after a one-week therapeutic retreat, with only 4 percent still within the clinical range afterwards (Church & Brooks, 2014). When EFT and other energy psychology methods were delivered in group and individual sessions to 218 male veterans and their spouses, at the end of the week, only 28 percent of the veterans remained within the clinical range. All improvements were maintained at follow-up, suggesting the therapeutic retention effects of EFT.

A systematic review assessing the evidence for 15 new or novel interventions for the treatment of PTSD (Metcalf et al., 2016) found four interventions that had moderate quality evidence from mostly small to moderate-sized randomized controlled trials. One of these was EFT. Another meta-analysis of seven studies investigating EFT in the treatment of PTSD found a very large treatment effect (weighted Cohen's d = 2.96, 95 percent CI 1.96–3.97; p < 0.001) for the studies that compared EFT to usual care or a wait list (Sebastian & Nelms, 2016). The review also found that a series of 4 to 10 EFT sessions was an efficacious treatment with no adverse effects for PTSD with a variety of populations (also discussed in the clinical guidelines now available).

Finally, a comparative review and meta-analysis have addressed the question of whether acupoint tapping is an essential ingredient in the intervention by comparing identical protocols with and without the acupoint tapping component (Church, Stapleton, Gallo, & Yang, 2018). The conditions that included the tapping protocol produced a significantly larger effect size than those with the other components but without tapping; moreover, the study indicated that the outcomes were not due to cognitive, exposure, and non-specific therapeutic elements of the protocol.

Physiological Outcomes

Recent research into EFT has focused on physiological outcomes; in particular, the stress hormone *cortisol* has been examined. In one study, 83 non-clinical adults were randomly assigned to either a single hour of EFT, a psychotherapy group receiving a supportive interview (SI), or a no-treatment (NT) group (Church, Yount, & Brooks, 2011). Salivary cortisol assays were performed immediately before and thirty minutes after the intervention. The EFT group showed clinically and statistically significant improvements in anxiety (–58.34 percent, p < .05), depression (–49.33 percent, p < .002), the overall severity of symptoms (–50.5 percent, p < .001), and symptom breadth across conditions –41.93 percent, p < .001). There were no significant changes in cortisol levels between SI (–14.25 percent, SE 2.61) and NT (–14.44 percent, SE 2.67); however, cortisol in the EFT group dropped significantly (–24.39 percent, SE 2.62), compared to cortisol in the SI and NT groups (p < .01). Furthermore, the reduced cortisol levels in the EFT group correlated with decreased severity in psychological symptoms.

Bach, Groesbeck, Stapleton, Sims, Blickheuser, and Church (2019) investigated EFT's mechanisms of action in the Central Nervous System (CNS) by measuring heart rate variability (HRV) and heart coherence (HC); the circulatory system using resting pulse rate (RPR) and blood pressure (BP); the endocrine system using cortisol; and the immune system using salivary immunoglobulin A (SigA). Participants (203) at six clinical EFT workshops were taught by a variety of instructors trained and certified in Clinical EFT, the evidence-based form of the technique. To measure physiological change, participants at one of these workshops (31) also received a comprehensive battery of medical tests. Psychological testing was similar at all six workshops, with pre- and post-measures and a follow-up during the subsequent year. Physiological measures were not assessed at follow-up, since data collection was performed via email.

At the end of treatment, significant declines were found in anxiety (–40 percent), depression (–35 percent), posttraumatic stress disorder (–32 percent), pain (–57 percent), and cravings (–74 percent). Happiness increased (+31 percent), as did salivary immunoglobulin A, an immune system biomarker (+113 percent). Significant improvements were found in Resting Heart Rate (–8 percent), cortisol (–37 percent), systolic Blood Pressure (–6 percent), and diastolic Blood Pressure (–8 percent). Positive trends were observed for Heart Rate Variability and Heart Coherence, and gains were maintained on follow-up, indicating that EFT results in positive health effects as well as increased mental well-being.

A pilot study that compared an hour-long EFT session with a placebo in four non-clinical participants (Maharaj, 2016) found differential expression in 72 genes associated with the suppression of cancer tumors, protection against ultraviolet radiation, regulation of type 2 diabetes insulin resistance, immunity from opportunistic infections, antiviral activity, synaptic connectivity between neurons, synthesis of both red and white blood cells, enhancement of male fertility, building white matter in the brain, metabolic regulation, neural plasticity, reinforcement of cell membranes, and the reduction of oxidative stress. Church, Yount, Rachlin, and Nelms (2016) also found that changes in the expression levels of six genes occurred after EFT. The genes identified in this study were involved in stress response pathways and are critical to the regulation of cellular immunity and inflammation. When this study was furthered by the investigation of microRNA levels in stored blood samples (Yount, Church, Rachlin, Blickheuser, & Cardonna, 2019), it found that remediation by EFT of psychological conditions, including depression and PTSD, was associated with a trend of reduced expression levels of microRNAs. Micro–RNAs regulate gene expression, which means that they alter the process. MicroRNAs can affect a third of all cellular mRNAs; thus, they have wide-ranging influence in biological processes, including embryonic development, cell proliferation, and metabolic homeostasis. This study, which showed that microRNAs play a role in mediating the physiological effects of EFT, demonstrated the feasibility of testing this role formally with a larger clinical population.

Session Details

Common EFT Processes

Acupoints in EFT are stimulated by tapping on them approximately seven times before moving on to the next point, using the index and middle fingers. The strength of tapping should be comfortable. Usually you only use the tapping technique when you have a problem, a feeling of distress, a feeling you do not like or want, or a belief you would like to change.

The EFT Setup Statement is always in the same format: "Even though I feel/have this … (insert your problem, thought, or feeling, perhaps a body sensation), I deeply and completely accept myself." When you say the tapping setup statement, you tap on the side of the hand, with two fingers from the other hand (see Figure 2); the Setup Statement is usually said three times before starting on the other eight EFT points, where you state the Reminder Phrase. This is always a shortened version of the Setup Statement (e.g., a single word that summarizes the client's concern, such as "this anger"). However, because the second part of the Setup Statement is about self-acceptance, clients are able to use other possible endings. For example: "Even though … I am open to the possibility of accepting myself … or I accept that I have these feelings."

Before and after each round of EFT (the 8 points outlined in Figure 1), it is imperative to ask, "How intense on a scale of 0 to 10 is the problem now? How do you know … (the intensity has gone up or down)?" Initially, the SUDS level may increase, as clients tune in to their problem (often for the first time).

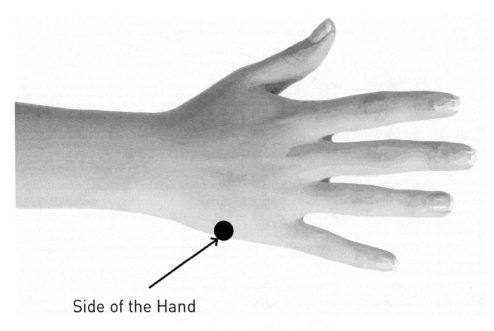

Side of the Hand

Figure 2: Side of Hand EFT Point

The Five Steps of EFT

1. Acknowledge that there is something the clients wish to change and then rate their distress/discomfort on a scale of 0–10.
2. State the problem in the setup statement while tapping on the karate chop point (3 times).
3. Tap through all 8 EFT points while saying a short reminder phrase, which is usually the main feeling or body sensation or thought.
4. Take a breath and re-rate the distress on a scale of 0–10.
5. Tap again from the eyebrow point until the rating is a zero. Only start again with the setup statement if the topic changes.

Example of a session. You tap on the side of the hand while saying, "Even though I have this headache in both temples, and I feel sick, I accept that I have this headache." Do this 3 times while tapping on the side of the hand. When you start tapping through the 8 points, you just say "this headache" or "I feel sick." When you finish one round of tapping (the 8 points), take a deep breath and rate your level of headache pain on a scale of 0–10 again. Start again at the eyebrow point and continue the rounds until you feel that the pain has subsided, or you rate it a zero or one.

The Importance of Being Specific

Tapping works best when you are very specific. Tapping on big global statements like "I always run late" may not result in much behavior change. You are better off to pick exact memories of running late and tap on what happened and how you feel when remembering it. You can also work backwards from the present time to the earliest memory, as this may be closer to the start of the behavior/pattern. You can also try and remember ever learning a behavior/pattern when you were quite young (e.g., by watching a family member), as you may have feelings/beliefs that you adopted by watching, rather than ever experiencing them yourself. You can still tap on those times when you learned from someone else.

Why do we state the negative? Newcomers to EFT may feel that tapping is affirming the problem at hand because they are focusing on it. However, the Setup Statement is stating the truth and acknowledging it, and for clients this may be the first time they have done so. Using EFT on a positive affirmation without clearing the distress first may bring only a palliative result. Research shows that the EFT technique calms the physiological response from the body, including hormones such as cortisol.

The generalization effect. After you address a few related events with EFT (e.g., the example above of running late), the process begins to generalize over all those problems. For instance, someone who has 100 traumatic memories of being abused usually finds that, after using EFT with a therapist, they all neutralize after addressing only 5–10 of the most significant ones.

Aspects

Aspects are parts of a memory or event that make up its entirety. EFT usually targets these individually. Sometimes they are emotions, body sensations, thoughts, smells, sounds, taste, and more. For example, a food craving could have many aspects:

- Smell, taste, sight, sound of the food
- Feeling in body/mouth as you eat the food
- Past memories of that food

If a client presents with a fear of flying, the aspects tapped on may include:

- The fear of turbulence and loss of control
- Aircraft or pilot failure
- Fear of terrorism
- The fear of tight spaces (claustrophobia) or heights

The Movie Technique

The Movie Technique is a staple process in EFT, as many clients have past memories or events that still impact their emotional state today. They may consciously know what these are, or, when they are tapping on a concern, a seemingly fleeting thought passes through their mind, sometimes related, sometimes unrelated. The memory that comes up may be representative of a root cause or decision moment, and the Movie Technique may be used. A summary of the major steps includes:

1. Giving the movie a title and rating the title for distress out of 10. The EFT process is used on the SUDS rating until it is low in number, as often the very title of a past memory prevents clients from being able to distance themselves from intense emotion, and this first step allows a gentle easing into the process.

2. Then clients are asked to imagine the memory on a movie screen that they are watching from their seats. They are asked to start the movie memory from a neutral point before anything distressing happened that day. Clients may choose to close their eyes.

3. They are instructed to play the movie memory slowly, stopping the movie every time a negative feeling, belief, or similar reaction comes up. They might open their eyes then and tap with the practitioner on that aspect or whatever they recalled in that moment. The usual EFT process consists of rating the distress out of 10 for that moment, and using the tapping process until the strength of the distress becomes very low in number.

4. Clients then close their eyes again, rewind the movie memory, and play it again from the neutral starting point and through the first aspects they just tapped on, in order to see if it still results in any distress. If it does, the EFT is repeated on anything new that has presented in that moment. If it does not, the clients keep playing the movie until the next increase in intensity, whereupon they tap with the practitioner on those aspects.

5. Clients continue until each rewind results in a neutral movie by the end.

Positive Tapping

Most people use EFT only when they feel a negative feeling they would like to reduce. But you can use tapping for positive statements as well. It is highly recommended that you do this only *after* you have reduced any negative feelings associated with a memory, thought, or feeling. You can then do some rounds of positive tapping to instill any new feeling or belief you would like to have. Examples might include:

"Even though I was really nervous about giving that talk next week, I now feel calm and confident" (you can use *calm and confident* as the reminder phrase).

"Even though I have had that headache for days, I now feel clear and focused" (reminder phrase is *clear and focused*).

Using "I CHOOSE" Statements

Dr. Patricia Carrington (2012) pioneered the "I choose" statements to help the beneficial changes from EFT become permanent and generalize to many aspects of life. The "I choose" phrase can be added to the end of the setup statement, as in:

"Even though I feel my mother never loved me, *I choose* to love myself anyway."

"Even though I'm nervous about giving that talk on Tuesday, *I choose* to be calm and confident."

What a Typical EFT Session Looks Like in a Clinical Setting

This section will now describe a typical EFT session. Prior to beginning a session, a practitioner may ask clients to complete a demographic and background questionnaire and/or psychological assessments.

Assessment

It is highly recommended that progress for any therapeutic or counseling approach be monitored with quality assessments. Certain psychological tests and materials are available only to those professionals who are appropriately trained to administer, score, and interpret those tests. Eligibility to purchase restricted materials is determined on the basis of training, education, and experience. Please consult your relevant training organization for more detail.

Recommended areas of assessment may include: mental health and wellbeing measures such as self-esteem, anxiety and depression, patient health surveys, trauma history inventories, pain measures, or other psychological symptom checklists. It is recommended that these be completed prior to the first session, and at repeated intervals with ongoing treatment (e.g., sessions 3, 6, 10). The use of ongoing assessments allows practitioners, therapists, and coaches to clarify and identify immediate areas of concern, and prioritize issues to work on. Assessment results can also be used to help clients understand their symptoms, and can assist with treatment evaluation and gaining insight into issues, fears, or concerns that clients may not be comfortable expressing in face-to-face sessions.

Session Overview

A typical session will be guided by what clients wish to use the EFT for (assuming this is the reason they have presented). The practitioner would ask them to tune into the problem and rate their current level of distress (SUDS rating) out of 10. The Setup Statement would be used to frame the problem, and then the Reminder Phrase would be used as the practitioner and clients tap through the eight points (see Figure 1). Please note that clients tap on their own body while the practitioner taps alongside them. It is not typical in Clinical EFT for the practitioner to tap directly on the clients, but rather encourage them to take responsibility for their own ability to regulate their emotions. In rare cases (e.g., extreme distress), and only with client permission, the practitioner may tap directly on the clients until they are able to regain control of their distress and tap on themselves (dependent on state/country practice regulations/laws).

Session example with insomnia. Evie had not slept well ever since her son had died four years before. When she sought support from an EFT practitioner, her pre-assessment revealed that she took hours to fall asleep every night, rarely succeeding before 2:00 a.m.; if she did fall asleep prior to that, she woke at 3:00 a.m., unable to return to sleep. The first session of EFT focused on her feelings of being frustrated about not sleeping well, and being easily awakened by the slightest sound. The tapping process included:

- Setup Statement: "Even though I am so frustrated with myself that last night I couldn't go to sleep easily, I deeply and completely accept myself."
- SUDS Rating: 10/10 for being frustrated
- Reminder Phrase: "so frustrated"

After five rounds of tapping, Evie's frustration was reduced to a 4 out of 10. and she started to cry. The memories that began to come to mind at this point were of the morning she found her son had died in his sleep (Sudden Infant Death Syndrome). The feelings she had in that moment, which were still very much present in her at that session, were grief, intense shock, and, later, a sense of personal blame that she had not awakened to any noise or checked on him in the middle of the night. Each of these was systematically worked through with the EFT process, in particular using the Movie Technique. The next three EFT sessions spread over three weeks addressed her self-blame, along with childhood memories where she had the same feeling (e.g., her parents divorced when she was four and she still blamed herself for their decision). After a month of EFT sessions

Evie reported she was falling asleep easily and not waking in the night. She felt refreshed and rested for the first time in four years.

Conclusion

A benefit often attributed to EFT is its ability to be used outside clinical settings as a safe and reliable self-help method for reducing distress. Another outstanding advantage of using EFT for a wide range of psychological and physical symptoms is its brevity and precision in achieving change very quickly. We are now also realizing the profound physiological changes that occur with this technique, as growing evidence is establishing EFT as safe and effective with a variety of populations and conditions.

Disclaimer

Emotional Freedom Techniques (EFT) is still considered experimental in nature, although it is gaining in scientific support. All information, books, workshops, and trainings are intended to promote awareness of the benefits of learning and applying EFT; however, the general public must take full responsibility for their use of it. This material is for your general knowledge only and is not a substitute for traditional medical attention, counseling, therapy, or advice from a qualified healthcare professional. Neither EFT nor the information here is intended to be used to diagnose, treat, cure, or prevent any disease or disorder. Please note that, if you begin tapping and find yourself overwhelmed, distressed, or becoming aware of previously forgotten memories, you may need to seek the professional help of a trained and experienced EFT practitioner. See www.petastapleton.com or www.eftuniverse.com for a list of practitioners.

A lack of results or progress may mean that you need professional assistance. If you have any concern regarding your health or mental state, it is recommended that you seek out advice or treatment from a qualified, licensed healthcare professional. Before making any dietary changes or discontinuing, reducing, or increasing prescription medications, it is recommended that you consult with a doctor, pharmacist, or other qualified medical or health professional first.

Acknowledgments

The author wishes truly to extend much love to Craig Weiner, Kate Helder, and Alina Frank for their feedback on this essay.

REFERENCES

Andrade, J., & Feinstein, D. (2004). Preliminary report of the first large-scale study of energy psychology. *Energy psychology interactive: Rapid interventions for lasting change.* Ashland, OR: Innersource.

Bach, D., Groesbeck, G., Stapleton, P., Sims, R., Blickheuser, K., & Church, D. (2019). Clinical EFT (Emotional Freedom Techniques) improves multiple physiological markers of health. *Journal of Evidence-Based Integrative Medicine, 24,* 1–12.

Baker, A.H., & Siegel, L.S. (2010). Emotional Freedom Techniques (EFT) reduce intense fears: A partial replication and extension of Wells et al. (2003). *Energy Psychology: Theory, Research, and Treatment, 2,* 13–30.

Baker, B.S., & Hoffman, C.J. (2014). Emotional Freedom Techniques (EFT) to reduce the side effects associated with tamoxifen and aromatase inhibitor use in women with breast cancer: A service evaluation. *European Journal of Integrative Medicine, 7*(2), 136–142.

Benor, D.J., Ledger, K., Toussaint, L., Hett, G., & Zaccaro, D. (2009). Pilot study of Emotional Freedom Techniques (EFT), Wholistic Hybrid derived from EMDR and EFT (WHEE) and Cognitive Behavioral Therapy (CBT) for treatment of test anxiety in university students. *Explore, 5*(6), 338–340.

Boath, E., Stewart, A., & Carryer, A. (2013). Is Emotional Freedom Techniques (EFT) generalizable? Comparing effects in sport science students versus complementary therapy students. *Energy Psychology Journal: Theory, Research, and Treatment, 5,* 29–34.

Bougea, A., Spandideas, N., Alexopoulos, E., Thomaides, T., Chrousos, G.P., & Darviri, C. (2013). Effect of the Emotional Freedom Techniques on perceived stress, quality of life, and cortisol salivary levels in tension-type headache sufferers: A randomized controlled trial. *Explore, 9,* 91–99.

Brattberg, G. (2008). Self-administered EFT (Emotional Freedom Techniques) in individuals with fibromyalgia: A randomized trial. *Integrative Medicine: A Clinician's Journal, 7,* 30–35.

Burk, L. (2010). Single session EFT (Emotional Freedom Techniques) for stress-related symptoms after motor vehicle accidents. *Energy Psychology: Theory, Research, and Treatment, 2,* 65–72.

Callahan, R., & Trubo, R. (2002). *Tapping the healer within: Using thought-field therapy to instantly conquer your fears, anxieties, and emotional distress.* New York, NY: McGraw-Hill Education.

Carrington, P. (2012). *EFT choices manual.* Retrieved from https://patcarrington.com/eft-choices-manual/

Chatwin, H., Stapleton, P.B., Porter, B., Devine, S., & Sheldon, T. (2016). The effectiveness of cognitive-behavioral therapy and emotional freedom techniques in reducing depression and anxiety among adults: A pilot study. *Integrative Medicine, 15*(2), 27–34.

Church, D. (2008, Oct. 24). *The effect of EFT (Emotional Freedom Techniques) on psychological symptoms: A limited replication.* Presented at Science and Consciousness, the Tenth Annual Energy Psychology Conference, Toronto, Canada.

Church, D. (2009a). The treatment of combat trauma in veterans using EFT (Emotional Freedom Techniques): A pilot protocol. *Traumatology, 15,* 55–65.

Church, D. (2009b). The effect of EFT (Emotional Freedom Techniques) on athletic performance: A randomized controlled blind trial. *The Open Sports Sciences Journal, 2,* 94–99.

Church, D. (2013). *The EFT manual* (3rd ed.). Santa Rosa, CA: Energy Psychology Press.

Church, D., & Brooks, A. J. (2010). The effect of a brief EFT (Emotional Freedom Techniques) self-intervention on anxiety, depression, pain and cravings in healthcare workers. *Integrative Medicine: A Clinician's Journal, 9,* 40–44.

Church, D., & Brooks, A. J. (2013). The effect of EFT (Emotional Freedom Techniques) on psychological symptoms in addiction treatment: A pilot study. *International Journal of Scientific Research and Reports, 2*(1), 315–323.

Church, D., & Brooks, A.J. (2014). CAM and energy psychology techniques remediate PTSD symptoms in veterans and spouses. *Explore: The Journal of Science and Healing, 10,* 24–33.

Church, D., De Asis, M.A., & Brooks, A.J. (2012). Brief group intervention using Emotional Freedom Techniques for depression in college students: A randomized controlled trial. *Depression Research and Treatment,* 1–7. Doi: 10.1155/2012/257172

Church, D., & Downs, D. (2012). Sports confidence and critical incident intensity after a brief application of Emotional Freedom Techniques: A pilot study. *The Sport Journal, 15.* Available from https://thesportjournal.org/article/sports-confidence-and-critical-incident-intensity-after-a-brief-application-of-emotional-freedom-techniques-a-pilot-study/

Church, D., Geronilla, L., & Dinter, I. (2009). Psychological symptom change in veterans after six sessions of Emotional Freedom Techniques (EFT): An observational study. *International Journal of Healing and Caring, 9*(1), 1–13.

Church, D., Hawk, C., Brooks, A., Toukolehto, O., Wren, M., Dinter, I., & Stein, P. (2013). Psychological trauma symptom improvement in veterans using EFT (Emotional Freedom Techniques): A randomized controlled trial. *Journal of Nervous and Mental Disease, 201,* 153–160.

Church, D., & Nelms, J. (2016). Pain, range of motion, and psychological symptoms in a population with frozen shoulder: A randomized controlled dismantling study of clinical EFT (Emotional Freedom Techniques). *Archives of Scientific Psychology, 4*(1), 38–48.

Church, D., Piña, O., Reategui, C., & Brooks, A. (2011). Single session reduction of the intensity of traumatic memories in abused adolescents after EFT: A randomized controlled pilot study. *Traumatology, 18*(3), 73–79.

Church, D., Stapleton, P., Gallo, F., & Yang, A. (2018). Is acupressure an active or inert ingredient in Emotional Freedom Techniques (EFT)? A meta-analysis of component studies. *Journal of Nervous and Mental Disease, 206*(10), 783–793.

Church, D., Stapleton, P., Mollon, P., Feinstein, D., Boath, E., Mackay, D., & Sims, R. (2018). Guidelines for the treatment of PTSD using clinical EFT (Emotional Freedom Techniques). *Healthcare, 6*(4), 146.

Church, D., Stern, S., Boath, E., Stewart, A., Feinstein, D., & Clond, M. (2017). Emotional Freedom Techniques (EFT) to treat PTSD in veterans: A review of the evidence, survey of practitioners, and proposed clinical guidelines. *The Permanente Journal, 21,* 16–100.

Church, D., Yount, G., & Brooks, A. (2011). The effect of Emotional Freedom Techniques (EFT) on stress biochemistry: A randomized controlled trial. *Journal of Nervous and Mental Disease, 200,* 891–896.

Church, D., Yount, G., Rachlin, K., Fox, L., & Nelms, J. (2016). Epigenetic effects of PTSD remediation in veterans using clinical EFT (Emotional Freedom Techniques): A randomized controlled trial. *American Journal of Health Promotion, 32*(1), 112–122.

Clond, M. (2016). Emotional Freedom Techniques for anxiety: A systematic review with meta-analysis. *Journal of Nervous and Mental Disease, 204*(5), 388–395.

Craig, G., & Fowlie, A. (1995). *Emotional Freedom Techniques: The manual.* Sea Ranch, CA: Authors.

Davison, M.L., Bershadsky, B., Bieber, J., Silversmith, D., Maruish, M.E., & Kane, R.L. (1997). Development of a brief, multidimensional, self-report instrument for treatment outcomes assessment in psychiatric settings: Preliminary findings. *Assessment, 4,* 259–275.

Feinstein, D. (2012). Acupoint stimulation in treating psychological disorders: Evidence of efficacy. *Review of General Psychology, 16,* 364–380.

Gaesser, A.H., & Orv, C.K. (2016). A randomized controlled comparison of Emotional Freedom Techniques and Cognitive-Behavioral Therapy to reduce adolescent anxiety: A pilot study. *Journal of Alternative Complementary Medicine, 23*(2), 102–108.

Geronilla, L., McWilliams, M., & Clond, M. (2014, April 17). EFT (Emotional Freedom Techniques) remediates PTSD and psychological symptoms in veterans: A randomized controlled replication trial. Presented at the Grand Rounds, Fort Hood, Killeen, TX.

Gurret, J. M., Caufour, C., Palmer-Hoffman, J., & Church, D. (2012). Post-earthquake rehabilitation of clinical PTSD in Haitian seminarians. *Energy Psychology: Theory, Research, and Treatment, 4,* 33–40.

Hartung, J., & Stein, P. (2012). Telephone delivery of EFT (Emotional Freedom Techniques) remediates PTSD symptoms in veterans. *Energy Psychology Journal, 4,* 33–40.

Hodge, P.M., & Jurgens, C.Y. (2011). Psychological and physiological symptoms of psoriasis after group EFT (Emotional Freedom Techniques) treatment: A pilot study. *Energy Psychology Journal, 3,* 13–24.

Jain, S., & Rubino, A. (2012). The effectiveness of Emotional Freedom Techniques (EFT) for optimal test performance: A randomized controlled trial. *Energy Psychology: Theory, Research, & Treatment, 4,* 13–24.

Jones, S., Thornton, J., & Andrews, H. (2011). Efficacy of EFT in reducing public speaking anxiety: A randomized controlled trial. *Energy Psychology: Theory, Research, Treatment, 3*(1), 19–32.

Karatzias, T., Power, K., Brown, K., McGoldrick, T., Begum, M., Young, J., Loughran, P., Chouliara, Z., & Adams, S. (2011). A controlled comparison of the effectiveness and efficiency of two psychological therapies for Posttraumatic Stress Disorder: Eye movement desensitization and reprocessing vs. Emotional Freedom Techniques. *Journal of Nervous and Mental Disease, 199,* 372–378.

Kober, A., Scheck, T., Greher, M., Lieba, F., Fleischhackl, R., Fleischhackl, S., Randunsky, F., & Hoerauf, K. (2002). Pre-hospital analgesia with acupressure in victims of minor trauma: A prospective, randomized, double-blinded trial. *Anesthesia and Analgesia, 95,* 723–727.

Lee, J.W., Chung, SY., & Kim, J.W. (2015). A comparison of emotional freedom techniques-insomnia (EFT-I) and sleep hygiene education (SHE) for insomnia in a geriatric population: A randomized controlled trial. *Journal of Energy Psychology; Theory, Research and Treatment, 7*(1), 22–29,

Llewellyn-Edwards, T., & Llewellyn-Edwards, M. (2012). The effect of EFT (Emotional Freedom Techniques) on soccer performance. *Fidelity: Journal for the National Council of Psychotherapy, 47,* 14–19.

Lubin, H., & Schneider, T. (2009). Change is possible: EFT (Emotional Freedom Techniques) with life-sentence and veteran prisoners at San Quentin State Prison. *Energy Psychology: Theory, Research, and Treatment, 1,* 83–88.

McCallion, F. (2012). Emotional Freedom Techniques for dyslexia: A case study. *Energy Psychology Journal, 4*(2), 35.

Maharaj, M.E. (2016). Differential gene expression after Emotional Freedom Techniques (EFT) treatment: A novel pilot protocol for salivary mRNA assessment. *Energy Psychology: Theory, Research, and Treatment, 8*(1), 17–32.

Maruish, M.E. (1999). Symptom Assessment-45 Questionnaire (SA-45). In M.E. Maruish (Ed.), *The use of psychological testing, treatment planning and outcomes assessment* (2nd ed.) (pp. 725–757). Mahwah, NJ: Erlbaum.

Metcalf, O., Varker, T., Forbes, D., Phelps, A., Dell, L., DiBattista, A., & O'Donnell, M. (2016). Efficacy of fifteen emerging interventions for the treatment of Posttraumatic Stress Disorder: A systematic review. *Journal of Traumatic Stress, 29*(1), 88–92.

Moritz, S., Aravena, S. C., Guczka, S., Schilling, L., Eichenberg, C., Raubart G., Seebeck, A., & Jelinek, L. (2011). Knock and it will be opened to you? An examination of meridian-tapping in Obsessive Compulsive Disorder (OCD). *Journal of Behaviour Therapy & Experimental Psychiatry, 42,* 81–88.

National Center for PTSD. (2008). PTSD Checklist. Retrieved from www.ncptsd.va.gov/ncmain/ncdocs/assmnts/ptsd_checklist_pcl.html

Nelms, J., & Castel, L. (2016). A systematic review and meta-analysis of randomized and non-randomized trials of clinical Emotional Freedom Techniques (EFT) for the treatment of depression. *Explore:The Journal of Science and Healing, 12*(6), 416–426.

Ortner, N., Palmer-Hoffman J., & Clond, M. (2014). Effects of Emotional Freedom Techniques (EFT) on the reduction of chronic pain in adults: A pilot study. *Energy Psychology: Theory, Research, and Treatment,* 6(2), 14–21

Palmer-Hoffman, J., & Brooks, A. (2011). Psychological symptom change after group application of Emotional Freedom Techniques. *Energy Psychology: Theory, Research, and Treatment, 3*(1), 57–72.

Rotheram, M., Maynard, I., Thomas, O., Bawden, M., & Francis, L. (2012). Preliminary evidence for the treatment of Type 1 'Yips': The efficacy of the Emotional Freedom Techniques. *The Sports Psychologist, 26,* 551–570.

Rowe, J. (2005). The effects of EFT on long-term psychological symptoms. *Counseling and Clinical Psychology Journal, 2,* 104.

Salas, M.M., Brooks, A.J., & Rowe, J.E. (2011). The immediate effect of a brief energy psychology intervention (Emotional Freedom Techniques) on specific phobias: A pilot study. *Explore: The Journal of Science and Healing, 7*(3), 155–161.

Sebastian, B., & Nelms, J. (2016). The effectiveness of Emotional Freedom Techniques in the treatment of Post-Traumatic Stress Disorder: A meta-analysis. *Explore: The Journal of Science and Healing, 13*(1), 16–25.

Sezgin, N., Ozcan, B., & Church, D. (2009). The effect of two psychophysiological techniques (Progressive Muscular Relaxation and Emotional Freedom Techniques) on test anxiety in high school students: A randomized blind controlled study. *International Journal of Healing and Caring, 9*(1), 23–29.

Stapleton, P., Bannatyne, A., Porter, B., Urzi, K.C., & Sheldon, T. (2016a). Food for thought: A randomised controlled trial of Emotional Freedom Techniques and Cognitive Behavioural Therapy in the treatment of food cravings. *Applied Psychology: Health and Well-Being, 8*(2), 232–257.

Stapleton, P.B., Chatwin, H., William, M., Hutton, A., Pain, A., Porter, B., & Sheldon, T. (2016b). A randomized clinical pilot trial: Do Emotional Freedom Techniques impact eating habits in 14 to 15 year olds, as well as self-esteem, self-compassion, and psychological distress? *Explore: The Journal of Science and Healing, 12*(2), 113–122.

Stapleton, P.B., Chatwin, H., Sheppard, L., & McSwan, J. (2016c). The lived experience of chronic pain and the impact of brief Emotional Freedom Techniques (EFT) group therapy on coping. *Energy Psychology: Research and Practice, 8*(2), 1–16.

Stapleton, P.B., Church, D., Sheldon, T., Porter, B., & Carlopio, C. (2013). Depression symptoms improve after successful weight loss with Emotional Freedom Techniques. *ISRN Psychiatry, 1,* 1–7.

Stapleton, P.B., Devine, S., Chatwin, H., Porter, B., & Sheldon, T. (2014). A feasibility study: Emotional Freedom Techniques for depression in adults. *Current Research in Psychology, 5*(1), 19–33.

Stapleton, P.B., Mackay, E., Chatwin, H., Murphy, D., Porter, B., Thibault, S., Sheldon, T., & Pidgeon, A. (2017). Effectiveness of a school-based Emotional Freedom Techniques intervention for promoting student well-being. *Adolescent Psychiatry, 7*(2), 112–126.

Stapleton, P.B., Sheldon, T., Porter, B., & Whitty, J. (2011). A randomized clinical trial of a meridian-based intervention for food cravings with six-month follow-up. *Behavior Change, 28*(1), 1–16.

Stapleton, P.B., Sheldon, T., & Porter, B. (2012a). Practical application of Emotional Freedom Techniques for food cravings. *International Journal of Healing and Caring, 12*(3), 1–9.

Stapleton, P.B., Sheldon, T., & Porter, B. (2012b). Clinical benefits of Emotional Freedom Techniques on food cravings at 12-months follow-up: A randomized controlled trial. *Energy Psychology: Theory, Research, and Treatment, 4*(1), 1–12.

Stein, P., & Brooks, A. (2011). Efficacy of EFT provided by coaches versus licensed therapists in veterans with PTSD. *Energy Psychology Journal: Theory, Research, & Treatment, 3*(1), 11–18.

Stewart, A., Boath, E., Carryer, A., Walton, I., & Hill, L. (2011). Can Emotional Freedom Techniques (EFT) be effective in the treatment of emotional conditions? Results of a service evaluation in Sandwell. *Journal of Psychological Therapies in Primary Care, 2,* 71–84.

Swingle, P. (2010, May). Emotional Freedom Techniques (EFT) as an effective adjunctive treatment in the neurotherapeutic treatment of seizure disorders. *Energy Psychology: Theory, Research, and Treatment, 2*(1), 29–38.

Swingle, P., Pulos, L., & Swingle, M.K. (2005). Neurophysiological indicators of EFT treatment of post traumatic stress. *Journal of Subtle Energies and Energy Medicine, 15,* 75–86.

Temple, G., & Mollon, P. (2011). Reducing anxiety in dental patients using EFT: A pilot study. *Energy Psychology: Theory, Research, and Treatment, 3*(2), 53–56.

Wells, S., Polglase, K., Andrews, H.B., Carrington, P., & Baker, A.H. (2003). Evaluation of a meridian-based intervention, Emotional Freedom Techniques (EFT), for reducing specific phobias of small animals. *Journal of Clinical Psychology, 59,* 943–966.

Wolpe, J. (1973). *The practice of behavior therapy* (2nd ed.). New York, NY: Pergamon Press.

Yount, G., Church, D., Rachlin, K., Blickheuser, K., & Cardonna, I. (2019). Do noncoding RNAs mediate the efficacy of energy psychology? *Global Advances in Health and Medicine, 8.* Doi: 10.1177/2164956119832500

Zhang, Y., Feng, B., Xie, J., Xu, F.X., & Chen, J. (2011). Clinical study on treatment of the earthquake-caused Post-Traumatic Stress Disorder by Cognitive-Behavior Therapy and acupoint stimulation. *Journal of Traditional Chinese Medicine, 1,* 60–63.

Re-Enter and Re-Imagine

A Client-Led Dreamworking Method

Christopher Sowton

Today, in 2018, I rejoice to see the multitude of effective and fascinating dream-working methods in use around the world. I would like to contribute my own method to this list, a method that is distinguished by its brevity and its orientation towards change rather than meaning. It is a method that health care practitioners can use within their already existing modes of treatment, without extensive re-schooling or changing course. Because this method involves helping a client re-enter a dream and imagine new possible outcomes, I have chosen a purely descriptive name for it—*Re-enter and Re-imagine* (RERI). This method has the following characteristics:

- *It is flexible*; it can be readily integrated into an already established mental health practice and can provide new insights that can then be utilized within the therapeutic treatment plan already in place.
- *It is brief*, consistently achieving useful results within 30 minutes or less.
- *It is non-interpretive*, freeing the practitioner from any expectation of producing an analysis of the dream.
- *It is experiential*; the method involves re-entering the dreamscape, re-experiencing the conditions and emotions of the dream, then changing the outcome from within. There is little or no time spent considering a dream from the "outside" and pondering what it might mean. The meaning component is not forced, yet a sense of meaning arises almost spontaneously and naturally during or shortly after the experiential work.
- *It is client-led*; the practitioner sets the stage for re-entering the dream and facilitates the process as it unfolds, but the new choices and outcomes are generated as much as possible by the dreamer/client.

I have been asked whether this method could be described as "simple." I have trouble answering that. On the one hand, it could be argued that nothing to do with dreams is really simple; dreams exhibit an almost infinite variety of content, a huge range and intensity of feeling, and a sense of deep inner intelligence that often feels almost divine. On the other hand, the method itself is, indeed, very simple. It has certain steps that unfold in a particular order, and because there is no burden to figure out what the dream "means," no great interpretive sophistication is required.

Dreamwork Methods That Involve Re-Entering a Dream and Changing the Outcome

If we were to categorize dreamwork methods, one category would include methods that involve re-entering a dream and changing the outcome. This category would include the RERI method, Imagery Rehearsal Therapy (IRT) developed by Joseph Neidhardt and Barry Krakow (Kellner, Neidhardt, Krakow, & Pathak, 1992),Tallulah Lyon's use of guided imagery for transforming nightmares (Lyons, 2016), the Nightmare Deconstruction and Reprocessing (NDR) developed by Patricia Spangler (Spangler & Hill, 2016), the Lucid Storytelling Technique taught by Clare Johnson (Johnson & Campbell, 2016a), Fariba Bogzaran's protocol for working with sleep paralysis (Krippner, Bogzaran, & DeCarvalho, 2002), the dream re-entry component of Robert Moss's Active Dreaming (Moss, 2011), and many others. These methods also bear an important general resemblance to many widespread practices that recruit the use of the imagination to generate and explore new possibilities in the service of healing and personal growth—these would include Jungian Active Imagination (Jung & Chodorow, 1997), Guided Imagery (Naparstek, 1994), Shamanic Journeying (Ingerman, 2004), and Soul Retrieval (Ingerman, 1991), to name a few. The common element in all these practices is that a deliberate attempt can be made to seek a solution to a problem using the creative power of the human imagination as a primary resource. Practitioners of these techniques do not *necessarily* seek to bring about a specific change; rather, they may be using the techniques for exploration, information gathering, or simply to have a fuller experience, but all these techniques *can* be applied in a change-oriented way.

Among the aforementioned techniques, Imagery Rehearsal Therapy (IRT) is the most widely studied and used within psychology and medicine. Its method is, in essence, very simple and straightforward: dreamers are asked to select a nightmare and write it down, then imagine changing it in any way they wish. In this way, a "new" dream is created with a better and less stressful outcome. This newly imagined dream is re-visited in the imagination (that is, rehearsed) over several days and weeks. Often the original disturbing nightmare will start to shift, reducing in frequency and intensity (Krippner, 2016).

In her dream groups and workshops for cancer patients Tallulah Lyons has worked extensively with the nightmares associated with severe illness (Lyons, 2016). Once the patient has re-entered the frightening dream, Lyons often invites him or her to imagine the presence of new figures:

> Invite a supportive companion or companions … now that your special animal/person/wizard/angel is here, ask him or her to guide you from the scary dream to a new dream where you feel good with yourself and with whatever is happening …you are totally safe … notice that the dream is changing … some things are becoming different … new things are happening and you are feeling and acting in a new way. When you're ready to come back, promise yourself you'll come back and reimagine this new dream … over and over again [Lyons, 2016, p. 55].

The invitation to summon helpers and allies is a core dreamworking technique, one that I use very frequently in my sessions. Very often nightmare sufferers cannot imagine anything but suffering alone, as they did in the original dream. They might never, on their own, conceive of the possibility that they could put out a call for help; thus, it is often the dreamworker's job to introduce this possibility. In cases where facilitative and guiding suggestions are needed in re-entry dreamwork, the "summoning of allies" would be one of the first things on the checklist.

Patricia Spangler has developed an offshoot of Clara Hill's Cognitive-Experiential Dream Model (CEDM), designed especially to work with post-traumatic nightmares; the technique is called Nightmare Deconstruction and Processing (NDR) (Spangler & Hill, 2016). Stage 3 of this technique is *rescripting*:

> The goal is to help dreamers gain mastery over the nightmare by rescripting the images related to the trauma, so that the emotions are less distressing, thus facilitating reconsolidation of trauma-related emotion.... After several sessions, once dreamers have gained some mastery over the nightmares, work can begin in making changes to their waking life [Spangler & Hill, 2015, p. 140].

Going in this order—changing the dream first, and only later translating these changes into waking life changes—is something that I have found to be clinically very useful. If imaginal work is done first, actualized changes tend to happen more readily, and often spontaneously.

Clare Johnson has found that teaching children to develop lucid dreaming abilities is one of the most effective ways to deal with recurring nightmares (Johnson & Campbell, 2016b); however, she adds:

> For children who do not immediately master the art of lucid dreaming, my Lucid Storytelling Technique allows a similar transformative process to take place in the waking state. When a child is helped to convert his nightmare into a waking version of a lucid dream, he can safely explore options for changing the dream story into something that makes him feel not terrified but empowered.... The dreaming mind has already created the best possible metaphors for the child's feelings about his situation. Stay within the metaphors by continuing to speak in the language of the dream, and gently help the child to see the dream as something that can be changed in any way they want to change it [Johnson & Campbell, 2016b, pp. 38–39].

Fariba Bogzaran's five-step protocol for working with sleep paralysis aims for a similar goal—to evolve a repetitive and frightening experience into something less troubling. Sleep paralysis, the phenomenon in which subjects believe that they are fully awake yet are unable to make any sound or movement, is usually repetitive, typically accompanied by great fear and distress. One aspect of Bogzaran's method involves working on the issue while clients are awake or semi-awake: "You can practice dream re-entry or observe the creation of a new dream. You might even decide to fully awaken" (Krippner, Bogzaran, & DeCarvalho, p. 50).

Robert Moss (2011) describes and teaches many practices that can help people engage their own dream life more fully and actively, one of which is dream re-entry:

> A simple and natural way to become a conscious dreamer is to use a remembered dream as the portal for a journey.... Why would you want to do such a thing? ... The best way to understand a dream is to recover more of the experience of the dream. Dreams are experiences, not texts, and a dream experience fully remembered is its own interpretation [Moss, 2011, p. 54–55].

In my work I have also found that this critical shift in emphasis—from standing *outside* the dream wondering what it might mean to going back *inside* the dream, experiencing it and working with it internally—has been exciting and rewarding. It brings a feeling of aliveness to the work that makes it much more engaging, and also much easier to do. It is often difficult to wean ourselves away from the interpretive mindset, however, as the first instinct for many of us when a dream appears is to ask: "What does it mean?" I encourage people to change this question to: "What does it want me to do?" whenever they catch themselves using the M word. If we engage the dream in some active way, the meaning component will usually dawn on us, unforced and often more authentically.

Helplessness versus Mastery

Practitioners of IRT have postulated that the central therapeutic factor is the increased sense of *mastery* over the nightmare, or within the nightmare (Krakow et al., 2001). This has certainly been my experience as well. Many dreams have a pervasive sense of helplessness or lack of agency; something unpleasant is happening, and there is nothing that can be done about it. The drama *happens to* the dreamer and is simply endured. As the dreamer's sense of egoic agency comes back online upon waking he or she often feels bewilderment—"Why on earth did I let that happen?" The sense of non-agency can be accompanied by emotions ranging anywhere from mild frustration to abject terror.

In most dreaming, this quality of non-agency and lack of critical awareness is the norm. An important exception is *lucid dreaming,* in which the dreamers become aware that they are in a dream, gain a sense of agency, and can subsequently influence the events of the dream, at least to some degree. Nightmare sufferers often take advantage of becoming lucid to escape a distressing dream situation, most commonly by forcing themselves to wake up. Thus it could be said that dreamwork techniques that involve re-entering and changing the dream bear an important resemblance to lucid dreaming, the key difference being that, in the former case, the changing of the dream is done while awake, not during sleep.

My experience has confirmed that the practice of re-entering a dream and changing the outcome can be effectively used with many types of dreams, not only the nightmares associated with trauma, PTSD, and sleep paralysis. In essence, we are enrolling the creative use of the imagination (a faculty that we all possess) to change something that is causing distress and shift it in a positive direction. This principle can be widely applied to most people and most dreams. However, it is particularly well-suited for certain types of dreams, namely, those that are tormenting, dissatisfying, or incomplete.

What Types of Dreams Should Be Selected to Work On?

There are some dreams that we would never wish to change. Some dreams bring a sense of beauty and wonder that asks only to be appreciated and held in awareness. Some dreams have already worked their magic, having wrought a change that does not require any further supportive efforts on our part. Some dreams are like messages that seem to call for careful attention and consideration. For these dreams, attempting to understand their meaning may be the most fruitful approach. Another large category of dream motifs is one that I call *ego check motifs,* because they provide feedback to our ego about our problematic behaviors and mindsets. We would not wish to change these dreams (or parts of dreams), since we would be over-riding their mirroring function and losing the corrective and compensatory benefit they offer us. With such dream motifs our best response is to try to accept the feedback and try it on, as uncomfortable as that may feel.

The dream content analysis research of Calvin Hall and Robert Van de Castle shows that "more dreams contain aggression than friendliness, failure rather than success, and misfortune rather than good fortune … it could be said that two thirds of dreams are unpleasant in nature" (Van de Castle, 1994, p. 298). Many dreams with unpleasant content are pointing to a critical failure of the imagination and of the adaptive function. The dreamer's imagination cannot generate a creative response to an important problem, either dreaming or awake. The dream offers a depiction of the problem, thus providing an accurate (usually metaphorical) setting in which to seek a new solution. We could say that the dream sets the stage, giving the imagination a chance to re-write a distressing or frustrating scene of the play. This invitation to try a re-write is one of the great benefits of having dreams and of working with them.

For me, selecting a dream to work on with the RERI method is usually guided by the question: *Can we consider this dream from the perspective that it is asking for something? If so, what might that be?* By taking this position, we are moving onto the cusp of generating something new. We are not focusing on what the dream might mean; rather, we are considering what changes it could set in motion. Any dream that has a sense of repetitiveness ("Oh, no! I just had my old college dream again!") is a good candidate for dreamwork. Something is stuck and re-playing itself. In most cases, such recurring anxious dreams are not bringing forth important information or useful warnings; they are arising from old brain loops that display a Groundhog Day–like quality of tenacious entrapment. They are begging for something to be done, yet, sadly, most people endure such dreams for a lifetime without ever considering that there could be a way out.

Any frightening dream is also a good candidate for re-entry work. I have met people who have endured decades of night-time terror, never once taking a pro-active position in relation to their dream tormentors, never imagining that such a stance could even be possible. It is, indeed, possible, in almost all cases, but it does require some imaginal work to be done. Similarly, any dream that engenders a sense of frustration, conflict, under-achievement, avoidance, disappointment, guilt, shame, or incompletion can be readily worked with. All such dreams can be seen to hold the question: "What if this could turn out differently? What then?" In short—any dream depicting a scene that is problematic in some way could lend itself to the use of the RERI technique. That is a lot of dreams!

As a practitioner, my clinical experience has taught me to watch out for the following situations, all of which particularly lend themselves to the RERI approach or a similar dreamworking method involving re-entry and changing of outcome:

1. Clients are terrorized and intimidated by a certain dream or dreams.
2. Clients are alienated from their dream life because of repeating negative content.
3. Clients repeatedly dream of an old scenario or an old emotional state that is no longer relevant to their waking life and brings forth no new information.
4. Clients present a dream or dreams highlighting an obstacle or challenge, with a sense of failure or frustration at not being able to overcome it.
5. Clients present a dream or dreams that refer to a troubling incompletion.

In all these cases it is, in my view, legitimate and valuable to attempt to change the dream story and create something new.

Steps of the Re-enter and Re-imagine Method

First, here are the steps, in summary:

1. Clients tell the dream.
2. Practitioners ask clarifying questions until they feel that a clear and complete account of the dream has been presented.
3. Practitioners propose re-entering the dream and considering possible new outcomes.
4. Clients and practitioners select a work point (or point of re-entry).
5. The practitioners invite the clients to re-enter the dream at that point, freeze the action, and bring in a sense of awareness and agency.
6. Practitioners ask the clients what they would like to do at this point.
7. The clients, using visual and feeling imagination, try out one or more new outcomes. The practitioners facilitate, if required, making specific suggestions only if the clients are stuck and cannot generate their own.
8. Once the clients have imagined a new outcome that feels good, the practitioners ask them to imagine the whole sequence, starting from the work point and moving through the newly generated scenes.
9. The practitioners invite the clients to come out of the dreamscape.
10. The practitioners ask if the clients have any spontaneous insight into the meaning of the dream, or how it might connect to their waking life. If so, these insights are discussed.
11. The practitioners invite the clients to rehearse the new dream sequence a few more times in the upcoming days or weeks.

First, the client tells the dream. The practitioner then takes a few minutes to ask questions that are intended only to get a full and clear account of the dream. I recommend using the *SEFA* acronym at this stage—*S for Setting* (the setting where the dreams takes place, which is often critical because it is a representation of where the dreamer is stuck); *E for Events* (the events and action that take place in the dream); *F for Feelings* (the feelings and emotions that the dreamer experiences in the dream, which are often left out of the dream report); and *A for Associations* (the dreamer's associations for each of the key figures that appear in the dream). For further information on how to elicit a clear, workable account of a dream, see Chapter 11 of the current author's book, *Dreamworking* (Sowton, 2017).

Next, both practitioner and client consider the dream from the perspective that it might be asking for change. To establish this perspective and obtain informed consent to work with the dream in this way, the practitioner might say something like: *Shall we go back into this dream and see what might happen?* If, for any reason, the client does not wish to re-enter the dream that wish must be respected; although, of course, the matter may be discussed, and important material may subsequently emerge.

The next step is to choose a re-entry point (or "work point," as I usually call it in session). The choice of the work point is important, and not always obvious; the best work point might occur anywhere in the chronological sequence of the dream. It is often near the beginning, but just as often right at the end. Here are my two main guidelines for choosing a good work point:

Choose a point with a heightened sense of drama. One kind of work point typically occurs near the beginning of a dream; it has energy, dynamism, and a sense of implicit choice. To use a classic example—the dream of a menacing figure at the door—the best work point would be just after the dreamer becomes aware of the figure's presence, but before he or she has begun scurrying around securing all the locks and entry points and trying to call the police. From this point there are many options: *Should I go to the door and see who is there? Should I converse with him? Could I let him in? Must I keep him out at all costs? Is the back door open? Should I flee from the house before he gets in? Should I hide? Call the police?* This dramatic sense of having several possible outcomes and not yet being committed to any one response is what makes a good work point. Dreamers may not be able to locate this polyvalent work point on their own because they have always been so frightened in the dream that they *always* reflexively lock the door and hide. In this case, it is the practitioner's job to present the possibility of a point in time *before* the fear reflex kicks in and takes over, to help the dreamers get a sense of that point (as yet very new and hypothetical) and experience it in their feeling body.

There is another natural work point that often yields good results, usually appearing right at the end of a dream just before waking. In this type there is no sense of choice; but only a terrible sense of paralysis and helplessness. There is no plan of action and no escape, so the dreamer can do nothing but wake up. Both of these potential points are characterized by a heightened sense of dramatic tension.

Another key consideration for choosing a work point is that it must not avoid or deny the existence of the problem the dream is depicting. In this work, it is important that we begin in a true place. If it is a place of terror, frustration, or distress, then so be it: that is where we begin to work. We do not avoid or gloss over this difficult place, as that would amount to denial and wishful thinking. In fact, we typically choose the point of re-entry into the dream with the awareness that we want to start right square in the middle of the problem. From there we will freeze the action, give ourselves a bit of time and space, then enlist our creative faculties to start generating possible new outcomes.

As an illustrative example, a few year ago I was working with Maria, a woman in her late 50s, who had lost her husband five years earlier. She had several dreams in which she was engaged in some activity, feeling quite happy and well … and then her husband appeared. He was there, but was not fully present and alive; he was like a ghostly shell of himself, and this saddened and frightened her greatly. In considering the best work point, we should not choose a point *before* the ghostly husband appears; if we do, we are avoiding the central problem of the dream, which is depicting one of the central problems of Maria's life. We would be losing the opportunity the dream is offering her, a chance to re-enter a place of unresolved grief and fear and consider trying on some new action or attitude.

What should be done in cases where the client suggests a work point, but the practitioner thinks a different one would yield better results? The practitioner can make a case for his choice and, if the client agrees, then the problem is solved. If the client expresses any reservation with his or her choice being over-ridden, then both should be tried, starting with the client's. In some cases, the dreamwork will proceed to a similar place, and in other cases, the contrasting result from the two experiences proves to be very illuminating.

In the next step the practitioner invites the client to re-enter the dream at the chosen work point. I have found it very helpful at this stage to say something that evokes a feeling of *slowing down or stopping the action*, so that the client feels a sense of having some time and space to think clearly. This, in turn, helps restore the critical sense of agency (if not yet mastery) to a dream ego that may have felt powerless and terrified within the dream scene. I will typically say something like: "Now freeze the action … give yourself time … and space … you have a clear mind and you can think about what you would like to do in this situation … (pause for 2–3 seconds)… What would you like to do?" The practitioner now sits back and waits to see what the client will come up with, and helps him or her follow this lead if any help is needed.

Going forward from here, let us use a real dream example to illustrate the method in action. Here is the dream of a 26-year-old man, Evan, whose life history was scarred by abuse and bullying:

> *I am inside a house with my girlfriend. We open the door to the back yard and step outside. There is a big loud party happening in the neighbor's yard right next door. I look over to see who is making all the noise and I lock eyes with a big man. The moment he sees me I start to get scared. Now he's coming over towards me! I take my girlfriend's hand and run back inside. We lock the sliding doors and move away so he won't be able to see us. Just then I see that Mark is inside with us, one of the guys who bullied me in public school. I feel very uneasy that he is in the house…. I don't know what to do…. I wake up.*

First off, a reminder: resist the temptation to think about what this dream might mean! You may have a good idea about what is going on here psychodynamically, and you may find it fascinating, but that is not the path we are taking. We are going to invite Evan to go back into the dream and do something on the inside.

Evan and I agreed on a work point right at the end of the dream, just before the feelings of fear and helplessness caused him to wake up. When I asked Evan what he would like to do at this point, he sat with his eyes closed for several moments. I could tell that he was "back in the dream" and was recalibrating the feeling landscape with a new sense of agency and empowerment. Since this process may take a bit of time, I generally do not interrupt it for up to 30 seconds or even more, unless I sense that the dreamer is lost or confused. After a time he said: "I'm feeling that Mark is the real problem. I'm afraid of him. He's the one I need to worry about, not the guy outside." I asked Evan what he would like to do in relation to Mark. "I'd like to confront him." I then asked Evan if he wanted some help confronting Mark (the invitation to summon allies mentioned earlier), or if he would like to do it on his own. Evan replied: "Well, he is a dangerous dude. Do you know he once threatened to kill me? I was terrified of him, everyone was. He was a seriously bad kid." I now sensed that Evan was feeling the need for some imaginal help. I considered first the other potentially helpful figures that were present in the dream—his girlfriend and the big guy outside the door. "Would you like your girlfriend to help you?" Evan shook his head, an immediate and clear "No." How about the big guy outside? There was a pause, as Evan considered this. There was a palpable shift in the energy; he was trying on something new and very important. "All right, let's try it." I suggested he go to the back door, unlock it, and see if the big guy was still there. "Yes, he's there." Would you like to invite him in? "He's already in. His name is John." How does it feel to have John with you? "It feels great. He's going to help me kick Mark's ass!" No further prompting was required from me; the whole scene was unfolding inside Evan's mind, like a new action-packed scene in a movie.

We are now at step 8 in the sequence, where the client has imagined a new outcome.

Now the practitioner checks in to confirm that it feels right and complete. This step can be facilitated with phrases such as: "How does that feel?," "Does that feel good?," and "Is there anything else you'd like to do?" Perhaps the most reliable clinical confirmation that things are on a good track is the emotionally felt and embodied sense that something good has happened. (I call this the "double resonance test," because it is a phenomenon of shared resonance occurring simultaneously in the emotional bodies of both the client and the practitioner.) After Evan confirmed verbally that he felt good about the new outcome, I asked him to go through the sequence again, starting from the work point and proceeding all the way to the end point of the newly changed outcome (Mark running away through the front door and down the street). This second pass-through is very helpful in consolidating the memory circuits associated with the new sequence and connecting them securely to the new feelings of empowerment and mastery. I have found it is most effective to do this while the client is still feeling the positive emotions of the new experience.

I then invited Evan to come out of the dream and return to the room where were sitting together. I asked him if he had any new insight about the dream (I tend to avoid using the word "meaning," for reasons which are probably evident by now, but I will often say something like: "Do you have any new sense now of how the dream might connect to your life?" or "Having done that … any new thoughts or insights?"). Evan did, indeed, have a very important and emotionally resonant insight after emerging from the dreamwork experience. "I've been carrying a fear of Mark, and other bullies, I guess, all my life. I think it makes me vulnerable to being abused again. I'm a bullying victim. I just have that in me." But now, I pointed out, something is different, now that John is with you. "Yes … the balance of power has shifted."

This spontaneous dawning of insight is one of the greatest delights of this style of dreamwork. There is no deliberate effort made to harvest meaning from the dream, yet meaning seems to arrive in its own time, on its own terms. The insights that arise have their roots in the emotional experience of the dreamwork and are felt in the body; they are not usually arrived at by thinking or by prior clinical experience, as is more often the case in analytical approaches to dreams.

In the final step the practitioner invites the client to re-visit the newly imagined sequence a few more times. How many re-visits is enough? I usually suggest three times over the next three days, but occasionally will suggest more, especially in cases of repeating nightmares. The science of neuroplasticity teaches us that if we want to change a deeply etched neural pathway we need to do some deep etching of our own. This is the "rehearsal" stage of the process; it can help evolve the new experience from a one-off imaginal event (which may be soon forgotten if it is not reinforced in some way) into a new and lasting potential rooted in the neurobiology of the dreamer's brain. As most practitioners know, a client's willingness and motivation to do the "homework" varies greatly from person to person. We can only extend the invitation with some encouraging energy behind it, and hope for the best.

Checking back in with a client following a powerful dreamworking session is a good practice. I try to do both a short-term check-in at the next session, and a long-term check-in, three to six months after the original experience. Both of these are helpful in manifesting the fullest potential of this kind of dreamwork. In the long term check-in I will ask, usually near the beginning of a session before other work has taken the stage: "Remember the dream you had back in the winter about Mark and John? How do you think that situation is now? Do you think Mark has been kept out of the house? Is John still with you?" I will use the terms and characters given in the dream to frame this enquiry rather than their psychologized translation into waking life, partly because the dream metaphors are easier to remember and re-engage. Evan does not need to go into his rational mind to assess how much progress he has made; in a well-rehearsed dream-work scene he need only re-visit the house in his mind's eye and his feeling body to get a reading on his inner John and his inner Mark. This kind of dreamwork scan can give both client and practitioner a quick and accurate sense of what has actually changed in the client's psyche with regard to that issue. Six months post-session Evan had a much clearer sense of how he had "kept John outside" by avoiding conflict and repressing his natural instincts to defend himself strongly when he felt his boundaries violated. He felt stronger, less passive, and much less likely to allow himself to be dominated or bullied.

Who Can Benefit from the RERI Method?

There is no particular age group or other demographic that stands out as being particularly well-suited for RERI dreamwork. The population that can benefit most is those people who have troubling dreams and want to do something about it. The acceptance of an orientation towards action is one pre-requisite. The willingness to do some "work" with the dreams is another. The ability to visualize is perhaps another, as some subjects report having difficulty re-entering their dream with any clear visual sense. (I typically will ask such people to "try it anyway," and surprisingly often things will start to come alive once they have delved in.) Apart from these three possible limitations, I have found the RERI technique to be widely applicable across cultures, ages, genders, and socio-economic lines (Sowton, 2017).

The approach is very well-suited for young dreamers, with the caveat that a parent (or two) must be co-trained along with the child to be an in-house facilitator of the technique. Parents of children with recurring nightmares, and their health care providers, are referred to an excellent new resource for children's dreamwork: *Sleep Monsters and Superheroes—Empowering Children through Creative Dreamplay* (Johnson & Campbell, 2016b). This recently published book is full of good practical suggestions, several of which involve dream re-entry and re-scripting. It is empowering not only for the young dreamers, but also for their parents, providing them with the bracing encouragement needed to tackle a problem that has often left them feeling agonized and helpless.

What Kind of Training and Certification Are Required to Practice RERI Dreamwork?

Dreamwork often falls through the cracks when it comes to training and certification. Paradoxically, while dreams have a rich and storied place in human history and healing traditions, they currently do not have a firm place in Western medicine and health care. Consequently, there is no clear path one can take to arrive at a career as a professional dreamworker, and there is no widely recognized certification for dreamworkers. There are many of us professional dreamworkers working away around the world, but the paths we have taken to get where we are have usually wandered in and out of a myriad of different schools, training programs, and/or decades of self-motivated learning. In addition, I think it is accurate to say that there are many skilled and competent "lay" practitioners of dreamwork, who have no officially recognized credentials.

In my view, the best way to approach the problem of how to become a trained dreamworker is to be aware of the common pitfalls and try to avoid them. The dangers and concerns that plague dreamworking are similar to those which apply in many other forms of psychotherapy. The ones I would caution most about are: (1) the tendency to rush to interpretation and to fit another person's dream into one's own interpretive model; (2) the tendency to project one's own psychological contents and associations onto another person's dream; (3) the fear of becoming "lost" while working with someone's dream; (4) the fear of causing harm by misinterpreting the dream; (5) the fear of triggering some intense emotional reaction while working with the dream and not knowing how to handle it; and (6) the possibility of becoming mired in one of the many complexities of the doctor-patient relationship—transference, counter-transference, dependence, conflict of interest, unconscious projection, etc. There can be no doubt that engaging in dreamwork can go very quickly into deep and emotional areas, thereby exposing a practitioner to all the risks mentioned above. Thus there is a responsibility to be well-prepared and to be willing to stay present with the client, facilitating whatever is unfolding as skillfully as possible.

So the question remains: What are the possible ways to acquire dreamworking skills? One good place to begin is by joining the IASD, The International Association for the Study of Dreams. The IASD is a very diverse association, welcoming to its membership and to its gatherings any person who has a serious interest in dreams. There are professionals and non-professionals, researchers, practitioners of all stripes, artists, and a lot of people who are simply interested in deepening their relationship with their own dream life. It is a hotbed of information about dreams, so that members who are seeking dreamwork training will soon find themselves presented with a rich assortment of options.

Several dreamwork training programs and models have been developed in the last three decades, including Loma Flowers's Dream Interview Method (Flowers, 2015), Clara Hill's Cognitive Experiential Dream Model (Hill, 2013), the Dream Tending Certificate Program at Pacifica Graduate Institute developed by Stephen Aizenstat, the Jungian Training Institutes, and many others. These resources notwithstanding, the place of dreamwork is still not widespread nor well established in academia, medicine, psychiatry, or psychology. For now, at least, most dreamworkers will be something else first (a naturopathic doctor, in my case), and develop a dreamworking component, while concurrently practicing another skill set with its own training and certification.

Evidence for the Effectiveness of Re-Entry Methods

The majority of the evidence base for the effectiveness of dreamwork methods involving re-entry and outcome change derives from IRT, which has held an established place within modern psychology and medicine for over 20 years. Several controlled studies have shown IRT to be effective in reducing nightmare frequency, intensity, and associated distress, while maintaining positive outcomes (Kellner, Neidhardt, Krakow, & Pathak, 1992; Neidhardt, Krakow, Kellner, & Pathak, 1992). In addition, Clara Hill's Cognitive Experiential Dream Model, which "was developed as a means of studying the effect of working with dreams in therapy," has shown in numerous studies that working with dreams enhances therapeutic outcomes in many different clinical settings (Spangler & Hill, 2015, pp.133–134).

Summary

The RERI method, with its relative simplicity and brevity, its avoidance of the interpretative stance, and its client-led format, can easily be integrated into an already existing mental health or counseling practice. It is well-suited for psychology, psychotherapy, social work, nursing, coaching, pastoral counseling, and any situation that allows for one-on-one client contact for twenty minutes or more.

REFERENCES

Flowers, L.K. (2015). Teaching dream interviewing for clinical practice. In M. Kramer & M. Glucksman (Eds.), *Dream research: Contributions to clinical practice* (pp. 14–26). New York, NY: Routledge.
Ingerman, S. (1991). *Soul retrieval: Mending the fragmented self.* San Francisco, CA: Harper San Francisco.
Ingerman, S. (2004). *Shamanic journeying: A beginner's guide.* Boulder, CO: Sounds True.
Johnson, C.R., & Campbell, J.M. (Eds.). (2016a). *Sleep monsters and superheroes: Empowering children through creative dreamplay.* Santa Barbara, CA: Praeger.
Johnson, C.R., & Campbell, J.M. (2016b). The healing power of story: Re-dreaming the dream. In C.R. Johnson, & J.M. Campbell (Eds.), *Sleep monsters and superheroes: Empowering children through creative dreamplay* (pp. 38–39). Santa Barbara, CA: Praeger.
Jung, C.G., & Chodorow, J. (Ed.). (1997). *Jung on Active Imagination.* New York, NY: Routledge.
Kellner, R., Neidhardt, J., Krakow, B., & Pathak, D. (1992). Changes in chronic nightmares after one session of desensitization or rehearsal instructions. *American Journal of Psychiatry, 149,* 659–663.
Krakow, B., Hollifield, M., Johnston, L., Koss, M., Schrader, R., Warner, T. ... & Prince, H. (2001). Imagery rehearsal therapy for chronic nightmares in sexual assault survivors with posttraumatic stress disorder: A randomized controlled trial. *Journal of the American Medical Association, 286,* 537–545.
Krippner, S. (2016). Working with post-traumatic stress disorder nightmares. In J. Lewis & S. Krippner. *Working with dreams and PTSD nightmares* (pp. 260–261). Santa Barbara, CA: Praeger.
Krippner, S., Bogzaran, F., & DeCarvalho, A. (2002). *Extraordinary dreams and how to work with them.* Albany, NY: SUNY Press.
Lyons, T. (2016). Dreamplay for children facing illness, injury, and physical handicaps. In C.R. Johnson & J.M. Campbell (Eds.), *Sleep monsters and superheroes: Empowering children through creative dreamplay* (pp. 53–66). Santa Barbara, CA: Praeger.
Moss, R. (2011). *Active dreaming.* Novato, CA: New World Library.
Naparstek, B. (1994). *Staying well with guided imagery.* New York, NY: Hachette.
Neidhardt, E.J., Krakow, B., Kellner, R., & Pathak, D. (1992). The beneficial effects of one treatment session and recording of nightmares on chronic nightmare sufferers. *Sleep, 15,* 470–473.
Sowton, C. (2017). *Dreamworking: How to listen to the inner guidance of your dreams.* Woodbury, MN: Llewellyn Publications.
Spangler, P.T., & Hill, C.E. (2016). Hill cognitive-experiential method. In J. Lewis & S. Krippner (Eds.), *Working with dreams and PTSD nightmares: 14 approaches for psychotherapists and counselors* (pp. 138–141). Santa Barbara, CA: Praeger.
Van de Castle, R.L. (1994). *Our dreaming mind.* New York, NY: Ballantine Books.

Bodymind Healing
Psychotherapy

Michael Mayer

Bodymind Healing Psychotherapy (Mayer, 2007a, 2009, 2012) is "an integral/transpersonal psychotherapy" (Cortright, 1997; Friedman & Hartelius, 2013; Walsh & Shapiro, 2006; Wilber, 2000;) that synthesizes Western, Eastern, and indigenous approaches to healing. Combining ancient wisdom traditions with modern psychology, *Bodymind Healing Psychotherapy* (BMHP) has a ten-dimension, holographic approach that includes: (1) Taoist Qigong Breathing techniques and hypnosis using *the River of Life* practice (Mayer, 2007a, 2007b, 2009); (2) Self-soothing (Kohut, 1971; Shore, 2003); (3) Focusing on Felt Meaning (Gendlin, 1978); (4) Psychodynamics; (5) Cognitive Restructuring using a body-oriented Subjective Units of Distress Scale (SUDS) (Beck, 1976; Shapiro, 1995); (6) Energy Psychology methods (Feinstein, 2012; Mayer, 2009, 2009b); (7) Belly Massage of Chi Nei Tsang (Chia, 1990); (8) Acupressure: Phenomenological Approach; (9) Practices from Bodymind Healing Qigong (Mayer, 2000, 2004, 2007a); and (10) Symbolic Process Approaches to Healing (Hillman 1975; Jung, 1961; Mayer, 1993, 2007a, 2012). Theory, methods, experiential exercises, and case examples illustrate how BMHP can be applied to various psychological conditions (Mayer, 2007a, 2009). After providing an overview of some of these methods, this essay shows how they synthesize into the practice of Bodymind Healing Psychotherapy. Addressing them occurs throughout the essay, most specifically under the case illustration on *panic disorder*.

Qigong in Psychotherapy

Qigong, one of the five branches of Traditional Chinese Medicine (Cohen, 1997), is one of the central elements of BMHP. The Qigong tradition (with medical, spiritual, and internal martial arts components) includes a treasure-house of practices that can aid psychotherapeutic healing. Regarding the behavioral health dimensions of incorporating Qigong into psychotherapy, Qigong can benefit the treatment of hypertension (Lee, Lee, Kim, & Ernst, 2010; Mayer, 1999, 2003, 2010; Yeh, Wang, Wayne, & Phillips, 2008), balance (Province et al., 1995), chronic pain (Bai et al., 2015), insomnia (Irwin, Olmstead, & Motivala, 2008), and various other psychological conditions (Abbott & Lavretsky, 2013).

Even though behavioral healthcare and psychotherapy are not necessarily separable disciplines, this essay focuses mostly on psychotherapy. For example, when BMHP uses Qigong methods (involving such elements as breathing, self-touch, and movement) with chronic pain, appropriate psychotherapeutic elements are intertwined including attitudes/cognitions/beliefs and appropriate imagery (Mayer, 1996). Or, when using Qigong to activate the parasympathetic nervous system to treat psychophysiological conditions (Mayer, 2007a; Rossi, 1986; Sapolsky, 1998) such as trauma (van der Kolk, 2014), BMHP implements an integral treatment approach combining Qigong and psychotherapy, using various arousal reduction methods (Schore, 2003).

Since the internal martial arts of Qigong are based in activating a relaxation response (Benson & Klippner, 1976) in life and death situations for survival purposes, it would be natural to suppose that thousands of years of evolution of such practices might have something to add to developing coping skills for modern people to deal with danger and to reduce stress. Qigong combines internal martial arts, spiritual approaches, and healing methods as a matter of theory, practice, and treatment. For example, its breathing methods have been used for self-defense to "sink the chi" (Ming, 1989), for activating a transcendent state of oneness (*wuji*), and for healing many disorders, including trauma (van der Kolk, 2014).

Regarding trauma treatment, BMHP uses an adaptation of Microcosmic Orbit Breathing (Mayer, 2007a; Wilhelm, 1931/1963) to help reverse sympathetic nervous system overreactivity by activating this state-specific (Tart, 1972) parasympathetic nervous system method (Mayer, 2007a; van der Kolk, 2014); moreover, BMHP incorporates this breathing method into an integrated treatment protocol that helps traumatized patients to regain a safety zone in their bodies, enhance development of a cohesiveness of self (Horner, 1990), and help them in unique embodied ways to find a new life stance (Mayer, 2004b, 2007a).

Such psychological benefits of Qigong are helpful not only to trauma patients, but to psychotherapeutic growth in general. For example, based on the fifteen ways outlined in BMHP (Mayer 2007a, pp. 255–258), Qigong is a complementary tool to (1) help those with reactive attachment styles to develop a cohesive center when the everyday issues of life assault or impinge upon their sensibilities, and, together with psychotherapy, it may provide a bodily base for developing affect modulation skills and affect tolerance; and (2) induce an altered state, helpful in issues with addiction.

More broadly speaking, even though, when appropriate, BMHP incorporates Qigong movements into psychotherapy (Mayer, 2004a; Wayne & Furst, 2013), in this approach the healing essence of Qigong is often brought into psychotherapy without using a Qigong movement, and without saying a word about Qigong (Mayer, 2007a, 2009a). For example, with no reference to Qigong, in a psychotherapy session a practitioner can introduce breathing methods (such as Qigong's Microcosmic Orbit Breathing) that simultaneously relax, re-energize, and re-empower (called *fongsung*); teach acu-point self-touch; and increase somatic awareness of the gestures that a person expresses at the moment of "felt shift" (Gendlin, 1978). These naturally arising gestures can serve as post-hypnotic anchors (Grinder & Bandler, 1981) to help to embody new life stances—indeed, these movements and postures are often similar to those practiced in Tai Chi/Qigong.

BMHP as an Integral, Transpersonal Psychotherapy

BMHP is more encompassing than a system that integrates Qigong and psychotherapy; it can be seen as a *transpersonal psychotherapy* (Boorstein, 1996; Cortright, 1997;

Mayer, 2007a, 2009a, 2015; Rodrigues & Friedman, 2013).[1] From this broader perspective, BMHP attempts to re-write the origin myth of psychotherapy. Mircea Eliade (1964) explains how the origin myth of anything determines the way it is seen and its destiny, adding that it creates a magical, incantational, hypnotic power. This certainly seems to be true with psychotherapy, in that an experimental psychologist, a Freudian, and a cognitive/behaviorist are able to "indoctrinate" adherents into their own view of psychotherapy's origin and purpose. For example, by saying that psychotherapy's origins are in modern psychotherapy, ancient wisdom traditions are not given their due. Different origin myths induce different realities, as can be seen by even the use of the word *psyche*, usually translated in psychology education as "mind"; however, as Hillman (1975) pointed out, *psyche* does not just mean "mind." In Greek, it translates as "soul." As the Western mystery tradition (Mathews & Mathews, 1986) teaches, the "soul," metaphorically speaking, is composed of four elements: fire (energy), earth (somatic psychology), air (cognitions and breath), and water (the affective dimension). Rooting psychotherapy in the soul of these elements creates an incantation into a more encompassing view that, for example, includes energetic (fire) and somatic (earth) dimensions.

Countering single-system psychotherapy origin myths, the astrological mandala is used to create an inclusive psychotherapeutic meta-system (Mayer 1977, 1984, 2007a), by taking the zodiac, composed of symbolic representations of the elements (fire, earth, air, water), and placing psychotherapy systems around the circle. The "mandala of psychotherapies" heals biases about what is the best or true origin of psychotherapy. The importance of this mandalic conceptualization is not to assign a type of therapy mechanistically to an astrological house or sign, but to develop heuristic, symbolic thinking; thus, at different times, a given school of psychotherapy can be at a different part of the zodiac.[2] Likewise, using tools from the mandala of ancient wisdom traditions, such as sound, touch, breath, symbolic stories, or mindfulness, may be the most appropriate healing choice at a certain time. BMHP interns are trained to imagine standing in the middle of a mandala that includes all psychotherapeutic schools and ancient wisdom traditions.[3] It is this breadth and depth that distinguish BMHP from other bodymind approaches to psychotherapy (Aposhyan, 2004).

Astrological Metaphor in Psychotherapy

One symbolic process method used in BMHP, when appropriate, is a non-deterministic approach to the use of astrological symbolism. A phenomenological theoretical perspective (Fingarette, 1965) bypasses the issue of correspondence between cosmos and personality. Astrological metaphors are used like a cosmological Rorschach projective technique, where symbols and myths are highlighted to help individuals focus on their life's meaning in an "astro-poetic" manner (Mayer 1977, 1984, 2012a).

BMHP and Couples Therapy

Beyond the scope of this essay, BMHP has an approach to couples therapy. For example, "the four elements" of the Western mystery tradition are adapted to teach couples "the elements of constructive communication": "Fire"—starting out communication with positive intention; "Air"—distinguishing the whole person from the part of the person's behavior with which one is having trouble; "Water"—expressing "I feel" versus "you are" statements; and "Earth"—"I want" statements that address the behavior, or way of being, that one person wants the other person to change. The couple is trained in empathetic listening skills to respond to each other's feelings in the Water phase of communication; the "I want phase" (Earth) is an opportunity to bargain. There is also a psychomythological component to BMHP couples therapy. Relationships are seen as a rite of initiation through the elements, while sharing stories from cross-cultural mythology helps reframe difficulties in relationship as opportunities for solving the dilemmas of the "temples of the elements" and the lessons on one's life journey down the river of one's life (Mayer, 1993).

The River of Life (ROL) Self-Hypnosis Induction

Though BMHP draws from the mandala of traditional and alternative therapies, an essential aspect of BMHP is the *River of Life* self-hypnosis method (Mayer, 2007a, 2007b, 2009). The ROL draws from Taoist Microcosmic Orbit Breathing (Luk, 1972; Wilhelm, 1931/1963), which focuses on the central channel of the body. A natural inhalation arises up the back (*Du Mei* channel), and a longer exhalation comes down the front of the body *(Ren Mei)*. This "long-breath" can be found by imagining that your exhalation is like a tire that has a slow leak in it, while someone is sitting on the tire. This can be differentiated from short-breath that is like a blow-out in a tire. Long-breath builds Qi, giving us a grounded yet light feeling. It is a natural exhalation through the nose[4] that is not really through the nose; it is more deep and internal, sinking down the front of the spine (*Ren* channel) to the belly (*Tan Tien*) in the very core of you. If you force the breath out of your nostrils as if trying to expel a bug caught there, this will be "short-breath." Long-breath is deep, smooth, non-forced, and calming, and generates a relaxed energized force *(fongsung)*; however, though it generates a strong internal force, if you put a feather in front of your nose it would barely move, or perhaps it would not move at all. Long-breath is also an entryway into "reeling silk" practices (Huang, 1974; Mayer, 2004a), one of the secrets of cultivating Qi with Tai Chi movements that are synchronized with the breath. It should be noted that patients do not need to learn all these particulars for the experience to have a beneficial effect.

BMHP adds a guided visualization of a river, a non-directive, integral component that allows individual images to arise, along with psychological methods that help to transmute "ice-blocks in the river." The ROL process has hypnotic, psychotherapeutic, and meditative dimensions.

Each different form of meditation, self-hypnosis, or somatically-oriented therapy is state-specific (Leskowitz, 2000; Rossi, 1986; Tart, 1972). Drawing from Gendlin's Focusing (1978, 1997) direct referent method, and similar to Ogden's sensory motor therapy (Ogden, Minton, & Pain, 2006) and bottom-up approaches (Taylor, Goehler, Galper, Innes, & Bourguignon 2010), BMHP is a bodymind-centered approach. However BMHP and the ROL contain state-specific dimensions that, for example, do the following: (1) constellate an embodied, observing self associated with the center-line of the body or the whole energetic field of the body (*wuji*), as compared, let's say, to mindfulness meditation that may constellate a different psychic vantage point (Kabat-Zinn, 2003); (2) activate the energy of the body in state-specific ways that simultaneously relax and energize (Mayer, 2009a, 2009c), (3) contribute to reducing arousal levels (Schore, 2003), and (4) add energetic healing dimensions to the relaxation response (Benson & Klippner, 1976). Further research would be necessary to determine how this state relates to Porges's (2001) polyvagal theory. Actually, the state-specific altered state activated by Qigong practice, in its broader dimensions, uses *yi* (translated as "intention") to "shape-shift" (Goodman, 1990; Gore, 1995; Mayer 2004a, 2007a) into embodied, hypnotherapeutic, psycho-energetic states from a universe of possibilities and elements of nature, e.g., animal forms (Feng, 2003) or trees (Lam, 1999; Mayer, 2004b, 2012b); (3) contain a unique integration of spiritually transcendent and psychologically transmuting dimensions; and (4) invoke a type of shamanic journey to the underworld (Eliade, 1964). However, here the pathway is an experiential journey into the personal and collective unconscious (Mayer, 2009a, 2012a).

The transcending/transmuting dialectic. The transcendent aspects of Microcosmic Orbit Breathing can be found at the end of the exhalation, at the navel *(Tan tien)*. According to Taoist theory, one may discover here "the Sea of Elixir," conceptualized and experienced as a relaxed state where one dissolves into a wider sea (Wilhelm, 1931/1963). Regardless of whether one regards this method as being a hypnotic-like induction or an actual channel, the felt experience of Microcosmic Orbit Breathing has clinical uses (McKeown, 2015). As discussed earlier, according to Qigong theory, the long exhalation (Lee, Lee, Kim, & Ernst, 2010; Liu & Chen, 2010) and the pause after exhalation help people to "sink their chi" (Ming, 1989, pp. 125–126). Some trauma therapists confirm this centuries-old wisdom, using exhalation to activate a parasympathetic nervous system response to help heal trauma (van der Kolk, 2014). In this author's clinical experience, applications of this type of breathing can add state-specific attributes to grounding and relaxation in cases of hypertension, insomnia, anxiety disorders, addictions, trauma, etc. (Mayer, 2007a, 2007b, 2009a).

The transmuting dimension of the River of Life can be activated by a person's "focusing" (Gendlin, 1978) on emerging somatic sensations while practicing "long breathing" (Luk, 1972; Mayer, 2007a). "As you are imagining the river of your life flowing down to where you are today, some feeling, blockage, and/or issue may arise. Note where in your body you feel that issue and what its quality is" (Mayer, 2009a, pp. 115–116). Then the practitioner "focuses" on the felt meaning of the block until new meaning, along with a felt shift happens. From there cognitive restructuring (Ellis, 2003) and other traditional and transpersonal psychotherapeutic interventions are used to facilitate the process of changing one's life stance. The person can imagine pouring the new meaning into the river of their central channel on their exhalation and embodying the new way of being down to their belly or feet.

Shape-shifting. BMHP brings the cross-cultural, somatic, psycho-mythological concept of *shape-shifting* to psychotherapy, positing that myths and practices of shape-shifting may be a primordial root of psychotherapy (Mayer, 2007a, 2009a, 2012a).

In shamanic literature, "shape-shifting" is linked to creation. In the Pacific Northwest, a creation myth tells of a Native American fisherman who finds a cave, where animals around a roaring fire play a game of "shape-shifting" into human beings (Gore, 1995). New embodied realities were created in indigenous cultures by assuming postures of stillness and using the imagination, long before contemporary schools of psychotherapy existed (Goodman, 1990). I call them "traditions of postural initiation" (Mayer, 2004a, 2012a).

In ancient Greece, Epimenides used "rituals … watching animals and following them in their movements to develop healing powers" (Kingsley, 1999, p. 215). In Epidaurus, at one of the world's oldest holistic healing centers, shape-shifting into another identity was an essential element of healing rituals. The Aesclepian priest advised the sick to go to the Dionysian theater to play a particular part in a play, or to wear a mask representing another person or animal or an element of nature (Papadakis, 1988). A new energy or healing pathway would be activated in the psyche (Meier, 1967). The Chinese tradition of Tai Chi Chuan can be taught as a way of postural initiation (Mayer 2004a, 2009a, 2012b).

Greek mythology is a treasure-house of shape-shifting stories that can be useful to narrative therapists in helping patients alter dysfunctional or fixated life stances. Zeus changes into a swan in order to seduce Leda, perhaps symbolically represent a man's need to let go of his godlike complex (Zeus) to find a more light-hearted manner (the swan) to approach a woman. Another Greek myth tells of Proteus, the old shape-shifting man of the sea, who changed his form from a lion to a snake, and from a leopard to a tree. When the Greek hero Menelaus needed information from Proteus to find his way home, he disguised himself as a seal until Proteus returned to his true form, whereupon Menelaus obtained the information he needed (Mayer, 2007a). BMHP uses body movements and postures, metaphors representing nature, and symbolic teaching stories to help the lost soul find its way home.

Contemporary psychotherapists may already unconsciously incorporate shape-shifting ideas when they use subpersonality work (Assagioli, 1965). A semi-joke is told in BMHP that we all just have one problem—that we use the word "I" incorrectly. So if people say, "I'm no good," the issue may be that the subpersonalities that believe they are "not good" is an introject from childhood. The "true I" knows differently. The role of psychotherapy then becomes one of helping individuals learn how to be mindful that "the I who we think is I" is not the true I. Healing comes from shape-shifting into the real I, similar to Menelaus finding his way home.

To facilitate shape-shifting, BMHP incorporates a "full-spectrum approach to symbolic process modalities" (Mayer 2009a, pp.109–132), addressing the imaginal, somatic, and energetic dimensions. It uses these three dimensions to incorporate symbolic processes into clinical practice through the following approaches: teaching stories, Qigong practices, directive and non-directive methods, hypnosis, dreamwork, astrological metaphors (Mayer, 1984, 1993, 2012), alchemical metaphors (Edinger, 1985), and, particularly, the River of Life and the Mythic Journey processes (Mayer, 1982, 2007a, 2009a).

Case Illustrations and Vignettes

Case Vignette: "Life Stance" with Social Phobia

Shape-shifting enhances psychotherapy, and vice versa. For example, one of my Standing Meditation Qigong students practiced the "Standing like a Tree" form of Qigong (*Zhan Zhuang*), which consists of imagining and practicing embodying the likeness of a tree (Mayer, 2004b). Sam (not his real name) asked me to end our Qigong relationship to begin psychotherapy with me. I learned he had a severe social phobia that was going to lead to his dropping out of his first year of college. As he was introduced to the River of Life practice, "focusing" on his fear of fellow students, he discovered it was rooted in the trauma of being physically and emotionally abused by his brother throughout his childhood. A culmination of the work he did in therapy came when his older brother again started to berate him verbally, saying, "I'm still better than you at everything." Sam was able to "stand up to him" and respond, "You're not better than me at everything; you're not better at being a kind brother." Sam marked this as the beginning of a change in his life-stance toward his brother, a "shape-shifting," if you will, into a new relationship where they communicated about the past—and apologies were made. From this new embodied life stance a new practice was anchored, helping him with his social phobia (Mayer, 2007a). He reported that Standing like a Tree together with psychotherapy helped him to find this new stance. Training in Standing Meditation as such is not, however, necessary to achieve this goal.

Case Illustration with BMHP: Panic Disorder

Shelly, a 23-year-old woman, knew nothing about Standing Meditation. Her case illustrates in more detail many of the integral/transpersonal dimensions of BMHP. Shelly presented with flat affect, showing no emotion, as she told me about her first job as a graphic artist for a big company:

> Whenever too many jobs back up, I have to leave my cubicle. I tell my fellow employees that I have to go to the bathroom, but in reality I'm sweating; heart palpitations and dizziness come over me like an unwanted plague. Sitting on the toilet seat in the bathroom with the door closed, I hope no one will discover what's going on with me.

Shelly was literally petrified that her boyfriend and friends would find out about her panic attacks and reject her. Before our therapy, Shelly suffered from adverse effects from her anxiety medications, so she wanted to find an approach that did not require medication. She reported that her psychiatrist "tried to push on me the idea that my issues related to the fact that I had been adopted in infancy." Shelly left treatment because she felt that her anxiety could not have anything to do with her early life, since she had a loving relationship with her adoptive parents.

Taoist Breathing Techniques and Hypnosis. Shelly wanted to control her symptoms related to being overwhelmed by the multi-tasking required at work. To help her find some symptom relief, I first taught Shelly Microcosmic Orbit Breathing. For most patients with whom I have tried this method, it is of major significance in reducing their panic attacks, bringing patients into their core, grounding them, and reducing arousal levels (Schore, 2003). But for Shelly it provided only minor relief in lowering her SUD scale by three points. (I later discovered that this was because of how critical she was of herself.)

Chi Nei Tsang—Belly Massage. Adding another medical Qigong method to the Microcosmic Orbit Breathing method was helpful to Shelly in obtaining further symptom relief. *Chi Nei Tsang* consists of pressing into points around the belly with a circle, stop-feel method (Chia, 1990; Mayer, 2007a). The following is an adaptation of the technique: As you are lying down, place your hands on your belly. Just feel your inhalations and exhalations; notice the way you normally breathe, and whether your hands rise or fall as you breathe in. The Taoists say that, in natural breathing, called diaphragmatic breathing, as the breath comes in, the stomach should inflate and the hands should rise. As you breathe out, your stomach should deflate, your pressing-in hands should follow the falling of the stomach; and then after the pause at the end of your exhalation you circle, stop, and feel.

For almost all of my anxiety-ridden patients this method significantly lowers SUD levels, and often helps patients to reduce or eliminate anxiety medications (Mayer, 2008). However, it is often the case that, if the psychological complex behind a life issue (for example, Shelly's self-criticalness) is not "worked through," the transcendent altered state accessed may not be long-lasting; and this was true for Shelly.

Transcending/transmuting Dialectic. I have called this two-sided coin "the transcending/transmuting dialectic" (Mayer, 2007a, p.106). Two important principles in transpersonal psychotherapy are that: (1) activating a state-specific altered state (Tart, 1972) can be a useful adjunct to psychotherapy and behavioral healthcare, helping to reduce or eliminate the need for medication and reduce arousal levels (Schore, 2003); and (2) transmuting traditions involve "working through" the deeper psychodynamic and cognitive roots of a psychological complex. The appropriate blending of these two traditions is a central aspect of BMHP (Mayer, 2007a, 2009a, 2012a).

Psychological methods help us to transmute the underlying complex, i.e., gain insight into etiology, develop new coping skills, activate new cognitive skills, transmute dysfunctional introjects, foster a compassionate relationship towards our issues, discover transformative meanings, and so on.

"Focusing" on the Felt Meaning of Anxiety. Gendlin's *Focusing* (Gendlin, 1978) is one such transmuting method. The process, as I have adapted and combined it with BMHP, consists of the following six steps: The first step involves learning to "clear a space" from painful feelings and the "subpersonality" (Assagioli, 1965) that is associated with those feelings. In practice, it adds to the Focusing technique the idea of imagining a river traveling down the "macrocosmic orbit" on the exhalation in order to further facilitate clearing a space away from these distressing feelings. Through this integration of Qigong and Focusing, a temporary, healing dissociation from the issue can be created. In this combined method, on the exhalation one can imagine negative feelings releasing down the river of breath and coalescing into an image of that subpersonality at a distance from oneself. This honors Focusing's emphasis on finding the right amount of "breathing room" from one's issues, not too close and not too far. It is from this "right distance" that a patient can get a "felt sense" of what this issue is "all about."

Secondly, the patient finds the "felt sense" of the issue. A "felt sense" can be distinguished from a feeling by the fact that it is unclear, is experienced as more holistic, and combines meaning with a body sense. The unclear sense in the body is a place where the meaning feels like it is "on the tip of our tongue." The difference between a feeling and a felt sense is like the difference between being immersed and drowning in the water of a feeling, versus sitting next to the river of our experience and noticing the rise of words or images that capture the essence of what that feeling state is all about. This involves not thinking about the issue, but directly referring to the body in this state-specific meditative state and allowing meanings to arise. (This is a key component of the transmuting dimension of the River of Life practice.)

Third, the patient practicing "Focusing" finds a "handle word or image" that opens the door to the description of that sense. Fourth, he/she "resonates" the emerging thoughts or images back with the body sense to see if the center of the target is hit. Fifth, questions are asked of the felt sense, such as "What is the worst thing about this issue?" "What is so important about this whole issue?" or "What is the crux of this issue?" The person waits until one of the images, words, or sounds gives the sense that the felt meaning of the issue has been discovered, whereupon a "felt shift" occurs. Sixth, the focuser "receives" the information that arose from the bodymind with appreciation, and explores where the information leads in terms of life changes.

As Shelly practiced the River of Life method, she "Focused" on the tension that blocked her inner river. She discovered a "held back" feeling in her jaw and heart. When she "resonated" (Gendlin's Fourth step) the words "held back" with this felt sense, new words emerged: "I feel 'ashamed' that I don't have it together." Shelly found "the crux of the felt meaning" of her panic, in response to my question, "What feels so scary about 'not having it together'?"

Psychodynamics. From Focusing, while practicing the ROL, the psychodynamic roots of her issue emerged. An image came to her mind of an infant being given away. As tears came to Shelly's eyes, she first said, "No, it couldn't be about this!" But as the tears turned into sobs, she realized that the deepest, earliest root of this issue was her feeling of being rejected by her birth parents. Though her past psychiatrist had been correct in his assessment, I believe that, because he told her *his* interpretation, rather than non-directively allowing it to come from her own bodymind, the interpretation produced a defensive reaction. She realized that the fear of being rejected by her friends nowadays felt similar to her fear that her adoptive parents would reject her if she did not meet their standards. We then worked on developing the re-parenting tools needed to soothe her.

Self-Soothing Using Acupressure Points. The "Tao of re-parenting" (Mayer, 2009a) uses the felt sense in the body and imagery to facilitate the re-parenting of childhood wounds. First, an image and felt sense of our parents soothing us is tried, but, if blocks exist, an archetypal image of a universal mother or father figure may aid the process.

Holding a pillow, Shelly tried to imagine her mother soothing her by being compassionate and non-judgmental about her not getting enough things done at work. Since her natural parents had rejected her, even though there was much love from her adoptive parents, Shelly realized she did not fully trust the unconditional love of the latter. Because she had a hard time finding a self-soothing figure in her personal life, she searched for an archetypal image that could accept her the way she was. Mother Teresa came to her mind, followed by a reduction in her anxiety level from a 7 to a 4 on an SUD scale of ten.

Chinese medicine, with its knowledge of the acupuncture and acupressure points, complements imagery work well. While using archetypal or personal healing imagery, the therapist can suggest that the patient touch an acupressure point on the heart (Conception Vessel17) with the right hand, and a point just below the navel (*Tan Tien,* acupoint CV6) with the left hand. CV 17, located four finger-widths up from the base of the breastbone in an indentation there, functions to "unbind the chest," according to Chinese medicine (Deadman & Al-Khafani, 1998, p. 518). Shelly touched this point, also called the *Sea of Tranquility* (Gach, 1990), with the middle finger of her right hand, made small circles, stopped, breathed, and felt the energy. With the middle finger of the left hand she similarly touched her belly (*Tan Tien*), which Taoists believe is the power center of the body.

Self-soothing is deemed by many psychodynamic psychotherapists to be important in repairing the Self (Kohut, 1971) and healing dysregulation (Schore, 2003). In conjunction with the ROL method, BMHP uses physical self-touch of the body, particularly on acupressure points on the heart and belly, to aid self-soothing and affect regulation.

One day, after my work with Shelly, synchronistically I saw a picture of "the *Chiltan*

Spirit Posture," which shows standing figures that have "one hand on the heart and the other on their belly" (Goodman, 1990).

I discovered that this posture was found in many indigenous cultures (Gore, 1995). Although we cannot be sure of what meanings these totem carvers intended, it can prove phenomenologically enlightening to follow the tradition of psychological archeology (Goodman, 1990) by exploring the holding of postures and hand gestures used by indigenous and cross-cultural traditions. BMHP proposes that drawing from psychotherapy's primordial origins can provide a deeper root system to aid all branches of modern psychotherapy. For example, touching the heart and belly has cross-cultural healing use in the chakras of Hinduism, the energy centers of Taoism, and indigenous cultures. Shelly reported that touching CV 17, using acupressure's circle, stop, and feel method (Gach, 1990), helped to lower her SUD level. Medical Qigong gives us many other points to help alleviate anxiety (Liu & Chen, 2010).[5]

Cognitive Restructuring. A transcendent altered state can be activated though touching acupressure energy points or doing various movement-based interventions; the transmuting dimension's working-through process is facilitated through "cognitive restructuring" (Ellis, 2003). Cognitive therapy techniques, such as voicing new truthful and constructive beliefs and measuring change with the SUD scale, have been combined with information reprocessing using eye movements (Shapiro, 1995) and with energy psychology interventions such as tapping (Callahan & Trubo, 2000; Craig & Fowlie, 1995; Feinstein, 2012, 2018). Although BMHP's integrative methodology uses such interventions when appropriate, BMHP has developed a parallel energy psychology tradition that uses the River of Life process, Qigong postures, and self-touch of acupressure points, along with cognitive restructuring as its preferred modalities (Mayer, 2005, 2009a, 2015).

A cognitive restructuring formula that BMHP uses is to first state a negative feeling/belief and then say, "Even though [fill in the blank]," and then find a more truthful and constructive belief and say, "This is an opportunity to [fill in the blank]." (Mayer, 2007a; Shapiro, 1995). Shelly began with the catastrophic negative belief, "Even though I feel that if anyone knows how messed up I am, I'll be rejected." Shelly's more truthful and constructive cognition was, "This is an opportunity to realize that I deserve to be loved for the way I am, vulnerable and all. I'm willing to take the risk to put out who I really am, and have people in my life who won't abandon me for who I am." The patient then imagines pouring this new

Chiltan Spirit Posture (from *Ecstatic Body Postures* by Belinda Gore, published by Inner Traditions International and Bear & Company, © 1995. All rights reserved. http://www.inner traditions.com. Reprinted with permission of the publisher).

belief, as if it is a healing potion, down their central channel of the "River of their Life" on their exhalation (Mayer 2007a, 2009a).

BMHP proposes that adding a somatic component (such as Gendlin's felt sense, the ROL, or acu-point self-touch) to cognitive therapy helps to develop new somatic anchors that lead to a more embodied, compassionate new life stance. When Shelly anchored this new cognition by feeling it enter the river of her central channel and going down to her feet, giving her a new life stance, while touching two acupressure points on her heart and belly, her face and breath relaxed, and her SUD level reduced to zero—even when she "Focused" on her fear in session. Shelly reported that using the ROL and self-touch methods outside of the session helped her to maintain a connection to this new life stance, reducing her SUD level there as well. After she had done the psychodynamic and cognitive transmuting inner work, the River of Life was more effective in affect regulation, helping her to "sink her chi" to her belly and down to the bottom of her feet.

This new way of being translated to Shelly's opening up and discussing her anxieties and panic attacks with her boyfriend, which led him to share a secret about his childhood abuse. Increased intimacy developed. Also, Shelly reported being better able to handle the job stressors in her work.

Regarding the symbolic process components of BMHP, just before our therapy, Shelly dreamed that her beautifully colored flower tattoo had turned grey. During our termination process, she had another dream that the flower's color had returned. She interpreted this to mean that trying to hide her fears and invalidating her vulnerabilities took the color out of her Self—and now her color was returning.

Similar to the tradition in the Aesclepian temple where a healing dream signaled it was time to leave, Shelly saw this dream as a signal to begin to terminate our therapy. We discussed how, when unwanted feelings were triggered outside of our sessions, self-touch of acu-points, the ROL method, and cognitive restructuring would help to provide an anchor (Grinder & Bandler, 1981) and increase her resiliency (Schore, 2003) to return to the grounded, centered state found in our sessions. Rather than a cure model of psychotherapy, this case illustrates the practice model of psychotherapy.

The holographic dimensions of BMHP are illustrated in this example because the transcendent dimensions of breathing and self-touch without the cognitive and psychodynamic levels were less complete; in addition, the cognitive and psychodynamic levels were less complete without breath and self-touch. Each integral dimension of BMHP contains the other: in breath and self-soothing is cognition, and cognitions are contained in the breath and self-soothing.

In our termination session, after about six months of therapy, Shelly said, "It's not that feelings of anxiety don't arise anymore, but they haven't turned into panic for a long time, because I'm able to soothe myself when they arise. I look at life's difficulties as an opportunity to practice 'sinking my Qi' and find the new life stance of accepting where I am, and soothe uncomfortable feelings."

Transcending/Transmuting Dialectic (continued)

The following brief case vignettes further show how the transcendent/transmuting dialectic is key to an integral BMHP. First, on stage, in front of about two hundred health professionals at our Health Medicine Forum, the medical doctor with whom I co-founded our clinic asked me to demonstrate my River of Life process with one of his patients. A local researcher from the nearby hospital measured the patient's systolic BP as 168 (Mayer, 1997). After about seven minutes of the ROL induction, the patient's BP went down to 128. The audience was impressed, as was I, since I was glad my own BP was not being measured before this big audience.

Robert, a company executive, heard about this presentation and came to our integrated medical clinic with high BP. He wanted to experience the "Qigong hypnosis thing." However, I assessed that he had much broader issues, when he told me about his conflicts with his wife, not having time to spend with his children, and sleeping only for a few hours a night due to his "workaholism." Robert reluctantly agreed to do a few sessions of psychotherapy. As we were doing the River of Life process, he felt a block in his inner river, a felt sense of "a disconnected wire of anxiety." An image arose of being at the dinner table with his four brothers and father. Robert remembered getting a "D" on his report card, when all his brothers laughed at him, saying that he would never amount to anything. Adding to his humiliation, one brother said, "But don't worry, when you get older you can always be a garbage man and pick up garbage at our estates." Tears came to his eyes in reply to my question, "Did you promise yourself anything at that point?" He said that he promised himself to "never rest" until he made more money than all of them together. Robert then made the connection between his current workaholism and his childhood promise about "not resting." His wife marked this as the beginning of his change. This inner work led him to develop a new stance toward life, to change his workaholic stance, becoming a more engaged partner to his wife and a better father, and living a more balanced life (Mayer, 2007a, pp. 171–174).

The Mythic Journey Process

The Mythic Journey Process (MJP) is a central component of Bodymind Healing Psychotherapy's symbolic process methods. Building upon the work of Joseph Campbell (1968), Sam Keen (1989), Carl Jung's active imagination process (1997), and James Hillman's Archetypal Psychology (1975), the Mythic Journey Process (Mayer, 1982, 1993, 2007a, 2009a) adds a somatic dimension to psycho-mythological inner work. The MJP consists of a person transposing a life problem into a story set in ancient times. To ground the mythic dimension somatically, the MJP uses Gendlin's Focusing, so that the storyteller continually refers back to the felt sense of the body. At the end of the process, a person grounds the newly discovered life stance through a spontaneously arising gesture, a Qigong/Tai Chi posture, or an animal movement. MJP can be used for relationship issues (Mayer, 1993), as well as for individual psychological issues (Mayer, 1982, 2007a, 2009a).

For example, a 40-year-old female patient, called Roberta, had longstanding passive/aggressive withdrawing tendencies with her husband. In her written MJP, she imagined the princess's "demon" as an ostrich hiding her head in the sand, a symbolic representation of withdrawing tendencies coming from her feelings of being discounted and denigrated by her parents, "the King and Queen." She felt a somatic constriction in her stomach (8 SUDS). In our therapy, which incorporated this psycho-mythological inner work, a spontaneous gesture emerged, when she pictured being attacked verbally by her husband. When I asked how she would like to respond to her husband, she put the backs of her hands together (like in a breast stroke clearing-the-water motion). I pointed out her gesture's similarity to a Crane movement in Hua Tao's Crane Qigong set. This Soaring Crane (Feng, 2003, p. 12) movement can have a medical Qigong purpose of clearing the heart chakra, a self-defense purpose of defending oneself against attack, and a psychological purpose of differentiating what is of danger and truly threatening from what is one's reactivity (Mayer, 2012b). In Roberta's MJP, she imagined herself meeting a Crane Qigong shaman who taught her to identify if something is harmful, and how to clear space for her heart's modulated expression. Roberta reported that this image, and the body sense and posture that went along with it, helped her to anchor and practice this embodied way of being when she became triggered by her old Ostrich-like behavior.

Some Naturally Arising Bodily Gestures
Leading to a New Life Stance

In my books, I report many examples of how anchoring naturally arising movements at a moment of felt shift in therapy can be useful in helping a patient to develop "a new life stance" (Mayer, 2007a, 2009a). Here are some examples:

1. A woman in one of my workshops, when working in an individual session with me on how to respond to a man who was giving her unwanted sexual attention, was going to "blast the guy." In conjunction with work on affect modulation skills with another therapist, and in response to my question, "How would you like to respond to this man if you were practicing your affect modulation skills?" she spontaneously made a flicking movement with the back of her hand. The gesture symbolized, say, that his "coming on to her wouldn't be a big deal." (The movement she made was exactly the same as a Tai Chi movement called "Fist Under Elbow.") She had no prior Tai Chi experience. When I pointed out the self-defense application of this gesture and asked what words would go along with it, she replied that she was going to say to the man, "Thanks for your interest, but I have a boyfriend, and I want to focus on the workshop." In other words, this posture helped her to anchor a stance that expressed the "affect modulation dial" (Mayer, 2007a, p. 216), one that was not overly assertive and yet established a boundary with kindness and strength.

2. A woman reported that her father always talked *at* her rather than *to* her, which led to five years of her not speaking to him. After six months of our therapy, she was ready to see her father again. In response to my question, "How would you like to approach him?" a spontaneous gesture arose. Her right hand was outstretched, palm-out, in front of her heart, and her left hand went palm-up next to her ribs. This posture, I pointed out, was similar to the posture Repulse Monkey in Tai Chi. We discussed how this posture balanced boundary setting and welcoming. This patient had never taken a Tai Chi class. After seeing her father for the first time in five years, the patient reported that, when he excessively talked *at* her, she was able to recall the Repulse Monkey mudra (hand gesture). She reported that it helped her to remember to set kind, non-reactive boundaries, as in: "Dad, I haven't seen you in years, how about listening to what's been going on for me?" She reported that this opened a conversation and clearing with her father, where he listened better and she was less reactive.

It should be said that a therapist can notice spontaneously arising gestures at key moments of therapy even with no training in Tai Chi/Qigong. By bringing patients' awareness to these postures, a somatic anchoring can take place, leading to practicing a new life stance. In other somatic psychotherapeutic methods (Levine, 1997; Ogden, Minton, & Pain, 2001), patient gestures are used to facilitate bodymind transformation. Then why learn Tai Chi or Qigong, one may ask? In this author's opinion, the study of Tai Chi, Qigong, and other traditions of "postural initiation" (Mayer, 2004a, p. 22) can expand the therapist's understanding of postures and deepen the embodiment of their healing purpose (Mayer, 2007a). Further comparison research would add to a more holistic paradigm in this pre-paradigmatic phase (Kuhn, 1996) of somatic psychotherapy's evolution regarding which methods are most efficacious, in what circumstances, for increasing a patient's somatic safety zone, decreasing dysregulation, and determining what state-specific qualities best facilitate the psychological transformation of various fixations and dysfunctions. Likewise, further comparative research could examine which of BMHP's full-spectrum of symbolic process approaches add, in what circumstances, to narrative approaches to psychotherapy.

Who Is Qualified to Practice BMHP?

There are elements of BMHP that can be practiced by any mental health professional. Standard of Care dictates that to practice any method a practitioner must have sufficient training. BMHP has many components that can be incorporated into a therapist's psychotherapeutic toolkit. The integral dimensions of BMHP can be learned through the book *BMHP* (Mayer, 2007a), online courses at Alliant University (http://bit.ly/2jwHwIM), through the Bodymind Healing Psychotherapy Certification Program (www.bodymindhealing.com/certificationprogram), and through workshops that are given throughout the country.

Some specific psychotherapeutic skills sets that are helpful to therapists in BMHP training are the following: (1) Cognitive restructuring with a Subjective Units of Distress Scale, (2) Gendlin's Focusing, (3) Symbolic Process, and (4) Tai Chi/Qigong or awareness of somatic gestures.

Evidence Base of BMHP

Many of the individual components of BMHP have a strong efficacy research base, for example, cognitive restructuring, Gendlin's Focusing, psychodynamics, and symbolic process modalities. Many methods of Energy Psychology, such as tapping acu-points while doing psychotherapy, are receiving increased recognition from respected journals (Feinstein, 2018). Likewise, the efficacy of Qigong has been documented (Jahnke, Larkey, Rogers, Etnier, & Lin, 2010; Wayne & Furst, 2013). Regarding efficacy measures used in BMHP, these two are the most common: (1) A Subjective Units of Distress (SUD) scale is usually employed to measure change; and (2) Some patients bring blood pressure monitors to their sessions. As reported above, the River of Life method dramatically reduced a person's blood pressure as measured by a hospital researcher; many other patients have reported similar results. Single-shot case illustrations are reported in the BMHP book showing applications of BMHP to such conditions as hypertension, anxiety, trauma, chronic pain, depression, and substance abuse. However, BMHP has not had the benefit of funding, which suggests that more robust research methodology measures could be applied to its overall integrative approach.

Associated Risks

Since BMHP is a type of somatically-oriented therapy, it can evoke deeper material than some other methods. Therefore, sufficient training in BMHP or in a therapist's chosen approach is fundamental. Likewise, for the patient, deeper material may emerge than in non-somatically oriented psychotherapy. The adept therapist will use appropriate assessment about how and when to apply certain elements of this process to help patients cope with the vicissitudes of life.

Shamanic Dimensions. BMHP can be viewed as a type of "journey to the underworld" (Eliade, 1964; Harner, 1990). However, instead of drums used to activate the journey, the patients' bodily felt sense guides them through the underworld of emotions. To use a metaphor from cross-cultural mythology, just as Theseus in the tale of the Minotaur used the thread of Ariadne tied to a post at the entrance to the underworld to guide him safely through the underground labyrinth, so does the BMHP patient establish a somatic safety zone by using: the River of Life, "the sinking of the chi," and hypnotic anchors such as an inner sanctuary or a specific stance to return to if difficult material arises.

By using the mandala of traditional/alternative therapies, including the ten holographic dimensions of BMHP and state-specific ancient wisdom traditions, this integral psychotherapy is oriented to cultivate a deep root system and to open a safe and wide pathway in the field of transformative psychotherapy.

Acknowledgments

In addition to the authors mentioned in this article and in my book who helped form Bodymind Healing Psychotherapy (BMHP), gratitude goes to: Sifu Master Fong Ha, and other Tai Chi/Qigong masters, who helped to give experiential grounding to BMHP's approach. Eugene Gendlin, Ph.D., for the opportunity to be his first East Bay Area Focusing Training Coordinator, in which capacity I served for ten years. Some locations where BMHP has been presented: Esalen Institute, The Alameda County Psychological Association/The California State Psychological Association. Professional community support: Bessel van der Kolk M.D., John Beebe M.D., David Feinstein, Ph.D., Dr. Kenneth Pelletier, and Stan Krippner Ph.D.

Notes

1. Here *transpersonal psychotherapy* is defined (Mayer, 2007, 2009, 2012) as follows: "Transpersonal Psychology, often called the fourth force of psychology (Freudian/neo-analytic; cognitive/behavioral/Humanistic/existential; Jungian/transpersonal), contains an integral psychotherapy that includes the mandala of all forms of psychotherapy as well as methods that focus specifically on connecting us with the wider whole of which we are a part. This experience of the wider whole can be accessed through energetic pathways (which can be activated through various altered states of consciousness practices: breathing, acu-point touch techniques, methods of postural initiation such as Qigong, spiritual practices from East/West/indigenous traditions, and symbolic process modes of healing)." It should be noted that the term "transpersonal" has been critiqued for overly focusing on altered states "beyond" the personal; but the term transpersonal means both beyond and "through" the personal (Rudhyar, 1970), i.e., containing transcendent and immanent aspects. Likewise, the tradition of transpersonal psychology has been criticized for having an imbalanced emphasis on ascending into higher states; but transpersonal psychology can contain an all vector approach containing ascending, descending, and relational elements (Daniels, 2009; Ferrer, 2011). It is in this broader sense that BMHP, in particular with its integral approach and its use of the transcending/transmuting dialectic (Mayer 2007), contributes specific clinical approaches, perspectives, and tools to transpersonal psychotherapy (Boorstein, 1996; Cortright, 1997; Mayer, 2007, 2009, 2015).

2. For example, behavioral psychology might be put into the 2nd house of Taurus, representing the physical embodiment of new behaviors; self-psychology might be placed in the 1st house, representative of Aries (the birth of a new self in springtime; the 3rd house or Gemini (the importance of communication in psychotherapy); or the 4th house or Cancer. Adding to the non-linear dimensions of BMHP, its ten layers are holographic, i.e., each of the parts is contained in all the other parts and in the whole, encompassing the psychodynamics of early home life; the 5th house, Leo (psychodrama); the 6th house, Virgo (health psychology); the 7th house, Libra (relational approaches); etc. For example, new beliefs (cognitions, 9th house, Sagittarius) are born from transmuting the early affective wounding (4th house, Cancer) and concomitant energy blocks and dysfunctional beliefs derived from early wounding and doing cognitive restructuring (9th house, Sagittarius) to find new, more constructive beliefs.

3. A more complete outlining of the mandala of psychotherapies can be found in *The Mystery of Personal Identity* (Mayer, 1984, reprinted 2012, pp. 106–109; *Bodymind Healing Psychotherapy,* pp. 34–35). Regarding the non-fixed nature of this symbolic process method of conceptualized systems of psychotherapy, a psychoanalytic approach can be seen to be in the 4th house of Cancer, emphasizing the feelings of one's early home life, or it can be seen to be in the 9th house (Sagittarius) of philosophy, due to the birth of a new meaning that comes from working through the early introjects absorbed from one's family of origin and reframing that meaning from an adult viewpoint.

4. Aspects of many old Taoist notions of breathing are being validated by modern science, For example, nose breathing versus mouth breathing has been shown to increase nitric oxide (NO), a bronchodilator and vasodilator that helps lower blood pressure and maintain homeostasis (balance) in the body. NO also sterilizes the air carried into the lungs, opens up the airways, and increases the amount of oxygen taken up in the blood (McKeon, 2015). For an online source for the importance of nose breathing, see J. Mercola at https://articles.mercola.com/sites/articles/archive/2016/07/30/buteyko-breathing.aspx. Other sources report that nose breathing slows the breathing rate, improves lung volume, and helps with a variety of disorders (L. Chaitow et al., 2014).

5. For example, Kidney-1 (located on the ball of the foot, in the middle, slightly in front of center, toward the toes) is particularly helpful for public speaking phobias. This point is also helpful for grounding energy, bringing it down from the head, at times when the ego experiences fragmentation under stress. The Kidney meridian in Chinese medicine is used to deal with the polarity of fear and vitality/strength.

References

Abbott, R., & Lavretsky, H. (2013). Tai Chi and Qigong for the treatment and prevention of mental disorders. *The psychiatric clinics of North America, 36*(1), 109–119.

Aposhyan, S. (2004). *Body-mind psychotherapy.* New York, NY: W.W. Norton.

Assagioli, R. (1965). *Psychosynthesis.* New York, NY: Viking Press.

Bai, Z., Guan, Z., Fan, Y., Liu, C., Yang, K., Ma, B., & Wu, B. (2015). The effects of Qigong for adults with chronic pain. *American Journal of Chinese Medicine, 43*(8) 1525–1539.

Beck, A. (1976). *Cognitive therapy and the emotional disorders.* New York, NY: International Universities Press.

Benson, H., & Klippner, M.Z. (1976). *The relaxation response.* New York, NY: HarperCollins.

Boorstein, S. (1996). *Transpersonal psychotherapy.* Albany, NY: SUNY Press.

Callahan, R., & Trubo, R. (2000). *Tapping the healer within: Using thought-field therapy.* New York, NY: McGraw-Hill Education.

Campbell, J. (1968). *The hero with a thousand faces.* Princeton, NJ: Princeton University Press.

Chaitow, L., Bradley, D., & Gilbert (2014). *Recognizing and treating breathing disorders: A multidisciplinary approach* (2nd ed.). London, UK: Churchill Livingston.

Chia, M. (1990). *Chi Nei Tsang: Chi massage for the vital organs.* Huntington, NY: Healing Tao Books.

Cohen, K. (1997). *The way of Qigong.* New York, NY: Random House.

Cortright, B. (1997). *Psychotherapy and spirit: Theory and practice in transpersonal psychotherapy.* Albany, NY: SUNY Press.

Craig, G., & Fowlie, A. (1995). *Emotional freedom techniques: The manual.* Sea Ranch, CA: Gary Craig.

Daniels, M. (2009). Perspectives and vectors in transpersonal development. *Transpersonal Psychology Review, 13* (1), 87–99.

Deadman, P., & Al-Khafani, M. (1998). *A manual of acupuncture.* Hove, UK: Journal of Chinese Medicine Publications.

Edinger, E. (1985). *Anatomy of the psyche: Alchemical symbolism in psychotherapy.* La Salle, IL: Open Court.

Eliade, M. (1964). *Shamanism: Archaic techniques of ecstasy* (Mythos: The Princeton/Bollingen Series in World Mythology). Princeton, NJ: Princeton University Press.

Ellis, A. (2003). Cognitive restructuring of the disputing of irrational beliefs. In W. Donohue, J. Fisher, & S. Hayes (Eds.), *Cognitive behavior therapy: Applying empirically supported techniques in your practice* (pp. 79–83). Hoboken, NJ: John Wiley & Sons.

Feinstein, D. (2012). Acupoint stimulation in treating psychological disorders: Evidence of efficacy. *Review of General Psychology, 16,* 364–380.

Feinstein, D. (2018, November). Energy psychology: Efficacy, speed, mechanisms. *EXPLORE: The Journal of Science and Healing*. Open access at https://doi.org/10.1016/j.explore.2018.11.003

Feng, A. (2003). *The five animal play Qigong*. Oakland, CA: Zhi Dao Guan Taoist Center.

Ferrar, J. (2011). Participatory spirituality and transpersonal theory: A ten-year retrospective. *The Journal of Transpersonal Psychology, 43* (1), 1–34.

Fingarette, H. (1965). *The self in transformation: Psychoanalysis, philosophy and the life of the spirit*. New York, NY: Harper Torchbooks.

Friedman, H., & Hartelius, G. (2013). *The Wiley-Blackwell handbook of transpersonal psychology*. West Sussex, UK: Wiley Blackwell.

Gach, M. (1990). *Acupressure potent points*. New York, NY: Bantam.

Gendlin, E. (1978). *Focusing*. New York, NY: Bantam Books.

Gendlin, E. (1997). *Experiencing the creation of meaning*. Evanston, IL: Northwestern University Press.

Goodman, F.D. (1990). *Where spirits ride the wind: Trance journeys and other ecstatic experiences*. Indianapolis, IN: University Press.

Gore, B. (1995). *Ecstatic body postures*. Santa Fe, NM: Bear & Co.

Grinder, J., & Bandler, R. (1981). *Trance-formations: Neuro-linguistic programming and the structure of hypnosis*. Moab, UT: Real People Press.

Harner, M. (1990). *The way of the shaman*. New York, NY: Harper One.

Hillman, J. (1975). *Revisioning psychology*. New York, NY: Harper & Row.

Horner, A. (1990). *The primacy of structure: Psychotherapy of underlying character pathology*. Northvale, NJ: Jason Aronson.

Huang, W. (1974). *Fundamentals of Tai Chi Chuan* (2nd ed.). Hong Kong, China: South Sky Book Company.

Irwin, M., Olmstead, R., & Motivala, S. (2008). Improving sleep quality in older adults with moderate sleep complications: Controlled trial of Tai Chi Chih, *Sleep, 31*(7), 1001–1008.

Jahnke, R., Larkey, L., Rogers, C., Etnier, J., & Lin, F. (2010). A comprehensive review of health benefits of Qigong and Tai Chi. *American Journal of Health Promotion: AJHP, 24*(6), e1–e25.

Jung, C. (1961). *Memories, dreams, reflections*. New York, NY: Vintage Books.

Jung, C. (1997). *Jung on Active Imagination*. Princeton: NJ: Princeton University Press.

Kabat-Zinn, J. (2003). Mindfulness-based interventions in context: Past, present and future. *Clinical Psychology: Science and Practice, 10*, 144–156.

Keen, S. (1989). *Your mythic journey*. New York, NY: Tarcher/Perigee.

Kohut, H. (1971). *The analysis of the self*. New York, NY: International Press.

Kuhn, T. (1996). *The structure of scientific revolutions*. Chicago, IL: University of Chicago Press.

Lam, K.C. (1999). *Chi Kung: The way of healing*. New York, NY: Broadway Books.

Lee, M.S., Lee, E.N., Kim, J.I., & Ernst, E. (2010), TC for Lowering resting BP in elderly: A systematic review. *Journal of Evaluation in Clinical Practice, 16*(4), 818–824.

Leskowitz, E. (2000). *Transpersonal hypnosis*. New York, NY: CRC Press.

Levine, P.A. (1997). *Waking the tiger: Healing trauma*. Berkeley, CA: North Atlantic.

Liu, T., & Chen, K. (2010). *Chinese medical Qigong*, Philadelphia, PA: Singing Dragon.

Luk, C. (1972). *Secrets of Chinese meditation*. New York, NY: Samuel Weiser.

Mathews, J., & Mathews, C. (1986). *The Western Way: A practical guide to the Western mystery tradition*. London. UK: Arcana Paperbacks.

Mayer, M. (1977). *A holistic perspective on meaning and identity: Astrological metaphor as a language of personality in psychotherapy*. (Doctoral dissertation). San Francisco, CA: Saybrook Institute.

Mayer, M. (1982). The mythic journey process. *The Focusing Folio 2*(2), 26–43.

Mayer, M. (1984, rev. 2012). *The mystery of personal identity*. San Diego, CA: ACS Publications.

Mayer, M. (1993). *Trials of the heart: Healing the wounds of intimacy*. Berkeley, CA: Celestial Arts.

Mayer, M. (1996). Qigong and behavioral medicine: An integrated approach to chronic pain. *Qi: The Journal of Eastern Health and Fitness, 6*(4), 20–31.

Mayer, M. (1997). Combining behavioral healthcare and Qigong with one chronic hypertensive adult. Mt. Diablo Hospital—Health Medicine Forum. Unpublished study. (Video available from Health Medicine Forum, Walnut Creek, CA, at www.alternativehealth.com).

Mayer, M. (1999). Qigong and hypertension: A critique of research. *Journal of Alternative and Complementary Medicine, 5*(4), 371–382.

Mayer, M. (2000). *Bodymind healing Qigong* (DVD). Orinda, CA: Bodymind Healing Center.

Mayer, M. (2003). Qigong clinical studies. In W.B. Jonas (Ed.), *Healing, intention, and energy medicine* (pp. 121–137). London, UK: Churchill Livingston.

Mayer, M. (2004a). *Secrets to living younger longer: The self-healing path of Qigong, standing meditation and Tai Chi*. Orinda, CA: Bodymind Healing Publications.

Mayer, M. (2004b). What do you stand for? *The Journal of Qigong in America, 1*, 2–13.

Mayer, M. (2005). Qigong: An age-old foundation of energy psychology. *The Energy Field, Association for Comprehensive Energy Psychology, 6*(4), 8.

Mayer, M. (2007a). *Bodymind healing psychotherapy: Ancient pathways to modern health.* Orinda, CA: Bodymind Healing Publications.

Mayer, M (2007b). River of Life CD, Orinda, CA: Bodymind Healing Publications. Available from https://gumroad.com/l/JcCe

Mayer, M. (2008). Mind-Body treatment for anxiety and panic disorders. *California State Journal of Oriental Medicine, 19*(1), 16–17, 27.

Mayer, M. (2009a). *Energy psychology: Self-healing practices for bodymind health,* Berkeley, CA: North Atlantic/Random House.

Mayer, M. (2009b, Winter). Bodymind healing in psychotherapy: Towards an integral, comprehensive energy psychology, *The Energy Field: The International Energy Psychology News and Articles,* p. 13. Available free online at www.bodymindhealing. com/

Mayer, M. (2009c). Energy medicine, *The Qigong Institute.* Article available online at http://qigonginstitute. org/html/papers/EnergyMedicine_EnergyPsychExcerpt.pdf

Mayer, M. (2010, February). Hypertension: An integral bodymind healing approach, *Natural Standard: the Authority on Integrative Medicine.* Available from http://bodymindhealing.com/store-2/downloadable-video-media/

Mayer, M. (2012a). *The path of a reluctant metaphysician: Stories and practices for troubled times.* Orinda, CA: Bodymind Healing Publications.

Mayer, M. (2012b, Summer). Tai Chi Chuan: A postmodern, metaphysical point of view. *Tai Chi Chuan and Oriental Arts.* Available from www.taichiunion.com

Mayer, M. (2015). Transforming energy psychology into a comprehensive transpersonal psychotherapy, solicited by *Blog for the Association for Transpersonal Psychology.* Available from http://acepblog.org/2015/01/09/transforming-energy-psychology-into-a-comprehensive-transpersonal-psychotherapy/

McKeown, P. (2015). *The oxygen advantage: The simple, scientifically proven breathing technique that will revolutionize your health and fitness.* New York, NY: William Morrow and Company.

Meier, C.A. (1967). *Ancient incubation and modern psychotherapy.* Evanston, IL: Northwestern University Press.

Mercola, J. (2016, July). Why nose breathing is so important for optimal health and fitness. Retrieved from https://articles.mercola.com/sites/articles/archive/2016/07/30/buteyko-breathing.aspx

Ming, Y. J. (1989). *The root of Chinese Chi Kung.* Wolfeboro, NH: YMAA Chi Kung Series.

Ogden, P., Minton, K., & Pain, P. (2006). *Trauma and the body: A sensorimotor approach to psychotherapy.* New York, NY: Norton.

Papadakis, T. (1988). *Epidauros.* Zurich, Switzerland: Verlag Schnell.

Porges, S. W. (2001). The polyvagal theory: Phylogenetic substrates of a social nervous system. *International Journal of Psychophysiology, 42*(2), 123–146.

Province, M.A., Hadley, E.C., Hornbrook, M.C., Lipsitz, L.A., Miller, J.P., Mulrow, C.D., Ory, M.G., Sattin, R.W., Tinetti, M.E., & Wolf, S.L. (1995). The effects of exercise on falls in elderly patients: A pre-planned meta-analysis of the FICSIT trials. *Journal of the American Medical Association,272*(17), 1341–1347.

Rodrigues, V., & Friedman, H. (2013). Transpersonal psychotherapies. In H. Friedman & G. Hartelius (Eds.), *The Wiley-Blackwell handbook of transpersonal psychology* (pp. 580–594). West Sussex, UK: Wiley Blackwell.

Rossi, E. (1986). *The psychobiology of mind-body healing: New concepts of therapeutic hypnosis.* New York, NY: Norton.

Rudhyar, D. (1970). *The astrology of personality.* Berkeley, CA: Shambhala.

Sapolsky, R.M. (1998). *Why zebras don't get ulcers: An updated guide to stress, stress-related diseases, and coping.* New York, NY: W.H. Freeman & Company.

Schore, A.N. (2003). *Affect regulation and the repair of the self.* New York, NY: W.W. Norton & Company.

Shapiro, F. (1995). *Eye movement desensitization and reprocessing.* New York, NY: Guilford Press.

Tart, C. (1972). States of consciousness and state-specific science, *Science, 176,* 1203–1210.

Taylor, A.G., Goehler, L.E., Galper, D.I., Innes, K.E., & Bourguignon, C. (2010). Top-down and bottom-up mechanisms in mind-body medicine: Development of an integrative framework for psychophysiological research. *Explore, 6*(1), 29–41.

Van der Kolk, B. (2014). *The body keeps the score: Brain, mind and body in the healing of trauma.* New York, NY: Viking.

Walsh, R., & Shapiro, S. (2006). The meeting of meditative disciplines and Western psychology. *American Psychologist, 61*(3), 227–239.

Wayne, P., & Furst, M. (2013). *The Harvard Medical School guide to Tai Chi.* Boston, MA: Shambhala.

Wilber, K. (2000). *Integral psychology: Consciousness, spirit, psychology, therapy.* Boulder, CO: Shambhala.

Wilhelm, R. (1931/1963). *The secret of the golden flower.* New York, NY: Harcourt, Brace & Jovanovich.

Yeh, G., Wang, C., Wayne, P., & Phillips, R.S. (2008). The effect of Tai Chi on BP: A systematic review. *Preventive Cardiology, 11*(2), 82–89.

Holistic Coaching
for Mental Health

Susan Turner Gabrielle

The field of coaching is a broad, comparatively young, and mostly unregulated discipline employed to support individuals, groups, or organizations that seek to initiate and make change. As such, defining what *coaching* is and is not has been somewhat problematic and depends partly on the external field applying the term; many still look to the coach as a trusted guide and mentor (Ives, 2008). As outlined by the International Coach Federation (ICF) (2016), one of the major professional organizations for coaches, "Professional coaching brings many wonderful benefits: fresh perspectives on personal challenges, enhanced decision-making skills, greater interpersonal effectiveness, and increased confidence" (para. 1). While coaching may utilize some elements of psychology, teaching, or counseling, in its purest form coaches look to individual clients to determine the focus of the coaching agenda (Williams & Menendez, 2015), though clients may also be directed to coaching through a physician, an employer, or an organizational structure. Even in these latter scenarios, however, a coach can be crucial in establishing a climate of trust and alliance in working together to problem-solve or accomplish set objectives, with the clients in the role of navigators, guiding their overall health. Regardless of the reason for coaching, as explained by Biswas-Diener (2009), there is the underlying belief that clients have the "innate capacity to grow and develop," with "a focus on mutually agreed upon goals, and an understanding that the relationship is relatively equal and collaborative" (pp. 544–545).

Different from therapeutic models found in psychiatry or psychology, coaching does not focus on pathology or situations of distress (Nash, 2013), nor lean on the coach as the expert who offers solutions to issues brought to the coaching session (Williams & Menendez, 2015). Indeed, as suggested by Williams and Menendez (2015), "Coaching is not about listening for problems ... it's about listening for possibilities, goals, dreams, aspirations" (p. 16). With that said, coaching may be thought of as similar to some forms of therapy, in that it has the facility to assist clients to recognize how they may be blocking access to their own resources and foundational inner wisdom, while allowing them the space to explore how to better use those sources for help.

This essay briefly examines the origins of coaching, how individuals come to places of change, and how one-on-one coaching—specifically, Holistic Coaching—may assist individuals in coming to places of better mental health.

Origins of Coaching and the Concept of Human Potential

Coaching, as a field of its own, began to be recognized in the mid–1990s, along with general changes occurring in the world of work. Companies, less and less, employed workers for their entire professional lives or paid into their retirement. Instead, employees found their jobs shipped overseas, reduced, or eliminated altogether through downsizing and cutbacks, which pushed them to take responsibility for their own best interests in terms of career development based on personal goals, as well as financial well-being (Flaherty, 2005).

According to Flaherty (2005) and Whitmore (1992/2010), even prior to this time-frame and as early as the 1980s, corporations were beginning to integrate coaching strategies used in the world of sports, especially those of mentoring, in which players were challenged and encouraged to reach for goals by the coach. Gallwey's *The Inner Game of Tennis* (1974) brought to light just how important mental attitude and inner resources were to the observable goals inherent in sports.

In sports as in business, Gallwey (1974) considered how individuals were faced with not only external opponents, but internal ones as well. He also recognized the idea of two competing selves: one self, the *teller*, was responsible for producing ideas, while the other, the *doer*, carried out the ideas. The teller, however, also acted as the inner judge, a critic who examined every step of the process for flaws, so that true potential was inhibited. Gallwey felt that the way to avoid this quashed potential was to learn to silence the critic, so that the doer could carry out actions independently and with more confidence. Using tennis as his model, he recommended that the players conduct their moves "unconsciously," or in what Csikszentmihalyi (1996) named the openness of the "flow" state, which was negatively affected by stress and pressure.

Even prior to Gallwey's application of sports coaching analogies to business, conceptions of fulfilling a sense of potential by understanding the self more fully were examined by humanistic psychology, the "third force." This movement attempted to move away from the early 20th-century focus on Freud's psychoanalytic therapy and the behaviorism theories of Skinner and Watson, all of which obfuscated a sense of growth and personal agency (Plotkin, 2013). Pioneers in humanistic psychology of the 1940s through the early 1970s, including Rogers, May, and Maslow (Moss, 2001), argued that the psychological field should return to its historical roots within philosophy, considering the individual as inherently good and able to turn to inner resources for guidance—assuming support from social structures (Spence, 2007). Of the rise of humanistic psychology, Keen (2001/2012) noted:

> Psychology should not be a science of behavior, but it should be a science of the mind, of mental life, of that subjective self we each are, and of how our experience flows from context to context, tied together by our values, which came from our personal memories, and identities, into a future of striving, and succeeding, and failing, and suffering, a future of challenge, and loss, and chance fates, and ghosts from the past—all of which ends up as who we each are… [p. 230].

Among the driving concepts of this time, known as the human potential movement (HPM) (Spence, 2007), was Maslow's (1943) needs scale, leading to what he referred to as self-actualization. He suggested that once an individual's basic needs for food, shelter, security (including employment), and meaningful relationships were met—at least in part—the person could then seek out higher levels of satisfaction, such as striving to fulfill untapped potential through the bettering of individual capacities. In much the same way coaching does now, the mid–20th-century HPM encouraged individuals to explore their inner resources and accept unlimited capacities for joy, creativity, and satisfaction in their lives, leading to physical and mental well-being.

In subsequent years, models from humanistic psychology and the HPM found their way into psychological treatments within the mainstream, aligned more along the lines of uncovering areas of personal growth and achievement over pathology (Williams & Menendez, 2015). Coaching may be seen to be a direct outgrowth of this movement. Furthermore, as related by Frisch, Lee, Metzger, Robinson, and Rosemarin (2012), with therapy's burgeoning acceptance, "some of those clinical practitioners were invited to apply their skills to the needs of corporate executives, even before executive coaching was labeled as a practice in its own right" (p. 24). In fact, the authors of *Becoming an Exceptional Coach* (Frisch et al., 2012) suggested that coaches become familiar with the ethical guidelines of helping professionals like therapists and counselors as directors for their own practices.

Finally, one other area within the field of psychology that has been especially influential on coaching and motivational behavioral change theories is positive psychology, developed by Seligman (2004). The field revived the ideas of humanistic psychologists like May (1975), who said that clients had the potential "to recognize their own possibilities, enlightening new aspects of themselves and their interpersonal relationships" (p. 108). As described by Curtis and Kelly (2013), "The goal of positive psychology is to help people fully realize their character strengths, competencies, and potential in life by imagining future possibilities as a means to enable human excellence" (p. 22).

Positive psychology focuses on positive emotions such as happiness and empathy, rather than on trauma and dysfunction (Jordan, 2013), and how those emotions may be put to work to improve the client's mental health and induce behavioral change, with evidence that concentration on the positive rather than on the negative is linked to well-being, as well as longer and fuller lives. Peterson and Seligman (2004) developed the Values in Action Inventory Survey (VIA-IS) in order to measure individuals' virtues and character strengths, as well as what they valued in their lives. This survey is frequently employed in coaching discovery sessions.

Given the continued changes to employment and heightened desires for meaningful and fulfilling lives, the coaching field has witnessed a meteoric rise. This is seen in increases of the numbers of coaches and the types of available coaching. Clayton (2011) pointed to at least 50,000 *executive coaches* all over the world, and coaches now additionally specialize in health and wellness, finances, life issues, and creativity, along with other areas. Such movement has brought professional changes to the field, with the establishment of training and education programs, ethical guidelines, and a growing body of literature (Merriam & Brockett, 2007).

Even as the field has expanded, Stober (2006) has noted that coaching is, more than anything else, about the capacity of individuals to experience growth and make meaningful changes in their lives. The field of coaching has consistently drawn from the person-centered humanistic principles of the early HPM and, more recently, positive psychology. In addition, Law (2013) wrote that bringing some psychological awareness to the coaching relationship can further aid in the success of coaching sessions. It holds clients in unconditional positive regard, while encouraging them to lead the way, as they seek out the changes that lead to better physical and mental health.

Holistic Coaching and Mental Health

Kets de Vries (2014) felt that the best way to serve coaching clients was to approach them holistically; as implied, the term *holistic* means whole or complete (Drapela, 1995). Holistic coaching, in some circles known as Integrative Wellness Coaching (IWC), is perhaps representative of the acknowledgment within more conventional forms of medicine that the seven pillars suggested by Gordon and Moss (2003) are indeed essential to the healing and wholeness of the individual, including that of mental health. These characteristics are: recognizing each person's incredible individuality; treating the person as a whole rather than a series of parts; inviting collaboration between patient and physician or other health professional; utilizing individuals' many resources for self-care, which moves far beyond conventional medicine's standard practices of drugs and surgery; understanding that there are many other systems of care that offer benefit to the patient; recognizing the influence of community support to provide encouragement not always found alone; and having spiritual practices that can make available a sense of meaning and hope to the client.

Holistic coaching may also be identified with health or wellness coaching; however, although health-related, it is typically broader in its reach. It can be different from life coaching, for example, as it may be less focused on intrinsically motivated values and personal goals, and more specifically related to overall wellness. Further, holistic coaching is important in bridging the gap between what allopathic or therapeutic personnel may prescribe for an individual and what the client may need (and/or ultimately want) in order to carry that prescription to completion. In that space, the coach is there to provide support during the process, creating a positive atmosphere in which clients are encouraged to make—and sustain—changes that have been identified to be to their benefit.

Though there are disagreements about exactly what qualifications should be prerequisite in holistic coaching, ultimately the coach is not in the role of educator or healthcare expert (Jordan, 2013), but instead places the client at the forefront to establish an individualized plan of management (Alexander, 2011), with goal-setting and accountability at the core. Practically speaking, however, coaching positions within organizations may also have educational or therapeutic duties, requiring coaches to be trained in areas like exercise physiology, have certification as dietitians, or even hold various licensures.

With that said, movement appears to be underway, in some form, toward person-centered holistic approaches, as corporations and businesses partner with clinics to employ not only physicians and nurse practitioners, but also nutrition, exercise, behavioral, and in some cases, complementary and alternative professionals. Maizes, Rakel, and Niemiec (2009) referred to this as a team-based approach, where holistic coaches might work alongside these professionals, helping clients determine what resources will be of most benefit in setting and maintaining health and well-being goals. It is an important part of a whole-being approach that understands that the more the clients have invested in self-care, the more likely they are to follow suggested healthcare guidelines.

Just like other forms of coaching, the holistic coach may use a variety of tools to assist clients in outlining clear agendas, such as the Wellness Wheel, Values in Action (VIA) assessments, or a wellness workbook like that of Travis and Ryan (2004). Once established, coaches may also point to mind-body resources to achieve the stated goals, if so desired, and especially if those therapies are more easily accessible in-house. As Jordan (2013) explained, such coaching moves beyond traditional health coaching or health education to embrace alternative techniques such as those suggested by Gordon and Moss (2003), i.e., hypnosis, meditation, acupuncture, and spiritual practices, among others. This implies a mind-body approach leading to better combined mental and physical well-being.

In the busyness of life, the coaching alliance allows for quiet moments of clarity for clients that they may not otherwise have, through whatever means are comfortable for them. This happens in the course of spending time truly listening *to* a person, in addition to listening *with*, and listening *for* (Williams & Menendez, 2015), a practice for which many conventional practitioners have little time or training. Additionally, such practitioners may come into a meeting as the "expert," stifling clients' ability to truly emote and work out issues for themselves, which is arguably a stronger mental position.

Individuals' Capacity for Change

Individuals who seek out coaching most often do so because they have expressed a desire to make changes in their lives (Longhurst, 2006). Given that Maslow (1987) and Rogers (1961), from a psychological perspective, both espoused the need for individuals to feel generally supported in their environments, coaches can be of genuine support to clients in their contemplation of how goals can be met creatively and positively (Orem, Binkert, & Clancy, 2007), integrating mind and body in the process. However, they also understood that social influences often thwarted the desires of the inner nature, causing people to behave within the strictures of common norms rather than as they may have preferred to do.

Sternberg and Kaufman (2010) revealed that cultural impacts, including traditional thinking and even environmental factors, could determine whether individuals had the ability to take risks and make changes based on creative thinking. At any stage, other inhibitors to original thinking, risk-taking, and change may include socioeconomic status, age, race, gender, birth order, and the number of difficulties a child has had within the family experience (Kohanyi, 2011). Yet, as Hennessey (2010) made clear, barriers to resources and difficult circumstances can also lead individuals to rely on internal sources of motivation and divergent thinking, or the ability to recognize several potential solutions to problems beyond one conventional answer (Kozbelt, Beghetto, & Runco, 2010).

Changes in thinking and action can be additionally problematic due to the individuality of each person. Processes, interventions, or programs that may incite change in one case fail to work in another, as researched by Vlaev and Dolan (2015). Behavior changes are at once challenging to make, then even more difficult to sustain (Bouton, 2014), regardless of whether the present conduct is detrimental to mental or physical health, to family dynamics, or to work situations (Kowalski, 2002). Bouton (2014) observed that nearly three-quarters of those who make changes to embrace healthier habits, such as eliminating drug use, return to those habits within a year of quitting, hinting at the difficulty of lasting change.

As examined by Miller and Rollnick (2013), it is important, when discussing change, that the *why* of change be considered before the *how* of change. Once clients enter a coaching relationship, for example, they may spend some time being ambivalent about change, or the pre-contemplation stage of discussion, prior to being ready for actual change; some clients, also, may not be clear on exactly what changes need to be made.

Once they actually begin to discuss the possibilities, the true issues may surface as part of process coaching (Kimsey-House, Kimsey-House, Sandahl, & Whitworth, 2011). The coach's job, then, is to bring the potential issue into the open, and allow coachees the container of space for discovery (Armstrong, 2012; Longhurst, 2006).

Even though coaching is not a therapeutic venue in the strictest sense, emotions are part of life, and are bound to surface (Nash, 2013). The emotions surrounding what clients choose to do or not do, and what they wish for instead, may to be explored as a means of determining what is really important to the client. Williams and Menendez (2015) referred to this as working with the "figure-ground" (p. 69), a term from Gestalt therapy. If a client states a goal, but the body language, tone of voice, or the sentiment around that goal says otherwise, then the client may be encouraged to dissect what is going on under the surface. Coaches are most effective when they are fully present and able to capture and validate the client's experience in their own language (Siminovitch & Van Eron, 2008). Marquardt (2011) found that coaches can truly be "catalyst[s] of action learning" (p. 101), which happens through establishment of trust, authenticity, and confidentiality, reflecting back to the client the places of learning and opportunities for growth as part of greater mental health.

Related to this point, Emson (2016) recognized, coaches can have awareness about the metaphorical language coachees use when describing both the coaching relationship and their lives overall. As argued by Lakoff and Johnson (2003), metaphors are not merely descriptive poetical and sense-making devices used by individuals to relate one concept to another (i.e., "time is money"), or used not only because we talk about ideas a certain way, but also because "we conceive of them that way—and we act according to the way we conceive of things" (p. 5). Quite often, metaphorical ideas are said and lived subconsciously, outside of reasoned thought. However, if the coaches are listening carefully, these ideas can be invaluable to them as information about how clients make meaning and mentally forms their identity. They can also be helpful to coaches as a way to avoid placing their own meaning onto clients, but instead hear firsthand how coachees relate to their worlds.

According to Sanna and Chang (2006), "Our thoughts, feelings, and behaviors over time inexorably intertwine and intermingle, determining varied reactions such as affect and emotions, judgments and decisions, and plans and future behaviors" (p. 3), understanding that much of behavior is simply unconscious—practiced and repeated patterns—and many individuals lack metacognitive awareness of their actions (Bernays, 1928). However, resistance to change has been shown to be a more complex process than merely a repetition of behaviors over time (Murtagh, Gatersleben, & Uzzell, 2012), and coaches can help clients become more aware of these processes.

Change as a Threat to Identity

Certainly, repeated behaviors can contribute to resistance to change, even when the individual has expressed a desire to do things differently. More importantly, perhaps, is the consideration that opposition to change may come from perceived threats to established identity. Identity, as given by Burke and Stets (2009), incorporates the qualities that make individuals unique and define who they are in relation to the role they play in society. Their identity is shaped, as individuals attempt to understand the self and make meaning of the experiences of the self within the environments it encounters (Proulx, Markman, & Lindberg, 2013), and by interaction with others over time (Breakwell, 1987). Furthermore, Piaget (1976) argued that humans adapt through assimilation and accommodation in order to make meaning and resolve disequilibrium of experience. As meaning is disrupted, meaning construction—and hence, identity—must be revised and reformed, with change being avoided or demanded accordingly (Breakwell, 1987). In addition, attachment to identity, environment, individual strength, freedom to change, and personality traits may all contribute to the acceptance of change (Petriglieri, 2011).

As explored by Neenan (2008), coaching clients frequently face defeating thoughts even before they begin, resulting in little true effort to make change in their lives. This, consequently, leads to few actual alterations or to changes that are not sustained. Clients may be plagued by inaction stemming from a sense of perfectionism, indecisiveness, or anxiety about right action, any of which may impede goal-setting and achievement, even if coachees have previously stated that they desire change. In this case, clients can be encouraged to examine "problem-perpetuating thinking" (p. 4), to think about their thinking, and to consider how more balanced mental activity will help them make desired changes.

Furthermore, if clients are initially unable to tap into their own inner strengths where more creative answers leading to change lie, a strategy suggested by Williams and Menendez (2015) is to have them "act as if" (p. 180), or to come up with alternative stories or choices, pretending, perhaps, that those alternatives are for a friend. To do so requires individuals to use the imaginal self to see the potential future, not as a suppressed identity, and to determine the course of action they might take based on all the choices of that reconsidered identity.

The Role of Coaching on Narrative Identity

Individuals have, throughout time, naturally and necessarily sought out the culture's mythologies, or storylines, to help them discover meaning and their unique position within the larger story (Vogel, 2012). Myths are important as a means of establishing identity, and of deconstructing and understanding behavior against generalized, cultural themes (Goldblatt, 2010). Krippner (1990) wrote that myths are "imaginative statements or stories that address important concerns and issues and that have direct consequences for people's behavior" (p. 3). Existential humanistic psychologist May (1991) observed that myth offered the ability to make meaning in an otherwise meaningless world. Without myths to guide the modern human experience, there would be no structure to hold a community and its people together; without them, instead of a sense of belonging, individuals become apprehensive, lose their moorings—their symbols—and are unable to translate the memory of a lifetime of existential experiences into their own myths of meaning (Tullett et al., 2013).

Whether human beings experience meaning-making individually, within groups, or through societal influences, the stories they tell themselves and that make up their lives are formed and cultivated as *narrative identities* (McAdams & McLean, 2013). Customs, habits, rituals, and ceremonies surrounding the meanings behind those narratives, in the form of daily activities, yearly celebrations, or lifelong-held beliefs, are developed and re-created continually (Leeming, 2001) and as individuals attempt to retain a sense of cohesiveness (McAdams & McLean, 2013). Therefore, any time changes occur, especially those that promote or demote the self-image, meaning must be re-formed and replaced, and the personal myth rewritten (Stevens, 1995).

Self-preservation and associated identity as narrative constructs are crucial aspects of behavior, and may go through many generational iterations before change occurs; in some cases, they are merely swept up as "new," but retain old characteristics (Todd, 2005). Adjustments to the storylines of identity are always taking place, as new situations are encountered and previous experience informs meaning and reaction. Going through old myths and replacing them with new ones call on the individual to be aware and open to change, with the hope that more fruitful situations and experiences await. As an example, and depending on the situation, holistic coaching may allow the client to create a healing narrative where none existed previously (Kreisberg et al., 2016). Feinstein and Krippner (1997) observed, "Mindfully weaving a carefully reformulated mythology into the fabric of your life is a concentrated act of personal empowerment" (p. 265).

Quite often, when individuals face challenges in their created mythologies and become aware that change is necessary, the attempts they make at transformation or evolution are met with resistance, whether within themselves, from others, or because of outside circumstances beyond their control (Owler, 2012). Furthermore, when effort is exerted for change, disruption of the identity occurs. Depending on the meaning assigned to the part of the identity that is attempting the change, dysfunctional behavior may be discarded because of the recognition that it is not serving the individual in the best way. Yet it may, instead, become even more entrenched if the self feels attacked and in danger of being lost (Murtagh, Gatersleben, & Uzzell, 2012).

Ideally, the holistic coaching model offers an opportunity for clients to discuss or "try on" new stories and potential changes to circumstances for the self, before actually taking the steps to do so, and this is done through the mutual dialogue exchange between the coach and coachee. As detailed by Armstrong (2012), the ancient Greek meaning of *dialogue* originally indicated the movement of ideas between individuals; indeed, as verbal creatures, it is how humans construct individual and social identity.

Key in this exchange is the ability of the coach to dialogue *with* the coachee in collaboration. Rather than the coach holding the role of expert, where a framework of meaning is imposed upon the client, true dialogue allows clients to generate meaning by making sense of their experience in the present moment, and then determine what they would like to do with that new meaning (Armstrong, 2012). This type of listening and dialogue is termed by Newnham-Kanas, Morrow, and Irwin (2010) as "dancing in the moment" (p. 29), permitting clients to direct the conversation organically and open the way for "aha!" moments where stories are rewritten and change can occur (Longhurst, 2006).

Though dialogue naturally implies a two-sided and equal conversation, Williams and Menendez (2015) proposed that there are times in coaching sessions when challenging the beliefs or mythologies of clients may be important, in order to break down barriers to change. For example, in the case of clients who believe things can only be done a certain way because that has been their previous experience, they may be challenged to consider alternatives. Coaches may also press the clients to think about different choices that they are not considering at the moment, or they may request directly that the clients do things completely differently from what they would normally do—with the caveat that the clients may refuse. It may be necessary to ask clients to justify their answers, or to keep records or a journal, or to press them for commitments to consider alternative possibilities in their lives.

Regardless, it is ultimately necessary to let clients lead the coaching agenda and determine goals (Williams & Menendez, 2015), whether the coach agrees or not. Coaches, like other helping professionals, have the potential to exert significant influence, causing clients to be pushed into uncomfortable and even unrealistic intents because they may want to please their coaches or feel that their own goals are too incremental. Even though coaching is goal-oriented by nature, objectives must be set that have the potential to encourage growth and meaning-making for the client (Grant, 2003), but that do not lead to repeated situations of failing to achieve goals. Here, coaches can be instrumental in verifying if goals are "SMART." Though the acronym varies slightly among its users, it typically refers to goals that are specific, meaningful, achievable, realistic, and time-based (Stober & Grant, 2006).

While the coaching relationship is centered on mutuality, in which the coach and the coachees are on equal footing, Moen and Kvalsund (2008) contended that the best coaching relationship should ultimately foster the independence of the coachees in order for them to take self-initiated actions. It is important to foster the conditions for internal motivation in clients, so that they are not dependent on the coach continually to help facilitate transformation (Owler, 2012). This evolution involves personal engagement and some understanding of the motivating factors underlying decision-making and permanent change.

"YNWA"

In some ways, coaching may be far less mentally threatening than psychotherapy, even if clients have been referred to coaching by medical professionals. Therapy, whether justified or not, can have negative connotations attached to it, and some are unwilling even to consider it (Williams & Menendez, 2015). Coaching has fewer of those associations, so it can be viewed as a more positively focused experience, putting the power in the client's hands as the expert.

Coaching delivery systems vary widely; they may be carried out in person, over the phone, by a medium such as Skype, or even by e-mail. Sessions may be as short as 10–20 minutes, or up to 50 minutes to two hours, though the latter is rarer; the number of meetings will often be arranged in advance. depending on the objective. Some coachees may employ the coach for a month, while others will meet for a year, working on several goals during that period.

Dennis et al. (2013) found that coaching done by telephone, with those who had chronic conditions such as diabetes, coronary artery disease, and others, saw improvements in health behavior, general health, confidence, and satisfaction. Likewise, Nothwehr (2013) learned that telephonic coaching could encourage lifestyle changes and positive behavior. Of over 150,000 coaching clients surveyed by the International Coach Federation in 2009, a majority reported benefits such as increased self-esteem and better work/life balance, while Hall (2013) noted the beneficial effects of mindfulness coaching in business.

McKeown, Roy, and Spandler (2015) discussed a song that is sung at certain sporting events titled, "You'll Never Walk Alone" (YNWA). It occurs during moments of intense emotion surrounding the sport, and has the effect of promoting commonality, or "the importance of solidarity, peer support, and alliances in overcoming adversity" (p. 361). They contended that the same metaphor, along with a sports mentality, could be applied in cases of mental health initiatives, finding that it worked particularly well with men. The professionals employed were referred to as coaches; they were not necessarily trained therapists or counselors, and were not distinguishable by dress. All participants were part of the coaching experience as support in small groups, which allowed for open dialogue related to mental health issues such as unemployment, depression, drug dependency, and relationship concerns. They found that men who were normally unlikely to seek out conventional healthcare services were more willing to experience the values of intervention in this form.

Finally, Thom et al. (2014) pointed to the use of coaches in a team-based approach, where they acted as liaisons between physicians and patients. Contrary to the idea that this would limit trusting interaction and relationship-building between doctor and client, the study found that the use of a health coach actually increased communication between the two. As a resource, coaching allowed clients to feel heard, and empowered them to pose questions they might not otherwise ask.

As can be seen in these examples, coaching can be utilized in a number of ways to the benefit of clients, whether by phone, in a small-group setting, or as an inter-office adjunct. The key, it seems, is that individuals are treated as whole but unique persons, and that they are allowed the opportunity to voice how they see themselves in the world and how they would like to move forward in their lives.

Conclusion

Clients are typically aware of circumstances when they are not living up to their fullest potential and may seek out coaching to help them live more complete experiences (Newnham-Kanas, Morrow, & Irwin, 2010), although they may be less aware of the reasons behind the choices they have previously made prior to coaching. As has been shown, the roles of meaning-making and identity are potential factors that are important considerations around whether goals leading to change are set, realized, or thwarted, and sustained or abandoned.

Coaching has, at its foundation, a humanistic, person-centered ideology, and looks to the client to set the agenda for how change is to be accomplished. Humanistic psychology also continues to influence coaching as a basic philosophical practice, including (a) a growth-oriented approach, (b) the practitioner-client relationship as a foundational source of change, (c) unconditional positive regard for the client, (d) a holistic view of the person and the human experience, and (e) the possibility of choice and accompanying responsibility (Stober, 2006). Neenan (2008) posited that it may also be helpful for the coach to understand the psychological basics of human motivation, as has been presented here, in order to help clients more effectively, especially those who may face situations of willful disregard in their health and well-being, even when (or maybe because of being) recommended by a physician for coaching.

Stoltzfus (2008) clarified that, while the agenda is the client's, the coaching experience is potentially powerful because it provides a clear framework for clients in which they must clearly identify objectives, make decisions about those objectives, and be held accountable to act on the choices based on those decisions. The coaching alliance is built on establishing authentic relationships with clients, which then lend themselves to true curiosity in the coaching session (Biswas-Diener, 2009); mutual trust leads to powerful questioning beneficial to the coachee, with an ongoing conviction that the client has the resources within to both generate and carry out goals. In that space, the coach is there to provide support during the process, creating a positive atmosphere in which coachees are encouraged to make—and sustain—changes that have been identified to be of importance to them and based on identified values.

As outlined by Williams and Menendez (2015), "The ICF defines coaching as partnering with clients in a thought provoking and creative process that inspires them to maximize their personal and professional potential…" (p. 1). The ways in which this may be accomplished are numerous, including examining meaning-making based on personal and global myths, and looking to metaphorical language, particularly as it influences action.

Especially when change is needed due to health reasons, as ordered by organizational managers, or personally desired by a client, coaching has the potential to provide support and accountability in meaningful ways (Grant, 2003) and across a variety of modalities. Coaches, such as Holistic or Integrative Wellness Coaches, see clients as resourceful and fully capable of achieving set goals, and set out to assist them in the process.

REFERENCES

Armstrong, H. (2012). Coaching as dialogue: Creating space for (mis)understandings. *International Journal of Evidence Based Coaching and Mentoring, 10*(1), 33–47.

Bernays, E. (1928). *Propaganda.* Retrieved from http://www.historyisaweapon.org/defcon1/bernprop.html

Biswas-Diener, R. (2009). Personal coaching as a positive intervention. *Journal of Clinical Psychology: In session, 65*(5), 544–553.

Bouton, M.E. (2014). Why behavior change is difficult to sustain. *Preventative Medicine, 68,* 29–36.

Breakwell, G. (1987). *Coping with threatened identities.* New York, NY: Routledge.

Burke, P., & Stets, J.E. (2009). *Identity theory.* New York, NY: Oxford University Press.

Clayton, T. (2011). *The lived experiences of executive coaches' interdisciplinary competencies* (Doctoral dissertation). Retrieved from ProQuest. (UMI Number: 3482867)

Csikszentmihalyi, M. (1996). *Creativity.* New York, NY: HarperCollins.

Curtis, D.F., & Kelly, L.L. (2013). Effect of a quality of life coaching intervention on psychological courage and self-determination. *International Journal of Evidence Based Coaching and Mentoring, 11*(1), 20–38.

Dennis, S.M., Harris, M., Lloyd, J., Davies, G.P., Faruqi, N., & Zwar, N. (2013). Do people with existing chronic conditions benefit from telephone coaching? A rapid review. *Australian Health Review, 37,* 381–388.

Drapela, V. (1995). *A review of personality theories* (2nd ed.). Springfield, IL: Charles C. Thomas.

Emson, N. (2016). Exploring metaphor use and its insight into sense making with executive coaching clients. *International Journal of Evidence Based Coaching and Mentoring, 20,* 59–75.

Feinstein, D., & Krippner, S. (1997). *The mythic path: Discovering the guiding stories of your past—Creating a vision of your future.* New York, NY: Jeremy P. Tarcher/Putnam Books.

Flaherty, J. (2005). *Coaching: Evoking excellence in others* (2nd ed.). Burlington, MA: Elsevier Butterworth-Heinemann.

Frisch, M.H., Lee, R.J., Metzger, K.L., Robinson, J., & Rosemarin, J. (2012). *Becoming an exceptional executive coach: Use your knowledge, experience, and intuition to help leaders excel.* New York, NY: American Management Association.

Gallwey, W.T. (1974). *The inner game of tennis.* New York, NY: Random House.

Goldblatt, P. (2010). Stories of longing and remembrance: The role of myth in making meaning. *MultiCultural Review, 19*(1), 37–41.

Grant, A.M. (2003). The impact of life coaching on goal attainment, metacognition and mental health. *Social Behavior and Personality, 31*(3), 253–263.

Hall, L. (2013). *Mindful coaching: How mindfulness can transform coaching practice.* London, UK: KoganPage.

International Coach Federation. (2009). Results of landmark ICF Global coaching client study released for international coaching week. Retrieved from http://coachfederation.org/prdetail.cfm?ItemNumber=1495&_ga=1.154551416.1328378703.1484273602

International Coach Federation. (2016). Benefits of using a coach. Retrieved from https://www.coachfederation.org/need/landing.cfm?ItemNumber=747&navItemNumber=565

Ives, Y. (2008). What is "coaching"? An exploration of conflicting paradigms. *International Journal of Evidence Based Coaching and Mentoring, 6*(2), 100–113.

Jordan, M. (2013). *How to be a health coach: An integrative wellness approach.* San Rafael, CA: Global Medicine Enterprises.

Keen, E. (2001/2012). Keeping the psyche in psychology. *The Humanistic Psychologist, 40,* 224–231.

Kets de Vries, M.F.R. (2014). Dream journeys: A new territory for executive coaching. *Consulting Psychology Journal: Practice and Research, 66*(2), 77–92.

Kimsey-House, H., Kimsey-House, K., Sandahl, P., & Whitworth, L. (2011). *Co-active coaching: Changing business, transforming lives* (3rd ed.). Boston, MA: Nicholas Brealey.

Kohanyi, A. (2011). Families and creativity. In M.A. Runco & S.R. Pritzker (Eds.), *The encyclopedia of creativity* (2nd ed.), Vol. 1, pp. 503–508. San Diego, CA: Academic Press.

Kowalski, K.M. (2002). How to cope with change. *Current Health, 29*(1), 6–11.

Kozbelt, A., Beghetto, R.A., & Runco, M.A. (2010). Theories of creativity. In J.C. Kaufman & R.J. Sternberg (Eds.), *The Cambridge handbook of creativity* (pp. 20–47). New York, NY: Cambridge University Press.

Kreisberg, J., Douds, A., Phillips, A., Ward, J.L., Stoddart, J., Flaherty, J., … & Marra, R. (2016). *Coaching and healing: Transcending the illness narrative.* Tucson, AZ: Integral Publishers.

Krippner, S. (Ed.). (1990). *Dreamtime and dreamwork: Decoding the language of the night.* Los Angeles, CA: Jeremy P. Tarcher

Lakoff, G., & Johnson, M. (2003). *Metaphors we live by.* Chicago, IL: University of Chicago Press.

Law, H. (2013). *The psychology of coaching, mentoring, and learning.* West Sussex, UK: Wiley-Blackwell.

Leeming, D.A. (2001). Myth and therapy. *Journal of Religion and Health, 40*(1), 115–119.

Longhurst, L. (2006). The 'aha' moment in co-active coaching and its effects on belief and behavioural changes. *International Journal of Evidence Based Coaching and Mentoring, 4*(2), 61–73.

Marquardt, M.J. (2011). The coach as catalyst for action learning. *Training and Management Development Method, 25*(1), 101–118.

Maslow, A.H. (1943). A theory of human motivation. *Psychological Review, 50,* 370–396.

Maslow, A.H. (1987). *Motivation and personality* (3rd ed.). New York, NY: Harper Row.

May, R. (1975). *The courage to create.* New York, NY: W.W. Norton & Co.

May, R. (1991). *The cry for myth.* New York, NY: W.W. Norton & Co.

McAdams, D.P., & McLean, K.C. (2013). Narrative identity. *Current Directions in Psychological Science, 22*(3), 233–238.

McKeown, M., Roy, A., & Spandler, H. (2015). "You'll never walk alone": Supportive social relations in a football and mental health project. *International Journal of Mental Health Nursing, 24,* 360–369.

Merriam, S.B., & Brockett, R.G. (2007). *Profession and practice of adult education: An introduction.* San Francisco, CA: Jossey-Bass.

Miller, W.R., & Rollnick, S. (2013). *Motivational interviewing.* New York, NY: The Guilford Press.

Moen, F., & Kvalsund, R. (2008). What communications or relational factors characterize the method, skills, and techniques of executive coaching? *International Journal of Coaching in Organizations, 6*(2), 102–127.

Moss, D. (2001). The roots and genealogy of humanistic psychology. In K. J. Schneider, J. F. T. Bugental, & J. F. Pierson (Eds.). *The handbook of humanistic psychology* (pp. 5–27). Thousand Oaks, CA: Sage.

Murtagh, N., Gatersleben, B., & Uzzell, D. (2012). Self-identity threat and resistance to change: Evidence from regular travel behavior. *Journal of Environmental Psychology, 32,* 318–326.

Nash, J. (2013). Coaching and mental health. In J. Passmore (Ed.), *Diversity in coaching: Working with gender, culture, race and age* (2nd ed.) (pp. 261–279). London, UK: Association for Coaching.

Neenan, M. (2008). From cognitive behaviour therapy (CBT) to cognitive behaviour coaching (CBC). *Journal of Rational-Emotive and Cognitive-Behaviour Therapy, 26,* 3–15.

Newnham-Kanas, C., Morrow, D., & Irwin, J.D. (2010). Motivational coaching: A functional juxtaposition of three methods for health behaviour change: Motivational interviewing, coaching, and skilled helping. *International Journal of Evidence Based Coaching and Mentoring, 8*(2), 27–48.

Nothwehr, F. (2013). People with unhealthy lifestyle behaviours benefit from remote coaching via mobile technology. *Evidence Based Nursing, 16*(1), 22–23.

Orem, S.L., Binkert, J., & Clancy, A.L. (2007). *Appreciative coaching.* San Francisco, CA: Jossey-Bass.

Owler, K. (2012). Facilitating internal motivation: Impacts of the life code matrix model on working life. *International Journal of Evidence Based Coaching and Mentoring, 10*(2), 65–75.

Peterson, C., & Seligman, M.E.P. (2004). *Character strengths and virtues: A handbook and classification.* Oxford, UK: Oxford University Press.

Petriglieri, J.L. (2011). *Threatened identities: Essays on the impact of identity threat on the dynamics of individuals' identities* (Doctoral dissertation). Retrieved from ProQuest. (UMI Number: 3503339)

Piaget, J. (1976). *To understand is to invent.* New York, NY: Penguin.

Plotkin, B. (2013). *Wild mind: A field guide to the human psyche.* Novato, CA: New World Library.

Proulx, T., Markman, K.D., & Lindberg, M.J. (2013). Introduction: The new science of meaning. In K.D. Markman, T. Proulx, & M.J. Lindberg (Eds.), *The psychology of meaning* (pp. 3–14). Washington, D.C.: American Psychological Association.

Rogers, C.R. (1961). *On becoming a person.* Boston, MA: Houghton Mifflin.

Sanna, L.J., & Chang, E.C. (2006). *Judgments over time: The interplay of thoughts, feelings, and behaviors.* London, UK: Oxford University Press.

Seligman, M.E.P. (2004). *Authentic happiness: Using the new positive psychology to realize your potential for lasting fulfilment.* New York, NY: Atria Book Publishing.

Siminovitch, D.E., & Van Eron, A.M. (2008). The power of presence and intentional use of self: Coaching for awareness, choice, and change. *The International Journal of Coaching in Organizations, 6*(3), 90–111.

Spence, G.B. (2007). Further development of evidence-based coaching: Lessons from the rise and fall of the human potential movement. *Australian Psychologist, 42*(4), 255–265.

Sternberg, R.J., & Kaufman J.C. (2010). Constraints on creativity: Obvious and not so obvious. In J.C. Kaufman & R.J. Sternberg (Eds.), *The Cambridge handbook of creativity (pp. 467–482).* New York, NY: Cambridge University Press.

Stevens, A. (1995). *Private myths: Dreams and dreaming.* Cambridge, MA: Harvard University Press.

Stober, D.R. (2006). Coaching from the humanistic perspective. In D.R. Stober & A.M. Grant (Eds.), *Evidence based coaching handbook: Putting best practices to work for your clients* (pp. 17–50). Hoboken, NJ: John Wiley & Sons.

Stober, D.R., & Grant, A.M. (2006). *Evidence based coaching handbook: Putting best practices to work for your clients.* Hoboken, NJ: John Wiley & Sons.

Stoltzfus, T. (2008). *Coaching questions: A coach's guide to powerful asking skills.* Virginia Beach, VA: Tony Stoltzfus.

Thom, D.H., Hessler, D., Willard-Grace, R., Bodenheimer, T., Najmabadi, A., Araujo, C., & Chen, E.H. (2014). Does health coaching change patients' trust in their primary care provider? *Patient Education and Counseling, 96,* 135–138.

Todd, J. (2005). Social transformation, collective categories, and identity change. *Theory and Society, 34,* 429–463.

Travis, J.W., & Ryan, R.S. (2004). *Wellness workbook: How to achieve enduring health and vitality* (3rd ed.). Berkeley, CA: Celestial Arts, Inc.

Tullett, A.M., Prentice, M.S., Teper, R., Nash, K.A., Inzlicht, M., & McGregor, I. (2013). Neural and motivational mechanics of meaning and threat. In K. D. Markman, T. Proulx, & M. J. Lindberg (Eds.), *The psychology of meaning* (pp. 401–419). Washington, D.C.: American Psychological Association.

Vlaev, I., & Dolan, P. (2015). Action change theory: A reinforcement learning perspective on behavior change. *Review of General Psychology, 19*(1), 69–95.

Vogel, M. (2012). Story matters: An inquiry into the role of narrative in coaching. *International Journal of Evidence Based Coaching and Mentoring, 10*(1), 1–12.

Whitmore, J. (1992/2010). *Coaching for performance.* London, UK: Nicholas Brealey Publishing.

Williams, P., & Menendez, D.S. (2015). *Becoming a professional life coach: Lessons from the Institute for Life Coach Training.* New York, NY: W.W. Norton.

The Role of Massage Therapy in Psychological Services

Evidence and Implications for Mental Health Practitioners

GRANT J. RICH

Several surveys, from the early 1990s and the early 2000s, show that approximately one third of the U.S. population utilizes some form of complementary and alternative medicine (CAM) (Barnes, Powell-Griner, McFann, & Nahin, 2004; Eisenberg et al., 1993). One such healing modality is massage therapy. In recent decades, psychologists have begun to explore the effects of massage therapy relevant to mental health. For instance, publishing in APA journals, Field (1998), Moyer, Rounds, and Hannum (2004), and Rich (2010) described the evidence for massage therapy for a variety of clinical conditions of relevance to psychology, including depressed and anxious moods, pain, enhancing immune function, increasing attentiveness, facilitating growth and development, and others. Despite such findings, many questions remained unanswered. This essay aims, first, to define and clarify massage therapy as a healing modality, and, second, discuss its implications for psychological services, including its efficacy for various psychological conditions, issues of interest to psychologists, and its suitability and potential limitations as a supplement to the work of such helping professionals. In addition, an overview of educational requirements, credentialing, and licensing will be offered, along with a description of a typical session.

Massage therapy, which has been documented in many world cultures, has been described as being present for thousands of years in locations such as China, India, Mesopotamia, Mesoamerica, Australia, various Pacific cultures, and ancient Greece and Rome (Calvert, 2002; Huber & Sandstrom, 2001). In North America, massage therapy was part of standard medical care well into the first half of the 20th century (Benjamin, 2015; Rich, 2010). It is worth noting that Sigmund Freud himself utilized massage early in his career, as described in *Studies on Hysteria* (Freud, 1893). The history of psychological examination of touch extends well into the 19th century, near the time of the founding of formal psychology, and includes its exploration by researchers in terms of sensation and perception/cognitive neuroscience (e.g., Heller & Schiff, 1991), human development (e.g., Field, 2006, 2014), social psychology (Hertenstein & Weiss, 2011), and clinical/counseling psychology (Dryden & Moyer, 2012). Recently, in the 21st century, several psychologists have examined the use of massage therapy as a subdiscipline of health psychology and CAM (e.g., Field, 2009; Hymel & Rich, 2014). Other valuable perspectives on healing touch come from medicine (e.g., Linden, 2014), history (e.g., Classen, 2005, 2012; Kripal, 2007), anthropology (e.g., Jablonksi, 2006; Montagu, 1986), and even literary studies (e.g., Krasner, 2010). The literature on massage therapy research, and touch research more generally, is broadly and diffusely distributed among several domains. In addition to psychology, and the fields mentioned above, relevant research is produced in such disciplines as physical therapy, occupational therapy, nursing, and public health. A few peer-reviewed, academic journals dedicated specifically to massage therapy and bodywork do exist, including the *Journal of Bodywork and Movement Therapies* (JBMT) (http://www.bodyworkmovementtherapies.com/) and the Massage Therapy Foundation's *International Journal of Therapeutic Massage and Bodywork* (IJTMB) (http://ijtmb.com).

Definitions of Massage Therapy

Complicating matters for psychologists seeking to understand the potential advantages and disadvantages of massage therapy as complementary and alternative medicine for holistic mental health care is the fact that there is a veritable plethora of techniques that fall under the umbrella term *massage*. For instance, the encyclopedia of bodywork describes more than two hundred different types of bodywork (Stillerman, 1996), and each of these techniques may vary along dimensions including type and depth of pressure, type and amount of training and education required to practice, and types of conditions for which the therapy is recommended or not recommended. Each of these therapies may be associated with different physiological and psychological effects, which suggests that researchers and consumers of massage therapy research should be cautious in determining what type of massage or bodywork is being described in any given study. By way of illustration, some definitions for three common massage and bodywork techniques will be offered. Reiki energy healing, Rolfing, and classic Swedish massage will now be described.

Claire (1995) defined *reiki* as "an ancient energetic healing technique utilizing the laying on of hands.... Reiki is a Japanese word that means 'universal life energy'" (p. 291). According to Claire, such practitioners work by either placing hands over important parts of the body or by visualizing special symbols, "enabling them to send healing energy, even at a distance" (p. 291). Stillerman (1996) connected spiritual discipline practices by Tibetan monks over two thousand years ago with the modern tradition of reiki championed by the Japanese monk Mikao Usui in the 19th century. There is comparatively little research on reiki and related "energy" techniques in the mainstream peer-reviewed psychology and medical literature. In addition, some research has been skeptical about the existence of such a detectable energy field. For instance, using experimental conditions, when Rosa, Rosa, Sarner, and Barrett (1998) examined the ability of therapeutic touch practitioners (a modality related to reiki) to detect the human energy field, they found that the practitioners performed no better than chance. A helpful, more recent review chapter of the research literature on reiki, written by psychologists, offered some contrasting, supporting evidence for its efficacy in certain situations, while also noting the need for caution, as training parameters for reiki practitioners are not universally standardized in the USA or internationally (Barnett, Shale, & Fisher, 2014). For example, some localities may require reiki practitioners to be certified or licensed as massage therapists, while in other jurisdictions different credentials or no credentials at all may be needed.

In contrast to reiki, which uses light touch or no touch at all, *Rolfing* is a type of bodywork that involves deep-tissue manipulation (Claire, 1995). Named for Dr. Ida Rolf, who earned a Ph.D. in biochemistry from Columbia University in 1920, Rolf, at the request of Fritz Perls, the Gestalt psychologist, began to teach at California's Esalen Institute in the 1960s (Benjamin, 2015; Claire, 1995; Kripal, 2007). Rolfing, which is also sometimes called Structural Integration, involves a series of ten bodywork sessions aimed at creating physical and emotional change, including body posture and movement. Much focus is devoted to the impact of gravity, the balance/alignment of body segments or blocks, and connective tissue/fascia (Knaster, 1996; Stillerman, 1996). Though there is written work by Rolfers themselves, including by Ida Rolf (1977/1989), there is a relative paucity of peer reviewed research in mainstream psychology and medical journals in support of Rolfing (e.g., Australian Government Department of Health, 2015). That said, research on fascia and bodywork more generally has become much more prevalent in recent years, with academic conferences and journal sections devoted to the topic (e.g., *Journal of Bodywork and Massage Therapy,* http://www.bodyworkmovementtherapies. com/). It should also be noted that officially Rolfers are trained at the Rolf Institute in Boulder, Colorado, though practitioners do train in closely related modalities, and may, for instance, refer to their work as *structural integration.* Another important point is that Rolfing is a different from Esalen massage. That is, while Rolfing is a deep tissue modality, which some clients may find painful at times, Esalen massage is known for its long, sweeping, gliding strokes and does not involved a standardized set of sessions (Gallace & Spence, 2014; Knaster, 1996; Stillerman, 1996).

In contrast to the light touch, lack of touch, or deep touch of reiki or Rolfing, classic Swedish massage therapy may justly be considered generally more moderate, though it too may occasionally include both light and deep techniques. Swedish massage, also known as Western massage, is the most familiar and popular type of massage therapy in North America and Europe (Stillerman, 1996). The technique as utilized today is typically credited to the Swedish gymnastics instructor, Per Henrik Ling (1776–1839), who described five basic massage strokes, linking his technique to anatomy and physiology (Stillerman, 1996). The Swedish Institute, the first Swedish massage school in the USA, was founded in 1916 and continues today. The five basic Swedish techniques had French labels; today they are commonly termed: effleurage (gliding strokes), pétrissage (kneading strokes), friction (rubbing, including rolling and wringing, both circular and cross-fiber), tapotement (percussion movements such as tapping, pincement, hacking, pounding, rapping, and clapping), and vibration (shaking, including rocking) (Salvo, 2007). Since most peer-reviewed research on massage therapy utilizes Swedish massage techniques, unless otherwise specified the research that follows in this article uses this modality.

Though there are many definitions of *massage therapy,* one helpful one is offered in a standard massage therapy text. As Holey and Cook (2004) defined it, "Massage is the manipulation of the soft tissues of the body by a trained therapist as a component of a holistic therapeutic intervention" (p. 6). Such a definition fits Swedish massage and Rolfing, but not all types or reiki or energy healing.

A typical Swedish massage therapy session usually lasts one hour, though in hospital or medical settings, especially when insurance reimbursement is involved, the session may be briefer, say, thirty minutes or even fifteen minutes. First-time clients typically sign waivers, complete health screenings to determine whether massage therapy is an appropriate healing modality or is contraindicated, and read or listen to educational materials to describe expectations and also policies about payment and inappropriate client behavior. Additionally, most massage therapists may utilize various pre-massage paper and pencil screenings to determine the client's type of condition and location of the problem. Further details on assessment measures, both those completed by clients and those utilized by the therapists (such as the McGill Pain Inventory, the Visual Analogue Scale, the Spielberger State-Trait Anxiety Measure, SOAP notes, etc.), may be found in publications by Dryden and Moyer (2012), Field (2006), Hertenstein and Weiss (2011), Salvo (2007), Thompson (2012), and Werner (2013).

The client undresses to a level of comfort (typically underwear, though some forms such as Esalen may have different norms traditionally) and is carefully draped on a massage table. The table may include headrests and bolsters for feet/arms, or other adaptations to accommodate different body types and sizes. A general relaxation session of massage therapy may include work during half of which the client is prone, and during the other half supine. Upper and lower arms and upper and lower legs are massaged, along with other sections of the body, including chest, torso, abdomen, back, as well as head (including face and scalp). Clients may offer feedback to the therapist concerning pressure, comfort, and other factors such as room temperature and their perceptions of the effectiveness of the treatment. Usually the massage therapist utilizes oils, powders, or gels, but clients may elect not to use such products, due to allergies or fears of ruining clothing, and so on. Typically, the therapist will utilize all five Swedish techniques (effleurage, pétrissage, friction, tapotement, and vibration). Though some therapists will follow a standardized manualized protocol, most therapists will adapt the treatment individually to the specific client's needs. After treatment, typically the clients are allowed several minutes alone in the room, to refocus attention and to dress. Sometimes payment is made before the therapy session, while some therapists prefer payment after a session, but typically all therapists ask for feedback on their work after the session concludes. Often, post-massage, discussion may include plans for whether future massage therapy is desired and/or advised.

Brief Survey of Psychological Effects of Massage Therapy

Modern massage research relevant to psychology focuses on a variety of clinical conditions and mental states. Of particular significance are the effects of massage therapy for depression, anxiety, posttraumatic stress, and pain (Rich, 2010, 2013), though the impact of massage therapy on a range of other clinical conditions has also been investigated (e.g., Field, 2006). Broadly speaking, massage therapy research has utilized both correlation and experimental approaches, with survey and questionnaire data as well as physiological data. Several scholars have written specifically on research methods for massage therapy (e.g., Andrade & Clifford, 2012; Hymel, 2005; Menard, 2002; 2003; Rich, 2002; Verhoef, 2012). One issue is the difficulty of creating double-blind studies, as of course, the massage therapist providing the treatment will know if she or he is or is not providing a massage (Rich, 2002); it should be emphasized that similar problems regarding the impossibility of double-blind studies also challenge research on psychotherapists (Seligman, 1995). Space precludes discussion of all the conditions for which massage therapy has shown some effectiveness; instead, three issues of interest to psychologists will be emphasized in this essay. First, the effects of massage therapy for depressed mood will be discussed, followed by consideration of the effects of massage therapy for anxious mood, and then for symptoms of posttraumatic stress. Readers interested in descriptions of massage therapy effects for a broad range of conditions are encouraged to seek out a review article in *American Psychologist*, and a book-length review of relevant published research, both by developmental psychologist and leading massage therapy researcher Tiffany Field (Field, 1998, 2006).

Ample research supports the effectiveness of massage therapy in reducing depressed mood. In a rare meta-analysis of massage therapy, Moyer, Rounds, and Hannum (2004) examined 37 studies, finding that reductions of depression and trait anxiety were the largest effects of massage therapy, following a treatment course of such therapy. Indeed, over ten massage therapy RCTs, using a total of 249 research participants, the post-treatment level of depression was lower than that of 73 percent of participants in the control group, which is considered in the meta-analysis literature to be a medium effect size (Moyer, 2012; Moyer, Rounds, & Hannum, 2004). Other reviews of the massage therapy literature on reduction of depressed mood support the conclusion of the meta-analysis. For instance, Yates (2004) found research demonstrating that massage therapy was associated with reductions in depressed mood in such samples as persons with fibromyalgia, back pain, burns, and breast cancer, and in children with diabetes. Field's (2000) own research examined reductions in depressed mood in such samples as adolescents with anorexia or bulimia, and anorexic women. Field has also documented reductions in depressed mood in depressed adolescent mothers (Field, Grizzle, Scafidi, & Schanberg, 1996). Though most massage therapy studies of depressed mood utilize paper-and-pencil assessments such as the Beck Depression Inventory or Profile of Mood States, some research has examined physiological markers such as cortisol and serotonin. For example, Field (2006) found reductions in urinary cortisol and norepinephrine levels in depressed child and adolescent psychiatric patients following massage therapy. Though such physiological data is notable, and suggests a biological mechanism by which massage therapy works to alleviate depressed mood, it is perhaps best viewed as preliminary. Indeed, some researchers (e.g., Moyer, 2012) remain skeptical that, for instance, the role of touch pressure in massage therapy in producing increased levels of such neurotransmitters involved in depression as serotonin and dopamine has been sufficiently established by research evidence, despite some work that argues for such an effect (e.g., Field, Diego, & Hernandez-Reif, 2007).

Though the physiological mechanisms by which massage therapy may alleviate depressed mood remain under debate, the effects of massage therapy on reducing depressed mood are so well supported that some massage therapy educators now alert massage therapy students and practitioners with comments such as the following by Werner (2015): "It is important to bear in mind, however, that massage may be so well received that the client may want to reduce or completely abandon his or her medications. It is vital that this does not happen without the oversight of the prescribing physician" (p. 184).

In addition to its effects on depressed mood, considerable research also supports the effectiveness of massage therapy for reducing anxiety. In a meta-analysis of 37 studies of massage therapy, Moyer, Rounds, and Hannum (2004) revealed that single applications of massage therapy were associated with reduced state anxiety, and also that reductions in trait anxiety (as well as depressed mood) following a treatment course of multiple massage therapy sessions were its largest effects. Indeed, in over 21 massage therapy RCTs, with a total of 1,026 participants, the authors found that the magnitude of the effect on state anxiety meant a reduction in state anxiety for the average research participant greater than 64 percent of that for participants in non-massage therapy comparison groups, considered a small to medium effect size by meta-analysis research standards (Moyer, 2012). In an analysis of trait anxiety, using a meta-analysis of seven massage therapy RCTs, with a total of 194 research participants, Moyer, Rounds, and Hannum (2004) found that, following a treatment course of multiple massage therapy sessions, trait anxiety in the average participant was lower than 77 percent of that in comparison groups research participants, an effect size considered medium to large in the meta-analysis literature (Moyer, 2012).

Given the relatively large number of studies examining the effects of massage therapy on anxiety, it is perhaps surprising that more studies have not specifically focused on massage therapy for posttraumatic stress. That said, the published research does support massage therapy for reducing symptoms of PTSD (Rich, 2013). For instance, Field, Seligman, Scafidi, and Schanberg (1996) examined sixty children aged 6 to 11 following Hurricane Andrew. Children in the massage group, compared to a control group, had lower anxiety and depression scores, greater happiness, and lower salivary cortisol; moreover, behavioral observations found that members of the massaged group were more relaxed. When Price (2012) examined evidence concerning massage therapy for adults with sexual trauma histories, she found several studies offering support for its value, as evidenced in part by high recruitment and retention rates for such massage therapy clients, as well as qualitative interview data in which participants who had received massage therapy reported satisfaction with their treatment. Price also reported some limited quantitative data in support of massage therapy as alleviating posttraumatic stress disorder symptoms; furthermore, based upon clinical experience, anecdotal evidence, and reviews of existing survey data, van der Kolk (2014) endorsed massage therapy as a valued treatment for various forms of posttraumatic stress, including that resulting from human-made and natural disasters and traumas. Such publications offer evidence that massage therapy is a promising treatment for posttraumatic stress, especially when additional data concerning massage therapy's effects on anxious mood are considered as well. Nevertheless, more research (including larger scale and mixed methods designs) on the use of massage therapy for posttraumatic stress is much needed, especially concerning such issues as individual differences in its efficacy for various types of clients and traumas, and issues such as whether massage therapist variables (such as therapist gender, years of experience, and type of education/training) influence massage therapy treatment efficacy for posttraumatic stress.

As massage educators become more aware of the research on massage therapy for anxiety and posttraumatic stress, massage textbooks have begun to include more discussion of the issue. For instance, Werner (2015) noted both risks and benefits, writing that:

> Some anxiety disorder patients have a history of physical or sexual abuse; this can create problematic reactions to touch. It is vital that these clients feel safe and in control within a massage environment.... It is vital to be flexible to meet the needs of clients with anxiety disorders. Adjustments like working through clothing, with another person in the room, or with the office door open may help them to feel safer. It is also important to remember that progress is not a smooth curve, and clients' needs may fluctuate from one session to the next [p. 176].

In sum, massage therapy effects have been documented for a range of clinical conditions and mental states. Its effects on depressed mood, anxious mood, and posttraumatic stress are among the most relevant and significant for most psychotherapists and agencies considering the use of massage therapy in psychological services.

Utilizing Chair Massage in Psychological Services

Though, traditionally, most modern era massage therapy in developed nations has been performed on special massage tables (similar to chiropractic or physical therapy tables), in recent decades, the use of specialty massage chairs has become more common. Their use offers a number of advantages, as well as some limitations. Such chairs are relatively lightweight and portable, permitting the massage therapist to bring massage therapy to clients easily and quickly, such as at a workplace, at institutions such as hospitals and universities, or in the field following natural or human-made disasters. The chairs are designed to allow clients to sit comfortably, while exposing back, arms, hands, and, to some degree, outer legs for the therapist's work. The fact that clients remain fully clothed offers advantages, including the therapist's ability to see more clients in a briefer time frame, as clients need not disrobe; the lack of need for dressing rooms; and the ability to work with clients who may be uncomfortable with any degree of disrobing (e.g., due to body image or trauma issues) that is common even with typical draping in a traditional table session. In addition, chair massage does not usually employ the oils, lubricants, and creams common to table massage, which might require client to shower or change clothing. A number of massage therapists have developed educational and training systems for chair massage, often based on Swedish techniques (e.g., Palmer, 2016; Stephens, 2007). Though continuing education units and trainings are widely available for seated massage, usually they are optional for practice for those already in possession of a state massage therapy license. It should also be noted that alternatives to the standard special massage chair include various massage cradles and headrests; these are often low-cost alternatives to a full chair, but require that the headrest or cradle be placed on a flat surface such as a desk or ordinary table. Such cradles and headrests, which offer yet another option for massage therapists, are extremely portable; for instance they will fit in standard luggage for international travel or in a shoulder or large handbag.

Though seated chair massage is widely used (e.g., Palmer, 2016; Salvo, 2007; Stephens, 2007), there is a relative paucity of research specifically focused on this type of delivery of massage therapy. That said, existing research is encouraging. An early study on the topic (Cady & Jones, 1997) examined the effectiveness on stress reduction of a fifteen-minute on-site seated chair massage at a workplace. Participants' blood pressure was measured pre- and post-workplace massage. Results found significant reductions in systolic and diastolic blood pressure after receiving the massage; however, there was no control group. Wowk, Culp, and Wakeling (1999) conducted a randomized, controlled study of the pain- and tension-reducing effects of a fifteen-minute workplace massage treatment versus seated rest for nurses in a large teaching hospital. Outcome measures included pulse, pain, and tension, as measured by the Visual Analogue Scale (VAS) and the Profile of Mood States (POMS). Results found that, post-treatment, VAS pain, VAS tension, and total POMS scores were significantly lower in the seated massage group than in the comparison seated rest group. Additionally, a significantly greater proportion of the massage group reported a sense of relaxation and had pain and tension relief persisting a day or longer after the massage.

Hodge, Robinson, Boehmer, and Klein (2002) also examined seated massage in a workplace setting. Using a randomized, controlled experimental design, and a sample of healthcare workers in a hospital setting, massage therapy was offered twice weekly for twenty minutes, while the control group received no specific intervention during break times of equal duration. The acupressure massage techniques utilized in this study relate to standard Swedish massage, with some specialty variations. Outcome measures included blood pressure, heart rate, the General Well-Being Scale (GWBS), the Spielberger State-Trait Anxiety Inventory (STAI), the Multidimensional Fatigue Inventory (MFI-20), the General Sleep Disturbance Scale (GSDS), and a test of cognition (the Symbol Digit Modalities Test: SMDT). For the massage group, results found decreases in systolic and diastolic blood pressure, decreased heart rate relative to pre-treatment heart rate, improved cognitive function, improved general well-being, decreases in depressed and anxious mood, and decreases in general sleep disturbances. Such studies point to possibly valuable effects in terms of job performance, absenteeism reduction, job satisfaction, and employer and employee cost savings, but as yet such variables are largely left unexamined by current research.

Seated chair massage also has often been utilized in the field following human-made and natural disasters. For instance, in his book-length analysis of post-trauma interventions, noted Harvard Medical School trauma researcher Bessel van der Kolk (2014) reported on a 2002 survey of 225 people who had escaped the Twin Towers on 9/11/2001; in response to being asked what had been most helpful in overcoming the effects of the experience, he noted that survivors mentioned, in the following order, acupuncture, massage, and yoga, and that massage was particularly popular with rescue workers. In addition, clinical and anecdotal evidence from psychologists, massage therapists, and clients among refugee populations in Jordan and the Middle East, and among post-earthquake survivors in Haiti, shows support for seated chair massage as a helpful intervention for reducing stress, anxiety, and depressed mood, and alleviating a number of posttraumatic effects (e.g., Rich, 2012a, 2012b, 2013). Rigorous research in such settings often presents many challenges, including costs, language, and cultural issues in international work, as well as ethical issues that must be examined. For instance, often massage therapists in post-disaster areas are focused on serving and helping the client population with seated chair massage, and are not concerned with conducting research. Additionally, in the days and months after a crisis, it is unlikely that protocols, budgets, university reviews and IRBs can be rapidly and appropriately conducted. Though recently researchers have been examining more closely policies and best practices in terms of ethics for international psychology, social science, and medical research, more work must be accomplished here for the discipline to progress ethically and effectively (e.g., Leach, Stevens, Lindsay, Ferrero, & Korkut, 2012).

Integrating Massage Therapy with Psychological Services: Education, Credentialing, Licensing and Other Issues to Consider

Psychologists with clients who utilize massage therapy or who may benefit from massage therapy should take care to familiarize themselves with it, both in terms of the research on its efficacy and in terms of what the potential benefits and limitations of massage therapy are (Barnett, Shale, & Fisher, 2014; Rich, 2010). Few psychologists currently are knowledgeable about the topic; indeed research with a sample of over 200 American Psychological Association members reported that only 10 percent of those sampled considered themselves to have good or expert knowledge of massage therapy (Bassman & Uellendhal, 2003).

Though massage therapy has a reputation as a safe therapy, there are some contraindications; among them are clients with skin infections, open wounds, weakened bones (osteoporosis), recent surgery, and bleeding disorders or use of blood-thinning medications. Especially clients who are pregnant or who have cancer should consult with their physician prior to beginning massage therapy treatment; indeed, such medical consultation may be suggested to all clients prior to initiating massage therapy treatment. In addition, safety issues (such as falls) can occur when clients get on or off of the massage table; this is especially a concern with elderly clients (Barnett, Shale, & Fisher, 2014; Rich, 2010; Salvo, 2007). Some clients who may have allergies or sensitivities to the massage creams and oils used are advised to mention such issues to the massage therapist, as many alternatives are possible (such as unscented lubricants).

To familiarize themselves with massage therapy, it is suggested that psychologists seek experience with receiving massage therapy themselves, as well as noting laws and credentialing rules that may apply to massage therapists in their geographic region. Currently, about forty-five of fifty U.S. states have statewide licensure or certification. Five of ten Canadian provinces have registration laws. These laws can vary, but, in the U.S., most states with statewide laws require five hundred hours of education, though a few require seven hundred and fifty or, in some circumstances, even one thousand hours. Several Canadian provinces require 2,200 hours. In the past, most massage schools were stand-alone specialty career schools, although, in the last decade or so, massage programs located in community colleges or even four-year colleges and universities have become increasingly common, offering the advantage that often at least some coursework transfers to other programs, such as nursing or associate degree credentials.

Typically, massage therapists must also pass an exam, often either the MBLEx or a state exam. In states without statewide licensure, situations may occur in which therapists in one town have graduated from educational programs and passed a national exam, while massage is practiced in a neighboring town by persons with no formal education or credentials, a situation that can be confusing to the general public and to helping professionals who are attempting to make referrals. To learn more about massage therapy credentialing, psychologists may visit the websites of state licensing and credentialing agencies, as well as the websites of major massage therapy professional organizations, including the American Massage Therapy Association (AMTA) (https://www.amtamassage.org/) and the National Certification Board for Therapeutic Massage and Bodywork (NCBTMB) (http://www.ncbtmb.org/). NCBTMB is transitioning from offering the NCBTMB national certification credential to the new BCTMB board certification credential, which, among other requirements, includes completion of 750 hours of education and CPR.

It is important to note that, while historically some psychotherapists advocated, and indeed used massage with their own psychotherapy clients (including Freud, 1893–1895/2010), most ethical codes and laws in the USA would certainly prohibit such simultaneously dual practice by a single practitioner of massage therapy and psychotherapy.

Reviewing the literature, Barnett, Shale, Elkins, and Fisher (2014) sensibly wrote, "although nonsexual touch may at times constitute appropriate boundary crossings in psychotherapy (e.g., a handshake in greeting, a hug of a grieving parent), the intimate and extended physical contact inherent in massage therapy would most likely be seen as an inappropriate and potentially harmful boundary violation for a psychologist" (p. 223). *The Ethical Use of Touch in Psychotherapy* (Hunter & Struve, 1998) and *Touch in Psychotherapy* (Smith, Clance, & Imes, 1998) are helpful resources for psychologists seeking more guidance on such issues as handshakes, hugs, and boundary crossings.

That said, there are indeed some legitimate researchers who continue to examine the possible role of more in-depth healing touch in psychotherapy and psychotherapy-like settings. Some such work may be identified by such related terms as *somatic psychotherapy* and *body psychotherapy* (e.g., Barratt, 2013; Greene & Goodrich-Dunn, 2014; Hefferon, 2013), and laws and ethical codes do vary internationally. Given that the massage therapy profession has several codes of ethics, those who are members of AMTA or credentialed by NCBTMB must abide by the ethical codes of these organizations, as well as relevant state ethical codes and laws. Several books have been written specifically for massage therapists seeking to better understand ethical issues involved in massage therapy; among the topics covered are dual relationships, boundaries, business ethics, sexuality, client misbehavior, issues regarding trauma, conflict resolution, disclosure, working with other professionals/referrals, and effective communication (e.g., Benjamin & Sohnen-Moe, 2005; Yardley-Nohr, 2007). Massage therapists will typically receive instruction in the course of their education about supporting clients if emotional reactions or other psychological issues emerge during massage therapy treatment; moreover, massage therapists often will have a brief unit in their education that focuses on psychological issues. Nevertheless, psychologists referring clients to a massage therapist may want to discuss such matters as scope of practice, plans for clients who have emotional reactions, and other such issues before the client's first massage therapy treatment.

Hunter and Struve (1998) found four common concerns of psychotherapists considering making a massage therapy referral: lack of psychotherapist knowledge about massage therapy, fear that bodyworkers may not have sufficient ethical guidelines to ensure client safety, fear that some massage therapists may attempt to conduct psychotherapy, and fear that some massage therapists may not understand or be aware of some clients' inability to set limits with authority figures. Rich (2010) suggested that psychologists consider asking some or all of the following questions of potential massage therapists prior to a client beginning treatment. The question topics may focus on learning about the training, certification, and insurance of the massage therapist, the types of massage styles or techniques the massage therapist will utilize, and how the particular massage therapist specifically approaches client draping and clothing and plans for clients' possible emotional reactions or needs for bathroom breaks during a massage therapy session. Barnett, Shale, Elkins, and Fisher (2014) added that, if a client's written and verbal permission are obtained, psychologists may find it effective to coordinate treatment with massage therapists; furthermore, in psychotherapy sessions, psychologists can monitor client progress in the massage therapy treatments, providing feedback to the massage therapist if necessary. Of course, all laws, policies, and ethical codes should be followed with respect to client confidentiality.

Massage therapy can be an effective and indeed enjoyable treatment; informal, anecdotal evidence suggests that more people likely look forward to their massage therapy appointments than to their dental appointments, for instance. However, attitudes regarding touch and massage therapy do vary, and there are numerous ways to assess such attitudes before making referrals. Massage therapy for sexual abuse and trauma survivors merits special attention and care. Publications by massage therapists and massage therapy researchers experienced with the issue offer helpful insights, pointing to the need for the massage therapists to check on the client's comfort level frequently during the massage, and the need to create a massage therapy environment in which the client feels safe and in control (Price, 2012; Rich, 2013; Werner, 2013). In terms of evaluating a psychotherapy client's attitudes to touch and massage, in addition to the psychologist discussing the issue with a client during psychotherapy, there are some assessment tools, both massage-specific ones such as ATOM (the Attitudes Toward Massage scale, Moyer & Rounds, 2009), and ones focused on touch more generally (Weiss & Niemann, 2011).

Additional reasons why psychotherapists should consider massage therapy for clients include the reality that there are frequently noncompliance and nonadherence issues with both psychotherapy and psychiatric medications (Taylor, 2015). Furthermore, on occasion a client may not be a candidate for psychiatric medication due to medical issues including multiple drug interactions, a reality that occurs especially in middle-aged and elderly clients as well as in those with chronic illnesses (Moyer, 2012; Rich, 2002). For some clients, medications or psychotherapists may be too costly or may be unavailable, as may be the case in certain developing nations or for clients who have no insurance or who face financial challenges. In such cases, massage therapy, as a CAM healing modality, offer some options that may, at least in part, facilitate enhanced health and well-being (Moyer, 2012; Rich, 2002, 2010).

Conclusions

In sum, massage therapy has a number of documented effects of relevance to psychology and related helping professions. Matching the right client with the right massage therapist, the right psychotherapist, and the right condition can be an effective combination. Though it is not a panacea, and though there are contraindications, evidence supports the use of massage therapy as a supplement to psychotherapy for reducing depressed or anxious mood and alleviating some symptoms of posttraumatic and other stress (e.g., Field, 1998, 2006; Moyer, Rounds, & Hannum, 2004; Rich, 2002, 2010, 2013). Massage therapy also has documented effects for other conditions of interest to psychologists, including those that boost immune function, reduce pain, enhance and promote growth (as in premature infants), and improve cognitive function (e.g., Field, 2006; Rich, 2002).

Future research ought to examine further the role of massage therapy for psychological services, including additional work exploring the use of seated chair massage in worksite settings, in institutions such as hospitals, community mental health settings, and schools, in correctional settings such as jails and prisons, in police and fire departments, and in local government agencies. Future research ought also to examine further the use of massage therapy from a lifespan development perspective, in that existing research does suggest some efficacy for infants (e.g., promoting growth for premature infants; improving sleep pattern), children (e.g., children with asthma or with autism), adolescents (e.g., aggressive adolescents, bulimic adolescents, and adolescents with attention deficit hyperactivity disorder), and the elderly (e.g., lessening depressed mood; improving behavior in the agitated elderly; improving daily functioning in Parkinson's disease patients) (Field, 2006; Rich, 2002; Yates, 2004). In some cases, massage therapy may improve mood and/or behavior, though the underlying disease may remain; thus research collaborations with physician, psychologist, and massage therapist colleagues is suggested to optimize research designs and to ensure that appropriate questions are asked and assessed. It is important not to confuse the fact that massage may alleviate *some* symptoms related to a condition, with the fact that it may not necessarily alleviate *all* symptoms.

In conclusion, it is evident that massage therapy is more than simply a spa luxury for the wealthy. Instead, massage therapy has many effects of significance and relevance to psychology and related helping disciplines, especially with respect to reductions in depressed and anxious mood, pain, and stress. With some caveats, it is physically and psychologically safe for most clients and is often comparatively affordable. Psychologists will find many appropriate applications of massage therapy, both via a standard massage table or with a special massage chair, in psychological services with a broad range of clients, conditions, and settings.

References

Andrade, C.K., & Clifford, P. (2012). Qualitative research methods. In T. Dryden & C.A. Moyer (Eds.), *Massage therapy: Integrating research and practice* (pp. 45–58). Champaign, IL: Human Kinetics.

Australian Government Department of Health. (2015). Review of the Australian Government Debate on Natural Therapies for Private Health Insurance. Retrieved from http://www. health.gov.au/internet/main/publishing.nsf/content/0E9129B3574FCA53CA257BF0001ACD11/$File/Natural%20Therapies%20Over view%20Report%20Final%20with%20copyright%2011%20March.pdf

Barnes, P.M., Powell-Griner, E., McFann, K., & Nahin, R.L. (2004). *Complementary and alternative medicine use among adults: United States, 2002. Advance data from vital and health statistics, No 343.* Hyattsville, MD: National Center for Health Statistics.

Barnett, J.E., Shale, A.J., Elkins, G., & Fisher, W. (2014). *Complementary and alternative medicine for psychologists.* Washington, D.C.: American Psychological Association.

Barratt, B.B. (2013). *The emergence of somatic psychology and bodymind therapy.* New York, NY: Palgrave.

Bassman, L.E., & Uellendhal, G. (2003). Complementary/alternative medicine: Ethical, professional, and practical challenges for psychologists. *Professional Psychology: Research and Practice, 34,* 264–270.

Benjamin, B. ., & Sohnen-Moe, C. (2005). The ethics of touch. Tucson, AZ: SMA.

Benjamin, P.J. (2015). *The emergence of the massage therapy profession in North America.* Toronto, CA: Curties-Overzet Publications.

Cady, S.H., & Jones, G.E. (1997). Massage therapy as workplace intervention for reduction of stress. *Perceptual and Motor Skills, 84,* 157–158.

Calvert, R. (2002). *The history of massage.* Rochester, VT: Healing Arts Press.

Claire, T. (1995). *Bodywork.* New York, NY: William Morrow.

Classen, C. (Ed.). (2005). *The book of touch.* New York, NY: Berg.

Classen, C. (2012). *The deepest sense: A cultural history of touch.* Urbana IL: University of Illinois Press.

Dryden, T., & Moyer, C.A. (Eds.). (2012). *Massage therapy: Integrating research and practice.* Champaign, IL: Human Kinetics.

Eisenberg, D.M., Kessler, R.C., Foster, C., Norlock, F.E., Calkins, D.R., & Delbanco, T.L. (1993). Unconventional medicine in the United States: Prevalence, costs, and patterns of use. *New England Journal of Medicine, 328*(4), 246–252.

Field, T. (1998). Massage therapy effects. *American Psychologist, 53,* 1270–1281.

Field, T. (2006). *Massage therapy research.* New York, NY: Elsevier.

Field, T. (2009). *Complementary and alternative therapies research.* Washington, D.C.: APA.

Field, T. (2014). *Touch* (2nd ed.). Cambridge, MA: MIT Press.

Field, T., Diego, C., & Hernandez-Reif, M. (2007). Massage therapy research. *Developmental Review, 27,* 75–89.

Field, T., Grizzle, N., Scafidi, F., & Schanberg, S. (1996). Massage and relaxation therapies' effects on depressed adolescent mothers. *Adolescence, 31,* 903–911.

Field, T., Seligman, S., Scafidi, S., & Schanberg, S. (1996). Alleviating posttraumatic stress in children following Hurricane Andrew. *Journal of Applied Developmental Psychology, 17,* 37–50.

Freud, S. (1893–1895/2010). Studies on hysteria. In I. Smith (Ed. & Trans.), *Freud—Complete works.* Retrieved from http://www.holybooks.com/sigmund-freud-the-complete-works/

Gallace, A., & Spence, C. (2014). *In touch with the future: The sense of touch from cognitive neuroscience to virtual reality.* New York, NY: Oxford University Press.

Greene, E., & Goodrich-Dunn, B. (2014). *The psychology of the body* (2nd ed.). Baltimore, MD: Lippincott, Williams, & Wilkins.

Hefferon, K. (2013). *Positive psychology and the body: The somatopsychic side to flourishing.* New York, NY: McGraw-Hill.

Heller, M.A., & Schiff, W. (Eds.). (1991). *The psychology of touch.* Hillsdale, NJ: Lawrence Erlbaum Associates.

Hertenstein, M.J., & Weiss, S.J. (Eds.). (2011). *The handbook of touch.* New York, NY: Springer.

Hodge, M., Robinson, C., Boehmer, J., & Klein, S. (2002). Employee outcomes following work-site acupressure and massage. In G. Rich (Ed.), *Massage therapy: The evidence for practice* (pp. 191–202). New York, NY: Mosby/Elsevier.

Huber, B., & Sandstrom, A.R. (Eds.). (2001). *Mesoamerican healers.* Austin, TX: University of Texas Press.

Hunter, M., & Struve, J. (1998). *The ethical use of touch in psychotherapy.* Thousand Oaks, CA: Sage.

Hymel, G. (2005). *Research methods for massage and holistic therapies.* New York, NY: Elsevier.

Hymel, G., & Rich, G. (2014). Health psychology as a context for massage therapy. *Journal of Bodywork and Movement Therapies, 18,* 174–182.

Hymel, G., & Rich, G. (in prep.). *Research methods* (Rev. ed.). London, UK: Elsevier.

Katz, J., Wowk, A., Culp, D., & Wakeling, H. (1999). A randomized, controlled study of the pain- and tension-reducing effects of 15 minute workplace massage treatments versus seated rest for nurses in a large teaching hospital. *Pain Research Management, 4*(2), 81–88.

Knaster, M. (1996). *Discovering the body's wisdom.* New York, NY: Bantam.

Krasner, J. (2010). *Home bodies: Tactile experience in domestic space.* Columbus: Ohio State University Press.

Kripal, J.J. (2007). *Esalen: America and the religion of no religion.* Chicago, IL: University of Chicago Press.

Jablonksi, N.J. (2006). *Skin: A natural history.* Berkeley: University of California Press.

Leach, M.M., Stevens, M.J., Lindsay, G., Ferrero, A., & Korkut, Y. (Eds.). (2012). *The Oxford handbook of international psychology ethics.* New York, NY: Oxford University Press.

Linden, D.J. (2015). *Touch: The science of hand, heart, and mind.* New York, NY: Penguin.

Menard, M.B. (2002). Methodological issues in the design and conduct of massage therapy research. In G. Rich (Ed.), *Massage therapy: The evidence for practice* (pp. 27–41). New York, NY: Mosby/Elsevier.

Menard, M.B. (2009). *Making sense of research: A guide to research literacy for complementary practitioners* (2nd ed.). Toronto, Canada: Curties-Overzet.

Moyer, C.A. (2012). Anxiety and depression. In T. Dryden & C.A. Moyer (Eds.), *Massage therapy: Integrating research and practice* (pp. 151–164). Champaign, IL: Human Kinetics.

Moyer, C.A., & Rounds, J. (2009). The Attitudes Towards Massage (ATOM) scale. *Journal of Bodywork and Movement Therapies, 13*(10), 22–33.

Moyer, C.A., Rounds, J., & Hannum, J.W. (2004). A meta-analysis of massage therapy research. *Psychological Bulletin, 130*(1), 3–18.

Montagu, A. (1986). *Touching* (3rd ed.). New York, NY: Harper & Row.

Palmer, D. (2016). Touchpro International: Chair massage. Retrieved from http://touchpro.com/

Price, C.J. (2012). Massage for adults with a history of sexual trauma. In T. Dryden & C.A. Moyer (Eds.), *Massage therapy: Integrating research and practice* (pp. 165–172). Champaign, IL: Human Kinetics.

Rich, G. (Ed.). (2002). *Massage therapy: The evidence for practice.* New York, NY: Mosby/Elsevier.

Rich, G. (2010). Massage therapy: Significance and relevance to professional practice. *Professional Psychology: Research and Practice, 41*(4), 325–332.

Rich, G. (2012a). *What mental health professionals should know about massage therapy: Research evidence for practice.* Paper presented at the 2nd Annual Symposium on Spirituality and Psychotherapy, Haiti.

Rich, G. (2012b). *Massage therapy for PTSD, anxiety, and depression.* Paper presented at the International Conference on Transgenerational Trauma, Amman, Jordan.

Rich, G. (2013). Massage therapy for PTSD, trauma, and anxiety. *Bulletin of Peoples' Friendship University of Russia: Series of Psychology and Pedagogy 3,* 60–66.

Rolf, I.P. (1977/1989). *Rolfing.* Rochester, VT: Healing Arts Press.

Rosa, E., Rosa, L., Sarner, S., & Barrett, S. (1998). A close look at therapeutic touch. *Journal of the American Medical Association, 279*(13), 1005–1010.

Salvo, S.G. (2007). *Massage therapy: Principles and practice* (3rd ed.). Philadelphia, PA: Elsevier.

Seligman, M.E.P. (1995). The effectiveness of psychotherapy. *American Psychologist, 50,* 965–974.

Stephens, R.R. (2006). *Therapeutic chair massage.* Baltimore, MD: Lippincott, Williams, & Wilkins.

Smith, E., Clance, P.R., & Imes, S. (1998). *Touch in psychotherapy.* New York, NY: Guilford Press.

Stillerman, E. (1996). *The encyclopedia of bodywork.* New York, NY: Facts on File.

Taylor, S.E. (2015). *Health psychology* (9th ed.). Boston, MA: McGraw-Hill.

Thompson, D. L. (2012). *Hands heal: Communication, documentation, and insurance billing for manual therapists* (4th ed.). Philadelphia, PA: Lippincott, Williams & Wilkins.

Van der Kolk, B. (2014). *The body keeps the score: Brain, mind, and body in the healing of trauma*. New York, NY: Viking.

Verhoef, M. (2012). Mixed methods research. In T. Dryden & C.A. Moyer (Eds.), *Massage therapy: Integrating research and practice* (pp. 59–70). Champaign, IL: Human Kinetics.

Weiss, S.J., & Niemann, S.K. (2011). Measurement of touch behavior. In M.J. Hertenstein & S.J. Weiss (Eds.), *The handbook of touch* (pp. 245–270). New York, NY: Springer.

Werner, R. (2013). *A massage therapist's guide to pathology* (5th ed.). Philadelphia, PA: Lippincott, Williams, & Wilkins.

Yardley-Nohr, T. (2007). *Ethics for massage therapists*. Baltimore, MD: Lippincott, Williams, & Wilkins.

Yoga Nidra

The Art of Deep Relaxation

NICK ATLAS

Yoga Nidra is an integrative practice of guided relaxation and meditative inquiry that invites practitioners to embody deeply, accept, and transform the conditions that lie at the root of their suffering. Yoga Nidra—which loosely translates as "dynamic sleep" (Satyananda,[1] 2006)—is typically "delivered" to a group by a trained instructor, though it may also be employed in a dyadic setting (e.g., in place of or as an adjunct to psychotherapy), or, ultimately, may be self-initiated. Similar to other mindfulness modalities, Yoga Nidra helps foster a sense of wholeness and wellbeing in every moment, and can become the foundation through which practitioners engage with the world.

Evidence-based research has demonstrated the effectiveness of Yoga Nidra in treating anxiety, hypertension, and depression (Eastman-Mueller, Wilson, Jung, Kimura, & Tarrant, 2013; Kumar, 2008); sleep disorders (Gutman et al., 2016), and chemical dependency (Temme, Fenster, & Ream, 2012). It may also aid in pain management (Nassif et al., 2014) and in enhancing wellbeing (Kumar, 2004; Rani et al., 2011). In addition, Yoga Nidra's far-reaching benefits have been successfully employed in the treatment of veterans suffering from posttraumatic stress disorder (PTSD) (Engel et al., 2007; Stankovic, 2011) and in persons with sexual trauma (Pence, Katz, Huffman, & Cojucar, 2014); as a natural remedy for patients with diabetes (Amita, Prabhakar, Manoi, Harminder, & Pavan, 2009), multiple sclerosis, and cancer (Pritchard, Elison-Bowers & Birdsall, 2010); and in schools to help children express their emotions and establish a healthy sense of self (Shapiro et al., 2015). An approach to non-dual meditation with ancient, tantric roots, Yoga Nidra is at the cutting edge of complementary and alternative medicine, while remaining accessible to a complete beginner.

At present, there are no licensing boards or minimum requirements governing the application of Yoga Nidra, nor is any graduate-level academic work required in order to become an instructor. Those wishing to achieve certification as a Yoga Nidra instructor may participate in a continuing education (CE) training course, of which a handful of reputable ones are available within the U.S. and abroad, though they vary in content and levels of scholarship. As one advances in the practice of Yoga Nidra, one not only learns to relax more deeply from moment to moment, but also may experience Yoga Nidra as a framework through which to view one's own psychospiritual progression toward self-realization. Consequently, Yoga Nidra is often called the "meditative heart of yoga" (Miller, 2010), and is frequently praised for its accessibility, elegance, and efficiency.

A Brief History

In contemporary settings, Yoga Nidra is generally understood to be a specific approach to meditation in which practitioners are directed to lie on their backs so as to receive guided relaxation from a trained instructor. As such, Yoga Nidra may be delivered in person, over the phone, or via the Internet, and is increasingly utilized by way of digital audio recordings. This modern interpretation is largely due to the proliferation efforts of Swami Satyananda's Bihar School of Yoga, which first published the book *Yoga Nidra* for an international audience in 1976 (Birch & Hargreaves, 2015), as well as the popularity and success of similar mind-body interventions such as Mindfulness-Based Stress Reduction (MBSR) (Kabat-Zinn, 2013).

The Sanskrit term *yoganidra*, however, has ancient underpinnings and has been used in a variety of contexts within the rich mythological and yogic traditions of India and Tibet. Though the term consists of two distinct words, *yoga* and *nidra*—the latter meaning "sleep"—the compound Sanskrit word may have several interpretations dependent upon its historical context (Birch & Hargreaves, 2015). The term *yoganidra* first appeared in the Hindu epic *Mahabharata* (c. 300 BCE to 300 CE) in reference to the Hindu god Vishnu's transcendental sleep between the *yugas* (cycles of the universe), but yoganidra was not implicated in any specific yoga practice or system therein. Several Shaiva and Buddhist Tantras (c. 500–700 CE) refer to yoganidra as a particular state of meditation that is both yoga and sleep—ostensibly the goal of Tibetan dream yoga (LaBerge, 2003; Norbu, 1992; Tenzin Wangyal, 1998; Wallace, 2012)—yet these teachings regarded yoganidra as a gnostic realization rather than as a practical technique.

By the 11th–12th centuries, yoganidra appeared in Hatha and Raja Yoga texts as synonymous with *samadhi* or *turiya*, a state of enlightenment occurring beyond the three ordinary states of waking, dreaming, and dreamless sleep, which is the subject of the significantly earlier *Mandukya Upanishad* (c. 300 BCE to 200 CE) (Easwaran, 2007). It was in these later texts that specific yoga systems were taught as a means to liberation (Birch & Hargreaves, 2015), including clear directives toward achieving yoganidra via meditative disciplines. Still, the meaning of yoganidra as samadhi persisted into the 17th–18th centuries, at which time the term *yoganidra* was applied to an obscure *asana* (posture), wherein the practitioners rest in a supine position and wrap their legs behind their head prior to falling asleep.

Ultimately, the term was re-appropriated and dissected by Satyananda (2006), who established Yoga Nidra as a hybridized system of yoga, drawing from a multitude of modern and medieval traditions, including Western relaxation therapies devised in the 19th century (Singleton, 2005). In the late 20th and early 21st centuries, several teachers (Atlas, 2017b; Miller, 2010) have adapted Satyananda's protocol to meet the demands of an increasingly secular and nascent audience, integrating the wisdom of various spiritual traditions and psychotherapeutic praxes.

Evidence-Based Research, Efficacy and Amenable Populations

Research on Yoga Nidra—both as a particular state of consciousness and as a therapeutic intervention—is scarce on account of its lacking an empirical definition (Parker, Bharati, & Fernandez, 2013) or a consensus as to what a Yoga Nidra protocol must entail. Still, a number of studies have demonstrated positive outcomes in both clinical and educational settings, while physiological studies have verified the effects of Yoga Nidra as on par with those of other mindfulness modalities (*ibid.*).

As noted above, Yoga Nidra has been proven effective as a remedy for anxiety, depression (Eastman-Mueller et al., 2013; Kumar, 2008), acute and chronic pain (Nassif et al., 2014; Rani et al., 2011), and chemical dependency (Temme, Fenster, & Ream, 2012); as a sleep therapy intervention (Gutman et al., 2016); and as a means to improve quality of life more generally (Kumar, 2004; Rani et al, 2011). Physiological studies have further demonstrated Yoga Nidra's potential to alter respiratory patterns and elicit calm in children exhibiting disruptive behavior (Jensen, Stevens, & Kenny, 2012); to increase dopamine tone (i.e., resulting in the experience of pleasure) (Kjaer et al., 2002) while lowering cortisol (i.e., stress) levels (Borchadt, Patterson & Seng, 2012); and to increase heart rate variability and parasympathetic arousal (i.e., relaxation response) in adults regardless of whether the practice is preceded by Hatha yoga (i.e., physical exercise, stretching, etc.) (Markil, Whitehurst, Jacobs, & Zoeller, 2012).

Perhaps the most promising research in this burgeoning field focuses on the applicability of Yoga Nidra as an adjunctive therapy for PTSD, particularly for combat veterans (Engel et al., 2007; Stankovic, 2011), but also for women suffering from sexual (Pence et al., 2014) and other complex traumas (Hartman, 2015). In 2007, a feasibility study conducted at Walter Reed Army Medical Center determinedYoga Nidra may be a beneficial and acceptable treatment approach for soldiers experiencing significant symptoms of PTSD" (Engel et al., 2007, p. 2). Subsequently, Walter Reed integrated Yoga Nidra into its ongoing treatment programs, while additional studies confirmed Yoga Nidra's efficacy in developing resilience among healthcare providers in clinical and related settings (Bingham, Peacock, Fritts, & Walter, 2011).

Though research has demonstrated the applicability of Yoga Nidra across a broad range of settings and diverse populations, it should be noted that practitioners suffering from PTSD symptoms—regardless of whether they have been clinically diagnosed—are always at risk for re-traumatization. As with any depth psychotherapeutic or meditative modality, even "healthy" practitioners who are asymptomatic are also at risk, as repressed, emotionally-charged material may surface during or following a session—in fact, this is ultimately what Yoga Nidra is designed to do. The benefit of routinized Yoga Nidra practice is that it affords practitioners a safe space and supportive network (e.g., the instructor/clinician, other group members, etc.) to meet, greet, and integrate the content of their unconscious in their own time and equipped with tools to proceed cautiously yet confidently. Still, potential instructors are strongly encouraged to receive training in Yoga Nidra and take due care prior to delivering the practice, especially if they intend to work with particularly sensitive populations that are at risk for re-traumatization, such as veterans, victims of abuse, those prone to depression and severe mental illness, etc.

Philosophy and Practice

Due in large part to Satyananda's efforts to create a systematized practice of Yoga Nidra, clinicians wishing to incorporate the technique within a therapeutic setting need only follow a brief, step-by-step, core protocol. Several contemporary schools (e.g., Evolutionary Education®, iRest®, Amrit Yoga®, Divine Sleep®, etc.) offer nuanced variations on the original seven-stage model described by Satyananda, and there is considerable flexibility and room for improvisation within and between models. Much of Yoga Nidra's adaptability rests on its affinity with yogic philosophy and, in particular, the yogic theory of *koshas* (subtle bodies or sheaths) that compose the *atman* (self). Thus, Yoga Nidra protocols typically trace the flow of awareness from sheath to sheath in an effort to embody deeply and accept the totality of the self with enhanced clarity and compassion.

The five principal koshas upon which the core Yoga Nidra protocol is based are: (1) the *annamaya* (gross/physical body or "body of food"); (2) the *pranamaya* (vital energy body or "body of breath"); (3) the *manomaya* (the emotional body); (4) the *vijnanamaya* (the body of thought); and (5) the *anandamaya* (the body of blissful joy). Miller (2010) added a sixth kosha called *asmitamaya*, or the body of the "ego-I," that witnesses the unfolding of awareness throughout the other five sheaths. According to kosha theory, transformations incurred in the subtler sheaths, such as the body of thought and emotions, will reverberate throughout the vital energy body and gross, physical structure, but not necessarily vice versa. This downwardly causal relationship is virtually identical to models of healing in many psychodynamic traditions and closely parallels additional Western, Eastern, and indigenous therapeutic paradigms in which physical disease is believed to be rooted in the mind (Grof, 1976).

Ultimately, Yoga Nidra protocols are designed to elicit sensation in one or several koshas, and to allow practitioners the opportunity to track sensations in the body while disidentifying from them. Traumas—or *samskaras*—are regarded as multidimensional imprints (*ibid.*) or blockages—i.e., they exist simultaneously as matter, energy, affect, and thought—that prevent the free flow of *prana* (life energy) through the self and stifle optimal health more generally. The goal of Yoga Nidra, then, is to unearth samskaras at their nexus and accept them without trying to change them, whereupon they may release their energetic charge. The newly liberated energy of the samskara is then reintegrated into the totality of one's being, resulting in greater self-awareness tending toward psychospiritual balance, wholeness, and enlightenment.

Satyananda's core, seven-stage protocol is as follows: (1) preparation; (2) resolve; (3) rotation of consciousness; (4) awareness of breath; (5) feelings and sensations; (6) visualization; and, (7) ending the practice. The preparation stage simply involves assuming a posture suitable for deep relaxation, such as *savasana* (corpse pose), in which the practitioner lies on a flat surface in a supine position. Neither Atlas (2017b) nor Miller (2010) restricted the practice to this posture, however, and both encouraged practitioners to assume any position in which they feel comfortable, including lying on their side or belly, sitting cross-legged on the ground or in a chair, standing, and even walking. It is not imperative that the technique be conducted on a hard surface, and many instructors occasionally make use of props such as pillows, bolsters, blankets, blocks, eye covers, etc.

In the resolve stage, practitioners are guided to formulate and internally voice a short, positive, intentional statement or *sankalpa*, such as "I am free from stress and anxiety," or "I will awaken to my highest potential." Miller (2010) suggested speaking the intention as an affirmation—as if the goal had already been met—while Satyananda does not explicitly comment against future-oriented statements, noting only that one's sankalpa will necessarily manifest over time. In either scenario, the setting of an auto-suggestive intention is a deviation from classical (i.e., medieval) yoga practices in which the practitioner aimed to extinguish the mind of sankalpa entirely, so as to enter into samadhi or deep meditative absorption (Birch & Hargreaves, 2015; Singleton, 2005). Subsequently, Atlas (2017b) preferred to offer the setting of intentions as an option, as well as the possibility of asking a question in need of resolution. According to the Evolutionary Education® model, how one chooses to present and integrate this, as well as all aspects of the Yoga Nidra practice, is at the sole discretion of the instructor and may be tailored to meet the needs and objectives of clients (*ibid.*).

Once the practitioner is settled and an intention has been formulated, the instructor begins to guide the practitioner to bring awareness to the various sheaths, beginning with the annamaya (gross/physical body). The third stage of Satyananda's protocol—the rotation of consciousness—entails shifting the mind from one part of the body to another in a definitive sequence. While there is no consensus on the optimum way to deliver this "body scan," instructors most often initiate a progressive relaxation of the body from head to toes or, conversely, from toes to head. The former approach is thought to be more grounding than the latter and is advisable when working with clients suffering from excessive rumination, hypertension, insomnia, and any other condition in which the head is especially volatile.

There is ample evidence for this sort of technique within classical yoga systems, wherein similar practices have been referred to for centuries as *nyasa* or *pratyahara* (i.e., the withdrawing of the senses) (Birch & Hargreaves, 2015). These and other antecedent rituals involved sequentially locating the breath along the body's *marmasthana* (vital points), *chakras* (multidimensional energy centers), and *nadis* (energy pathways), so as to awaken *prana* (vital energy). Rama (1984) described both a thirty-one point and sixty-one point practice of *shavayatra*, or "inner traveling through the body," that may be taught as an adjunct to the corporeal, progressive relaxation of limbs, trunk, and so on. Regardless of one's "map" of the body and style of delivery—for example, one need not utilize any Sanskrit terminology, etc.—it is advised that instructors routinize their sequence, at least initially, so that clients develop an internalized, autogenic response (Schultz & Luthe, 1965) that will allow for easier access to and tranquility within the body during ensuing sessions.

While autogenics (*ibid.*) and similar progressive relaxation techniques (e.g., see Benson & Klipper, 1975) may encourage practitioners to "relax" each part of their body, Atlas (2017b) and Miller (2010) preferred to have clients "welcome" or "invite" the impression of their body as sensation, thereby placating any supplemental anxiety surrounding whether a client is indeed capable of relaxing on demand. Satyananda advocated for a more methodical approach, proffering explicit directions to shift attention quickly between "right hand thumb, second finger, third finger" and so on. Again, there are no steadfast rules regarding the exact language used in this process—it is largely situation-specific—nor are there clear guidelines as to how long the process should take, though anywhere from five to fifteen minutes is recommended.

The fourth stage of the core protocol—awareness of breath—corresponds with the *pranamaya* (body of breath) and typically is dedicated to monitoring one's breath without attempts to manipulate it (Satyananda, 2006). In this stage, instructors/clinicians may guide clients to listen to the sound of their own breath; to feel the rise and fall of their belly; to sense the passage of air through their nostrils, throat, chest, abdomen, etc.; and, on occasion, to count both the in-breath and out-breath as a means to stabilizing attention. More liberal or experimental approaches to Yoga Nidra, however, may use this stage as an opportunity to integrate additional breathing practices or *pranayam*, such as extending exhalation so that it is twice the length of inhalation, focusing on alternating sides of the body, visualizing breathing through alternate nostrils, breathing into the chakras, etc. (Atlas, 2017b; Miller, 2010).

In stage five, practitioners are invited to attend to "feelings and sensations" associated with the *manomaya* or emotional body. In this stage, the instructor may ask practitioners to "welcome the feeling 'tone' of their emotions" into awareness, emphasizing that such tones may arise pre-verbally as undifferentiated sensations and that there is no need to name or judge them. Again, there is considerable flexibility here in terms of how this stage may be navigated, and seasoned instructors will likely adapt their approach based upon their familiarity with their clients and their clients' familiarity with the process.

For example, the invitation to "feel sensation as it is" may remain open-ended or regimented (e.g., practitioners may elicit a predefined series of emotions over several practices). Instructors may also invite practitioners to imagine opposite sensations and to move back and forth between the two. Creating a binary serves the purpose of drawing out both feelings and is especially useful when practitioners are working with repressed emotions that are ephemeral and difficult to bring to the surface. According to Satyananda (2006), working with pairs of opposite feelings "harmonizes the opposite hemispheres of the brain," balances "basic drives," and may bring about emotional catharsis "as memories of profound feelings are relived" (p. 72). Such theories are corroborated by emerging studies on neural "reconsolidation" (Ecker, Ticic, & Hulley, 2012) or "reconditioning" (Graham, 2013), whereby the utilization of opposites may unlock habitual neural signatures and release the emotional and—correlatively—bioelectrical charge associated with a traumatic memory or outmoded belief, before rewiring the brain in novel ways.

Stage six of Satyananda's protocol—visualization—involves the instructor guiding practitioners to imagine any number of images and scenarios so as to train focus and elicit repressed, disturbing thoughts and/or imagery. According to Satyananda, when one initially attempts to visualize and sustain the image of a deity (e.g., Jesus, Buddha, etc.), an esoteric symbol (e.g., a cross, a golden egg, the chakras, etc.), or a peaceful environment (e.g., a mountain, ocean, forest, etc.), painful material will naturally surface and can then be removed from the *vijnanamaya*, or body of thought. While neither Atlas (2017b) nor Miller (2010) prohibited the use of visualization, the comparable stage in their respective protocols is one of open invitation to experience thoughts and images that may arise unprovoked, or to invoke thoughts or beliefs about themselves or the world that the practitioners may already be exploring in their lives. Regardless of the specific protocol, the implicit intention to remove samskaras so as to relax more deeply and embody deeper states of self-awareness persists.

While Satyananda ended the practice at stage seven by inviting peaceful imagery and arousing the *anandamaya* (body of bliss), Miller (2010) included two additional stages (making ten overall), including the *asmitamaya* (witness or body of the ego–I) and a state he called *sahaj*—or, a natural state of being where everything is perceived just as it is. It should be stressed that Miller's inclusion of these stages serves as an invitation to perceive the self at increasingly subtle depths, but does not guarantee that practitioners will experience the *satchidananda* (truth-consciousness-bliss) characteristic of samadhi.

Atlas (2017a; 2017b), meanwhile, employed a hybrid, six-stage model that emphasizes a gradual oscillation between the "path of expansion," or experience of the body as limitless and free, versus the "path of contraction" into the body's suffering. A dream researcher, Atlas (*ibid.*) also made use of dreams as a primary messenger of unconscious material awaiting integration, encouraging lucid dreaming as a vehicle for profound healing, transformation, and heightened self-awareness during both sleep and waking states.

Administering Yoga Nidra in a Clinical Setting

The following is a step-by-step guide to administering an introductory-level Yoga Nidra session within a clinical setting, either one-on-one or with a group. As with any depth psychotherapeutic modality, and as has been repeatedly stressed, it is recommended that instructors/clinicians develop at least a modicum of proficiency in their personal practice—with the help of continuing education trainings, for example—prior to employing the modality with clients. The reasoning behind this is that clients receiving the practice are likely to encounter new sensations and emotions, unearth repressed thoughts and feelings, discover varying degrees of meditation, and generate questions related to their unique experiences. Thus, it is advisable that instructors/clinicians know the terrain in an embodied way, so as to respond to a host of potential outcomes with greater insight and authenticity.

Once an instructor/clinician feels prepared to offer his or her services as a Yoga Nidra guide, the first step is to make the client(s) aware of the opportunity to receive Yoga Nidra either as part of or in place of a "typical" therapy session. The notion that the practice is received is an important distinction to make, as—at least initially—clients will have no other responsibility than to relax in a comfortable position and follow the sounds of the instructor's/clinician's voice. This may be a departure from more conversational, therapeutic modalities as well as from brief, guided meditations (e.g., "grounding" or "centering" exercises at the beginning or end of a therapy session).

An ideal length for guided Yoga Nidra is anywhere from fifteen to thirty-five minutes. Practices tending toward the shorter end of this range (e.g., see the sample protocol included in this section) may consolidate the entire core protocol or present just the first few stages, as they are designed to provide enough time and space for clients to "drop" out of their heads and into their bodies. Longer practices afford the opportunity to progress through the latter stages of the protocol so as to bring attention to the koshas (sheaths); to address anything of interest that may arise (e.g., sensations, emotions, thoughts, imagery, intuitions, etc.); and, on occasion, to experience the restorative benefits of Stage One and Stage Two sleep. Prior to beginning the practice, clients should also be made aware of the possibility that difficult feelings and sensations may surface as well. While obtaining informed consent and making clients aware of the potential risks associated with meditation are imperative, instructors/clinicians ought to remain vigilant at all times throughout the practice, monitoring their clients' bodily cues and any other signs of physical and/or emotional distress.

After clients have consented to receiving Yoga Nidra and have been informed of their duties as active listeners, the instructor should further clarify that, while client are welcome to shift positions during the practice, Yoga Nidra is most effective when one remains still for the duration. Furthermore, clients need not try to change anything during the course of the practice, which is undertaken with an implicit intention of deeply embodied self-acceptance, integration, and wholeness (Atlas, 2017a; 2017b). In other words, it is neither the responsibility of the instructor/clinician nor the clients to try to heal or fix anything; rather, the goal of each party is to remain present with what is. The instructor/clinician may also suggest that clients attempt to access and hover at the edge of sleep or hypnagogic state (Maury, 1848), a unique, boundary-thin (Hartmann, 1989) state of consciousness similar to a lucid dream, which has been demonstrated to promote physical and psychological healing (Atlas, 2017a). While not essential, the instructor/clinician may occasionally remind clients of these intentions throughout the course of the experience.

Clients receiving Yoga Nidra should be encouraged to assume a comfortable position. As noted above, Yoga Nidra is typically practiced in savasana (corpse pose), wherein clients lie on their backs (e.g., on a mat or couch) with their hands resting a few inches from their sides and their open palms facing upward. Ideally, a small pillow or cushion is placed under their heads, allowing their foreheads to rest slightly higher than their chins—which helps to maintain alertness; an additional cushion (e.g., a yoga bolster or pillow) may be placed under their knees for extra support. Clients may also wish to use an eye cover to block out light and/or blanket to maintain body heat. In lieu of savasana, the instructor/clinician may suggest alternative positions, such as lying on one's side or belly, sitting upright, standing, walking, etc., and clients' hands may also rest against their bodies (e.g., one hand over their belly and one over their heart) or anywhere they feel drawn.

Once a resting position has been established, the instructor/clinician should employ an especially calm, authentic voice and demeanor—no doubt the result of extensive personal practice—encouraging clients to take two or three deep breaths, "expanding [their] belly as [they] inhale and naturally softening [their] belly as [they] exhale" (Atlas, 2017b, p. 70). The instructor may also recommend that clients audibly sigh from time to time, which tends to elicit a sense of calm, especially if clients are prone to rumination. After a minute or two, the clients are likely to have settled into their role, and the instructor should begin the formal protocol. Again, while there is considerable variation and room for improvisation within any one approach, a consistent routine will allow clients to access the deep relaxation of Yoga Nidra more quickly on account of their familiarity with the protocol and subsequent, autogenic response, as well as the instructor's ease of delivery.

Similar to Satyananda's "resolve" (Satyananda, 2006) stage, or the "sankalpa" (i.e., setting of intentions) stage of iRest® (Miller, 2010), Evolutionary Education®'s introductory-level protocol begins with "Centering" (Atlas, 2017b). Centering contains three distinct phases: invoking the "ally"; aligning with the "highest and best" or one's sense of the divine; and, setting intentions or asking a question (Atlas, 2017b). In the first phase, the instructor should spend two-three minutes guiding clients to welcome their ally or "inner resource" (Miller, 2010)—an image, memory, and/or felt sense of a soothing presence, such as a loved one, a favorite pet, a special object, a place in nature, etc. Clients should be guided to choose something reliable, whether living, deceased, or imaginary, that will *consistently* evoke deeply rooted feelings of peace, safety, security, groundedness, joy, etc. Thus, romantic partners do not make great allies in Yoga Nidra; smiling dogs, memories of walks on the beach, and the smell of Grandma's chocolate chip cookies do. If clients have difficulty honing in on an ally, the instructor may suggest that the experience of receiving Yoga Nidra itself—provided it is a positive one—can serve as an ally.

The purpose of the ally is to create an affective lifeline that will help clients anchor their attention in their body, in the present moment, and in something pleasing, should they feel overwhelmed by their experience. Though Miller (2010) invited the inner resource at a slightly later stage in the protocol, Atlas (2017b) established the ally first and foremost, thereafter equipping clients with a valuable tool that they may summon at any moment during the practice and/or in their life. The instructor may also occasionally invite the ally back into the experience, perhaps during the middle portion of the practice as well as at the end, so that clients develop familiarity with it and grow accustomed to summoning it on their own.

Next, the instructor may wish to orient clients to their larger sense of self by asking them to welcome or open to "the highest and best," their "sense of the divine," a "connection to source" (Atlas, 2017b) or a "heartfelt desire" (Miller, 2010), emphasizing that there is no specific way to achieve this. This technique serves the purpose of placing individuals in the world, providing them time and space to attune with intuitive and/or spiritual modes of being, and engaging their trust and faith, all of which appear to play a role in psychospiritual transformation (Atlas, 2017a). The instructor may further request that clients "listen to any messages from [the] unconscious that may be helpful" (Atlas, 2017b, p. 71) for them, while advising them not to be concerned if no such messages arise.

In the next phase of the protocol, the instructor may devote an additional minute or so guiding clients to set an intention or intentions for their practice. Ideally, clients will employ evocative language or mental imagery as if to embed their intention(s) in the depths of their being, orienting their larger self toward their desired goal(s). As noted above, Miller (2010) suggested speaking intentions as positive affirmations (e.g., I have achieved "x"…) rather than wishes yet to be fulfilled. The best intentions are those pertaining to short-term, attainable goals that, upon actualization, strengthen clients' morale and naturally lead to increased success in this process. As noted above, Atlas (2017b) also offered practitioners the opportunity to ask a question in need of resolution, which inspires deep listening and an openness to the unknown rather than goal-orientation.

Once the three phases of Centering (i.e., invoking the ally, connecting to source, and setting intentions) have been established, the instructor begins the most fundamental stage of the practice: the body scan (i.e., the *annamaya* stage). There are an infinite number of ways to administer a body scan, though most will begin at the toes and progress toward the head (see the example below), or begin at the head and finish at the toes. Similarly, some body scans may emphasize awareness of the right foot/arm/leg versus the left foot/arm/leg, for example, while others may ask clients to become aware of both feet/arms/legs in unison, or employ a combination of approaches. As noted above, Satyananda's rotation of consciousness stage emphasizes a definitive, terse sequence, while other approaches (e.g., Atlas, 2017b; Miller, 2010) may be considerably more improvisational and drawn out. A typical body scan may take anywhere from five to fifteen minutes to complete, and, in the case of an introductory practice such as this one, may constitute the majority of the protocol. Furthermore, a good body scan will flow effortlessly from section to section, so as to help clients elicit a sense of interconnectedness within their being. Thus, due care should be taken to avoid having the body scan sound too mechanical, which may prevent clients from relaxing deeply into the global sense of awareness and expansive presence that lies at the heart of Yoga Nidra. While it is not inappropriate to read from a script, the most effective body scan is one that emerges poetically from the instructors' embodied presence, wisdom, and experience in practicing Yoga Nidra themselves (Atlas, 2017b).

When inviting clients to feel parts of their body piece by piece, the instructor ought to incorporate inclusive language whenever possible. For example, repeatedly asking clients to "relax" various parts of their bodies may be alienating if they have trouble letting go of tension. To avoid this issue, instructors might suggest that clients "welcome" the sensation of their feet, "soften" their ankles, "slacken" their calves, "feel" their legs as pure sensation, and so on. Asking clients to relax is certainly appropriate, and it may be possible to gauge whether it is effective within a given practice (by reading body language, for example); however, expanding the possibilities to invite awareness of the body without the pressure of having to attain relaxation can be quite liberating for some clients.

Below is an example of a body scan that I have found to be effective. It may be read to clients verbatim or improvised at the instructor's discretion. Included in the example are brief pauses that may follow individual prompts (separated by "…")—allowing clients a momentary lull to embody themselves, plunge more deeply into relaxation, and unfurl into meditative absorption—as well as extended pauses (e.g., anywhere from one to five minutes) that enable clients to have their own experience free from interruption. Following the three-part Centering stage, the instructor/clinician may proceed as follows:

"Imagine a healing energy welling up beneath the soles of your feet, pervading your toes … soles and tops of your feet … your heels, ankles … calves and shins … knees, in back and in front … thighs … hips … and hip sockets…. Imagine feeling into the marrow of your bones, the very centers of your bones, everything soft and slack. Welcoming the sensation of your entire right leg … your left leg … and feeling both legs completely released and relaxed, as if separate from the rest of your body" [pause momentarily before proceeding].

"Welcoming sensation in the tips of your fingers … traveling upward through your palms and backs of your hands … softening your wrists … forearms … elbows … upper arms and shoulders … relaxing your shoulder sockets … softening the marrows of your bones … everything soft and heavy … both arms soft and slack, as if separate from the rest of your body" [extended pause].

"Feel your pelvis … the weight of your pelvis … welcoming sensation in your root … groin … tailbone and sacrum … the base of your spine … lower abdomen and belly … feeling your lower back … middle back … and upper back … feeling your spine like a thread of silk … your solar plexus and sternum … ribs … chest … and collarbone, in back and in front … the back of your neck and your throat … imagine your throat opening like a flower … releasing the weight of your head … all the muscles and bones of your face … softening your jaw … and the bones of your cheeks … the orbits of your eyes … centers of your eyes … softening your brow … forehead … temples … and your scalp … feeling your whole body, soft and slack [extended pause].

"Imagine softening the space all around your body … beyond left and right … above you … and beneath you … beyond the crown of your head … and several inches beneath the soles of your feet" [extended pause] … "welcoming your whole body as pure sensation … pure energy … soft and slack … open and expansive … transparent and receptive" [extended pause] … "and imagining your body inside of you … inside of awareness … open … spacious … limitless awareness … without border or boundary … without center or periphery … just being … pure being, here … without the need to change anything … or do anything … everything just as it is [pause for several moments until you are ready to end the practice].

"Welcoming your ally—this trusted companion on your journey … and with it, sparking good feelings in your body … a sense of peace … safety … security … well-being … a touch of joy … and letting it crack an inner smile ... notice where it arises from ... and allowing it to radiate out through your whole being into eternity [extended pause].

"You might take a moment or two to look back over your experience as if you were emerging from a dream ... taking note of anything of interest ... any messages you may have received ... and anything you may wish to return to or set in motion in your practice, or in the rest of your life [extended pause] ... you might also revisit your intention or intentions, or set new intentions [extended pause] ... and taking a moment to open to the highest ... the highest and best for yourself ... for everyone you know... for all of life [extended pause].

"And, in the next moment or two, taking two or three slightly deeper breaths into your belly ... you might place your hands against your body, perhaps a hand over your chest and another over your belly, or anywhere that they feel drawn ... you might wiggle your fingers and toes a little bit ... you could give yourself a rub, or a hug, a stretch or a yawn ... and before sitting up, take a moment on one side ... have a breath or two here ... and when you do decide to sit up, try to do so slowly, maintaining the healing resonance in your body."

After allowing clients a few moments to collect themselves, it is advised that instructors/clinicians spend several minutes checking-in and, depending upon the setting and time permitting, discussing the experience or anything pressing for the client. A simple, body-centered practice such as the one outlined above has the potential to open up a wealth of insights that may be used as jumping-off points for psychotherapy, counseling, and a host of other therapeutic methods. If and when the session is nearing a close, the instructor/clinician should make absolutely certain that clients are grounded, focused, and alert prior to their exiting, especially if they must operate a vehicle or engage in a similar activity.

Training

At present, there are no minimum education requirements that must be met in order to practice or administer Yoga Nidra, nor does one need to attain any sort of licensure. It is advised, however, that aspiring instructors procure some form of continuing education, especially for the purposes of progressing in the protocol and exploring the nuances of Yoga Nidra. At the time of publication, an increasing number of organizations—including Evolutionary Education®, iRest®, Amrit Yoga®, etc.—and instructors-at-large offer certification courses in Yoga Nidra, each with its own slant on the practice and often with some overlap among them. Furthermore, it should be stressed that neither instructors/clinicians nor clients need to have any formal yoga experience, as Yoga Nidra is accessible to complete beginners and, as has been emphasized herein, derives from ancient yogic philosophy. At the same time, it has virtually nothing to do with modern-day versions of yoga that are almost entirely relegated to physical fitness. Those interested in pursuing advanced training in Yoga Nidra are further invited to contact the author for more information.

Conclusion

At present, the yoga industry is among the fastest-growing commercial industries in the world (Walton, 2016). In recent years, however, yoga has become virtually synonymous with vigorous stretching, while much of its ancient philosophy and many of its technologies for deeper, psychospiritual transformation have been left by the wayside. Mindfulness-based practices have also been consumed with increased vigor, especially in the West, though they, too, are often stripped of their Buddhist heritage and viewed as quick and efficient coping mechanisms rather than profound, depth psychologies. In the author's personal experience, a slight shift in attitude, awareness of tradition, and acknowledgment of various avenues into the psyche can make the difference between a superficial meditation practice and one that is inherently therapeutic, dynamic, transcendent, and capable of imparting lasting health in both mind and body. Yoga Nidra, which requires no formal training in yoga, is one such practice that cuts through the façade of spirituality by inviting practitioners to relax more deeply, to come face-to-face with themselves, to embody their suffering, and to accept courageously the deepest parts of who they are. Well suited for classrooms, mental health clinics, private practice, and a host of other venues, Yoga Nidra will surely find its way into mainstream dialogue in the years to come, reaping significant benefits for those who embrace it and share it within their communities.

NOTE

1. As this essay is intended for a broad audience spanning several disciplines, I have dispensed with all diacritical notes from the original Sanskrit, Tibetan, etc., opting for the closest Standard English spellings wherever possible.

REFERENCES

Amita, S., Prabhakar, S., Manoi, I., Harminder, S. & Pavan, T. (2009). Effect of yoga-nidra on blood glucose level in diabetic patients. *Indian Journal of Physiology and Pharmacology, 53*(1), 97–101.

Atlas, N. (2017a). *Lucid dreaming and the path to freedom: A transpersonal phenomenological inquiry.* (Unpublished dissertation.) Carrollton, GA: University of West Georgia.

Atlas, N. (2017b). *Yoga psychology teacher training manual.* Carrollton: Evolutionary Education Press.

Benson, H., & Klipper, M. (1975). *The relaxation response.* New York, NY: HarperTorch.

Bingham, M.O., Peacock, W.P., Fritts, M.J. & Walter, J.A.G. (2011). The effects of Intergrative Restoration (iRest®) on sleep and perceived stress in military medical center healthcare providers: A pilot study for developing staff resilience. Poster session at Samueli Institute, Alexandria, VA. Retrieved from http://www.irest.us/sites/default/files/CCF_Poster_BAMC_Study

Birch, J., & Hargreaves, J. (2015). Yoganidrā: An understanding of the history and context. Retrieved from https://www.irest.us/sites/default/files/Yoganidra%20Birch%20 and%20Hargreaves

Eastman-Mueller, H., Wilson, T., Jung, A., Kimura, A. & Tarrant, J. (2013). iRest yoga-nidra on the college campus: Changes in stress, depression, worry, and mindfulness. *International Journal of Yoga Therapy, 23*(2), 15–24.

Easwaran, E. (Trans.) (2007). *The upanishads* (2nd ed.). Tomales, CA: Nilgiri Press.

Ecker, B., Ticic, R. & Hulley, L. (2012). *Unlocking the emotional brain.* New York, NY: Routledge.

Engel, C., Goertz, C., Cockfield, D., Armstrong, D., Jonas, W., Walter, J., Fritts, M., Greene, R., Carnes, R., Gore, K., & Miller, R. (2007). Yoga nidra as an adjunctive therapy for post-traumatic stress disorder: A feasibility study. Poster session at the Samueli Institute and Walter Reed Army Medical Center, Washington, D.C. Retrieved from http://www. irest.us/sites/default/files/WRAMH_PTSD_YN_Results_0

Graham, L. (2013). *Bouncing back: Rewiring your brain for maximum resilience and well-being.* Novato, CA: New World Library.

Grof, S. (1976). *Realms of the human unconscious: Observations from LSD research.* New York, NY: Dutton.

Gutman, S.A., Gregory, K.A., Sadlier-Brown, M.M., Schlissel, M.A., Schubert, A.M., Westover, L.A., & Miller, R. (2016). Comparative effectiveness of three occupational therapy sleep interventions: A randomized controlled study. *OTJR: Occupation, Participation and Health,* 1–9. Retrieved from https://www.irest.us/sites/default/files/Sleep_Interventions_Study_Pub_16

Hartman, C. (2015). Exploring the experiences of women with complex trauma and the practice of iRest-yoga nidra. (Unpublished doctoral dissertation). San Francisco, CA: California Institute for Integral Studies. Retrieved from http://www.irest.us/sites/default/files/iRest%20and%20Women%20with%20Complex%20Trauma

Hartmann, E. (1989). Boundaries of dreams, boundaries of dreamers: Thin and thick boundaries as a new personality measure. *Psychiatric Journal of the University of Ottawa, 14*(4), 557–560.

Jensen, P.S., Stevens, P.J., & Kenny, D.T. (2012). Respiratory patterns in students enrolled in schools for disruptive behavior before, during, and after *yoga nidra* relaxation. *Journal of Child and Family Studies, 21*(4), 667–681.

Kabat-Zinn, J. (2013). *Full catastrophe living: Using the wisdom of your body and mind to face stress, pain, and illness*. New York, NY: Bantam Books.

Kumar, K. (2004). Yoga nidra and its impact on students' well being. Yoga-Mimansa, 36(1), 31–35.

Kumar, K. (2008). A study on the impact on stress and anxiety through *Yoga nidra*. *Indian Journal of Traditional Knowledge, 7*(3), 401–404.

LaBerge, S. (2003). Lucid dreaming and the yoga of the dream state: A psychophysiological perspective. In B. A. Wallace (Ed.), *Buddhism and science, breaking new ground* (pp. 233–258). New York, NY: Columbia University Press.

Markil, N., Whitehurst, M., Jacobs, P.L., & Zoeller, R.F. (2012). Yoga nidra relaxation increases heart rate variability and is unaffected by a prior bout of hatha yoga. *The Journal of Alternative and Complementary Medicine, 18*(10), 953–958.

Maury, A. (1848). Des hallucinations hypnagogiques, ou des erreurs des sens dans l'état intermédiaire entre la veille et le sommeil. *Annales Medico-Psychologiques du système nerveux, 11*, 26–40.

Miller, R. (2010). *Yoga nidra: A meditative practice for deep relaxation and healing*. Louisville, CO: Sounds True.

Nassif, T.H., Norris, D.O., Soltes, K.L., Blackman, M.R., Chapman, J.C., & Sandbrink, F. (2014). Evaluating the effectiveness of mindfulness meditation (iRest) for chronic musculoskeletal pain in U.S. veterans using the Defense and Veterans Pain Rating Scale. Poster session presented at the War Related Illness and Injury Study Center, Washington, D.C. Retrieved from http://www.irest.us/sites/default/files/AA PM%20Poster%20Final

Norbu, N. (1992). *Dream yoga and the practice of natural light*. Ithica, NY: Snow Lion Publications.

Parker, S., Bharati, S.V., & Fernandez, M. (2013). Defining Yoga-Nidra: Traditional accounts, physiological research, and future directions. *International Journal of Yoga Therapy, 23*(1), 11–16.

Pence, P.G., Katz, L.S., Huffman, C., & Cojucar, G. (2014). Delivering Integrative Restoration—Yoga nidra meditation (iRest®) to women with sexual trauma at a veteran's medical center: A pilot study. *International Journal of Yoga Therapy, 24*, 53–62.

Pritchard, M., Elison-Bowers, P., & Birdsall, B. (2010). Impact of Integrative Restoration (iRest) meditation on perceived stress levels in multiple sclerosis and cancer outpatients. *Stress and Health, 26*, 233–237.

Rama, S.S. (1984). *Exercise without movement: Manual One*. Honesdale, PA: Himalayan International Institute.

Rani, K., Tiwari, S.C., Singh, U., Agrawal, G.G., Ghildiyal, A., & Srivastava, N. (2011). Impact of *Yoga Nidra* on psychological general wellbeing in patients with menstrual irregularities: A randomized controlled trial. *International Journal of Yoga, 4*(1), 20–25.

Satyananda, S. (2006). *Yoga nidra*. Bihar, India: Yoga Publications Trust.

Schultz, J.H., & Luthe, W. (1965). *Autogenic training*. New York, NY: Grune & Stratton.

Shapiro, S., Lyons, K.E., Miller, R.C., Butler, B., Vieten, C., & Zelazo, P.D. (2015). Contemplation in the classroom: A new direction for improving childhood education. *Educational Psychology Review, 27*(1), 1–30.

Singleton, M. (2005). Salvation through relaxation: Proprioceptive therapy and its relationship to yoga. *Journal of Contemporary Religion, 20*(3), 289–304.

Stankovic, L. (2011). Transforming trauma: A qualitative feasibility study of Integrative Restoration (iRest) yoga nidra on combat-related post-traumatic stress disorder. *International Journal of Yoga Therapy, 21*, 23–37.

Temme, L.J., Fenster, J., & Ream, G.L. (2012). Evaluation of meditation in the treatment of chemical dependency. *Journal of Social Work Practice in the Addictions, 12*(3), 264–281.

Tenzin Wangyal, R. (1998). *The Tibetan yogas of dream and sleep*. Ithaca, NY: Snow Lion Publications.

Wallace, B.A. (2012). *Dreaming yourself awake: Lucid dreaming and Tibetan dream yoga for insight and transformation*. Boston, MA: Shambhala.

Walton, A.G. (2016, March 15). How yoga is spreading in the U.S. Forbes.com. Retrieved from https://www.forbes.com/sites/alicegwalton/2016/03/15/how-yoga-is-spreading-in-the-u-s/#4635d753449f

Mindfulness Meditation

Principles and Applications for Holistic Healing

Nitin Anand, Mahendra Prakash Sharma,
Amanpreet Kaur *and* Priya Kayastha Anand

Introduction to the Concept of Mindfulness Meditation

Mindfulness, or Vipassana meditation, is one of India's most ancient meditative techniques originating from traditional Buddhist meditation practices. It was rediscovered by Gautam Buddha 2500 years ago. In particular, mindfulness is focused on cultivation of attention and awareness through meditation. Mindfulness can be defined as "the awareness that emerges through paying attention on purpose, in the present moment, and non-judgmentally to the unfolding of experience moment by moment" (Kabat-Zinn, 2003). Indeed, mindfulness is understood to be at the core of Buddhist meditation practices. The word *Vipassana* is a combination of two words, "Vi," and "Passana." "Vi" means "in a special way," and "Passana" means "to see, to observe." It is also known as insight, awareness, or mindfulness meditation (Langer & Moldoveanu, 2000). Thus, mindfulness is the non-judgmental observation of the ongoing stream of internal and external stimuli as they arise. In other words, it is a state of "bare attention," which requires one to remain psychologically present with whatever happens in and around, without adding or subtracting from it in any way (Nairn, 1999).

People who are mindful focus their minds precisely on the activity which they are doing at the very moment, whether it is working in an office, interacting with people, studying, cleaning the house, or playing with one's children. Irrespective of the activity in which we are engaged, we can practice mindfulness. It empowers people with the ability to respond consciously rather than to react automatically to ongoing events. All of us in our own ways are mindful to one degree or another, in each of the passing moments of time. It is an inherent capacity of humans to be aware of themselves and the existing environmental experiences. Moreover, Buddha has mentioned that one way to achieve an end of suffering is to practice mindfulness meditation.

Mindfulness meditation is also known as an open monitoring type of meditation, wherein the individual simply registers or becomes aware of the emerging and fading away of mental events while maintaining a detached emotional state. In mindfulness meditation, the practice is to develop equal and non-judgmental distribution of one's attention among all the mental events occurring in one's awareness at each moment. In other words, our thoughts, feelings, perceptions, desires or will, and memories are to be observed in a detached manner as just a mental phenomenon arising in our awareness and eventually passing away, as long as people do not get engage with it. This can be understood from the principle of impermanence, which imparts us with the ability to observe things as they really are present in the moment. As everything is perishable and nothing is permanent, so we need to observe mental events in a detached manner without clinging to them.

When we behave in an unmindful manner, we are in the grip of the conditioning of the sensorial mind by not being in the present moment or by being judgmental of our thoughts, feelings, perceptions, and desires, which further provoke mental processes or events inside us. This provocation occurs when thoughts, feelings, perceptions, and desires escape our non-judgmental awareness and insist on interaction with our minds. Memory, as still another mental event, adds further elaborations to these four mental events by generating numerous reactions that are not based on the facts of the present moment. These reactions take the mind away from present-moment awareness and non-judgmental observation. When individuals practice mindfulness, then they can turn these phenomena into events for non-judgmental observation, after which mindfulness diffuses them and overcomes the unmindful or unwholesome responses (Bodhi, 2000).

Mindfulness meditation helps in maintaining a continuous state of awareness, which is different from the fragmented awareness under which the sensorial mind usually operates. This continuous state of awareness helps in attaining knowledge about self, which guides individuals in choosing actions in daily life. These actions become wise actions rather than just a discharge of one's impulses. Mindfulness meditation can be likened to an ongoing movie rather than just a photo shot.

A detached manner of awareness can be gradually developed via mindfulness meditation, wherein the individual learns to operate largely in an awareness mode rather than being in a reactive mode towards the ever-emerging stream of thoughts, feelings, perceptions, desires or will, and memories. The process of mindfulness meditation involves cultivation of bare attention, disengagement from mental events, and shifting from the sensorial conditioning of the mind. The fundamental wisdom in meditative philosophies suggests that meditation is not confined just to the prayer rooms; rather, this whole life is a meditation.

Origins of Mindfulness

Mindfulness meditation has its origins in Theravada and Mahayana Buddhism. The construct of mindfulness awareness originated in the earliest Buddhist documents, but it is neither religious nor esoteric in nature (Brown, 1999). It is known that descriptions of meditation are found in the Rig-Veda [Rig-Veda: X: 129], which was composed many centuries before Buddha (Brereton, 1999; Kalupahana, 2006). Furthermore, early Buddhist texts also corroborate the information about the presence of meditative practices even before Buddha. In the biography of Buddha, as per our awareness, a few of the Buddha's teachers were trained in the Vedic system of yoga (Kalupahana, 1994; Santina, 1997). Buddha was raised in both the shramanic and brahminic (Vedic & Upanishadic) traditions. This upbringing helped him to identify and integrate the philosophical discrepancies among these traditions, which contributed significantly towards their subsequent fusion.

Theravada, the key scripture of Buddhism, consists of these core aspects of integration of these traditions. The meditative method propagated by Buddha is known as mindfulness meditation. In Pali (an ancient language of India), it is known as Vipassana, which means "to see things in a special way"—that is, as they really are, not just as they seem to be influenced by the mental events (thoughts, feelings, perceptions, desires, and memories) (Vipassana Research Institute, 2005). Buddha's most significant contribution was the integration of the existing philosophies in a manner that is comprehensible to a larger population. He presented the philosophy, techniques, and meditation practices in a pragmatic and a user-friendly manner. He also developed meditation into a method of healing, proposing its use for the enhancement of the community's health and wellness.

In the ancient times of India, between the Maurya and the Gupta Dynasties (2nd century BCE to 5th century BCE), meditation became more accessible to the common man. Before this period, meditative practices were pursued mostly by a few select people in the relative social isolation offered by the forests and the mountains. This development explains the great popularity of the Theravada traditions of thought and the spread of mindfulness meditation and other meditative practices beyond India, particularly after the Buddha's era. Meditative practices are now followed in the Southeast Asian countries of Burma, Cambodia, Vietnam, and Thailand, while the Mahayana traditions have been practiced in China, Korea, Japan, and Vietnam. The Vajrayana traditions of Buddhist thought have followers primarily in Tibet, followed by Mongolia, Nepal, Bhutan, and the Ladakh region of India.

According to the abhidhammic scheme of meditation, it is understood that the mind is considered to be just another sense organ, the sixth one following the eyes, ears, nose, tongue, and skin. In this school of thought, our thoughts, feelings, perceptions, desires, and memories are understood as mental events or experiences, rather than as real facts of life. Similarly, the principle of impermanence enlightens us that nothing is permanent, and all events are transitory. Thus, as everything is perishable, so we need to observe mental events in a detached manner without clinging to them. These mental events, like tides of the ocean, constantly arise in our stream of awareness, peak, and eventually dissipate. The Buddhist traditions have contributed to the emphasis on simple and effective ways to cultivate and refine the capacity of attention and awareness and extend it to all aspects of life. Mindfulness surely received its most comprehensive, well-defined articulation and development within the traditions of Buddhism over 2500 years ago. Mindfulness remains the central technique for cultivating attention and awareness, which underlie all streams of Buddhist meditative practices.

In sum, mindfulness meditation is the fundamental framework that connects all streams of Buddhist meditative practices. One needs to understand that the various traditions of Buddhist thought have numerous sub-traditions and associated texts, which have an impact on the practice of mindfulness (Goldstein, 2002). However, as explained by Buddha, mindfulness is the central technique or teaching on which all the various forms and traditions of Buddhism rest. At the same time, the core concept of mindfulness has been explained across two discourses by Gautam Buddha, namely, in the *Anapanasati Sutra* (Rosenberg, 1998) and the *Satipathana Sutra* (Thera, 1962), which are the principal teachings upon which the foundation of various forms and traditions of meditative practices exists.

The perspective of mindfulness hypothesizes the conceptualization of how the unexamined behaviors of an untrained mind can contribute significantly and directly to human suffering, both one's own and that of others. It also suggests that alleviation of that suffering through meditative practices occurs by offering calmness and clarity to the mind, opening the self to ongoing experiences, and enhancing awareness, attention, and human behaviors. Gautam Buddha is said to have attained enlightenment after meditating under a pipal tree, now known as the Bodhi tree in Bodh Gaya, India, after which he became known as the Buddha, or the "Awakened One."

Mindfulness: Evolving Interest in Research and Practice

In the last decade, there has been a growing interest in the application of mindfulness to various clinical and mental health conditions. This emergent trend is evident from the outcomes of an ever-increasing number of research studies on mindfulness and its impact on clinical syndromes, which have been approved for funding and publication. Moreover, a considerable number of doctoral researchers are taking up this field of intervention and studying its effects on various clinical conditions, which suggest that this research area is triggering significant research interest. The factors underlying this interest appear to be primarily driven by the sense that new dimensions of therapeutic benefits and newer understandings about mind-body interactions might arise through evaluation of its impact on mental health conditions.

In one of the earliest studies, mindfulness as a technique was utilized as part of dialectical behavior therapy (DBT; Linehan, 1993a) and in combination with cognitive therapy, an approach that has come to be known as Mindfulness-Based Cognitive Therapy (MBCT; Segal, Williams, & Teasdale, 2013). Following the publication of these research studies, mindfulness has inspired researchers to utilize the technique across various medical and mental health conditions. Yet, mindfulness should be recognized mainly as a technique of meditative practice, not solely understood or seized upon as the next promising cognitive behavioral technique, which has been decontextualized and accommodated into a behaviorist paradigm with the aim of effecting desirable change Goyal, A.K. (2012).

Baer (2003) has suggested several mechanisms that may explain how mindfulness skills can lead to stress reduction, along with cognitive and behavioral changes, an evaluation that has made the scientific community even more interested in mindfulness. These mechanisms are exposure (prolonged non-judgmental exposure leads to desensitization, with a reduction in emotional response over time); cognitive change (understanding that experiences are not always accurate reflections of reality); self-management (promoting the use of a range of coping skills); relaxation (induces relaxation with non-judgmental observation of current conditions); and acceptance (experiencing events fully without defense, as they are, and without trying to change, escape, or avoid them).

Mindfulness: Principles and Mechanisms of Change

The available literature suggests that there are sets of different but interacting mechanisms in mindfulness meditation that can lead to symptom reduction, as well as cognitive and behavioral change. However, many of the proposed mechanisms have not been empirically studied and remain hypothetical in nature (Kocovski, Segal, & Battista, 2009). A growing body of evidence indicates that mindfulness does have a number of positive effects on well-being and on minimizing the distress caused by medical and psychological disorders. The current understanding of mindfulness meditation involves chiefly the processes of attention, non-judgmental awareness, defusion, acceptance, and exposure to sensations, thoughts, emotions, perceptions, desires, and memories, along with awareness regarding their process of ongoing change.

Attention, Metacognition and Decentering

Unlike concentrative meditative practices, in mindfulness meditation attention is paid not to a single stimulus (object, word, or sound) but to *observation* of constantly changing internal or external stimuli as they arise. It is also known as *open monitoring*, wherein individuals attempt to remain attentive to the emergence and fading away of the mental events while maintaining a detached emotional state (Baer, 2003). Mindfulness meditation training inherently requires that individuals alter their field of attention in a manner that is more present-moment focused towards thoughts, feelings, perceptions, desires, and memories.

To facilitate attention to the present moment, the usual mindfulness meditative exercise that is initiated is called the *body scan technique*, wherein instruction initially involves focusing attention on the incoming and outgoing breath to make people come into contact with the present moment. Once individuals are able to comprehend and focus attention on the unending cycle of incoming and outgoing breath, they are gradually instructed to be aware of their body as a whole. They are also gradually instructed to be introspectively aware of their sensations, thoughts, and feelings as they arise, before returning their attention to their breath (Woods, 2009). The monitoring of thought processes, which includes the focus of attention, is termed *metacognition*. This monitoring is a necessary condition for active direction of attention. The ability to sustain the metacognitive processes facilitates the development of "decentering" from thoughts and emotions, such that thoughts and related events are understood as transitory mental events rather than necessarily as direct representations of reality. The development of this ability leads to formation of metacognitive insights about mental events (Bishop et al., 2004; Teasdale, 1999).

Non-Judgmental Awareness, Acceptance and Cognitive Flexibility

The phenomena (cognitions, emotions, perceptions, or sensations) that emerge in the individual's mind during mindfulness practice are observed carefully and attentively, but they are not evaluated in dichotomous categories such as good or bad, true or false, healthy or sick, or important or trivial (Marlatt & Kristeller, 1999). If individuals become judgmental of their experiences, that will lead to an increased tendency to amplify their effects. Rather than evaluating one's cognitive and emotional experiences, mindfulness teaches us simply to be aware of them through reducing habitual tendencies to place mental experiences into dichotomous categories. Mindfulness meditation is viewed as a state that enhances the available range and adaptability of cognitive and behavioral actions, which, in turn, offer opportunities to develop awareness of ongoing mental events (Hayes & Wilson, 2003).

The non-judgmental awareness mode enhances "cognitive flexibility" (Roemer & Orsillo, 2003), increases the openness to experience mental events, and reduces the tendency to label some experiences as "unpleasant" (Mamig, 2006). This non-judgmental awareness assists people with their difficulties in life and further enhances their acceptance-based behavior. Hayes (1994) suggested that acceptance involves experiencing events fully and without defense, as they are, while Kabat-Zinn (1990) described acceptance as one of several foundations of mindfulness practice. Treatments incorporating mindfulness meditation strongly emphasize acceptance of symptoms as they are, rather than avoidance or suppression of them (Baer, 2003; Brown & Ryan, 2003; Hayes & Wilson 1993). Therefore, mindfulness meditation training also provides a method for teaching acceptance skills.

Exposure, Approach and Desensitization

It has been proposed that the practice of mindfulness functions as an exposure to internal experiences, including sensations, cognitions, and emotions (Baer, 2003; Kabat-Zinn, 1982; Linehan, 1993a). Similarly, Shapiro, Carlson, Astin, and Freedman (2006) suggested that willingness to remain in contact with unpleasant internal experiences is an important outcome of mindfulness practice. Practitioners of mindfulness are instructed to meet unpleasant emotions (such as fear, sadness, anger, and aversion) by turning towards them, rather than turning away (Santorelli, 2000). When individuals focus their awareness on unpleasant cognitions, emotions, desires, and memories in a non-judgmental manner, mindfulness can help prevent avoidance or escape from these mental events (experiential avoidance). When individuals fully experience their feared cognitions or emotions without engaging in avoidance behaviors, they can better formulate more effective coping strategies. Thus, mindfulness can play an important role in extinction of the fear response (Baer, 2003; Kocovski, Segal, & Battista, 2009). Linehan (1993a, 1993b) suggested that prolonged observation of current thoughts and emotions, without trying to avoid or escape them, can be seen as an example of exposure, which should encourage the extinction of fear responses and avoidance behaviors previously elicited by these stimuli (mental events). Thus, it seems that the practice of mindfulness skills can improve the ability to tolerate negative emotional states, foster global desensitization to formally stressful stimuli, and enhance habituation skills to cope with negative states in an effective manner.

Re-perceiving, Cognitive Change and Positive Reappraisal

Mindfulness practices (intention, attention, and attitude) lead to an increase in clarity and objectivity when viewing moment-by-moment internal and external experiences in a non-judgmental manner (Shapiro, Carlson, Astin, & Freedman, 2006). Thus, mindfulness results in the enhancement of four areas, namely: self-regulation; values clarification; exposure; and cognitive, emotional, and behavioral flexibility. This fundamental shift in perspective has been theorized to lead to dis-identification with one's thoughts, emotions, and perceptions (Grabovac, Lau, & Willet, 2011). Mindfulness focuses on changing one's relationship to one's thoughts and feelings, viewing thoughts as merely thoughts and not as reality or facts (Segal, Williams, & Teasdale, 2013). The focus is not on changing the content of mental events; rather, it is on changing people's relationships with their internal responses to mental events, resulting in cognitive, emotional, and behavioral changes.

Positive reappraisal, which happens as a result of cognitive change and re-perceiving, is understood to be the key mediator of therapeutic change (Garland, Gaylord, & Frederickson, 2011). Mindfulness is identified as a tool to be used for the construction of a positive reappraisal. One possible concern is that such an emphasis, which is embedded in the narrative experience of self over time, may actually increase an individual's vulnerability to becoming entangled with cognitive processes underlying mood and anxiety symptoms, as it reinforces the narrative experience of self (Grabovac, Lau, & Willet, 2011).

Self-management, Relaxation and Control

Several researchers have noted that the improved self-observation that results from mindfulness meditative practices may promote the use of a range of effective coping skills (Kabat-Zinn, 1982; Kristeller & Hallett, 1999; Linehan, 1993b) for better self-care and self-management. Some authors (Goldenberg et al., 1994; Kabat-Zinn et al., 1998) have suggested that meditation often induces relaxation, which may contribute to the management of various medical and psychological disorders. However, the core purpose of mindfulness training is not to induce relaxation, but rather to teach non-judgmental observation of current mental events or conditions, which might include autonomic arousal, racing thoughts, muscle tension, and other mental phenomena incompatible with relaxation (Baer, 2003). Evidence also suggests that relaxation is not unique to meditation, but is common to many relaxation strategies (Shapiro, 1982). Thus, although practice of mindfulness exercises may lead to relaxation, this outcome may not be the primary reason for engaging in mindfulness meditative practices.

Conventional theories propose that a fundamental component of anxiety-provoking situations is that individuals perceive these situations as being out of their control (Mineka & Thomas, 1999). However, mindfulness-based approaches differ significantly from conventional approaches in their philosophy regarding attempts to control internal responses. Mindfulness tends to lead to a change in perspective about the sense of self and a revision in first-person subjective experience (Hölzel et al., 2011). It has been postulated that paying close attention to the transitory nature of the sense of self leads to the "deconstruction of the self," as individuals become aware of the momentary nature of thoughts, emotions, and sensations (Epstein, 1988). In place of identification with the static self, there emerges a tendency within individuals to identify with the phenomenon of "experiencing" themselves in an ongoing transitory state (Hölzel et al., 2011).

Methods of Mindfulness Meditation

Mindfulness meditation has been used in various forms in different mindfulness-based interventions, although the underlying mechanisms and principles remain the same. Mindfulness practice is essentially experiential, which involves both formal and informal meditation practices (Hick, 2010). Formal practices could be carried out at varying periods of time on a regular basis (for example, sitting meditation, body scan, etc.), while informal practices are aimed at developing a continuity of awareness in a non-judgmental manner in all activities of daily living (for example, mindful walking, mindful eating, etc.) (Kabat-Zinn, 2003). One has to set-up time and space for the formal practices, while informal practices are carried out as a way of life. One can be meditative in each passing moment of life. To attain a meditative state, cultivation of a lifestyle that facilitates meditative status is needed. The lifestyle recommended is one of moderation—the middle way, rather than the extreme. Below we make an attempt to describe the various methods of mindfulness practice.

Mindfulness-Based Stress Reduction (MBSR)

Meditation techniques were originally intended to develop spiritual understanding, awareness, and experience of ultimate reality. However, Psychologist Jon Kabat-Zinn (1982) has been instrumental in bringing mindfulness meditation into medical settings as a therapeutic approach. He developed the Mindfulness-Based Stress Reduction (MBSR) program, which involves integration of systematic training of mindfulness into an accessible and implementable format for individuals undergoing chronic pain and stress-related disorders. The MBSR program is a well-defined approach, skill-based and psychoeducational in nature, with considerable in-session experience and discussion. It is a group-based educational and secular program conducted as an 8- to 10-week course for groups of up to 30 participants who meet weekly for 2–2.5 hours for instruction and practice in mindfulness meditation skills, along with discussion of stress, coping, and homework assignments (Baer, 2003).

A brief 8-week MBSR session summary is outlined below:

- Week 1: Mindful Eating (Raisin experiment), Automatic Pilot; Body and Breath Meditation
- Week 2: Body Scan meditation; difference between "thinking" and "sensing" mind
- Week 3: Hatha Yoga postures—mindfulness of bodily sensations during gentle movements and stretching
- Week 4: Sounds & Thoughts meditation; decentered stance to thoughts and feelings
- Week 5: Exploring difficulties that arise in life from time to time; spirit of openness, compassion, and curiosity
- Week 6: Cultivating loving-kindness and compassion through a "befriending meditation" and acts of generosity in daily life; finding peace in a frantic world
- Week 7: Making connections between daily routines, activities, behavior, and moods; making skillful choices with kindness, creativity, and greater resilience
- Week 8: Weaving mindfulness into your daily life.

Only a few of the above-mentioned techniques in the 8-week program are described below (Williams & Penman, 2011), as descriptions of all of them in detail would be outside the purview of this essay.

Several mindfulness meditation skills are taught as part of MBSR. For example, the *body scan* is a 45-minute exercise in which attention is directed sequentially to numerous areas of the body, while participants are lying down with their eyes closed. Sensations in each area are carefully observed. In *sitting meditation*, participants are instructed to sit in a relaxed but attentive posture, with eyes closed and focus directed to the sensations of breathing and sense of the body as a whole. Hatha yoga postures are used to teach mindfulness of bodily sensations during gentle movements and stretching. Participants also practice *mindfulness* during ordinary activities such as walking, standing, and eating. In addition, they are instructed to practice these skills outside of group meetings for at least 45 minutes per day, six days per week. Audiotapes are also used early in the treatment to facilitate the training in mindfulness, but participants are encouraged to practice without tapes after a few weeks (Baer, 2003). The main purpose of the formal and informal practices of mindfulness meditation is to make people aware, or attentive towards the present moment, to inculcate a skill to observe things as they are without reacting to them or making any judgments, which leads to better well-being, coping, and personal fulfillment. In sum, mindfulness meditation is widely used for the self-management of stress and emotional distress in patients with a wide range of stress-related disorders; it also helps reduce symptoms of stress in non-clinical populations (Bishop, 2002).

Mindfulness-Based Cognitive Therapy (MBCT)

Teasdale, Segal, and Williams (1995) had proposed that the skills of attentional control taught in mindfulness meditation could be beneficial in preventing the relapse into major depressive episodes. The Mindfulness-Based Cognitive Therapy (MBCT) program is a manualized 8-week sequence, wherein 2- to 2.5-hour-long sessions are held in groups on a weekly basis (Segal, Williams, & Teasdale, 2013).

MBCT sessions are preceded by a pre-course orientation and assessment session. Based significantly on Kabat-Zinn's (1990) MBSR program, it integrates elements of cognitive therapy with mindfulness meditation in order to facilitate development of a decentered view of one's thoughts and emotions, including statements such as "thoughts are not facts" (Baer, 2003).

MBCT offers a structured schedule of home practice, involving 45 minutes per day of formal mindfulness practice, some informal practice opportunities in daily life, and some recording of observations of one's experiences. Session handouts and recordings are also given, usually as part of the program. Each session starts with a formal practice (body scan, mindful movement, or sitting meditation practice). Generally, there is a group exercise or exploration that investigates the theme of the week. Short mindfulness practices such as Three-Minute Breathing Space, Mindful Stretching, or Mindful Walking are integrated with other elements to reconnect the participants to an enhanced level of awareness of direct experiencing. Stories and poems related to the themes are included to offer new perspectives on life. Each session closes with a short mindfulness practice.

A summary of an 8-week MBCT sessions may be seen at a glance below:

- Week 1: Automatic Pilot: Raisin experiment (Mindful Eating); Body scan meditation; Group introduction
- Week 2: Dealing with Barriers: Body scan meditation; 10 minutes of mindfulness of breathing; thoughts and feelings exercise; keeping a record of experiences of pleasant events
- Week 3: Mindfulness of the Breath (and the body in movement): Mindful movement; three-minute breathing space; awareness of breath, body, and pleasant experiences

- Week 4: Staying Present: Five-minute mindfulness of seeing or hearing; Sitting meditation; three-minute breathing space; defining, exploring territory of "depression"
- Week 5: Acceptance and Allowing/letting be: Sitting meditation; three-minute breathing space; and present-moment experience.
- Week 6: Thoughts are not facts: Sitting meditation; three-minute breathing space; awareness of breath and body; moods, thoughts, and alternative viewpoint exercise; reflection and work on personal relapse; action plan preparation
- Week 7: How can I best take care of myself?: Sitting meditation—awareness of breath, body, sounds, thoughts, and emotions; link between activity and mood; daily activities of pleasure and mastery; identifying relapse signatures; breathing space; and developing an action plan
- Week 8: Using what has been learned to deal with future moods: Body scan; Ending meditation; review of early warning signs; review of whole course; formal and informal practices; plans for home practice [Crane, 2013].

Other important interventions incorporating mindfulness training are discussed below.

Acceptance and Commitment Therapy (ACT)

ACT, which was compiled by Hayes, is conceptually based in contemporary behavior analysis (Hayes & Wilson, 1993). Experiential mindfulness exercises are used as part of ACT. Metaphors are employed to help guide the patients to use the mindfulness exercises, with a focus on four ACT processes: acceptance, defusion, focus on the present moment, and a transcendent sense of self (Dahl, Wilson, Luciano, & Hayes, 2005). Although ACT does not describe its treatment methods in terms of mindfulness or meditation, it deserves mention here because several of its strategies are consistent with the mindfulness-based interventions described above. Clients in ACT are taught to recognize an observing self, who is capable of watching their own bodily sensations, thoughts, and emotions. They are encouraged to see these phenomena as separate from the person having them. For example, they are taught to say, "I'm having the thought that I'm a bad person," rather than "I'm a bad person" (Kohlenberg, Hayes, & Tsai, 1993, p. 588). They are also encouraged to experience thoughts and emotions as they come, without judging, evaluating, or attempting to change or avoid them, with a view to enhancing their psychological flexibility (Hayes, 1994). For example, "Leaves on a stream" is a metaphor exercise where all four ACT processes that are thought to define mindfulness are put into perspective.

Dialectical Behavior Therapy (DBT)

DBT is an approach originally developed for treatment of borderline personality disorder (Linehan, 1993a, 1993b). It is based on a dialectical world view, which postulates that reality consists of opposing forces (Baer, 2003; Linehan, 1993a). In DBT, the most central dialectic is the relationship between acceptance and change. Clients are encouraged to accept themselves as they are, while work is done to change their behaviors and environments in order to build a better life for them. It includes a wide range of cognitive and behavioral treatment procedures, most of which are designed to change thoughts, emotions, or behaviors. Mindfulness skills are taught in DBT within the context of synthesizing acceptance and change. Linehan (1993a, 1993b) has described three mindfulness "what" skills, and three mindfulness "how" skills.

The clients learn mindfulness skills in a year-long, weekly skill group, which also covers interpersonal effectiveness, emotion regulation, and distress tolerance skills apart from mindfulness skills. However, the DBT approach does not outline a specific frequency or duration of mindfulness practice, unlike MBSR or MBCT. Several variations on observing the breath are taught, including following the breath in and out, counting breaths, coordinating breathing with footsteps while walking, and following the breath while listening to music (Baer, 2003). Some exercises encourage mindful awareness during everyday activities—for example, attempting to be mindful while making tea, washing dishes or clothes, cleaning house, or taking a bath.

Meta-Cognitive Therapy (MCT)

MCT, which was developed by Wells (2011), is based on the principle that metacognition is responsible for understanding how cognition operates and how it generates the conscious experiences that people have with regard to themselves and the world. Metacognition shapes appraisals, regulation of thoughts and emotions, and strategies used. Cognitive Attentional Syndrome (CAS), which consists of worry, rumination, fixated attention, and unhelpful self-regulatory strategies and coping behaviors, is of interest here (Wells, 2011). CAS maintains the individual's sense of threat by indulging in a toxic style of thinking that underlies the psychological disorder. Detached Mindfulness (DM), which is used as a technique in MCT, has two important features: mindfulness and detachment. The aim of DM is to shift the focus of patients away from the object mode of experiencing to a metacognitive mode of awareness. It significantly helps patients to escape from the influence of their thoughts.

The psychological elements of DM as described by Wells (2011) are the following: Meta-awareness, cognitive decentering, attentional detachment and control, low conceptual processing, low goal-directed coping, and altered self-awareness. DM has some similarity with mindfulness meditation, but it is also different from that approach. DM does not involve meditation and does not even require a regular practice. Rather, it concentrates on developing "meta-awareness of thoughts," separating meta-awareness from detachment.

The ten techniques used in MCT to promote a state of DM (Wells, 2005) are the following: Metacognitive guidance, Free-Association Task, Tiger Task, Suppression-Counter Suppression Experiment, Clouds Metaphor, Recalcitrant Child Metaphor, Passenger Train Metaphor, Verbal loop, Detachment: the observing self, and the Daydreaming technique. Socratic dialogue is also used, and homework assignments are given as part of teaching DM. For example the instructor might use one of more of these phrases, "to experience the thoughts as if experiencing clouds passing you by in the sky"; "are you the belief or the person observing the belief?"; "mind is like a busy station and thoughts and feelings are trains passing through. Just be a bystander and watch your thoughts pass through without engaging with them."

Assessment of Mindfulness

Within the past few years, self-report questionnaires for the assessment of mindfulness have begun to appear in the research literature. Each available mindfulness questionnaire represents an attempt to operationalize mindfulness by having participants self-report items that capture its essence. These self-report measures have shown promising psychometric characteristics and have contributed to the understanding of mindfulness constructs and the changes that occur as individuals practice mindfulness meditation (Baer, Walsh, & Lykins, 2009).

The five most important and commonly used measures in clinical practice are discussed below:

1. **The Mindful Attention Awareness Scale** (**MAAS**; Brown & Ryan, 2003). The MAAS is a 15-item instrument, reverse-scored, on a 6-point scale (from 1 = almost always, to 6 = almost never), measuring the general tendency to be attentive to and aware of present-moment experiences in daily life. It has a single-factor structure and yields a single total score. Participants rate how often they have experiences of acting on automatic pilot, being preoccupied, and not paying attention to the present moment. For example, "I find myself doing things without paying attention," and "I break or spill things because of carelessness, not paying attention, or thinking of something else." The authors reported internal consistency (coefficient alpha) of .82, along with expected convergent and discriminant validity correlations. The MAAS appears to have appropriate application in research examining the role of mindfulness in the psychological well-being of college students, working adults, and cancer patients, with or without comparisons to nonclinical controls.

2. **The Freiburg Mindfulness Inventory** (**FMI**; Buchheld, Grossman, & Walach, 2001). The FMI is a 30-item instrument designed to assess non-judgmental present-moment observation and openness to negative-experience aspects of mindfulness. It was developed with participants in mindfulness meditation retreats and is designed for use with experienced meditators. Items are rated on a 4-point Likert-type scale (rarely to almost always). Items include, "I watch my feelings without becoming lost in them," and "I am open to the experience of the present moment." The authors reported internal consistencies of .93 in individuals who completed the inventory at the beginning and end of intensive meditation retreats lasting from 3 to 14 days. The authors suggested that the scale should be interpreted unidimensionally, recommending use of a single total score.

3. **The Kentucky Inventory of Mindfulness Skills** (**KIMS**; Baer, Smith, & Allen, 2004). The KIMS is a 39-item instrument designed to measure four elements of mindfulness: observing, describing, acting with awareness, and accepting without judgment. Items include, "I notice when my moods begin to change" (observe); "I'm good at finding words to describe my feelings" (describe); "When I do things, my mind wanders off and I'm easily distracted" (act with awareness); and "I tell myself that I shouldn't be feeling the way I'm feeling" (accept without judgment). Items are rated on a 5-point Likert-type scale (never or very rarely true, to always or almost always true). The instrument, which is based largely on the DBT conceptualization of mindfulness skills, measures a general tendency to be mindful in daily life and does not require experience with meditation. Internal consistencies range from .76

to .91 for the four subscales. Scores for three of the four scales were found to be significantly lower in a sample of individuals with borderline personality disorder than in a student sample (Baer et al., 2004). A short-form version of the KIMS is also available.

 4. **Toronto Mindfulness Scale (TMS;** Lau et al., 2006). The TMS is a 13-item, two-factor (Curiosity and Decentering), uniquely "state-oriented" scale for use immediately following a meditation experience, which has been validated in a number of clinical contexts. The items of Factor 1 (Curiosity) reflect an attitude of wanting to learn more about one's experiences. The items of Factor 2 (Decentering) reflect a shift from identifying personally with thoughts and feelings, to relating to one's experience in a wider field of awareness. Since the TMS assesses the level of mindfulness during a single point in time, it may not reflect a respondent's true or average capacity to evoke a state of mindfulness.

 5. **Five Facet Mindfulness Questionnaire (FFMQ**; Baer, Smith, Hopkins, Krietemeyer, & Toney, 2006). This instrument was derived from a factor analysis of questionnaires measuring a trait-like general tendency to be mindful in daily life. It consists of 39 items assessing five facets of mindfulness: observing, describing, acting with awareness, non-reactivity to inner experience, and non-judging of inner experience. Items are rated on a 5-point Likert-type scale ranging from 1 (never or very rarely true) to 5 (very often or always true). The FFMQ has been shown to have good internal consistency and significant relationships in the predicted directions, with a variety of constructs related to mindfulness (Baer et al., 2006). Research suggests that consideration of multiple facets of mindfulness is helpful in understanding the relationship between mindfulness and psychological adjustment.

It should be noted that no single method or measure can provide a complete picture of the characteristics it is designed to measure (Baer, Walsh, & Lykins, 2009). Each measure appears to yield useful data that may not be provided by others (Meyers et al., 2001). The construct of mindfulness is such that it is challenging to formulate it into concrete, operational, and universally accepted definitions, which are a pre-requisite for performing scientific assessment.

Applications of Mindfulness Meditation

Meditation techniques were originally intended to develop spiritual understanding, awareness, and experience of ultimate reality. However, psychologist Jon Kabat-Zinn (1982) has been instrumental in bringing mindfulness meditation into medical settings as a therapeutic approach. As noted above, he developed the Mindfulness-Based Stress Reduction (MBSR) program, which involves systematic training to facilitate adaptation to medical illness and stress-related disorders. It is widely used for the self-management of stress and emotional distress in patients with a wide range of stress-related disorders, as well as to reduce symptoms of stress in non-clinical populations (Bishop, 2002; Kabat-Zinn & Chapman-Waldrop, 1988).

From a research perspective, a number of early studies, reviewed by Baer (2003), have attempted to investigate the validity and short- and long-term clinical effectiveness of the MBSR intervention in patients with a wide range of medical conditions, including chronic pain, anxiety disorders, moderate to severe psoriasis, cancer, prostate cancer, HIV, coronary heart disease, obesity, and stress-related conditions (Carlson, Speca, Patel, & Goodey, 2003; Kabat-Zinn, 1982; Kabat-Zinn, Lipworth, & Burney, 1985; Kabat-Zinn, Lipworth, Burney, & Sellers, 1987; Kabat-Zinn & Chapman-Waldrop, 1988; Kabat-Zinn et al., 1992; Miller, Fletcher, & Kabat-Zinn, 1995; Parswani, 2007; Robinson, Mathews, & Witek-Janusek, 2002; Salmon, Santorelli, & Kabat-Zinn, 1998; Speca, Carlson, Goodey, & Angen, 2000).

In the next section we discuss the applications of MBSR for major medical conditions that are also a public health concern.

Applications of Mindfulness-Based Stress Reduction Programs with Medical Conditions Mindfulness-Based Stress Reduction Program for Overeating and Obesity

The mindfulness-based eating awareness training program was developed by incorporating elements of mindfulness-based stress reduction (MBSR), CBT, and guided eating meditations. These eating awareness programs, which integrate mindfulness meditation with the objective of increasing general physiological and psychological self-regulation and mindfulness, appear to be well suited to the complicated matrix of physiological, cognitive, emotional, and behavioral dysregulation witnessed in dysfunctional eating.

The MB-EAT program (Kristeller & Hallett, 1999; Kristeller & Wolever, 2011; Kristeller, Quillian-Wolever, & Sheets, 2014) includes mindfulness meditation techniques that are incorporated into daily routine activities related to food craving and eating, in order to address issues related to shape, weight, and self-regulatory mechanisms of eating such as appetite and feelings of gastric and sensory satiety. Mindfulness meditation is designed to enhance awareness of automatic physiological and psychological eating patterns and simultaneously to enable patients to learn ways to stay away from the physiological, cognitive, emotional, and behavioral patterns of dysregulation. MB-EAT also works towards heightening awareness about individuals' healthy patterns of responding to hunger and satiety cues and towards using such awareness in helping them make wise choices about nutrition and physical activity (Kristeller, Baer, & Quillian-Wolever, 2006).

MB-EAT has proven to be effective in causing a significant decline in disordered eating. According to the original published study (Kristeller & Hallett, 1999), there was a significant decline in the number of eating binges per week, with only 4 out of 20 participants meeting the criterion of Binge Eating Disorder at the time of follow-up. Measures of depression and anxiety also decreased from clinical to subclinical ranges. The original study (Kristeller & Hallett, 1999) was an open-label, non-randomized study with an extended follow-up. This has been succeeded by a randomized controlled trial funded by the NIH, which has shown similar findings (Kristeller, Quillian-Wolever, & Sheets, 2014).

MB-EAT would be effective for those individuals who do not improve with cognitive behavioral interventions. The literature suggests that around 50 percent of individuals diagnosed with bulimia find cognitive-behavioral therapy (CBT) effective in eliminating binge eating and purging, and it reduces it in many others. MB-EAT also minimizes dysfunctional dieting and improves the distorted body image (Wilson, 2005).

Mindfulness-Based Stress Reduction Program
for Chronic Pain

Mindfulness meditation practices can specifically address the phenomenology of pain, which is a culmination of a mind-body experience. A Mindfulness-Based Stress Reduction Program (MBSR) can train individuals with chronic pain to develop a wiser relationship with the subjective experience of that pain.

Individuals with a practice of mindfulness learn to observe pain in a non-judgmental manner, by becoming aware of the pain sensations, thoughts, feelings, perceptions, and impulses, which change with each passing moment. In this process, they also learn to de-link thoughts, feelings, perceptions, associated memories, and behavioral responses from the physical sensations of pain. Thus, over time, with the practice of mindfulness, individuals become more aware, more willing to observe the sensations of pain without offering any judgment to these sensations; moreover, they are able to experience pain sensations more readily, rather than emphasizing efforts to avoid them.

Mindfulness-Based Stress Reduction programs have been able to offer relief from chronic pain and suffering, while enhancing functioning and improving quality of life experiences for people suffering from chronic pain. The published literature indicates that around 14 randomized controlled trials have been conducted to-date, out of which 12 RCTs have offered MBSR programs and 2 of them have offered Mindfulness-Based Cognitive Therapy (MBCT). MBSR has been shown to offer significant decline in chronic pain in conditions of fibromyalgia (Astin, Shapiro, Eisenberg, & Forys, 2003), chronic headache (Cathcart, Galatis, Immink, Proeve, & Petkov, 2013; Day et al., 2014), rheumatoid arthritis (Pradhan et al., 2007; Zautra et al., 2008); and chronic low back pain (Morone, Greco, & Weiner, 2008).

Mindfulness-Based Stress Reduction
Programs and Cancer

MBSR programs have been offered as intervention for individuals living with cancer. As per a recent review of published literature (Carlson, 2012), around 43 individual intervention studies offering MBSR to those living with cancer have been published. Recent meta-analytic research that evaluated 10 studies reported a medium-sized effect on psychosocial outcome variables (d = 0.48) (Ledesma & Kumano, 2009). The first published study to evaluate the effects of MBSR on cancer patients, by Speca, Carlson, Goodey, and Angen, (2000), was a randomized controlled trial with a wait-list condition having 89 subjects. Results indicated, overall, less mood disturbance, tension, depression, anger, and concentration problems, compared to control subjects following the intervention.

Mindfulness meditation techniques have been applied to mental health conditions as well, showing promising results in alleviating symptoms and improving patients' abilities to cope with the stressors of daily life. Intervention based on mindfulness has been found to be efficacious in dealing with chronic pain (Kabat-Zinn, 1982, 1985, 1987; Randolph, Caldera, Tacone, & Greak, 1999), depression (Teasdale, Segal, & Williams, 1995; 2000), and anxiety disorders (Miller, Fletcher, & Kabat-Zinn, 1995). These were the initial efforts made by researchers in the application of mindfulness to mental health conditions. As of now, mindfulness-based cognitive behavioral interventions have been applied in various clinical conditions—namely, depression, recurrent depression, generalized anxiety disorder, social anxiety disorder, and obsessive-compulsive disorder.

Applications of Mindfulness Meditation in Mental Health

Mindfulness-based interventions have been reported to be efficacious in a variety of stress-related medical conditions, as well as with medical conditions related to emotional disorders (Bishop et al., 2004; Ludwig & Kabat-Zinn, 2008). The majority of people who have undergone mindfulness-based treatment programs have shown significant reductions in both physical and psychological symptoms (Kabat-Zinn et al., 1998; Kristeller & Hallett, 1999; Miller, Fletcher, & Kabat-Zinn, 1995). According to a recent *meta-analysis* of systematic reviews of *RCTs*, evidence has supported the use of mindfulness programs to alleviate symptoms of a variety of *mental* and physical disorders (Gotink et al., 2015). Other reviews reported similar findings (Garland, Froeliger, & Howard, 2014; Sharma & Rush, 2014). Furthermore, mindfulness meditation appears to bring about *favorable structural changes in the brain* and may also prevent or delay the onset of *mild cognitive impairment* and *Alzheimer's* disease (Hölzel, et al. 2011; Posner, Tang, & Lynch, 2014).

Mindfulness and Depression

Research has suggested that mindfulness cultivated during MBSR and MBCT decreases ruminative thinking by switching emotional processing modes through intentional redeployment of attention and dysfunctional beliefs, while significantly increasing meta-cognitive awareness with respect to negative thoughts and feelings (Ramel, Goldin, Carmona, & McQuaid, 2004; Teasdale, 1999) that significantly reduced relapses into depression (Teasdale et al., 2002). The MBCT program and other mindfulness-based interventions have been successful in treatment of depression and relapse prevention in young adults as well (Kenny & Williams, 2007).

Applications of Mindfulness Meditation in the Indian Population

Mindfulness-based interventions in the Indian setting have been applied to various clinical and non-clinical populations for such purposes as evaluation of the impact of mindfulness on acceptance and spiritual intelligence among individuals with depression (Nangia & Sharma, 2011). Most of the mindfulness-based interventions have been carried out on adult clinical populations for anxiety disorders (Sharma, Mao, & Sudhir, 2012), coronary heart disease (Parswani, Sharma, & Iyengar, 2013), obsessive-compulsive disorder with predominant obsessions (Sharma, Goyal, Salam, & Kumar, 2012), smoking (Sharma & Sharma, 2013), and depression (Sharma, Sudhir, & Narayan, 2013).

A few studies have been carried out on such non-clinical populations as IT professionals (Kaur, 2010), adolescents (in order to enhance well-being) (Anand & Sharma, 2011), and paramilitary personnel (Majgi, 2009; Majgi, Sharma, & Sudhir, 2006). Another application was in the form of a mindfulness-based program for management of aggression among youth (Sharma, Sharma, & Marimuthu, 2016). Thus, according to the available research evidence, it can be said that mindfulness-based intervention programs have reported significant and lasting reductions in both physical and psychological symptoms, and that they can be applied effectively in the treatment of a wide range of mental and physical health problems.

Some researchers have tried to study the effect of mindfulness-based stress reduction intervention on reducing stress and increasing quality of life and self-compassion in healthcare professionals (Shapiro, Astin, Bishop, & Cordova, 2005). To-date, none apart from mindfulness-based interventions (Goodman & Schorling, 2012) have been shown to help large numbers of distressed providers, nor have any preventive measures been demonstrably successful.

Mindfulness Meditation Delivery Requirements

Individuals can learn mindfulness for enhancing their awareness of self and subjective well-being. However, when it comes to delivery of mindfulness mediation for health and mental health conditions, it is advisable to undergo structured training. In the Indian setting, individuals are required to attain at least a master's degree in Psychology, Clinical Psychology, or Counseling and Psychotherapy, or an equivalent of the master's degree in Psychology or Allied Disciplines of Mental Health, before they can undergo training in mindfulness meditation techniques with the objective of learning about their delivery in a healthcare setting. In addition to attaining academic qualifications, practitioners are also required to register themselves with the Rehabilitation Council of India as mental health professionals in order to obtain a license to offer psychological services and practice within mental health settings. The titles of the licensing agencies in mental health would understandably vary across the world, but in India, training in mindfulness-based interventions is offered at the Department of Clinical Psychology, National Institute of Mental Health and Neuro Sciences (NIMHANS), Bangalore, within a master's program in Clinical Psychology and also through workshops on mindfulness-based interventions for individuals with a master's degree in Clinical Psychology.

Conclusions and Future Directions

The existent published research literature on mindfulness-based interventions for medical and psychological disorders hints at the enormous potential of this intervention. It is highly likely that upcoming mindfulness interventions will be methodologically rigorous and sound and would offer relief from suffering to a larger set of individuals, namely, those who are continuing to suffer from illnesses despite existing therapeutic interventions. It is also clear that there appear to be challenges to teaching mindfulness to others in a credible manner, if the teacher or instructor is not practicing mindfulness in his or her own life. It is to be understood that mindfulness is not a therapeutic method of intervention that professionals normally encounter in their own lives through a didactic mechanism of learning, which they can then share with others for their benefit.

Indeed, mindfulness is an ongoing effort to develop the skill of being aware of the present moment in a non-judgmental manner; clearly, it continuously undergoes refinement through life. Thus, teachers themselves must practice mindfulness as a way of observing life and having a grounded understanding that all mental experiences inclusive of thoughts, feelings, perceptions, desires or will, and memories are transitory in nature, so that all of them need to be observed in a neutral and detached manner. Whereas mindfulness meditation holds a lot of promise for offering therapeutic intervention for numerous medical and psychological disorders, at the same time it comes with challenges for clinicians and researchers in the acquisition, design, delivery, and evaluation of mindfulness-based interventions. It appears deceptively simple at times, and yet it is a highly complex approach for effectively integrating it at a conceptual and therapeutic level with other existing therapeutic modalities and clinical practices in the fields of medicine and clinical psychology.

Individuals with illnesses also need to overcome the challenge of maintaining sufficient motivation and keenness to acquire the skill of mindfulness meditation. This challenge for patients lies in part in the ability of the mental health professionals and clinicians themselves to acquire mindfulness meditation skills successfully and accurately. Clearly, the therapeutic technique is such that, in order to pass on these skills to others, professionals need to learn and integrate the skills themselves in an effective manner. Thus, mindfulness heals and relieves all who learn it for the purpose of self-discovery or to pass it on to patients who are suffering from various illnesses.

In addition to the challenges mindfulness poses in its acquisition and delivery, it offers enormous amounts of flexibility in terms of both its content and delivery. This is because mindfulness is grounded in the meditative practice of being present in the moment in a non-judgmental manner, which is itself grounded in aspects of silence, stillness, self-introspection, emotional sensitivity, and acceptance of the entire range of emotional expression. In this process of mindfulness acquisition, there is a universal acknowledgment of seeking happiness, well-being, resilience, and peace of mind, body, and soul for all the people involved whether professionals or people suffering from illnesses (Kabat-Zinn, 1990; Santorelli, 1999).

REFERENCES

Anand, U., & Sharma, M.P. (2011). Impact of a mindfulness-based stress reduction program on stress and well-being in adolescents: A study at a school setting. *Journal of the Indian Association for Child/Adolescent Mental Health, 7*(3), 73–97.

Astin, J.A., Shapiro, S.L., Eisenberg, D.M., & Forys, K.L. (2003). Mind-body medicine: State of the science, implications for practice. *Journal of the American Board of Family Medicine, 16*(2), 131–147.

Baer, R.A. (2003). Mindfulness training as a clinical intervention: A conceptual and empirical review. *Clinical Psychology: Science and practice, 10*(2), 125–143.

Baer, R.A., Smith, G.T., & Allen, K.B. (2004). Assessment of mindfulness by self-report: The Kentucky Inventory of Mindfulness Skills. *Assessment, 11*(3), 191–206.

Baer, R.A., Smith, G.T., Hopkins, J., Krietemeyer, J., & Toney, L. (2006). Using self-report assessment methods to explore facets of mindfulness. *Assessment, 13*(1), 27–45.

Baer, R.A., Walsh, E., & Lykins, E.L. (2009). Assessment of mindfulness. In *Clinical handbook of mindfulness* (pp. 153–168). New York, NY: Springer.

Bishop, S.R. (2002). What do we really know about mindfulness-based stress reduction? *Psychosomatic Medicine, 64,* 71–84.

Bishop, S.R., Lau, M., Shapiro, S., Carlson, L., Anderson, N.D., Carmody, J., & Devins, G. (2004). Mindfulness: A proposed operational definition. *Clinical psychology: Science and practice, 11*(3), 230–241.

Bodhi. (2000). *The noble eightfold path: Way to the end of suffering.* Onalaska, WA: Pariyatti Publications..

Brereton, J.P. (1999). Edifying puzzlement: RGVEDA 10. 129 and the uses of Enigma. *Journal of the American Oriental Society, 119*(2), 248–260.

Brown, J.R. (1999). *Psycho spiritual openings of meditating pain patients: A phenomenological study.* (Doctoral Dissertation). Santa Barbara, CA: Pacifica Graduate Institute.

Brown, K.W., & Ryan, R.M. (2003). The benefits of being present: Mindfulness and its role in psychological well-being. *Journal of Personality and Social Psychology, 84,* 822–848.

Buchheld, N., Grossman, P., & Walach, H. (2001). Measuring mindfulness in insight meditation (Vipassana) and meditation-based psychotherapy: The development of the Freiburg Mindfulness Inventory (FMI). *Journal for Meditation and Meditation Research, 1*(1), 11–34.

Carlson, L.E. (2012). Mindfulness-based interventions for physical conditions: A narrative review evaluating levels of evidence. *ISRN Psychiatry,* 1–21.

Carlson, L.E., Speca, M., Patel, K.D., & Goodey, E. (2003). Mindfulness-based stress reduction in relation to quality of life, mood, symptoms of stress, and immune parameters in breast and prostate cancer outpatients. *Psychosomatic Medicine, 65,* 571–581.

Cathcart, S., Galatis, N., Immink, M., Proeve, M., & Petkov, J. (2014). Brief mindfulness-based therapy for chronic tension-type headache: A randomized controlled pilot study. *Behavioural and Cognitive Psychotherapy, 42*(1), 1–15.

Crane, R. (2013). *Mindfulness-based cognitive therapy: Distinctive features.* Abingdon-on-Thames, UK: Routledge.

Dahl, J., Wilson, K.G., Luciano, C., & Hayes, S.C. (2005). *Acceptance and commitment therapy for chronic pain.* Reno, NV: Context Press.

Day, M.A., Thorn, B.E., Ward, L.C., Rubin, N., Hickman, S.D., Scogin, F., & Kilgo, G.R. (2014). Mindfulness-based cognitive therapy for the treatment of headache pain: A pilot study. *The Clinical Journal of Pain, 30*(2), 152–161.

Epstein, M. (1988). The deconstruction of the self: Ego and "egolessness" in Buddhist insight meditation. *The Journal of Transpersonal Psychology, 20,* 61–69.

Garland, E.L., Gaylord, S.A., & Fredrickson, B.L. (2011). Positive reappraisal mediates the stress-reductive effects of mindfulness: An upward spiral process. *Mindfulness, 2*(1), 59–67.

Garland, E.L., Froeliger, B., & Howard, M. (2014). Mindfulness training targets neurocognitive mechanisms of addiction at the attention-appraisal-emotion interface. *Frontiers in Psychiatry, 4,* 173.

Goldenberg, D.L., Kaplan, K.H., Nadeau, M.G., Brodeur, C., Smith, S., & Schmid, C.H. (1994). A controlled study of a stress-reduction, cognitive-behavioral treatment program in fibromyalgia. *Journal of Musculoskeletal Pain, 2,* 53–66.

Goldstein, J. (2002). *One dharma: The emerging Western Buddhism.* San Francisco, CA: HarperCollins.

Gotink, R.A., Chu, P., Buschbach, J.J., Benson, H., Fricchione, G.L., & Hunink, M.M. (2015). Standardised mindfulness-based interventions in healthcare: An overview of systematic reviews and meta-analyses of RCTs. *PloS One, 10*(4), e0124344.

Goyal, A.K. (2012). *Mindfulness Based Cognitive Behaviour Therapy in Obsessive Compulsive Disorder* (Unpublished Ph.D. Thesis). Bangalore, India: National Institute of Mental Health and Neuro Sciences.

Grabovac, A.D., Lau, M.A., & Willett, B.R. (2011). Mechanisms of mindfulness: A Buddhist psychological model. *Mindfulness, 2*(3), 154–166.

Hayes, S.C. (1994). Content, context, and the types of psychological acceptance. In S.C. Hayes, N.S. Jacobson, V.M. Follette, & M.J. Dougher (Eds.), *Acceptance and change: Content and context in psychotherapy* (pp. 13–32). Reno, NV: Context Press.

Hayes, S.C., & Wilson, K.G. (1993). Some applied implications of a contemporary analytic account of verbal events. *The Behavior Analyst, 16,* 283–301.

Hayes, S.C., & Wilson, K.G. (2003). Mindfulness: Method and process. *Clinical Psychology: Science and Practice, 10*(2), 161–165.

Hick, S.F. (2010). Cultivating therapeutic relationships: The role of mindfulness. In S.F. Hick & T. Bien (Eds.), *Mindfulness and the therapeutic relationship* (pp. 21–35). New York, NY: Guilford Press.

Hölzel, B.K., Carmody, J., Vangel, M., Congleton, C., Yerramsetti, S.M., Gard, T., & Lazar, S.W. (2011). Mindfulness practice leads to increases in regional brain gray matter density. *Psychiatry Research, 191,* 36–43.

Kabat-Zinn, J. (1982). An outpatient program in behavioral medicine for chronic pain patients based on the practice of mindfulness meditation: Theoretical considerations and preliminary results. *General Hospital Psychiatry, 4,* 33–47.

Kabat-Zinn, J. (1990). *Full catastrophe living: Using the wisdom of your body and mind to face stress, pain, and illness.* New York, NY: Delacorte.

Kabat-Zinn, J. (2003). Mindfulness-based interventions in context: Past, present, and future. *Clinical Psychology: Science and Practice, 10*(2), 144–156.

Kabat-Zinn, J., & Chapman-Waldrop, A. (1988). Compliance with an outpatient stress reduction program: Rates and predictors of completion. *Journal of Behavioral Medicine, 11,* 333- 352.

Kabat-Zinn, J., Lipworth, L., & Burney, R. (1985). The clinical use of mindfulness meditation for the self-regulation of chronic pain. *Journal of Behavioral Medicine, 8,* 163–190.

Kabat-Zinn, J., Lipworth, L., Burney, R., & Sellers, W. (1987). Four-year follow-up of a meditation-based program for the self-regulation of chronic pain: Treatment outcomes and compliance. *Clinical Journal of Pain, 2*(3), 159–173.

Kabat-Zinn, J., Massion, A.O., Kristeller, J., Peterson, L.G., Fletcher, K., Pbert, L., et al. (1992). Effectiveness of a meditation-based stress reduction program in the treatment of anxiety disorders. *American Journal of Psychiatry, 149*, 936–943.

Kabat-Zinn, J., Wheeler, E., Light, T., Skillings, Z., Scharf, M.J., Cropley, T.G., Hosmer, D., & Bernhard, J.D. (1998). Influence of a mindfulness meditation-based stress reduction intervention on rates of skin clearing in patients with moderate to severe psoriasis undergoing phototherapy (UVB) and photochemotherapy (PUVA). *Psychosomatic Medicine, 50*, 625–632.

Kalupahana, D.J. (1994). *A history of Buddhist philosophy*. New Delhi, India: Motilal Banarsidass.

Kalupahana, D. (2006). *Mulamadhyamakakarika of Nagarjuna*. New Delhi, India: Motilal Banarsidass.

Kaur, M. (2010). *Mindfulness Integrated Cognitive Behavioral Intervention in Workplace Stress* (Unpublished Master's Thesis). Bangalore, India: National Institute of Mental Health and Neuro Sciences.

Kenny, M.A., & Williams, J.M.G. (2007). Treatment-resistant depressed patients show a good response to mindfulness-based cognitive therapy. *Behaviour Research and Therapy, 45*(3), 617–625.

Kocovski, N.L., Segal, Z.V., & Battista, S.R. (2009). Mindfulness and psychopathology: Problem formulation. In F. Didonna (Ed.), *Clinical handbook of mindfulness* (pp. 85–98). New York, NY: Springer.

Kohlenberg, R.J., Hayes, S.C., & Tsai, M. (1993). Radical behavioral psychotherapy: Two contemporary examples. *Clinical Psychology Review, 13*, 579–592.

Kristeller, J.L., & Wolever, R.Q. (2011). Mindfulness-based eating awareness training for treating binge eating disorder: The conceptual foundation. *Eating Disorders, 19*(1), 49–61.

Kristeller, J.L., & Hallett, C.B. (1999). An exploratory study of a meditation-based intervention for binge eating disorder. *Journal of Health Psychology, 4*, 357–363.

Kristeller, J.L., Baer, R.A., & Quillian-Wolever, R. (2006). Mindfulness-based approaches to eating disorders. In R. A. Baer (Ed.), *Mindfulness and acceptance-based interventions: Conceptualization, application, and empirical support* (pp. 75–91). Oxford, UK: Academic Press (Elsevier).

Kristeller, J., Quillian-Wolever, R., & Sheets, V. (2014). Mindfulness-Based Eating Awareness Training (MB-EAT) for binge eating: A randomized clinical trial. *Mindfulness, 5*(3), 282–297.

Langer, E.J., & Moldoveanu, M. (2000). The construct of mindfulness. *Journal of Social Issues, 1*, 229–305.

Lau, M.A., Bishop, S.R., Segal, Z.V., Buis, T., Anderson, N.D., Carlson, L., ... & Devins, G. (2006). The Toronto Mindfulness Scale: Development and validation. *Journal of Clinical Psychology, 62*(12), 1445–1467.

Ledesma, D., & Kumano, H. (2009). Mindfulness-based stress reduction and cancer: A meta-analysis. *Psychooncology, 18*(6), 571–579.

Linehan, M.M. (1993a). *Cognitive-behavioral treatment of borderline personality disorder*. New York, NY: Guilford Press.

Linehan, M.M. (1993b). *Skills training manual for treating borderline personality disorder*. New York, NY: Guilford Press.

Ludwig, D.S., & Kabat-Zinn, J. (2008). Mindfulness in medicine. *JAMA, 300*(11), 1350–1352.

Majgi, P. (2009). *Efficacy of Mindfulness-Based Cognitive Behavioural Intervention in reducing stress in paramilitary force personnel* (Unpublished Ph.D. Thesis).

Majgi, P., Sharma, M.P., & Sudhir, P. (2006). Mindfulness based stress reduction program for paramilitary personnel. In U. Kumar (Ed.), *Recent developments in psychology* (pp. 115–125). New Delhi, India: Defense Institute of Psychological Research.

Marlatt, G.A., & Kristeller, J.L. (1999). Mindfulness and meditation. In W.R. Miller (Ed.), *Integrating spirituality into treatment* (pp. 67–84). Washington, D.C.: American Psychological Association.

Meyer, G.J., Finn, S.E., Eyde, L.D., Kay, G.G., Moreland, K.L., Dies, R.R., ... & Reed, G.M. (2001). Psychological testing and psychological assessment: A review of evidence and issues. *American Psychologist, 56*(2), 128.

Miller, J., Fletcher, K., & Kabat-Zinn, J. (1995). Three-year follow-up and clinical implications of a mindfulness-based stress reduction intervention in the treatment of anxiety disorders. *General Hospital Psychiatry, 17*(3), 192–200.

Mineka, S., & Thomas, C. (1999). Mechanisms of change in exposure therapy for anxiety disorders. In T. Dalgleish & M.J. Power (Eds.), *Handbook of cognition and emotion* (pp. 747–764). Chichester, UK: John Wiley & Sons.

Morone, N.E., Greco, C.M., & Weiner, D.K. (2008). Mindfulness meditation for the treatment of chronic low back pain in older adults: A randomized controlled pilot study. *Pain, 134*(3), 310–319.

Nairn, R. (1999). *What is meditation? Buddhism of everyone*. London, UK: Shambhala.

Nangia, D., & Sharma, M.P. (2011–2012). *Effects of mindfulness-based cognitive therapy on mindfulness skills, acceptance and spiritual intelligence in patients with depression. Amity Journal of Applied Psychology, 2*(2) and *3*(1), 85–90.

Parswani, M. (2007). *Mindfulness-based stress reduction program in coronary heart disease*. (Ph.D. Thesis submitted). Bangalore, India: NIMHANS.

Parswani, M.J., Sharma, M.P., & Iyengar, S.S. (2013, July–Dec.). Mindfulness-based stress reduction program in coronary heart disease: A randomized control trial. *International Journal of Yoga, 6*(2), 111–117.

Posner, M.I., Tang, Y.Y., & Lynch, G. (2014). Mechanisms of white matter change induced by meditation training. *Frontiers in Psychology, 5*, 1220.

Pradhan, E.K., Baumgarten, M., Langenberg, P., Handwerger, B., Gilpin, A.K., Magyari, T., Hochberg, M.C., & Berman, B.M. (2007). Effect of Mindfulness-Based Stress Reduction in rheumatoid arthritis patients. *Arthritis and Rheumatism, 57*(7), 1134–1142.

Ramel, W., Goldin, P.R., Carmona, P.E., & McQuaid, J.R. (2004). Effects of mindfulness meditation on cognitive processes and affect in patients with past depression. *Journal of Cognitive Therapy and Research, 28*, 433–455.

Randolph, P., Caldera, Y.M., Tacone, A.M., & Greak, B.L. (1999). The long-term combined effects of medical treatment and a mindfulness-based behavioral program for the multidisciplinary management of chronic pain in West Texas. *Pain Digest, 9*, 103–112.

Robinson, F.P, Mathews, H.L., & Witek-Janusek, L. (2002). The effects of MBSR program on perceived stress, mood, endocrine functions, immunity and functional health in individuals affected with HIV. *Journal of Alternative and Complementary Medicine, 8*, 719–730.

Roemer, L., & Orsillo, S.M. (2003). Mindfulness: A promising intervention strategy in need of further study. *Clinical Psychology: Science and Practice, 10*(2), 172–178.

Rosenberg, L. (1998). *Breath by breath: The liberating practice of insight meditation.* Boston, MA: Shambhala.

Salmon, P., Santorelli, S.F., and Kabat-Zinn, J. (1998). Intervention elements promoting high adherence to mindfulness based stress reduction programs in the clinical behavioral medicine setting. In S.A. Shumaker, E.B. Schron, J.K. Ockene, & W.L. McBee (Eds.), *Handbook of health behavior change* (2nd ed.) (pp. 239–266). New York, NY: Springer.

Santina, P.D. (1997). *The tree of enlightenment: An introduction to the major traditions of Buddhism.* Chico, CA: Buddha Dharma Education Association.

Santorelli, S. (2000). *Heal thy self: Lessons on mindfulness in medicine.* New York, NY: Three Rivers Press.

Segal, Z.V., Williams, J.M.G., & Teasdale, J.D. (2013). *Mindfulness-based cognitive therapy for depression: A new approach to preventing relapse* (rev. ed.). New York, NY: Guilford Press.

Shapiro, D.H. (1982). Overview: Clinical and physiological comparisons of meditation with other self-control strategies. *American Journal of Psychiatry, 139*, 267–274.

Shapiro, S.L., Carlson, L.E., Astin, J.A., & Freedman, B. (2006). Mechanisms of mindfulness. *Journal of Clinical Psychology, 62*, 373–386.

Sharma, M., & Rush, S.E. (2014). Mindfulness-based stress reduction as a stress management intervention for healthy individuals: A systematic review. *Journal of Evidence-Based Complementary and Alternative Medicine, 19*(4), 271–286.

Sharma, M.K., Sharma, M.P., & Marimuthu, P. (2016). Mindfulness-based program for management of aggression among youth: A follow-up study. *Indian Journal of Psychological Medicine, 38*, 213–216.

Sharma, M.P. (2002). Vipassana meditation: The art and science of mindfulness. In J.P. Balodhi (Ed.), *Application of Oriental philosophical thoughts in mental health* (pp. 69–74). Bangalore, India: NIMHANS.

Sharma, M.P., Goyal, A., Salam, K.P., & Kumar, D. (2012). Mindfulness-based cognitive behaviour therapy in OCD: A case series. *Archives of Indian Psychiatry, 1,* 9–15.

Sharma, M.P., Kumaraiah, V., Mishra, H., & Balodhi, J.H. (1990). Therapeutic effects of Vipassana meditation in tension headaches. *Journal of Personality and Clinical Studies, 6*, 201–206.

Sharma, M.P., Mao, A., & Sudhir, P.M. (2012). Mindfulness-based cognitive behavior therapy in patients with anxiety disorders: A case series. *Indian Journal of Psychological Medicine, 34*(3), 263–269.

Sharma, M.P., & Sharma, M.K. (2013). Mindfulness, an integrated approach for cessation of smoking in the workplace. *International Journal of Yoga, 6*(1), 80.

Sharma, M.P., Sudhir, P.M., & Narayan, R. (2013). Effectiveness of mindfulness-based cognitive therapy in persons with depression: A preliminary investigation. *Journal of the Indian Academy of Applied Psychology, 39*(1), 57–64.

Speca, M., Carlson, L.E., Goodey, E., & Angen, M. (2000). A randomized, wait-list controlled clinical trial: The effect of a mindfulness meditation-based stress reduction program on mood and symptoms of stress in cancer outpatients. *Psychosomatic Medicine, 62*(5), 613–622.

Teasdale, J.D. (1999). Metacognition, mindfulness, and the modification of mood disorders. *Clinical Psychology and Psychotherapy, 6*, 146–155.

Teasdale, J.D., Moore, R., Hayhurst, H., Pope, M., Williams, S., & Segal, Z.V. (2002). Metacognitive awareness and prevention of relapse in depression: Empirical evidence. *Journal of Consulting and Clinical Psychology, 70*, 275–287.

Teasdale, J.D., Segal, Z., & Williams, J.M. (1995). How does cognitive therapy prevent depressive relapse and why should attentional control (mindfulness) training help? *Behavioral Research Therapy, 33*(1), 25–39.

Teasdale, J.D., Segal, Z.V., Williams, J.M., Ridgeway, V.A., Soulsby, J.M., & Lau, M.A. (2000). Prevention of relapse/recurrence in major depression by mindfulness-based cognitive therapy. *Journal of Consulting and Clinical Psychology, 68*(4), 615–623.

Thera, N. (1962). *The heart of Buddhist meditation.* New York, NY: Weiser.

Vipassana Research Institute. (2005). *Realizing change: Vipassana meditation in Aaction*. Igatpuri, India: Vipassana Research Institute.

Wells, A. (2005). Detached mindfulness in cognitive therapy: A metacognitive analysis and ten techniques. *Journal of Rational-Emotive and Cognitive-Behavior Therapy, 23*(4), 337–355.

Wells, A. (2011). *Metacognitive therapy for anxiety and depression*. New York, NY: Guilford Press.

Williams, M., & Penman, D. (2011). *Mindfulness: A practical guide to finding peace in a frantic world*. London, UK: Hachette.

Woods, S. L. (2009). Training professionals in mindfulness: The heart of teaching. In In F. Didonna (Ed.), *Clinical handbook of mindfulness* (pp. 463–475). New York, NY: Springer.

Zautra, A.J., Davis, M.C., Reich, J.W., Nicassario, P., Tennen, H., Finan, P., Kratz, A., Parrish, B., & Irwin, M.R. (2008). Comparison of cognitive behavioral and mindfulness meditation interventions on adaptation to rheumatoid arthritis for patients with and without history of recurrent depression. *Journal of Consulting Clinical Psychology, 76*(3), 408–421.

Presence in Place

Exploring Well-Being Through Mindfulness
and Spirituality at Grand Canyon National Park
and Other Natural Settings

DAVID S.B. MITCHELL, KANIKA A.M. MAGEE
CHRISTOPHER N. CROSS, JULES P. HARRELL
and FATIMAH L.C. JACKSON

Background

Through their serenity and majesty, natural environments can invite us into holistic presence in mind, body, and spirit. The National Park Service (NPS), which functions as steward for an abundance of natural spaces across the United States, maintains and cultivates a number of these sites as well as educates the populace about them. The Grand Canyon National Park is arguably one of the most captivating of these settings.

Healthy Parks Healthy People is a global movement that concentrates on the power of the National Parks and public lands to facilitate a healthy, civil society. The NPS's Healthy Parks Healthy People U.S. program was established in 2011 to reflect the role of the parks and public lands as a significant strategy for health restoration, stress reduction, and, hence, disease prevention by promoting and sustaining access to the outdoors.

Partly extended from a larger report on recognizing the presence of non-native, ethnic minorities, and exploring means of mindfully and spiritually engaging with the Park (Jackson, Harrell, Mitchell, & Cross, 2016), this essay takes the inquiring traveler on a contemplative and spiritual journey through natural settings to help support the promotion of enhanced presence and well-being.

Personality in Place: Openness, Absorption
and the Grand Canyon

Compared to those of many other members of the animal kingdom, human sensory receptors, including the ones in our eyes, nose, and ears are quite ordinary. The outstanding feature of human perception is the brain's capacity to operate on input that sensory receptors send its way. When we encounter a wondrous event of the magnitude of the Grand Canyon, a singular psychological peak experience may take place. Several psychological processes in the form of stages and traits contribute to the likelihood of such an occurrence.

Psychologists commonly acknowledge openness to thinking about new experiences as a distinct dimension of the human personality (DeYoung, 2014). The openness to experience trait encompasses one's level of attraction to novel stimuli and preferences for encounters with new, abstract, or concrete situations. People vary with respect to their willingness to actively seek out new sources of input from the environment and to consider unique and innovative ideas. Those high in openness tend to engage in activities that are variegated and distinctive.

Absorption refers to the tendency to become fully engaged in the object of one's attention (Bouchard & Walker, 2017; Tellegen & Atkinson, 1974). It is a consistent marker of the openness trait (DeYoung, 2014). People high in openness tend to experience more frequent and intense absorbed states.

When absorption takes the form of a transient psychological state, it is comprised of episodes where an individual's cognitive capacities virtually merge with the object of one's attention. One is virtually impervious to distraction, as the boundaries between the self and the external world dissipate. Absorption also manifests in a more enduring form. Those high in trait absorption experience episodes of fully-engaged attention more frequently.

An array of situations prompts the expression of behaviors related to any particular trait. Even individuals who possess relatively low levels of trait absorption may experience absorbed episodes in highly engaging environments. One need not be high in trait absorption, for instance, to be fully engaged by the vistas of the Grand Canyon.

Abraham Maslow (1968) described Being, or B-Cognition, as a characteristic of human peak experiences. He stated that B-Cognition involves circumstances "where the precept is wholly attended to … complete absorption" (p. 74). Cognitive experiences of this kind are more common in those Maslow called self-actualized—that is, fulfilled individuals. Such experiences make us more fully human.

The Grand Canyon, with its expanse and beauty, stands as a unique and enhanced stimulus situation. Playing to the strengths of the human nervous system, it is precisely the kind of experience that will elicit absorbed episodes, even in those not particularly open to new experiences or high in trait absorption. Such fully engaged states are a high form of human expression and represent the joining of a geographical wonder with a biological one.

Process Overview

To engage in the processes and reflections that we suggest here, no prior training is required of the therapist or traveler: individuals can lead themselves through the process. However, prior exposure to contemplative and spiritual practices is helpful, as these activities and techniques can help individuals to exercise their awareness and/or attentional capacity.

Notwithstanding previous exposure or experience, the most important antecedent of engaging in our suggestions here is one's intention to commune with nature. We invite those involved in this process to refer to themselves as "travelers," as the term connotes being on a journey and open to the freshness and wonder of new experience. Travelers are particularly encouraged to do the practices suggested in this essay that feel most affirming, absorbing, and actualizing for them in a variety of natural settings.

As is the case with many contemplative and spiritual practices, engaging in these practices with others is strongly recommended. If willing and able, individuals such as family members or friends can be identified to participate. The point of traveling along with others cannot be overemphasized, particularly with regard to communities of color seeking to acquaint themselves with the outdoors. The literature on the Afro-cultural ethos of communalism, for example, suggests that, in general throughout the Black diaspora, emphasis is placed on behaviors and activities that affirm interdependence, sharing, group duty, and an identity that is rooted in group membership (Boykin, Jagers, Ellison, & Albury, 1997). Research on communalism typically focuses on the effectiveness of small groups of three to four people in promoting beneficial cognitive outcomes. An oft-cited African proverb states, "It takes a village to raise a child"; when it comes to the benefits of companionship, improving one's mental health may be no different. Similar to the text from prompts used in communalism research, all those present are encouraged to work for the benefit of each other before, during, and after the visit. Travelers should share reflections on their experience with others (e.g., therapists) soon after their visits. Journaling about the experience can be another powerful way to retain some of the experience as well as serve as a marker of pitfalls and progress over time.

Prior to the journey, the traveler should identify a natural setting to visit and with which to engage, whether it is a local park, a state hiking trail, or the Grand Canyon itself. Additionally, actions such as verbally stating one's intention to visit and be present with the site, utilizing mental imagery of oneself enjoying the site, and creating affirmations about the intended efficacy of the intervention can potentially help support cognitive restructuring. Activities like these can build up a sense of the upcoming experience as being something that is new, and can help support a mindset of well-being during the journey. It is in part through consciously assimilating actions such as these that the traveler can engage in a more centering experience, regardless of the physical destination of the site itself.

The mindfulness and spirituality-related recommendations suggested here can be enacted in a side-by-side manner, helping to buttress other travelers. This practice can be achieved in the following manner, particularly if travelers choose the Grand Canyon itself as a site: Earth in Mind (mindfulness) and Entry (spirituality); Earth's Visage, Earth's Voice, etc. (mindfulness), Engagement (spirituality); Reflections (mindfulness) and Effect (spirituality). Companions visiting the site with travelers are encouraged to read out loud (e.g., from the book or from the app discussed below) to travelers the meditations recommended here.

Therapists supporting travelers on their journeys can offer a pre-test/post-test treatment methodology to assess whether mindful attitudes, a feeling of communing with and sensitivity toward nature, and spirituality, are maintained before and after the intervention. The Five Facet Mindfulness Questionnaire (FFMQ; Baer et al., 2008), the Connectedness to Nature Scale (CNS; Mayer & Frantz, 2004), and Galilea's (1982) tripartite conceptualization of spiritual experience, offers helpful source material for such evaluation. The first two measures are Likert-scale, self-report questionnaires. Galilea's (1982) work suggests that a spiritual awakening is reflected by a shift in perspective followed by a change in action, and that the spiritual experience is a conversion experience.

Zinnbauer and Pargament's (1998) study of religious conversion demonstrates similar traits, highlighting the enduring agreement that this experience indeed involves a radical shift and a new concept of self. The language of religious conversion can be taken parallel to that of transformation, to note the presence of similar traits and experiences beyond a specific religious context. Shults and Sandage (2006), provides a framework for a spiritual transformation, which involves a profound integrative change in how a person relates to the sacred (Sandage & Moe, 2013; Shults & Sandage, 2006). To identify its occurrence, one must ponder a macro-level shift that will also be reflected through micro-level actions. The person experiencing the spiritual conversion will report an expanded concept of self, viewing oneself not just through the narrow lens of humanity, but through a lens of a higher purpose and calling. In this sense, a person not only transcends physical space, but can overcome and transcend the limitations, injustices, and oppression of the world, instead recognizing the beauty and potential inherent in life. This experience is referred to as a conversion—a conversion of self-concept and of all of society.

Signs that a conversion is in progress or has occurred include prayer and meditative acts. A person having this experience will report increases and/or deeper experiences of prayer exercises including body prayer, meditation, object focus, *lectio divina*, journaling, humming, and singing. The conversion is further demonstrated when it is followed by outward acts, including social outreach, volunteerism, acts of kindness, giving, and challenging inequality. The progression can be synopsized as: experience (conversion), reflect (spiritual practice), and project (community orientation). As such, the inquiring therapist can ask about the following: (1) the practices in which the traveler engaged prior to, and as a result of the visit(s); and (2) whether the traveler felt that a conversion or changed way of being and viewing had occurred in several areas (e.g., a new view of self/personal value, of nature/environment, or of community). Queries can be open- or closed-ended in nature.

Mindfulness in Place: Engaging with Body, Engaging with Earth

In its current Western context, *mindfulness* is often conceptualized as a secular practice and attitude, devoid of any particular religious or general spiritual precepts. However, its roots in Eastern thought are anything but absent of such qualities, and it is through cultivating mindfulness that greater degrees of compassion, insight, and gratitude can potentially be generated. Such a perspective and practice can be attained as we continuously invite ourselves to enter into presence within ourselves and with the current space that we occupy.

Baer et al. (2008) have suggested that there are five aspects of a mindful mindset which appear in the literature: observing experience, describing experience, acting with awareness, not judging inner experience, and not reacting to inner experience. As a whole, dispositional mindfulness has been linked to a number of holistic mental, physical, and relational health factors, including openness to experience (Brown & Ryan, 2003), spirituality (Carmody, Reed, Kristeller, & Merriam, 2008; Greeson et al., 2011), and connectedness to nature (Howell, Dopko, Passmore, & Buro, 2011). The latter has been defined as "individuals' experiential sense of oneness with the natural world" (Mayer & Frantz, 2004, p. 504). Howell and colleagues (2011) proposed that mindfulness may help bring about increased sensory awareness while in outdoor settings, and that connectedness to nature may increase as a result.

One potential reason for the benefits of becoming mindfully engaged in natural spaces may lie in positive distraction (Nolen-Hoeksema, Wisco, & Lyubomirsky, 2008), wherein self-reinforcing activities that allow a person to become more fully absorbed and engaged can lead to a number of beneficial outcomes. Indeed, outcomes like reduced rumination have been observed in individuals as a result of spending time in natural settings as opposed to urban ones (Bratman, Hamilton, Hahn, Daily, & Gross, 2015). Due to the fact that mindful cultivation requires attentional effort, working on centering ourselves with aids can definitely help. Some research supports the idea that even mere exposure to images of nature can do just that (Lymeus, Lundgren, & Hartig, 2016). Given studies such as these, there is reason to consider that dedicated time spent in natural settings can result in greater quality and quantity of health-related outcomes.

Mindful Process Defined

The brief mindfulness meditations proposed here focus on grounding oneself through sensory experience and can be used easily in any open, natural setting. Checking-in with ever-changing inner and outer states is part and parcel of the process.

At the end of each of the following meditations, the traveler is asked to take several full, deep breaths. This is achieved most effectively by gently pushing the lower abdomen out to breathe in, and then gently pulling the lower abdomen in to breathe out. Doing this with each meditation can aid in the process of presence-building. All meditations except for the "Earth's Visage" should ideally be done in a seated (or standing with assistance) posture with the eyes closed. This is where having others present to help hold us accountable can be quite helpful.

The following "Earth in Mind" meditation is to be done before a traveler leaves to visit a site, while the meditations that follow it are to be done at the actual site.

Earth in Mind. The name of this meditation fittingly converges with the title of a book that, among other things, deals with *biophilia*, a hypothesized predisposition or desire for humans to seek out experiences that provoke the aforementioned connectedness with nature (Orr, 2004). Before traveling to the site that you have chosen, close your eyes for a moment. Look inwardly and notice what feelings and thoughts come up for you. See if you can observe for a moment what things come up for you internally, from displeasure to excitement, as you think about the site that you have chosen to visit. Taking note of your inner life, even for a short amount of time, can help make the encounter more memorable for you as you move forward and look back on this experience. If there is any tension present now or during the visit, see if you can visualize it leaving your body and mind with your out-breath. If attention is wandering now or during the visit, see if you can attempt to bring it back to the intention of the meditation. When you are ready to bring this meditation to a close, take three more full, deep breaths with your lower abdomen—once … twice … three times—and open your eyes.

Each of the following brief meditations, which can come after the above meditation, focuses on one of the senses. Similar to the work of Kabat-Zinn (2005) and others, this is done to support the traveler in anchoring in the present moment. Similar to the approach used within Mindfulness-Based Stress Reduction courses (http://www.umass med.edu/cfm/mindfulness-based-programs/), we encourage travelers to aim for at least five to eight site visits. Depending on their physical characteristics and salient features, some sites will vary in their appeal to each of our senses; however, travelers are encouraged to engage in all of the meditations during each visit to a given site. These meditations are as follows:

Earth's Visage. This brief meditation asks us, "What do we see?" Every day, we find out a great deal about the spaces and places we are in by using our eyes. Take a moment to look around you. What is the first thing that catches your eye? Maybe it is a rock, a cloud, a bird, or the movement of water in a creek. Spend a few moments gazing at it, noticing its color, texture, depth, and even its distance from you. What colors or patterns stand out to you the most? As we watch and hold this thing in our visual attention, we may be reminded of a simple truth: everything changes. Notice if what you are looking at changes in any small or big ways: whether it moves, ripples, flies away, or whether the light and shadow on its surface change in any way. Visiting the same site at different times of the day or year can remind us of this simple truth. A slightly different face of the earth is brought into view each time we visit. Each time, we open our eyes with a beginner's mind. If we practice beholding the Earth as it is, it is possible that its beauty may become that much easier to see. Do this for as long or as short a time as you feel comfortable. When you are ready to bring this meditation to a close, take three full, deep breaths with your lower abdomen.

Earth's Voice. This brief meditation asks us, "What do we hear?" Perhaps our second most important sense is that of hearing. What we hear in rural and natural settings is often quite different from what we hear in more urban settings. For this meditation, close your eyes and bring your attention to your ears. Take note of the sounds in this place. Take note of the silence. If your ears pick up anything in particular—the song of a bird, the rustling of leaves, or the movement of water over rock and earth—see if you can hear the full range of vibrations that come to you. Do you hear any silence in between the sounds? At some point, can you no longer hear a sound that came to you? Just notice what is reaching you through your ears, and hold that in your attention as it comes and goes. Do this for as long or as short a time as you feel comfortable. When you are ready to bring this meditation to a close, take three full, deep breaths with your lower abdomen and open your eyes.

Earth's Breath. This brief meditation asks us, "What do we smell?" The sense of smell is wondrous. The faintest aroma can bring back memories from years ago in a flash. Whether it is perfumes or colognes, cookies or pies, strong smells can help us form and recall memories rather well. For this meditation, close your eyes and let your attention center on your nostrils and the air flowing in and out of them. You may even have a sense of the air as it moves beyond your nose: passing through the airways in your throat, or tickling the space above your upper lip. Now try flaring your nostrils as you breathe in, and relaxing them as you breathe out. Do this once, twice, three times. Let your nose know the space around you, taking in as much as it can. Notice the taste of the air—its temperature—its "tingliness." How does your body respond to the movement of nostrils and air? The scent may be very faint or rather pungent. Flowers, trees, people, animals, even the ground itself produce aromas that are all brought to us by the wind, by the breath of the Earth. Take note of the feel of this breath as it enters and exits your nose—its dryness or coolness, heat or moistness. Notice it. Remember it. And just let it be as it is. Breathing in, and breathing out. Do this for as long or as short a time as you feel comfortable. When you are ready to bring this meditation to a close, take three full, deep breaths with your lower abdomen and open your eyes.

Earth's Skin. This brief meditation asks us, "What do we feel with our hands?" Look around you and allow your eyes to rest on something that you can touch and that catches your attention. It may be any number of things: a tree limb, a flower, a pinecone, or a rock at your feet. After you see that thing, walk over to it and place your hands on its surface. You may hold it in your hands or simply let your hands rest on it. After closing your eyes, feel the shape of this thing and it's mass. Let your fingers and palms take in its texture and temperature—whatever coolness, softness, hardness, or roughness is there. Perhaps there is bumpiness, smoothness, or prickliness. Maybe there is even moistness in or around it. Whatever is present; just take it in as much as you can with your hands. Let your skin be with the Earth's skin for a moment. When you are ready to bring this meditation to a close, take three full, deep breaths with your lower abdomen, open your eyes, and release whatever you were holding or touching from your grasp.

Earth's Backbone. This brief meditation asks us, "What do we feel with our feet?" Find a relatively level place to stand or sit. If you sit, you can cross your legs, but it is preferable that you sit in such a way that you can place your feet flat and firm on the ground beneath you. You may keep your feet enclosed in shoes, sandals, or socks, or take off whatever you have on them. After closing your eyes, see if you can bring your attention to the feel of your feet. Pay particular attention to how the soles of your feet feel—whether they are hot or cold, tense or relaxed, dry or moist. Notice the feel of the ground beneath your soles. Notice what you can of its texture, its softness or firmness. It may be sandy, rocky, grassy, gravely, or even "dirty." Even if the ground beneath you shifts slightly, search through your feet for the solidity underneath that. Do you feel the Earth supporting your body? The Earth's backbone is old and strong. Feel it push back against your presence with its force and its strength. Do this for as long or as short a time as you feel comfortable. When you are ready to bring this meditation to a close, take three full, deep breaths with your lower abdomen and open your eyes.

In all, though there is no direct data on the use of these particular meditations within the Grand Canyon, there is evidence to suggest salutary links between mindfulness, outdoor experience, and various cognitive, emotional, and relational outcomes. Findings from Attention Restoration Theory (ART) suggest that mildly evocative natural stimuli help to rejuvenate aspects of working memory and attention (Berman, Jonides, & Kaplan, 2008; Ohly, White, Wheeler, Bethel, Okoumunne, Nikolaou, & Garside, 2016), while simply walking in nature can improve cognitive and affective function (Bratman, Daily, Levy, & Gross, 2015; Bratman, Hamilton, Hahn, Daily, & Gross, 2015). Moreover, evidence suggests that green spaces within urban environments can lead to decreased affective arousal during exposure as well as heightened meditative and engaged states after departing such environments (Aspinall, Mavros, Coyne, & Roe, 2015). More exposure to natural beauty has been shown to lead to more prosocial behavior as a result of heightened positive affect while in natural settings (Zhang, Piff, Iyer, Koleva, & Keltner, 2014). However, the potentially absorptive and awe-invoking experience of natural environs such as the Grand Canyon should also be able to invoke experiences of flow (Berman & Berman, 2005) and prosocial behavior (Piff, Dietze, Feinberg, Stancato, & Keltner, 2015).

Moreover, mindfulness and other contemplative activities within natural settings (e.g., forest bathing) have been shown to promote emotional restoration (Van Gordon, Shonin, & Richardson, 2018; Park, Tsunetsugu, Kasetani, Kagawa, & Miyazaki, 2010). At this junction, willingness to be still and to open oneself as fully to present experience is all that is required of the traveler. Upon finishing these meditations, travelers are encouraged to reflect on the process with any companions, focusing on what they found to be most helpful, most challenging, and most salient about the experience.

Spirituality in Place: Entry, Engagement and Effect

Mindful states such as those supported by the previous process can potentially invoke a greater sense of awe and wonder that borders on the spiritual. *Spirituality* is a word that often evokes one of two responses: a pondering sigh that invites a deeper conversation around its meaning, or a complete withdrawal and avoidance. For some it is embedded within religious experience and belief, while for others it is completely disconnected from and independent of such experience and belief. Within this context, it is no surprise that Bernard McGinn (1993) acknowledged 35 definitions of *spirituality*.

Spirituality is a lived experience that connects to self, community, and the intangible as found for some in dreams, hopes, the impossible, and the transcendent. McGinn (1993) referred to spirituality as an "element in human nature and experience," which, as such, reflects shared, common elements and unique individual experience. Hence, spirituality as a discipline is typically approached from one of three lenses: historical, anthropological, or theological (McGinn, 1993).

The historical framework views spirituality from the perspective of tradition: how an individual's or group's historical context influences perspective and experience. It looks at the long reach of history in the formation of culture and the impact of history in shaping understanding and perspective.

The theological approach to spirituality is rooted in religious traditions or belief systems. This approach informs spirituality as a deeper experience with, expression of, or appreciation for a higher power or self. It offers an opportunity for people of faith to connect through the lens of their faith, whether through an encounter visiting such sites as Angel's Peak, Vishnu's Temple, or some other marker that we find in grandiose spaces such as within the Grand Canyon.

The anthropological approach, which will offer the primary context for this discussion, requires a merger between psychology and culture, as it is concerned with the experiences of individuals who are within a cultural context and have a unique identity. It requires an awareness of the implications of cultural trends on individuals and of their background, socioeconomic class, race and ethnicity, and other defining markers that inform their experiences. This approach, which offers opportunities to celebrate the full breadth of diversity, provides a framework for the broad experiences of all races, ethnicities, and nationalities as they explore the spiritual dimensions of the Grand Canyon.

Spiritual experiences include transcendence, contemplation, interiority, and ecstasy/ecstatic experiences, among others. Common mechanisms that have been applied to mediate spiritual experience include prayer, meditation, repetition (e.g., *lectio divina*), music, visualizations, object focus (e.g., art, prayer beads), fasting, pilgrimage, music and sounds (e.g., bells), incense/smells, and readings. This conversation with the Canyon may begin as meditation and then overflow into contemplation; moreover, it is a conversation that will hopefully continue beyond a physical presence in the Canyon itself. While the process below explicitly discusses the Canyon, the suggested method, as well as reflections, can be implicitly used to immerse oneself in other natural settings as well.

Spiritual Process Defined

Based on the work of African American mystic Howard Thurman, Holmes (2004) divided contemplative experience into three categories: entry, engagement, and effect. These three categories will be used as a basis for experiencing the Canyon. Holmes stated, "Entry denotes a shift from the everyday world to the liminal space that worship creates … a transition from the everyday world to an altered reality … [the] everyday socially constructed world recedes and joy unspeakable unfolds" (pp. 29–30).

The entry to the Canyon must be viewed as a seminal part of the experience. The journey to the Grand Canyon is lengthy—and, if one chooses the long drive from Las Vegas or Phoenix, it may also be referred to as arduous. There are long stretches of road without basic conveniences like restrooms, hotels, and McDonald's. In the penetrating sun, the drive could easily be viewed as a deterrent. Yet these will be the primary access routes for most visitors, as the nearest airports are quite small. Spirituality however, views life as a journey that draws one deeper into an experience of holiness, and not as an end in itself.

Indeed, such a journey is an ongoing experience in which people can be deliberately aware and present. Infused with meaning, it is no longer simply a lengthy drive; it is a part of the experience that begins to allow travelers to detach themselves from the assumptions and norms of a materialistic culture, attending instead to the natural surroundings that are encountered. Along the drive, travelers might notice the changing atmosphere, and the transition from homes and businesses to trees and farms. Greet the boulders that stand guard along the sides of the road and the mountains that both climb and descend in the same motion. Each flower meadow, along with the seemingly endless rows of rolling hills experienced as one, winds around the roads being traveled up and down, providing an entry into another land and experience. While it is an individual and subjective experience, it can also be shared with others in the car while on the road. It places one into contact with life through cattle and livestock and through flower meadows and pine trees—and an occasional mountain goat or elk that may have found its way to the roadside.

The layers of urban culture might fall away, making room for something new. The cacophony of sounds dissipates, allowing one to hear something grand. The distractions of life still themselves, honing one's ability to focus and see beyond the self and into a new reality. This is the journey that invites one into the spirit, it invites one into meditation, and it invites one into the deep. In this deep place, the traveler may notice the sun showing between the trees, see the moon standing above the hills, and graze the curves that mark each stage of the journey inward to the Canyon.

This entry, and all subsequent steps, can be marked by meditation, poetry, or song. When jazz saxophonist John Coltrane rendered "A Love Supreme" and "Favorite Things," he offered selections that connect with the human spirit. This, or another music selection, may be fitting for the drive and the experience.

"Engagement refers to the willingness to involve body and spirit in the encounter with the Holy ... participants may be ecstatic or silent.... During these times, sounds are not interferences; rather they are guides to those on the contemplative journey" (Holmes, 2004, p. 30). In addition to the journey itself, each site or lookout point within the Canyon offers an opportunity to engage the divine. Some of these sites are highlighted below.

Hopi House. After a long climb up to an altitude of 7,400 feet, one emerges onto the Canyon rim—a colorful expanse that goes on for as far as the eye can see or the mind can imagine. The ridges and hills begin and end, going deeper and farther at each new distance. They are the embodiment of the journey that the traveler is called to encounter.

The Hopi House is an affirmation of the significance of the Canyon to multiple groups of people, with cultural reflections inscribed throughout the house. It provides an opportunity to reflect on the sacredness of this space in many times and cultures, and offers insight into the worship this space may have invoked. It is a unifying space that acknowledges significance through time and culture as an indication that, regardless of the current time or specific culture, a shared experience of sacredness, a shared celebration of spirit, can occur.

Lipan Point. Listen to the wind and let it carry you away. This amazing escape offers a unique impression of the Canyon that is not only visual but auditory, for the wind whistles through the air and brushes gently yet firmly across each face. The site offers a safe experience for viewing and listening, and a more adventurous opportunity to step to the edge of the Canyon. This "safe edge" has another tier not far below, but, from a distance, it looks like an expanse that is the depth of the Canyon itself. This is a place to sit, to listen, and to be. It is unencumbered by manmade structures and offers a "nothing but nature" perspective on the Canyon.

Travelers must decide if they are to step out into what seems like an unproven cliff with an uncertain end. Once the step is taken, however, it becomes clearer, and the glory that is apparent from the edge is beyond that which could be viewed from the safer distance. The journey to the edge was worth it. From this space, peace can be found and the soul enlivened. This space calls out to the traveler: Step to nature's edge—and let it be well with your soul.

Duck on a Rock. Recognizing that each "sight" is a stage along the journey, the traveler must take notice of the leaning trees, telling their stories of the cycle of life, of regeneration and renewal. For this is not about the destination, but the journey itself. This spot, perhaps more so than others, demonstrates that each site is what the traveler makes of it. Some have looked out and seen a duck; others look and ask, "Where is the duck?" The value of the experience is in sharing what some travelers have encountered without hindering each traveler to interpret and experience it independently and uniquely.

Valhalla Overlook. This is the place where it all comes together: the nations meet; the sights, sounds, and smells abound; and the cultures connect. It is where the tree sap and flowers present bold fragrances, and the ridges and valleys of the mountain are more pronounced and apparent. If the rest of the Canyon speaks, this is the part that yells. There can be a feeling of sensory overload that might be soaked in gradually. It may be a location to visit and revisit throughout the Canyon experience.

Shoshone Trail. Discover this beautiful and well-defined trail that provides a perfect place for a meditative walk, prayer, or reflection. Walking through this site at dawn is particularly breathtaking. After about 15–20 minutes of the silent witness of trees—some standing, some fallen—and the discussion of birds, the traveler emerges into an opening where the sun can be seen rising through the trees. As the silent streams of light peek through, the location calls to the traveler to sit, to stay, to stretch, to be, in its midst.

The length and solitude of the walk perhaps make this the most effective place to hear the sounds of the birds as they chirp to one another and peck on the wood. A chorus of sounds surrounds the traveler along the walk, making it both silent and melodic simultaneously.

"Effect is often specific to the participating person or community. Those caught up in this intimacy … explain that the experience expands their knowledge, awakens a palpable and actionable love, and is either profoundly restorative … or inspires action. The action can be restorative of personal relationships or proactive for the needs of the community" [Holmes, 2004, pp. 30–31].

This is the awakening of the inner self. It is an interiority that is naturally sought and can be found in the varied colors of the Canyon rocks, in the parched trees of the most recent burn, in the silent walks along shrub-lined trails, and in the silent majesty of the elk who call this space home. This is an opportunity to discover beauty and to be restored to nature, to creation.

Wake up early to feel the cool air and hear the nothingness of sound, yet feel the warmth of the spirit and hear the symphony of creation in it. This is an age of doing, yet this is a place of being. Learn to be. Travelers must give themselves permission to be—still, aware, silent, holy. This is the breath of creation. These are the sounds of the garden. This is the place of formation that allows travelers to return changed, renewed, and enlivened. Life is different because of this restored, newly found, poignant connection.

Technology in Place: A Mobile App Concept

Since the dawn of the Digital Era, technology and social media have been brought to individuals by the development of cyber platforms. This is particularly the case with the relatively recent advent of mobile apps. The technologically-driven age within which we live offers up a multitude of mobile apps and wearable technologies that have emerged recently to aid consumers in achieving more meditative and healthy states. For example, of the 560 mobile apps linked to mindfulness in Apple iTunes, the top-rated app was Calm (Huberty, Green, et al., 2019). It has been rated the happiest app in the world (Center for Humane Technology, n.d.), followed by Headspace (Headspace, n.d.) and the Insight Timer (Insight Timer, n.d.). The Calm app, which focuses on meditation and relaxation, has been downloaded millions of times and has over 700,000 five-star ratings. It has several functions all aimed to mitigate stress and positively affect mood, primarily through meditation and music.

Another notable app is Oprah Winfrey and Deepak Chopra's Meditation Experience app (Winfrey & Chopra, n.d.). It is a more streamlined version of the Calm app and focuses on themed-meditations to be completed daily over a period of several weeks. Research from the science division of Calm has shown its ability to reduce stress among college students and even improve mood in cancer patients (Huberty, Green et al. 2019;

Huberty, Eckert, et al. 2019). Taken together, mindfulness technology, available with the advent of "smartphones," has been shown to be an effective way to address stress and positively impact mood.

It is through using health-promoting technologies such as these that travelers can find other ways to help themselves cultivate well-being. However, an app that interfaces directly with the spaces within the National Parks is currently not available. In collaboration with several colleagues, our research team has developed the wireframe and concept for *My NPS*, a dynamic mobile app that would be multipurpose for visitors to all parks within the United States National Park system (Jackson et al., 2016). In other words, our app would provide a tailored approach to maximize being present in the location of the Grand Canyon where the user is situated. It is our goal that all visitors who utilize the app—regardless of nationality, ethnicity, or religion—will feel minimal bias or barriers while connecting more deeply with the Canyon. To accomplish this, we will use only images of nature in and around the Canyon to maintain the focus. In addition, we would have a feature for users to be guided through the mindfulness meditations described earlier in this essay. Images such as those used in the app could be useful tools of contemplation on which to focus while reflecting on entry, engagement, and effect in the spirituality process or in the site arrival of the mindfulness process. This could be a powerful tool allowing users to access mediatations in real-time as they continue along their pilgrimage or journey to the Canyon sites that we have discussed here (e.g., Hopi House, etc.). Our research team traveled to each of these sites and chose them for their sensorial salience; however, any site can help the engaged traveler generate varying degrees of connectedness. Our goal is to allow users to engage with the app as a conduit to connecting more deeply with the spirit of the environment around. We believe that this method of connecting with something as powerful and awe-inspiring as the Grand Canyon would promote a selfless appreciation for centeredness and wonder.

App Process Defined

The flow of user interaction with the app would proceed as follows. Upon or before entrance to the Grand Canyon, users would download the app onto their smartphone or mobile device. Once downloaded, the home screen would be populated with general information about the National Park Service in general and the Park specifically, with a selection tab titled, "Mindfulness and Spirituality in the Grand Canyon." A new screen would surface, giving an introduction to the topic and showcasing a map of the Grand Canyon with markers at specific sites. For example, one of the sites would be Shoshone Trail; upon selection, the menu for mindfulness meditations (e.g., Earth's Visage, etc.) would appear for users either to read or listen to as a guided meditation. Once completed, travelers would be instructed to type into a mobile notepad what they experienced. This contemplative engagement at specific locations could be repeated at each site that is visited. Once the travelers complete the pilgrimage or journey, meditations could be listened to or read again to revisit that previous sense of centeredness along with companions, on one's own, or in the presence of one's therapist. The currently proposed functionality of the *My NPS* app does not allow for interface with settings outside of the Park. However, we encourage travelers and their therapists, should they have them, to consider the feasibility of using mobile technology in general as a potentially aid in their quest to become more centered and whole.

Final Thoughts and Recommendations

Given the preceding discussion about the use of absorption, mindfulness, spirituality, and technology in natural spaces, there is a general process that we suggest which travelers can follow to help them be more fully present when experiencing a natural setting/site. The process does not require prior licensure, education, or training, and revolves around the aforementioned states of entry, engagement, and effect (Holmes, 2004).

The traveler begins with a desire to "knock on nature's door," whether that be with the intention of going for a walk, taking a longer hike, or considering a longer excursion into the outdoors. That desire becomes the impetus for plans to set aside time to engage in the experience through whatever particular spiritual practice the traveler chooses. After the plan is made, it must then be initiated: the traveler sets out on the journey by vehicle or by foot. While approaching the location of choice, the traveler is asked to be attentive to the sensations and intentions that are present. After arriving, it is suggested that in the first few moments before engaging with the space (e.g., prior to getting out of a car), the traveler does the Earth in Mind meditation exercise and then sets any intentions that she wants to utilize as an aid to communion in and with that space. This is the essence of what entry looks like in our process.

Next, the traveler enters the area and takes note of which senses are most evoked by the surroundings. Expansive spaces such as the Grand Canyon are so richly and awesomely evocative that the traveler should take time to first absorbe the totality of the sensory experience. After being in the space for several moments, gently bring awareness to at least one aspect of our experience that has attracted our attention. Perhaps attention has been captured by the gentle sound of the breeze blowing through the trees, or by the trickling of a stream that runs next to the trail. Noticing and focusing on the salience of at least one aspect of sensory experience in such spaces is a wonderful invitation to ground oneself in the moment. Choosing the meditation most suited for that modality (e.g., the Earth's Voice meditation due to noticing the wind rustling the tree leaves), the traveler can then proceed. At this junction, travelers are invited to do the following: (a) close their eyes and take three deep, diaphragmatic breaths, (b) ask themselves the attention-focused question posed within a given meditation (e.g., "What do we hear?"), (c) open their eyes and maintain that attentional stance for as long as they are comfortable at a given site (i.e., at the Canyon or elsewhere outdoors), and then (d) close their eyes and end with three more deep, diaphragmatic breaths. If travelers have additional time, they can read through or listen to the whole of the selected meditation prompt on their smartphones or in excerpts from this essay to guide them. They can also engage in more than one prompt should they have the desire and time to do so. Using such guides may help us to ground ourselves in both the spaciousness as well as the specificity of the experience. This is the essence of what engagement looks like in our process.

Lastly, providing ourselves with time for reflection is an integral part of effect. As such, before leaving the space, travelers are invited to reflect on emotions, lingering sensations, and other salient sensory, affective, and cognitive aspects of the experience that they just had. Journaling is a worthwhile tool that travelers can use to aid in this process, and should be done before leaving the site, while the experience is still fresh in one's mind, body, and spirit. Journal entries can be made on one's smartphone or with pen and paper, and can be shared with others such as fellow travelers, friends, family, therapists, or some combination thereof. Such sharing can help to prepare travelers for a more relaxed and fulfilling return to daily life as well as for future engagement with natural settings, be they different ones or the location that they just visited. Similar to rites of passage and the hero's journey that have been with us since time immemorial (Campbell, 1949/2004; van Gennep, 1960/2004), this experience of visiting natural settings is a circular one that invites us away from urban spaces into transpersonal, transitional natural ones, and then back again. It is through such a journey that we can cultivate newfound communion with ourselves, as well as with and within the world around us. As we reflect on our presence in natural spaces, it is important that we retain an open, accepting, and even playful stance to repeating and returning to such settings to experience them anew. Seeking relational (e.g., through words of affirmation and dialogic engagement) and physical (e.g., through asking others to travel with us) support from those around us can be essential to helping us cultivate mindfulness and to step into our journeys while being fully present and in the moment, whether we are seeking entry for the first time or for the hundredth. This is the essence of what effect looks like in our process. Importantly, it is also the foundation for future experiences which begin with entry into those natural and numinous spaces beyond.

In all, there is strong evidence to suggest that interventions such as those suggested herein may be of benefit to people's well-being. The unmatched majesty of the Grand Canyon inspired the creation of this essay and the belief that, regardless of creed or color, everyone can connect with the powerful presence of nature. The process suggested above serves as one potential method to support efforts toward the collective grounding and connection of consciousness to natural settings. It is through continually inviting ourselves to participate in such intentional (and perhaps at times technology-mediated) experiences with the great outdoors that we hope to support the cultivation of mental health in a holistic manner. We can do so by allowing ourselves to be present in place through the majesty that is around—as well as within—us all.

REFERENCES

Aspinall, P., Mavros, P., Coyne, R., & Roe, J. (2015). The urban brain: Analysing outdoor physical activity with mobile EEG. *British Journal of Sports Medicine, 49*(4), 272–276.

Baer, R.A., Smith, G.T., Lykins, E., Button, D., Krietemeyer, J., Sauer, S. & Williams, J.M.G. (2008). Construct validity of the Five Facet Mindfulness Questionnaire in meditating and nonmeditating samples. *Assessment, 15*(3), 329–342.

Berman, D.S., & Davis-Berman, J. (2005). Positive psychology and outdoor education. *Journal of Experiential Education, 28*(1), 17–24.

Berman, M.G., Jonides, J., & Kaplan, S. (2008). The cognitive benefits of interacting with nature. *Psychological Science, 19*(12), 1207–1212.

Bouchard, T.J., & Walker, N. (2017). The recaptured scale technique applied to the Multidimensional Personality Questionnaire constructs: A replication across item formats and gender. *Personality and Individual Differences, 109*, 77–82.

Boykin, A.W., Jagers, R.J., Ellison, C.M., & Albury, A. (1997). Communalism: Conceptualization and measurement of an Afrocultural social orientation. *Journal of Black Studies, 27*(3), 409–418.

Bratman, G.N., Daily, G.C., Levy, B.J., & Gross, J.J. (2015). The benefits of nature experience: Improved affect and cognition. *Landscape and Urban Planning, 138*, 41–50.

Bratman, G.N., Hamilton, J.P., Hahn, K.S., Daily, G.C., & Gross, J.J. (2015). Nature experience reduces rumination and subgenual prefrontal cortex activation. *Proceedings of the National Academy of Sciences of the United States of America, 112*(28), 8567–8572.

Brown, K.W., & Ryan, R.M. (2003). The benefits of being present: Mindfulness and its role in psychological well-being. *Journal of Personality and Social Psychology, 84*(4), 822–848.

Campbell, J. (1949/2004). *The hero with a thousand faces* (Commemorative edition). Princeton, NJ: Princeton University Press.

Carmody, J., Reed, G., Kristeller, J., & Merriam, P. (2008). Mindfulness, spirituality, and health-related symptoms. *Journal of Psychosomatic Research, 64*, 393–403.

Center for Humane Technology. (n.d.). App ratings. Retrieved from https://humanetech.com/resources/app-ratings/

DeYoung, C.G. (2014). Openness/Intellect: A dimension of personality reflecting cognitive exploration. In M.L. Cooper & R.J. Larsen (Eds.), *APA handbook of personality and social psychology: Personality processes and individual differences, 4*, 369–399. Washington, D.C.: American Psychological Association.

Galilea, S. (1982). *The way of living faith.* San Francisco, CA: Harper & Row.

Greeson, J.M., Webber, D.M., Smoski, M.J., Brantley, J.G., Ekblad, A.G., & Wolever, R.Q. (2010). Changes in spirituality partly explain health-related quality of life outcomes after Mindfulness-Based Stress Reduction. *Journal of Behavioral Medicine, 34*, 508–518.

Headspace. (n.d.). *Your guide to health and happiness.* Retrieved from https://www.headspace.com/

Holmes, B. (2004). *Joy unspeakable: Contemplative practices of the black church.* Minneapolis, MN: Fortress Press.

Howell, A.J., Dopko, R.L., Passmore, H.A., & Buro, K. (2011). Nature connectedness: Associations with well-being and mindfulness. *Personality and Individual Differences, 51*(2), 166–171.

Huberty J., Eckert, R., Larkey, L., Kurka, J., Rodríguez De Jesús, S.A., Yoo, W., & Mesa, R. (2019). Smartphone-Based meditation for myeloproliferative neoplasm patients:Feasibility study to inform future trials. *JMIR Formative Research, 3*(2):e12662.

Huberty, J, Green, J., Glissmann, C., Larkey, L., Puzia, M. & Lee, C. (2019). Efficacy of the mindfulness meditation mobile app "Calm" to reduce stress among college students: Randomized controlled trial. *JMIR Mhealth and Uhealth, 7*(6):e14273.

Insight Timer. (n.d.). *#1 free app for meditation & sleep.* Retrieved from https://insighttimer.com/

Jackson, F., Harrell, J.P., Mitchell, D.S.B., & Cross, C. (2016). The Grand Canyon: Discovery of lost and untold stories of non-native American ethnic minorities from the 15th to 20th centuries and the conscious exploration of mindfulness and spirituality. *Grand Canyon National Park Historic Diversity Research in Coordination with Healthy Parks Healthy People Program* (Technical report), 1–108. Washington, D.C.: Cobb Research Laboratory.

Kabat-Zinn, J. (2005). *Coming to our senses: Healing ourselves and the world through mindfulness.* Ashland, OR: Blackstone Audio.

Lymeus, F., Lundgren, T., & Hartig, T. (2016). Attentional effort of beginning mindfulness training is offset with practice directed toward images of natural scenery. *Environment and Behavior, 49*(5), 1–24.

Maslow, A.H. (1968). *Toward a psychology of being.* New York, NY: Van Nostrand.

Mayer, F.S., & Frantz, C.M. (2004). The Connectedness to Nature Scale: A measure of individuals' feeling in community with nature. *Journal of Environmental Psychology, 24*(4), 503–515.

McGinn, B. (1993). The letter and the spirit: Spirituality as an academic discipline. *Christian Spirituality Bulletin, 1*(2), 2–9.

Nolen-Hoeksema, S., Wisco, B.E., & Lyubomirsky, S. (2008). Rethinking rumination. *Perspectives on Psychological Science, 3*(5), 400–424.

Ohly, H., White, M.P., Wheeler, B.W., Bethel, A., Ukoumunne, O.C., Nikolaou, V., & Garside, R. (2016). Attention Restoration Theory: A systematic review of the attention restoration potential of exposure to natural environments. *Journal of Toxicology and Environmental Health, Part B, 19*(7), 305–343.

Orr, D.W. (2004). *Earth in mind: On education, environment, and the human prospect.* Washington, D.C.: Island Press.

Park, B.J., Tsunetsugu, Y., Kasetani, T., Kagawa, T., & Miyazaki, Y. (2010). The physiological effects of Shinrin-yoku (taking in the forest atmosphere or forest bathing): Evidence from field experiments in 24 forests across Japan. *Environmental Health and Preventive Medicine, 15*(1), 18.

Piff, P.K., Dietze, P., Feinberg, M., Stancato, D.M., & Keltner, D. (2015). Awe, the small self, and prosocial behavior. *Journal of Personality and Social Psychology, 108*(6), 883.

Sandage, S.J., & Moe, S.P. (2013). Spiritual experience: Conversion and transformation. *APA handbook of psychology, religion, and spirituality, 1,* 407–422.

Shults, F.L., & Sandage, S.J. (2006). *Transforming spirituality: Integrating theology and psychology.* Grand Rapids, MI: Baker Academic.

Tellegen, A., & Atkinson, G. (1974). Openness to absorbing and self-altering experiences ("Absorption"), a trait related to hypnotic susceptibility. *Journal of Abnormal Psychology, 83*, 268–277.

Van Gennep, A. (1960/2004). *The rites of passage.* London, UK: Routledge.

Van Gordon, W., Shonin, E., & Richardson, M. (2018). Mindfulness and nature. *Mindfulness, 9*(5), 1655–1658.

Winfrey, O., & Chopra, D. (n.d.). Meditation experience mobile app. (software). Available from https://chopracentermeditation.com/mobileapp

Zhang, J.W., Piff, P.K., Iyer, R., Koleva, S., & Keltner, D. (2014). An occasion for unselfing: Beautiful nature leads to prosociality. *Journal of Environmental Psychology, 37*, 61–72.

Zinnbauer, B.J., & Pargament, K.I. (1998). Spiritual conversion: A study of religious change among college students. *Journal for the Scientific Study of Religion, 37*(1), 161–180.

Grounding and Communication as an Integrative Therapy

Caifang Zhu

Meditation-Initiated Integrative Therapy (MIIT) began as an approach that integrated meditative practices and selected psychotherapies (Zhu, 2012). The meditative practice in MIIT fell into three stages, namely, following one's breath, observing the discriminative mind, and observing the nondual and non-discriminative mind (Zhu, 2011b). The selected psychotherapies included cognitive behavioral therapy, psychodynamic psychotherapy, somatic psychotherapy, humanistic psychotherapy, and expressive arts therapy.

A typical session, both in an individual case and in a group setting, entailed a formal meditation, either sitting or walking or both, followed by therapeutic conversations drawing on appropriate topics. MIIT later evolved into Grounding and Communication (GAC) as an integrative therapy, where *grounding* refers to meditation, and *communication* refers to therapeutic conversations and interactions. In GAC, a humanistic orientation is highlighted by empathic listening, with the subsequent responses characterizing the basic tone of therapeutic communication. Nonetheless, the empathic understanding and acceptance of the client's thoughts, emotions, and behaviors may be balanced at times by necessary challenges to a client's dysfunctional belief system. These challenges draw upon Rational Emotive Behavior Therapy (REBT) (Ellis & Ellis, 2019) and Cognitive-Behavior Therapy (CBT) (Beck & Weishaar, 2005).

Grounding is not merely practiced independently; it can be used any time in any circumstances by the well-trained therapist to enhance therapeutic communication in the counseling session. Case presentations, involving one individual case and one experience of group counseling, are given in this essay. Both MIIT and GAC (Grounding and Communication) have received only preliminary empirical studies, but years of clinical work show that MIIT and GAC appear to be effective with anxiety, depression, obsessive-compulsive disorder, and deficits in social and interpersonal relationships, among others.

From MIIT to GAC

Grounding and Communication (GAC) is an integral transpersonal model that can be used to enhance the well-being of average individuals. It can also be used for its therapeutic effect on mental health disorders. It is an updated version of Meditation-Initiated Integrative Therapy (MIIT) (Zhu, 2012).

MIIT is similar to Mindfulness-Based Stress Reduction, or MBSR (Kabat-Zinn, 2013), and Mindfulness-Based Cognitive Therapy, or MBCT (Segal, Williams, & Teasdale, 2002), in that MIIT also employs formal meditation practice as an important integral part of its model. However, MIIT differs from MBSR and MBCT in several ways. First, MBSR and MBCT seem to place their training mostly into mindfulness practice, with MBCT also dealing with cognitive issues. *Mindfulness*, as defined by Jon Kabat-Zinn (1994), "means paying attention in a particular way: on purpose, in the present moment, and non-judgmentally" (p. 4). Meditation in MIIT, however, is taught in a three-stage model for beginning, intermediate, and advanced practitioners. At the beginning stage, practitioners basically learn the method called *suixi* in Chinese, which literally means following your breathing, inhaling and exhaling (Rosenberg, 1998; Zhiyi, 2018). At the intermediate level, practitioners learn the method called *guan wangxin*, meaning observing the discriminative, judgmental mind. At the advanced stage, practitioners learn to observe the nondual, non-discriminative, non-judgmental mind known as *guan zhenxin*, which is perhaps best symbolized by the Circle or Zero in the famed ox-herding Pictures of Chan Buddhism (Sheng-yen, 2001; Xu, 2007).

Second, MIIT allows individual clients or group participants to recollect what shifted from their unconscious to their conscious awareness. The recalled contents serve as clues to the manifestation of the unconscious for practitioners to analyze or process.

Third, meditation in MIIT may invite practitioners to bring their particular problem into the process of meditation. When that problem becomes the object of meditation, additional insights are likely to come up from the unconscious. This involves the same mechanism as does the manner of investigating a *koan* in the traditional practice of Chan/Zen that hopefully will result in a breakthrough or awakening (Zhu, 2011a, 2019). Such a breakthrough effect may come quickly or may take a much longer time. The meditation session itself, however, can be part of a relaxing and therapeutic practice regulating the body, the thoughts, and the emotions, as well as the interconnections among mind, body, and spirit (Zhu, 2012).

GAC, as an updated version of MIIT, is a psycho-spiritual and integral model for healing and growth. On the one hand, it uses a mind-body-spirit holistic regulation practice in order to achieve well-being characterized by harmony, serenity, and, at advanced stages, oneness or liberation. On the other hand, it features an intervention on the emergence of unconscious contents during meditation as clues or insights for therapeutic effects. The post-meditation therapeutic communication takes place in a framework integrating humanistic psychotherapy, cognitive behavior therapy, psychodynamic therapy, somatic psychotherapy, and expressive arts therapy, among others.

In group counseling (*counseling* is used here interchangeably with *psychotherapy*), GAC normally operates according to the following procedure.

During meditation proper, these are the suggested phases:

1. seated meditation with basic instructions given to novice practitioners
2. relaxation; unconscious contents emerging into conscious awareness
3. seeing clues and gaining insights about problems

In post-meditation sessions:

4. exposure/catharsis verbally or non-verbally (e.g., expressive arts)
5. empathic listening and responses, association, analysis
6. training on dealing with maladaptive thoughts and behaviors, with homework

Both MIIT and GAC at the beginning stages normally ask participants to meditate for 10 to 15 minutes. At intermediate and advanced stages, the meditation time will increase incrementally to 25 to 30 minutes for workshops, and of even greater length for individual clients. Regardless of stages, no specific posture is required, although different sitting postures are demonstrated and the half-lotus posture is encouraged for intermediate and advanced practitioners.

In group counseling, Stage 5 is not guaranteed for all the members in a particular session. The operation of individual counseling (therapeutic communication) in a group may begin with a volunteer, who is taken through the basic meditation instructions for beginning stage practitioners:

- assuming a comfortable and relaxed posture in a non-interfering setting that is neither too bright nor completely dark
- simply observing the inhaling or exhaling of one's breath while maintaining an overall awareness of sitting grounded on the cushion or chair
- just patiently bringing attention back to observing inhaling or exhaling if attentiveness is lost
- being aware of what is going on in thoughts, emotions, and body without being trapped or distracted

In the updated MIIT, which is the GAC model, the post-meditation therapeutic communication takes Carl Rogers's person-centered humanistic perspective as the overarching style (Rogers, 1951, 1961). Empathic listening and non-directive responses are frequently employed by the counselor or therapist. Congruence is emphasized as well. For Rogers, congruence was epitomized in his one-time consultation in a demonstration with Mark during Rogers's visit to South Africa in 1982 (Farber, Brink, & Raskin, 1996). Nonviolent Communication (NVC), a development based on Rogerian humanistic psychology and psychotherapy, is also included in the post-meditation interaction with clients. Nonviolent Communication, created by Rogers's student Marshall Rosenberg (2015), highlights the practice of empathic listening and honest responses. It specifically features observing, feeling, awareness of needs, and requesting assistance.

The change from MIIT to GAC emphasized the importance of the role of interpersonal communication in an honest, empathic, and equal way. In contemporary China, traditionally-minded people may not be sufficiently aware of this process, and the use of a volunteer is a teaching device for them.

Intermediate and Advanced Stage Meditation

Meditation at the beginning stage of MIIT or GAC is focused on the practice of breathing. In traditional Buddhist teachings, breathing is seen as a psycho-spiritual practice. There are two basic procedures: counting the number of breaths, or simply following the breath, inhaling and exhaling. Such teachings are an important component of meditation in the *Pali Canon* that guides the practice and beliefs in Southeast and South Asian Buddhist countries and communities. The best known *suttas* that feature the teaching of following one's breath are two very short classical texts, the *Anapanasati Sutta* (Mindfulness of Breathing) and the *Satipathana Sutta* (Four Establishments of Mindfulness). The very beginning of the sixteen meditations in *Anapanasati Sutta*, teaches:

> While breathing in long, one knows: "I breathe in long." While breathing out long, one knows: "I breathe out long." While breathing in short, one knows: "I breathe in short." While breathing out short, one knows: "I breathe out short." One trains oneself, "Sensitive to the whole body, I breathe in. Sensitive to the whole body, I breathe out" [Rosenberg, 1998, pp. 7–8].

Likewise, the beginning of the *Satipathana Sutta* states much the same, except for the difference of phrasing due to a translation preference:

> He breathes in, aware that he breathes in. He breathes out, aware that he breathes out. When he breathes in a long breath, he knows, "I am breathing in a long breath." When he breathes out a long breath, he knows, "I am breathing out a long breath.… Breathing in, I am aware of my whole body. Breathing out, I am aware of my whole body. Breathing in, I calm my body Breathing out, I calm my body" [Thich Nhat Hanh, 2006, p. 16].

In both the MIIT and GAC models, the beginning stage meditation centers around the breathing practices, based on the above teachings. The purpose is to develop the awareness of and intimacy with one's own physical and emotional presence and to avoid a disassociation of the cognitive mind from emotion and sensation. Once this stage is practiced sufficiently, the practitioner moves on to the intermediate level. Here, MIIT or GAC shifts the practice of following breathing, remaining aware of sensations and feelings, to observing the discriminative mind.

Later, parts of both the *Anapanasati Sutta* and the *Satipathana Sutta* contain several teachings on this practice. In the *Satipathana Sutta*, the third meditation practice is known as the mindfulness or observation of mind, which manifests in 16 different psychological configurations: desiring and not desiring; hating and not hating; being ignorant and not being ignorant; being collected and not collected; being distracted and not distracted; being expansive and not expansive; being surpassable and unsurpassable; being concentrated and unconcentrated; being freed and not freed. Here is a quotation:

> When his mind is desiring, the practitioner is aware, "My mind is desiring." When his mind is not desiring, he is aware, "My mind is not desiring." When his mind is hating something, he is aware, "My mind is hating" [Thich Nhat Hanh, 2006, p. 23].

The practice of observing such mental activities coming and going, arising and disappearing, leads to the understanding of the impermanence of the discriminative mind. Practitioners, therefore, do not want to be caught up in worldly considerations and discriminative thoughts. Instead, they seek to attain deliverance that keeps them on the path of liberation.

At the advanced stage, the priority of practice is the experience of the nondual or non-discriminative mind (the "true mind"), where one's awareness is simply the oneness of all that is. Such a state is perhaps best symbolized by the Circle or Zero in the illustrated Ox-herding Pictures of the Chan Buddhism tradition (Sheng-yen, 2001). It represents a great leap forward, breaking through all kinds of psychological bondages or restrictions, all kinds of what psychodynamic psychology calls *defense mechanisms* (Mitchell & Black, 1995). It is an enlightenment, a liberation. It is an enlightenment that can illuminate all the darkness of the unconscious. It might be mentioned that Carl Jung, following years of reflection, agreed that the unconscious could be illuminated in this way (Young-Eisendrath & Middeldorf, 2002).

Practitioners at this stage seem to resemble what Jung described as the archetypes of holistic persons, well-developed and with balanced mind-body-spirit. According to Wilber's (2000) schemata of ten stages of consciousness development, meditation is placed at the advanced stage. Both MIIT and GAC have stages that correspond to Wilber's transpersonal stages of the psychic, subtle, and causal (nondual). In the Chan Buddhist tradition, these correspond to the eighth, ninth, and tenth traditional Ox-herding Pictures. The eighth picture is symbolized by a Circle or Zero meaning that both the herder and ox are forgotten, or experienced as oneness (Zhu, 2011a).

The ninth picture, known as reverting to the origin and returning to the source, simply portrays trees and flowers in the natural world. It suggests that the mind of the enlightened person sees things as they are naturally, without projections. When practitioners come out of formal meditation, they are said to "enter the marketplace with blissful hands," which illustrates the tenth picture of "a rotund, smiling, self-contented" person (Sheng-yen, 2001, p. 219). This person, a bodhisattva presumably, carries a cloth bag to collect psycho-spiritual sufferings of people in need of assistance, much like an extraordinary psychotherapist, as a container of the client's frustration and despair.

Practitioners of this kind do not live on a solitary mountain, but return to everyday life as helping professionals in their society. They belong to what Maslow (1964) called self-realized and transpersonal people. They should not be categorized as "spiritual bypassers" who ignore the suffering of their fellow humans (Friedman, 1983; Welwood, 2002). When giving a workshop on transpersonal psychology in Beijing from September 21 to 23, 2018, Stanley Krippner stated that a treatment goal of transpersonal psychotherapy might include encouraging clients to make connections to the transpersonal elements in their lives, including simple acts of kindness and awe.

Case Presentations

My clients are either individuals or participants in 12-week group counseling sessions or 3-day workshops. In the following, I will present one case of individual counseling and one case of group counseling, using the MIIT or GAC model.

Individual Case: In the case of individual counseling, a one-hour session might not begin with instructed meditation. If it appears useful and is accepted, it will be introduced at an appropriate time during the session. Otherwise, the first one or two sessions consist mainly of listening to the client in order to gather basic information, which is used to assess and conceptualize the case and its treatment. Meanwhile, building a therapeutic alliance is the first and foremost task I need to prioritize during the beginning couple of sessions.

C is a young man in his late 20s, married with a child, although he lives apart from them. He received his college education in Northeast China but has been working in Beijing for several years, while his wife and child still live in his hometown in Northeast China. His expertise is in the telecommunications industry. When he came to seek consultation with me, his chief complaint was his obsessive thoughts that colleagues in his office have been staring at him or his computer screen in order to steal his programming design. He was also obsessed with the thought that his eye-contact with others would frighten them. He gave me an example: Once on a public bus he looked at a passenger in his eyes for about 20 seconds, and the passenger looked away, appearing somewhat scared.

In the first session of counseling, I listened to him with empathic responses to establish a therapeutic alliance. In addition, I wanted to see if I could make a general assessment of his obsessive-compulsive disorder.

In the third session, I started to use the cognitive-behavioral approach for the first half of the session and followed it up with walking meditation in the second half. The Socratic way of inquiry was used regarding the client's belief that his eye-contact was frightening to others. "You said you looked at the passenger's eyes for 20 seconds and scared him. Do you think staring at a stranger for 20 seconds is a normal length that average people can accept? Do you think you can stand that yourself?" So, through the Socratic dialogue, I tried to remind him of his dysfunctional thinking and convey this message to him: it is not that his eye-contact is always scary, but that the length of his looking into the eyes of the stranger is apparently too long for comfort.

He asked me whether I felt uncomfortable when he eye-contacted me. I said I did not feel uncomfortable and scared at all. I invited him to ask his friends for feedback about the effect of his eye-contact. Gradually, he realized that he was obsessed with cognitive distortion, and then his dysfunctional way of thinking became modified.

After 25 to 30 minutes of communication on the cognitive dimension, client C acknowledged that he began to understand his problematic way of thinking, however, he was still worried that he could not help behaving that way. Every morning before entering his office, he would use the bathroom so that he would not have to use it again during his whole morning of work. He said he would be obsessed with the thought that everyone would stare at him in an unfriendly way if he rose from the seat of his cubicle in the public office to walk to the bathroom. In other words, he would control his physiological needs and interpersonal chances so that he could avoid imagined conflicts with his fellow workers.

At this time I asked him if he would like to do some role-play or behavioral exposure with me. Given the initial therapeutic relationship of trust he seemed to have in me, he said he was willing to do some exercises with me to explore the issue. With my brief instruction, he sat in the chair in front of the computer on my desk, and then rose from the chair to walk in the direction of an imagined bathroom in my office. When obsessive thoughts came to his mind, I asked him to take three deep breaths and then pay attention to walking, particularly to the process of lifting and grounding each footstep. As a practice in the counseling session, I asked him to slow down the walking meditation, or mindful walking, as much as possible, so that he might have enough time to relax and shift his attention from the obsessive thoughts to the simple physical sensation of walking.

After about 10 minutes of "snail walk," a very slow-paced walking meditation, he said that he felt relaxed, fairly free from the intrusive thoughts of others staring at him. He said such a relaxed experience was something he had never had over the previous years. He said his former therapists with a psychoanalytic orientation never engaged him in physical or behavioral exercises in a mindful or meditative way. I encouraged him to do such an exercise on a daily basis as his homework, and he agreed. After working with me for ten sessions, C stated that he had setbacks sometimes, but overall he had been making significant progress. C was pleased with these gradual, positive changes.

Group Counseling Case: Since summer 2014, I have led eight groups in Beijing to practice MIIT or GCA. The size of the group varies from 7 to 12 and the group counseling takes place once a week, mostly over the weekend. Each group meeting lasts 2.5 hours, on average. With a few exceptions, the overwhelming majority of the participants are functioning well, professionally and socially. The ages of the participants range from the mid–20s to the late 50s, and the ratio of females to males is about 3:1. About 90 percent of the participants have a bachelor's degree or above.

The last group I finished working with lasted from mid–July through mid–October 2018. A well-established psychological counseling center in Beijing organized this event. Most of the eight participants in this recent group were clients at my counseling center. One participant dropped out due to her scheduled travels and conferences at home and abroad. Among the other seven participants two were male and five were female. Their ages ranged from the late 20s to the early 60s.

One male named H was in his late 20s, the only child of his parents. He was unable to hold down a job or socialize with others due to his severely diminished interpersonal relationships. He said he simply dislikes to meet and interact with people. He used to teach high school students, but said he would simply teach the class but not communicate and socialize with students on an individual level. In his narrative of his early life as a child, H had an accident that involved a brain concussion. His parents sent him to North America for a college education. However, he felt very isolated and lonely, and had very few friends.

Another participant in the group, Q, was a female in her mid–30s. Like the young man H mentioned above, she is also single, with virtually no social life. She worked at home and was paid for transcribing recorded lectures and similar work. She had siblings (an elder brother and elder sister), and she had been living with her elder sister in a rented apartment. She complained that her parents, who were farmers, had favored her elder brother and sister and neglected her. She felt that at one time she was forced by her brother to join the family reunion dinner on the Chinese New Year's Eve. Since then she had little communication with the rest of the family. Her social life was limited to contacts with her sister, who over weekends would bring her to places of interest or social occasions.

As noted above, Grounding and Communication consists of two major components, namely, meditation and therapeutic communication. In communication, the empathic way of humanistic psychology is balanced and integrated with other approaches, including the appropriate challenges used in cognitive-behavioral therapy (CBT). For example, communication plays a key role in the dialectics of acceptance and challenge found in Dialectical Behavior Therapy (Linehan,1993). Communication is critical in the acceptance and committed action phase of Acceptance and Commitment Therapy (Hayes, Strosahl, & Wilson, 2012). In each of the 12 weekly sessions (two hours each session) on Sunday mornings, the participants would begin with sitting practice for 10–15 minutes. Instructions in meditation, focused on following their breath, were given prior to their sitting either on a mat or on a chair, according to their own choice. Following the meditation, all participants were given a piece of blank paper and oil pastels to express linguistically or artistically what they had experienced in the silent meditation. No logic, order, or grammar was needed for their expressions. After presenting on several life issues, I invited a volunteer from the group to pick three items she or he thought were especially significant and wanted to explore. Therapeutic counseling proceeded from there.

In another design used more frequently at post-beginning levels, participants are asked to watch their cognitive process, or to concentrate mentally on a targeted issue. They are asked to watch their mental process, random thoughts, emotions, and images surfacing from the unconscious. In concentrating on the targeted issue with which one is, or was, having difficulties, one might be able to see clues or ideas leading to a solution of the problem being investigated. In a GAC weekend workshop I gave in Zurich, Switzerland, in March 2019, ten of the eighteen attendees reported having an insight during the 20-minute meditation session that helped to solve their targeted problem.

When the meditation period is over, communication with a sense of groundedness begins. In the first six sessions, the communication process is chiefly the learning of non-violent communication (NVC) (Rosenberg, 1998). Given that the very first session of this group counseling was an overall introduction to an extended audience, the actual NVC learning began in the second session. Instead of jumping to the first of the four elements (observing, feeling, needs, and requesting), Rosenberg taught, "I began to teach empathic listening as a prerequisite (meditation practice is seen as a prerequisite for empathic listening)." Empathic listening and non-directive responses are taught and practiced in pairs in the group.

H did not say a word to the extended group in the very first session, which he and his father both attended. The second session includes a paired exercise of empathic listening as one talks about his or her complaint and the other listens empathically. During this session, H seemed to be comfortable and engaged with his partner. After 10 minutes of role-play (for five minutes one listens empathically, and for another five minutes one speaks in turn), H shared with the whole group that for the first time he felt he would like to start talking to people. When he was speaking to his partner, and earlier to the whole group, he felt he was listened to empathically and thus felt respected as a person. His previous experience had led him to think he was a "nobody, like the air" when he was talking to others, because he felt he was not listened to. As a result, he felt neglected, ignored, interrupted, ridiculed, and doubted.

From this group experience onward, and with a continued milieu of empathic listening and honest responses, H continued to reveal himself by sharing his thoughts, feelings, and experiences as well as responding to fellow group members. H shared his unsuccessful experiences while studying in Canada, and of trying to make friends with fellow churchgoers in Beijing. He shared his communication with his parents, whom he loved but from whom he did not obtain empathic understanding and encouragement.

Towards the end of the 12-week group counseling, H made a date with an international female student who was studying in Beijing. Although he was disappointed at the outcome of the date, he had nonetheless moved out of his habitual comfort zone of isolation. H began to feel increasingly natural and confident in social activities and interpersonal relationships.

As for Q, similar changes happened shortly after nonviolent communication practice began with empathic listening in the group. For many years she had low self-esteem, believing she was unintelligent, not good looking, and unworthy of being listened to. In the paired practice of empathic listening, Q listened to her partner and was listened to empathically by her partner. She was moved to tears a few times while sharing their practice of mutual listening. She was not as verbally expressive as H, but was more emotional. The group learned to respect her and be patient by waiting silently and empathically when she broke into tears in the midst of sharing and the recollection of painful experiences. Gradually, her voice grew clearer, louder, and more confident.

In the later sessions I gave her a homework task: finding a friend with whom to have lunch over the weekend. Q reported the difficulty of doing such homework and asked if she could ask fellow participants of our group to have dinner. I agreed with her request, and so did the fellow members. Towards the end of all the 12 sessions, Q was apparently more comfortable and interested in inviting others to, or responding to, social engagements. About six months later, when I contacted Q for approval of citing her case for this essay, she said that, although her work environment remains more or less the same, her "inner world has been much more peaceful, less entangled" since the group counseling.

A Preliminary Empirical Study

This preliminary study was a survey done with the sixth MIIT group I led from April through July 2016. Nine participants were recruited, but one dropped out after two sessions due to the breakout of an episodic personality disorder. Five of the eight remaining participants were female, three were male. Their ages ranged from the late 20s through the early 50s. Three of them are professionals in counseling psychology, two in either the telecommunications industry or business administration, one a high school teacher, one a homemaker, and one an administrative assistant.

The pre-test before the MIIT group counseling was administered to all eight participants using two inventories, the Toronto Mindfulness Scale (2004) and the Life Satisfaction Index B. Twelve weeks later, a post-test was administered to the same eight persons, but one of them did not return the survey forms.

Five of the seven valid samples of the Life Satisfaction Index B showed improvement in each of their individual scores, and two of them declined slightly. Consequently, the average score of the whole sample increased by 0.9. Among the valid samples of the Toronto Mindfulness Scales, four showed improvement, while the other three showed a decline in each of the individual scores. The average score of the seven samples dropped by 0.4. To sum up, in this preliminary small-scale study, we found that the average mindfulness score dropped slightly, but the average score of life satisfaction increased somewhat.

How do we explain this phenomenon? Perhaps we can say that, towards the end of the MIIT group counseling, participants became more willing and comfortable to express or share their feelings and thoughts. They enjoyed such a process especially when there was an environment of empathic listening and understanding. For most beginners of mindfulness meditation practice, the increased frequency of expression and interaction might result in a slight decrease of their mindfulness, unless their training included mindful communication right from the onset. Such a change, nonetheless, could have made them feel more or less satisfied in their lives. In future empirical experiments, with consideration to standardization, the sample size needs significantly to increase. See Table 1 below for an overview of the pre and post-test data.

Qualifications for Using GAC

To practice and use GAC for the purpose of enhancing general well-being requires no specific professional qualifications or credentials. To use it as a therapeutic approach

Data for the Pre- and Post-test

Participants	Toronto Mindfulness Scale		Life Satisfaction Index B	
	Pre-MIIT	Post-MIIT	Pre-MIIT	Post-MIIT
A	35	29	13	11
B	43	33	16	15
C	23	30	18	22
D	14	24	11	14
E	34	/	17	/
F	33	24	13	14
G	32	33	9	10
H	27	35	11	15
Average score	30.1	29.7	13.5	14.4

Table 1: Pre- and Post-test Study Data

with clients, one needs, first, to be a licensed mental health professional (psychologist, therapist/counselor, nurse, social worker, or member of the clergy trained in pastoral counseling). One needs to go through a 12-week, small-group training that teaches basic meditation practice and eclectic ways of therapeutic communication.

At this time, the 12-week GAC training is provided only through the Beijing Clear-Orientation Center for Counseling and Meditation. An alternative to such a group training is a certificate of 8-week mindfulness training (e.g., MBSR, MBCT).

Since 2014, as Director of the Beijing Clear-Orientation Center, I have led eight groups who experimented with MIIT and GAC. This does not include dozens of my other MIIT or GAC workshops ranging from 2 to 3 hours to 2 to 3 days. The size of each group varied from 7 to 12 participants. The group usually meets once a week for average of 2.5 hours, some groups meeting for 3 hours, some for 2 hours, and others for 2.5 hours.

From my observations and limited empirical study, it appears that MIIT and GAC are effective in treating anxiety, depression, deficits in interpersonal relations and social skills, and obsessive and compulsive disorders. Both approaches demonstrate how they can add useful dimensions to more conventional types of psychotherapy.

REFERENCES

Beck, A.T., & Weishaar, M.E. (2005). Cognitive therapy. In R.J. Corsini & D. Wedding (Eds.), *Current psychotherapies* (7th ed.), pp. 238–268. Belmont, CA: Brooks/Cole.

Ellis, A., & Ellis, D.J. (2019). *Rational emotive behavior therapy* (2nd ed.). Washington, D.C.: American Psychological Association.

Farber, B.A., Brink, D.C., & Raskin, P.M. (1996). *The psychotherapy of Carl Rogers: Cases and commentary.* New York, NY: Guilford Press.

Friedman, H. (1983). The self-expansiveness level form: A conceptualization and measurement of a transpersonal construct. *Journal of Transpersonal Psychology, 15*(1), 37–50.

Hayes, S.C., Strosahl, K.D., & Wilson, K.G. (2012). *Acceptance and commitment therapy: The process and practice of mindful change* (2nd ed.). New York, NY: Guilford Press.

Kabat-Zinn, J. (1994). *Wherever you go, there you are: Mindfulness meditation in everyday life.* New York, NY: Hyperion.

Kabat-Zinn, J. (2013). *Full catastrophe living: How to cope with stress, pain and illness using mindfulness meditation* (Rev. ed.). London, UK: Piatkus.

Linehan, M.M. (1993). *Skills training manual for treating borderline personality disorder.* New York, NY: Guilford Press.

Maslow, A.H. (1964). *Religions, values and peak-experiences.* Columbus: Ohio State University Press.

Mitchell, S., & Black, M. (1995). *Freud and beyond: A history of modern psychoanalytic thought.* New York, NY: Basic Books.

Rogers, C.R. (1951). *Client-centered therapy.* New York, NY: Houghton Mifflin, College Division.

Rogers, C.R. (1961). *On becoming a person.* New York, NY: Houghton Mifflin.

Rosenberg, M.B. (2015). *Nonviolent Communication: A language of life* (3rd ed.). Encinitas, CA: PuddleDancer Press.

Rosenberg, L. (1998). *Breath by breath: The liberating practice of insight meditation.* Boston, MA: Shambhala.

Segal, Z.V., Williams, J.M.G., & Teasdale, J.D. (2002). *Mindfulness-based cognitive therapy for depression: A new approach to preventing relapse.* New York, NY: Guilford Press.

Sheng-yen, with D. Stevenson. (2001). *Hoofprint of the ox: Principles of the Chan Buddhist path as taught by a modern Chinese master.* New York, NY: Oxford University Press.

Thich Nhat Hanh. (2006). *Transforming and healing: Sutra on the four establishments of mindfulness.* Berkeley, CA: Parallax Press.

Welwood, J. (2002). *Toward a psychology of awakening.* Boston, MA: Shambhala.

Wilber, K. (2000). *Integral psychology: Consciousness, spirit, psychology, therapy.* Boston, MA: Shambhala.

Xu, G.X. (2007). *Psychological Chan/Zen: A psychotherapy for Easterners.* Shanghai, China: Wenhui Press.

Young-Eisendrath, P., & Middeldorf, J. (2002). The Jung-Hisamatsu conversation. In P. Young-Eisendrath & S. Muramoto (Eds.), *Awakening and insight: Zen Buddhism and psychotherapy.* New York, NY: Brunner-Routledge.

Zhiyi. (2018). *The essentials of practicing concentration and observation meditations.* Retrieved from the website of the Chinese Buddhism Electronic Text Association, http://tripitaka.cbeta.org/T46n1915_001

Zhu, C. (2011a). The hermeneutics of Chan Buddhism: Reading koans from the *Blue Cliff Record. Asian Philosophy, 21*(4), 373–393.

Zhu, C. (2011b). Three stages of meditation-initiated integrative growth. Retrieved from http://blog.sina.com.cn/s/blog_715972430100qjt7.html

Zhu, C. (2012). Ordinary mind: Meditation Initiated Integrative Therapy (MIIT). In T. G. Plante (Ed.), *Religion, spirituality and positive psychology: Understanding the psychological fruits of faith.* Pp. 159–76. Santa Barbara, CA: Praeger

Zhu, C. (in press). Chan meditation. In M. Farias, D. Brazier, & M. Lalljee (Eds.), *Oxford Handbook of Meditation.* New York, NY: Oxford University Press.

PART 4

Multicultural and Indigenous Interventions

Medicinal Drumming
and Holistic Healing

Sal Núñez

Since time immemorial cultures have formulated approaches to heal the mind, body, heart, and spirit. In indigenous communities, healing ceremonies regularly involve community participation and a ritualized process officiated by an elder-healer. Frequently the procedure includes the use of elements, such as sacred medicinal plants (especially psychedelics), song, dance, storytelling, rhythms, fasting and more, which generate shifts in consciousness. In specific healing ceremonies, the alteration in state of consciousness is purposeful and primary to the therapeutic process. Other important features in healing ceremonies are belief and faith (Azar, 2010), because these states of mind aid in the activation of the inherent healing system. Healing ceremonies also include an intentional process designed to prepare the participant to receive the medicine and commune with Spirit or cosmic energy.

Traditional healing approaches and ceremony are a complex and holistic system of healthcare deeply rooted in spiritual views and energy (Struthers, Eschiti, & Patchell, 2004). Because the *Medicinal Drumming Praxis* evolved from indigenous wisdom, Afro-Puerto Rican healing rhythms, and conventional psychology, individuals interested in learning the model must be willing to explore the foundations of indigenous medicine, ceremony, traditional epistemology, transpersonal potential, and spiritual energy.

Education Required to Deliver Intervention

Since this model derives from earth- and spiritual-based therapeutic approaches, a degree from an academic institution is helpful, especially if it is in psychology or music, but not necessary to learn and practice. An ideal candidate or practitioner would possess or be able to develop specific qualities, knowledge, and skills. Essential qualities include emotional maturity and an open mind, cultural humility, emotional regulation, and musical aptitude or interest. Knowledge of plant medicine and the clinical application of rhythm, song, and sound is also important. Familiarity with the process by which to induce trance states is also helpful. Similarly, skill in managing group dynamics within a ceremonial process is vital. Because the drum is centerpiece to the model, the facilitator must also be confident playing a hand drum in a group setting. Since therapists and musicians, particularly percussionists, possess some of these skills, they tend to be ideal candidates for learning the model, but learning is not limited to these individuals.

Training

Training in medicinal drumming is offered through the Community Mental Health Certificate Program at City College of San Francisco, funded by a grant from the San Francisco Department of Public Health, Mental Health Services Act. The medicinal drumming program consists of an 18-week apprenticeship comprised of four hours of rehearsal and experiential work once per week. During this time, learners are required to practice rudimentary hand drumming techniques and simple rhythms for a minimum of 30 minutes every day. They are taught how to strengthen intuition and heighten their sense of mindfulness while engaging in regular periods of self-reflection. Learners also devote time to exploring transpersonal potential and how to preserve the integrity of indigenous wisdom, ceremony, and scientific credibility. During this brief period, learners are taught the basic procedures of the model and evaluated to determine their ability to move to the next level of learning and practice. The next level involves exposure to more intricate aspects of ceremony and cofacilitating therapeutic drumming circles in the community. As with any other skill set, the graduates must continue practicing and receiving support over the course of years, in order to develop competency, proficiency, and eventually mastery. Since the medicinal drumming model lies outside the standard academic training of mental health practitioners, training in the model is necessary.

Other places to seek training as a drumming group facilitator (not medicinal drumming) are posted on the internet. Currently there are a number of commercially-based recreational and wellness models available to the general public. Training models generally range from a weekend workshop to a week-long session, while others are lengthier. Once individuals complete these relatively short programs, they are "certified" to facilitate recreational drumming circles, commonly without support or supervision. When skillfully facilitated, recreational and wellness drumming circles are joyful and rejuvenating, and may promote a temporary sense of well-being. Yet there are significant differences between recreational and ceremonially healing circles, as only the latter involve a ceremonial framework and process guided by indigenous medicine and wisdom, transpersonal potential, spiritual energy, and the power of traditional rhythms and songs.

The ideal way to learn an indigenous-based healing model is to study with the People from whom the model was born. Due to colonization, medical monopolization, and unfamiliarity with indigenous medicine, the medicinal power of the drum within a ceremonial process is not clearly understood. Any individuals can pick up a drum, strike it, create sound, and as a result consider themselves prepared to lead a drumming circle, and some people do. Most often, when this occurs, the results are dissonant, disorganized, and unproductive. This parallels the idea that, just because people can utter words, merely on that merit they are qualified to facilitate deep psychotherapy.

Credentialing or Licensing Agencies

During the first session of the training, learners are encouraged to become familiar with and pursue a deeper understanding of the earth-based medicine associated with their genealogy. Because indigenous people worldwide share similar healing concepts and principles, guiding learners through the process of discovery or rediscovery of their earth-based genealogy serves as one protective factor in maintaining the integrity of the model. For the graduates of medicinal drumming, credentialing occurs through the process of continued mentorship and support, an expressed and observed commitment to maintaining indigenous wisdom, conversations with and guidance by community elders, and community acceptance.

Overview of Evidence-Based Research and Potential Risks

Healing drumming circles have existed cross-culturally for millennia. The longitudinal use of these models suggests that these therapeutic interventions are effective, at least within their respective communities. Obviously, the time, energy, and resources invested in maintaining such traditions would be of significant waste unless the practices were meaningful. For Western science, anecdotal reports do not hold the same value as scientific outcomes; yet this does not mean that an intervention is not effective, rather that it has not been studied under controlled circumstances. Be that as it may, there is something to learn from data that are consistent in reports over the course of centuries and across cultures. Because this model is holistic and multilayered, vast literature has been written about it. The following is a small sample of the evidence supporting the practice.

Scientific Data

Water is a conduit of sound, which travels four times faster in water than in air. Because the most abundant compound of the human body is water (Mayo Clinic Staff, 2014; USGS, 2015), the body is naturally predisposed to the effects of sound vibrations. For instance, vibroacoustic and vibrotactile therapies use sound vibrations as deep tissue massage to help reduce stress, anxiety, insomnia, and pain (Hoope, 2001; Tajadura-Jiménez, Valjamae, & Vastfjall, 2008; Walters, 1996; Wigram, 1995). Not only does the human body respond to sound, but so does the brain, whose hemispheres are easily synchronized through entrainment, resulting in hemispheric synchronization (Jovanov & Maxfield, 2011; Maxfield, 1991; Neher, 1962; Tierney & Kraus, 2015).

Hemispheric synchronization is accomplished by a variety of means, for example, exposure to binaural beats, photic driving, sonic driving, or repetitive rhythmic patterns such as those produced by drumming (Farmer, 2009; Maxfield, 1991; Neher, 1962; Tierney & Kraus, 2015). Hemispheric synchronization stimulates the release of hormones and neurotransmitters such as dehydroepiandrosterone (DHEA) (Bittman et al., 2001) and serotonin, respectively, which enhance well-being. It also produces cortical coherence, lucid thinking, heightened intuition and awareness, and altered states of consciousness (Jovanov & Maxfield, 2011). Because consciousness manifests as vibrations, patterned rhythms can be used to shift the field we term *consciousness* (Maxfield, 1991; McCraty, Deyhle, & Childre, 2012; Morris, 2010).

Measurable states of consciousness drumming will prompt shifts from Beta to Alpha or Theta states (Maxfield, 1991; Neher, 1962; Tierney & Kraus, 2015). Movement from a

Beta to an Alpha state results in a sense of relaxation and, in turn, more flexibility in cognitive processing. This state is occasionally referred to as *being in the zone*. A Theta state is accompanied by sensorial experiences and hypnogogic effects, which not only include lucid thought, but also serve as a portal to access non-ordinary dimensions of consciousness (Maxfield, 1991; Jovanov & Maxfield, 2011; Tierney & Kraus, 2015) and the spiritual realm. When experienced within a safe environment and frame, these neurological shifts promote health, wellness, and positive mood shifts towards elation (Kaplan, 2000; Núñez, 2006). However, individuals have reported transient unpleasant physical sensations, tension, and dizziness during what appears to be the Theta state of consciousness. It is not known whether or not this is attributed to drumming or if it is a phenomenon inherent to Theta.

Rhythms are based on intervals of sound and silence, and are geometric sound configurations that resonate with the human constitution, brain, and bio-energetic field. When encoded with emotional content and intentionality, whether constructive or destructive, vibrational frequencies become vehicles that propagate the encoded content across space (Hagelin et al., 1999; Jahn & Dunne, 2005; McCraty, Deyhle, & Childre, 2012; Morris, 2010). These intentionally encoded frequencies transmit their regenerative capacity through the manipulation of tempo, dynamics, and timing, without the support of melody (Laukka, 2000), but most importantly through vibro-acoustic, sentient, and spiritual processes. A common example of the effects of these actions is observed when an audience is moved by music, not due to a performer's technical ability, but rather by their prowess in arousing emotion. These instances, which may be described as mystical or magical, involve a shared energetic dynamic, or the manifestation of Spirit.

Because the human body is a natural resonator, and drumming and voice generate harmonic frequencies, organs, tissues, bones, and fluids absorb the vibratory energy emitted by the drums and resonate to the expressed activity of the source. For example, vibrations in the approximate range of 60 Hz facilitate secretions on bronchial drainage and alleviation of broncho-spasm (Wigram, 1995). Rhythmic patterns and frequencies also stimulate the vagus nerve (Brown & Gerbarg, 2012; Kalyani et al., 2011) and hold the potential to facilitate systemic coherence, i.e., the synchronization of cortical, cardiovascular, and respiratory functioning.

Shifts in respiratory and cardiovascular activity result from the aerobic elements of drumming. These actions increase oxygenated blood that helps nurture physiology with life-generating energy. Regular exercise, such as aerobics or sustained drumming, strengthens the heart and, over time, may decrease blood pressure (Whelton, Chin, Xin, & He, 2002). Drumming increases body temperature, stimulates sweating (which helps secrete toxins from the body), and triggers hormonal fluctuations, each with their specific benefits. Hormonal fluctuations include decreased levels of cortisol and increased dehydroepiandrosterine (Bittman et al., 2001). Drumming also induces relaxation and reduction of stress and anxiety, and increases group cohesion (Núñez, 2006).

Consonant vocalizations synergize the energy created by drumming. When used in concert with drumming or a cappella, they enhance relaxation, stimulate physiological responses, deepen a state of consciousness, and elevate mood (Núñez, 2016). Simple vocalizations also entrain the brain and provoke the movement of emotional energy (Diamond, 1983, 2002).

The symbols, the geometric configuration of the circle, colorful cloths, and the elements all translate meaning to the participants. Symbols transmit an archetypal energy that can yield strength, support the processing of emotions, or be used for whatever purpose needed by an individual or group. The key for using symbols rests in the manner by which they are introduced and the meaning they possess for individuals. The circle(s) in which individuals sit serve as psychological and spiritual containers that support safety and trust, physically creating a sacred perimeter in which potentialities are manifested. Colors occur on a spectrum where each is defined by its electromagnetic wavelength or frequency. Different wavelengths or colors, though in part subjective and culturally rooted, influence mood and stimulate physiological reactions. Some colors are best suited to invoke calm and others to raise blood pressure and metabolic functioning (Kuhbandner & Pekrun, 2013; Lewis, Haviland-Jones, & Feldman Barret, 2010; Wang, Shu, & Mo, 2014). Elements such as the flickering of fire trigger shifts in brain wave activity (Fábián et al., 2009; Glicksohn 1986; Neher, 1962) and are conducive to trance induction. When elements such as water, air, fire, and earth are paired appropriately with plant medicine, colors, and rhythms, synergy evolves and facilitates a spiritual experience and connection with higher consciousness.

The aroma of medicinal plants such as rosemary, lavender, tobacco, sage, and others activates the olfactory bulb, which stimulates mood, emotion, and memory. The active ingredients of each plant promote the inherent healing capacity of the body and stimulate change by the action of their biochemical properties. For example, rosemary serves to invigorate the senses as well as to enhance positive mood, and may be a neuroprotective agent (Satoh et al., 2008). Lavender is soothing and helps to shift mood to a relaxed and pleasant state (Sayorwan et al., 2012). In addition to the benefits of their fragrance, medicinal plants channel life through the altar by means of their color and life-generating frequencies emanating from the spirit of the plants. Visually, olfactorily, and energetically, plants and other elements bridge the energetic current of the group with Mother Earth and cosmic consciousness.

The intimacy generated by the ceremonial process fosters community, networking, new relationships, and renewed affection between the participants (Goudreau, Weber-Pillwax, Cote-Meek, Madill, & Wilson, 2008; Núñez, 2006; Sideroff & Angel, 2013). Psychological bonding and group cohesion inspire mingling post-ceremony, when individuals tend to share resources, develop plans to stay connected, and make themselves available to support each other. If behavioral manifestations are indicators of physiological causality, it is plausible that the participants are responding not only to a subjective spiritual experience, but also to a potential wave of oxytocin, as evidenced by the unconditional positive regard towards others.

Populations and Conditions Effective in Treating

Historically and cross-culturally, medicinal drumming ceremonies have been used as interventions for a variety of issues and conditions. During the time of slavery in the Caribbean, medicinal drumming ceremonies were used to commune with Spirit and inspire hope and strength, as well as an intervention to decompress from the trauma of bondage. Today, medicinal drumming is still used to inspire hope and strength, commune with Spirit, decrease stress and anxiety, process trauma, elevate mood, and increase community cohesion. Over the past 18 years, medicinal drumming has been used in clinical settings with children, adolescents, families, adults, and older adults. It has also been used in county jails and juvenile detention centers to help residents decompress from the challenges of incarceration, process trauma, inspire hope, and strengthen community.

Medicinal Drumming Praxis: An Overview

The medicinal drumming praxis adheres to a standard format involving the following stages: (a) creation and establishment of sacred space; (b) introduction to the process, tools, and technology; (c) movement through the stages of engagement; (d) alignment and attunement; (e) restoration; and (f) closure. When operationalizing the model, each stage is comprised of segments and steps which, when approached sequentially, generate energetic ebb and flow and engender balance and restoration.

In medicinal drumming, the guide (facilitator) is responsible for the integrity of the praxis and ensuring the appropriate delivery of the method in a manner accountable to the participating community. Due to the brevity of this essay, a detailed overview of the guide's role is not possible, but it appears intertwined throughout the following description of the praxis.

Creating and Establishing Sacred Space

In collaboration with the community, the guide is responsible for creating and maintaining sacred space, which becomes the ceremonial container. The ceremonial space is comprised of an altar in the center, surrounded by intrinsic circles of chairs, and drums selectively placed within the circle, all organized to produce visual symmetry. Creating this space requires clear instructions from the guide and focused action from the community, which stimulate behavioral shifts to foster group cohesion.

After the space has been created, the participants are invited to sit in the circle where the guide formally introduces self and elders, welcomes the community, briefs them on what to expect, and answers questions. The guide then leads the group through a ritualized process that involves: acknowledging the seven directions; invoking spiritual energy; smudging the space, people, and drums; establishing safety and trust; and promoting a collective experience.

An important element of this stage is to draw and transform the group's attention into absorbed concentration by gradually slowing the actions of the group. This may be accomplished by the guides using slow circular motions as they smudge the drums and group, by pairing medicinal plants with a breathing exercise, or deliberately speaking more slowly and pausing longer while addressing the group. This is comparable to inducing a hypnotic state intended to quiet the mind and promote a collective shift into an Alpha state of consciousness.

In order to accomplish the above, the guide must be centered, calm, and in a contemplative state (Schenck & Churchill, 2012). Concurrently, the guide must be attentive to and responsible for the proper unfolding of the sequential events that serve as foundation to the process. Thus, the systematic navigation through the stage creates an experiential containment for the process to unfold. Included within the procedural steps of this stage, and in addition to the above, are the use of plant medicine, invocations, and affirmations, establishing intent, and acknowledging the presence of all participants. The primary purpose of these rituals is to produce collective experiences that engage the senses of the participating community and stimulate absorbed concentration.

Introduction to the Process, Tools and Technology

The process, which refers to the procedural aspects of the ceremony, involves sharing information, maneuvering rhythms, songs, and stories, managing plant medicine, and using other tools in a manner congruent with the energetic current of the group. The process also involves seamlessly ushering the group through the different stages of the ceremony in a manner that aligns with the energetic current of the group. The energetic current is comprised of the rational emotive expressions, behavioral manifestations, and spiritual energy awakened by the process.

The tools utilized during the ceremony include, but are not limited to, drums, medicinal plants, altars, symbols, and elements. During the introduction, the guide provides an overview of the tools and their purpose. The intent is to demystify preconceived notions regarding a ceremonial setting, move those new to the praxis into a position of familiarity and put them at ease, and role-model respect.

Each tool possesses a technology that, when properly awakened and appropriately combined with others, creates a synergistic effect (Sobiecki, 2012) that stimulates the curative energy inherent within each group participant. As the guide crafts synergy and progressively engages the group through the drumming ceremony, the collective energy begins to amplify and strengthens the encoded intentions. Crafting synergy is a vital component of the praxis, as the combination of rhythms, plant medicine, song, and words moves the group towards balance and revitalization. The appropriate combination of technologies stimulates neurological, cardiovascular, and endocrine activity; emotional decompression, and other health and wellness responses.

Movement through the Stages of Engagement

After introducing the process, tools, and technology, the guide ushers the group into physical contact with the tools. The guide invites group members to retrieve drums from the center of the circle, where they have been placed during the creation of the ceremonial space. Prior to retrieving the drums, participants are instructed to not awaken (strike) the drums after returning to their seats. Retrieving the drums occurs in an orderly manner and by designated rows if participants are in concentric circles. This process promotes mindfulness and assists the group in experiencing the behavioral results of collective intentionality, which is the capacity to direct mental faculty onto an object or event. With youth, this procedure assists with the development of impulse control and emotional regulation.

Once all group members are seated, the guide slowly and intentionally journeys the group through the initial contact with the drums, which occurs in a manner that builds the confidence in each group member and strengthens group cohesion. During this segment, the guide coaches the group on several rudimentary but essential musical elements such as hand care, creating basic tones, maintaining consistent tempo, use of volume and intensity, and responding to hand signals. This process leads to a sense of group comfort with the drums, further unity, and preparation for transitioning into the collective drumming rounds (*toques*).

Once the group has become comfortable with the drums, the guide introduces an opening rhythm, usually one designed to further ground the group. Prior to initiating the rhythm, the guide informs the group of its curative aspects and invites group members to consider its use for health and wellness, for establishing an intention that they may affirm during the toque, or for whatever purpose is necessary. During this segment, the guide may also address the historical and cosmological context of the rhythm along with pertinent scientifically-based information that underscores its healing properties.

To initiate the rhythm, the guide usually begins by having the group clap out the rhythm and then transfers the rhythm onto the drums. However, there are other ways to transmit a patterned rhythm to a large group, for example by singing it or vocalizing percussive sounds. Routinely, rhythms are presented in rudimentary form, so that the community may execute them with relative ease and focus on the experience rather than on rhythmic complexity. Similarly, rhythms are initiated in slow tempo to assist the group in accommodating and synchronizing the rhythm. From this point on, rhythms are paired with intention, song, and plant medicine to amplify synergy.

Subsequently the guide introduces additional rhythms in a progression that aligns with and supports the movement of the energetic current of the group. The additional rhythms are chosen to match and attune with the evolving collective energy. For example, if the guide has perceived that the group has a significant amount of unrestrained energy, while playing the initial rhythm, the guide may follow with a high-intensity rhythm to release energy and foster the group's journey towards balance.

Intermittently, and as part of the stages of engagement, the guide provides information, invites the participants to share brief comments, and engages the group in songs, chants, or story, each intended to produce a particular effect. For example, after a high-intensity rhythm intended to release imbalanced energy, a slow "call and response" song may be used to calm the sympathetic nervous system. Likewise, a lullaby may be used to soothe any agitation (Clare, 2014; Garunkstiene, Buinauskiene, Uloziene, & Markuniene, 2014) experienced by the group after a participant has divulged traumatic material. At junctures where traumatic experiences are shared, the guide intentionally shifts the process to focus on moving the traumatic energy. This requires the use of certain tools, rhythms, and songs, as well as the group's intentionality, to synergize the effects of the tools and intervention.

Within the medicinal drumming praxis, it is important to keep melodies simple so as to focus on releasing energy through the intentional collective experience. Within the ceremonial setting, singing and yelling are associated with a cathartic process. Depending on the desired effect, the guide will engage the group in chanting or "call and response," while drumming or a cappella, whichever is more in line with the energetic current of the group. Chanting induces trance, while "call and response" augments attention.

Alignment/Attunement

Commonly, this is the stage where group members begin to verbalize experiencing a sense of clarity, relaxation, vitality, and hope. During this stage, the guide further attunes to the current of the group and, through tempo and musical dynamics, reflects the current of energy back to the group, as a feedback loop. As this segment builds towards a peak, the guide pays particular attention to deepening group synchronicity. This is achieved by introducing certain vocalizations, collective synchronized breathing, vocal discharge (group yell), and clearly accentuated endings to the drumming rounds. The combinations of these elements lead to a cathartic experience and shift towards restoration.

Restoration

During the energetic peak, the group reverberates in rhythmic synchronicity and in alignment with its extended environment. At this stage, group members frequently verbalize experiencing clarity, deepened connection, relaxation and energy, and more sensitivity to environmental stimuli. At this point in the ceremony, the guide points out behavioral indicators that substantiate a shift in collective energy, such as the group's accomplished synchronicity, along with its ability to sustain tempo and regulate musical dynamics. Group members are also invited to share briefly their state of being. The guide pays attention to positive statements and affirmations shared by the group members, weaving these into a feedback dialogue to validate the behavioral, physiological, and psychic transformations reported by the group. As with any therapeutic approach, the statements and affirmations are chosen with care to align with the current generated by the group. This process not only mirrors to group members what they have generated, but also helps anchor their experiences and achievements into a constructive frame. Once the stage has reached its highest point, experienced as the peak in energy, the guide begins to usher the group towards closure.

Closure

The guide introduces a final rhythm or song, explaining its meaning, purpose, and intent. Cognitively, the final rhythm or song is used to bridge and ground the collective back into the here and now. Physiologically, the purpose is to help soothe residual arousal or acute sympathetic activity. Emotionally, the intention is to impress upon consciousness that which one would like to see manifested in the world for self or whatever constructive purpose may be significant. This final rhythm or song is delivered in a slower tempo and usually is faded out instead of ending in an accentuated manner. Thereafter, group members are led through a brief breathing exercise and encouraged to sense their life-force energy and affirm their subjective selves. After completing the exercise, the guide instructs the participants to deliver all drums to the center of the ceremonial space and return to their seats.

Once this is done, the guide invites group members to consider how they might use and re-access the energy and experiential state achieved during the ceremony. If it appears that it may be helpful to the group, the guide may offer ideas or suggestions on how to reactivate the achieved state. For example, the guide may invite group members to feel their pulses and then to use them as a way to recall the feelings attained in the group. Depending on the nature of the group, the guide may use visualization, contingency, or conditioned pairing as methods to extend the experience and effects beyond the ceremony. For example, the guide may introduce a guided visualization and in-vivo process, pairing the aroma of a particular medicinal plant with a positive physiological and emotional state. Later, the participants can reactivate the state by exposure to the aroma or by recreating the visualization. Subsequently, the guide informs the group that potential reverberating effects of the ceremony may include enhanced sensitivity to color, sound or movement, unordinary or vivid dreams, intuitive clarity, and a sense of deeper connection to self, others, and the environment.

Depending on the size of the group, the guide will invite participants to share a brief closing comment, or state one word that summarizes how they feel, what they may be experiencing, or an intent they want to affirm. This occurs in an organized manner and moves throughout the group in a clockwise fashion, one person at a time, each with an option to pass. Once completed, the guide thanks the group members for sharing their energy, words, and contributions to the collective, encourages them to consider network-ing to extend the community beyond the ceremony, and then ushers the group towards the final segment of closure.

Contingent on the cultural composition of the group, the guide will briefly explain the purpose and meaning of the closing procedure and answer any related questions. Then the guide acknowledges elders and invites them to share closing words. The guide then leads the group through the process of acknowledging the seven directions, life source, and spiritual energy present during the ceremony.

The final collective act involves two steps: one is standing in a circle to experience the flow of life-force energy generated by the collective current, followed by creating sound to propel the energy into the ether. The first step is accomplished by all individuals vigorously rubbing their own hands together, followed by their placing their left palms facing upward and the right palms facing downward, then placing one hand above and another below the hands of their neighbors at approximately one inch apart. The group is then asked to sense and focus on the energy harnessed, which flows through the space between their hands. This energy is normally experienced and manifested as heat, light tingles, a magnetic pull, or other sensations. Thereafter, the group members are asked to, at the count of three, throw their hands up into the air and shout their names or pro-ject their intentions. This creates a final collective act, marking the closure of the group process. Once this final event is completed, the community is invited to socialize and assist with clearing the space.

Clearing the space, specifically the altar, involves intention and particular consid-eration to appropriately disposing of any elements, such as water, plants, fire, etc., used during the ceremony. This is performed by individuals who are familiar with such prac-tices or who have been instructed on the proper procedure. The appropriate disposing of the elements used in the ceremony is done privately and symbolizes the conclusion of the ceremony.

References

Azar, B. (2010). A reason to believe. *American Psychological Association Monitor, 41*(11), 52–56.

Bittman, B., Berk, L., Felten, D. Westengard, J., Simonton, O., Pappas, J., & Ninehourser, M. (2001). Composite effects of group drumming music therapy on modulation of neuroendocrine-immune parameters in normal subjects. *Alternative Therapies, 17*(3), 201–207.

Brown, R.P., & Gerbarg, P.L. (2012). *The healing power of the breath: Simple techniques to reduce stress and anxiety, enhance concentration and balance your emotions.* Boston, MA: Shambhala Publications.

Clare, M. (2014). Soothing sounds: Reducing agitation with music therapy. *British Journal of Healthcare Assis-tance, 8*(4), 190–195.

Diamond, J. (1983). *The life energy in music: Notes of music and sound.* New York, NY: Archaeus Press.

Diamond, L. (2002). The therapeutic power of music. In S. Shannon (Ed.), *Handbook of complementary and alternative therapies in mental health* (pp. 517–537). San Diego, CA: Academic Press.

Fábián, T.K., Kovács, K.J., Gótai, L., Beck, A., Krause, W.R., & Fejérdy, P. (2009). Photo-acoustic stimulation: Theoretical background and ten years of clinical experience. *Contemporary Hypnosis, 26*(4), 225–233.

Farmer, S.D. (2009). *Earth magic: Ancient shamanic wisdom for healing yourself, others, and the planet.* Carlsbad, CA: Hay House.

Garunkstiene, R., Buinauskiene, J., Uloziene, I., & Markuniene, E. (2014). Controlled trial of live versus recorded lullabies in preterm infants. *Nordic Journal of Music Therapy, 23*(1), 71–88.

Glicksohn, J. (1986). Photic driving and altered states of consciousness: An exploratory study. Imagination. *Cognition and Personality, 6*(2), 167–182.

Goudreau, G., Weber-Pillwax, C., Cote-Meek, S., Madill, H., & Wilson, S. (2008). Hand drumming: Health promoting experiences of Aboriginal women from a Northern Ontario urban community. *Journal of Aboriginal Health, 4*(1), 72–83.

Hagelin, J.S., Rainforth, M.V., Orme-Johnson, D.W., Cavanaugh, K.L., Alexander, C.N., Shatkin, S.F., Davies, J.L., Hughes, A.O., & Ross, E. (1999). Effects of group practice of the transcendental meditation program on preventing violent crime in Washington, D.C.: Results of the National Demonstration Project, June-July, 1993. *Social Indicators Research, 47*(2), 153–201.

Hoope, J. (2001). An introduction to vibroacoustic therapy and an examination of its place in music therapy practice. *British Journal of Music Therapy, 15*(2), 69–77.

Jahn, R.G., & Dunne, B.J. (2005). The PEAR proposition. *Journal of Scientific Exploration, 19*(2), 195–246.

Jovanov, E., & Maxfield, M.C. (2011). Entraining the brain and body. In J. Berger & G. Turow (Eds.), *Music, science, and the rhythmic brain: Cultural and clinical implications* (pp. 31–48). New York, NY: Routledge.

Kalyani, B.G., Venkatasubramanian, G., Arasappa, R., Rao, N.P., Kalmady, S.V., Behere, R.V., Rao, H., Vasudev, M.K., & Gangadhar, B.N. (2011). Neurohemodynamic correlates of "OM" chanting: A pilot functional magnetic resonance imaging study. *International Journal of Yoga, 4*(1), 3–6.

Kaplan, C.D. (2000). *The short term effects of small group hand drumming on mood, group cohesiveness and rhythm perception.* (Doctoral dissertation). Retrieved from Dissertation Abstracts International, 60(11), 5822.

Kuhbandner, C., & Pekrun, R. (2013). Joint effects of emotion and color on memory. *Emotion, 13*(3), 375–379.

Laukka, P. (2000). Emotional expression in drumming performance. *Psychology of Music, 28*(2), 181–189.

Lewis, M., Haviland-Jones, J.M., & Feldman Barrett, L. (Eds.). (2010). *Handbook of emotions* (4th ed.). New York, NY: The Guilford Press.

Maxfield, M.C. (1991). *Effects of rhythmic drumming on EEG and subjective experience.* (Unpublished doctoral dissertation). Menlo Park, CA: Institute of Transpersonal Psychology.

Mayo Clinic Staff. (2014). *Water: How much should you drink every day?* Mayo Clinic. Retrieved from http://www.mayoclinic.org/healthy-lifestyle/nutrition-and-healthy-eating/in-depth/water/art-20044256%20-%2042k

McCraty, R., Deyhle, A., & Childre, D. (2012). The global coherence initiative: Creating a coherent planetary standing wave. *Global Advances in Health and Medicine, 1*(1), 64–77.

Morris, S.M. (2010). Achieving collective coherence: Group effects on heart rate variability coherence and heart rhythm synchronization. *Alternative Therapies, 16*(4), 62–74.

Neher, A. (1962). A physiological explanation of unusual behavior in ceremonies involving drums. *Human Biology, 34*(2), 151–160.

Núñez, S. (2006). *Effects of drumming on anxiety in Latino male youth.* (Doctoral dissertation). Available from ProQuest Dissertations and Theses database. (UMI No. 3204911).

Núñez, S. (2016). Medicinal drumming: An ancient and modern day healing approach. *NeuroQuantology, 14*(2), 226–241.

Satoh, T., Kosaka, K., Itoh, K., Kobayashi, A., Yamamoto, M., Shimojo, Y., Kitajima, C., Cui, J., Kamins, J., Okamoto, S., Izumi, M., Shirasawa, T., & Lipton, S.A. (2008). Carnosic acid, catechol-type electrophilic compound, protects neurons both in vitro and in vivo through activation of the Keap1/Nrf2 pathway via S-alkylation of targeted cysteines on Keap1. *Journal of Neurochemistry, 104*(4), 1116–1131.

Sayorwan, W., Siripornpanich, V., Piriyapunyaporn, T., Hongratanaworakit, T., Kotchabhakdi, N., & Ruangrungsi, N. (2012). The effects of lavender oil inhalation on emotional states, autonomic nervous system, and brain electrical activity. *Journal of Medical Association Thailand, 95*(4), 598–606.

Schenck, D., & Churchill, L.R. (2012). *Healers: Extraordinary clinicians at work.* New York, NY: Oxford University Press.

Sideroff, S., & Angel, S. (2013). The use of drumming in the development of self-trust and healing in the therapeutic process. *Annals of Psychotherapy and Integrative Health, 16*(2), 70–81.

Sobiecki, J.F. (2012). Psychoactive Ubulawu spiritual medicines and healing dynamics in the initiation process of southern Bantu diviners. *Journal of Psychoactive Drugs, 44*(3), 216–223.

Struthers, R., Eschiti, V., & Patchell, B. (2004). Traditional indigenous healing: Part I. *Complementary Therapies in Nursing & Midwifery, 10*, 141–149.

Tajadura-Jiménez, A., Valjamae, A., & Vastfjall, D. (2008). Self-representation in mediated environments: The experience of emotions by modulated auditory-vibrotactile heartbeat. *Cyber Psychology and Behavior, 11*(1), 33–38.

Tierney, A., & Kraus, N. (2015). Neural entrainment to the rhythmic structure of music. *Journal of Cognitive Neuroscience, 27*(2), 400–408.

U.S. Geological Survey. (2015). Water Science School. *The water in you.* Retrieved from http://water.usgs.gov/edu/propertyyou.html

Walters, C.L. (1996). The psychological and physiological effects of vibrotactile stimulation, via asomatron, on patients awaiting scheduled gynecological surgery. *Journal of Music Therapy, 33*(4), 261–287.

Wang, T., Shu, S., & Mo, L. (2014). Blue or red? The effects of colour on the emotions of Chinese people. *Asian Journal of Social Psychology, 17*(2), 152–158.

Whelton, S.P., Chin, A., Xin, X., & He, J. (2002). Effect of aerobic exercise on blood pressure: A meta-analysis of randomized, controlled trials. *Annals of Internal Medicine, 136*(7), 493–503.

Wigram, T. (1995). The psychological and physiological effects of low frequency sound in music. *Music Therapy Perspectives, 13*, 16–23.

Practicing Medicine Wheel for Holistic Healing

Kathryn LaFevers Evans, Three Eagles

When patients come to a practitioner for help, their problem can often be summed up as physical, mental, or spiritual fragmentation. They are in some sense broken open, not whole. The practitioners' job, in a nutshell, is to renew their patients' sense of wholeness, their experience of inner and outer unity. Medicine Wheel is, therefore, not only a practical tool with which to mend a patient's mental health, but also a transformative practice with which to re-weave a patient's soul, or the whole person.

Minimum Education Requirements to Practice Medicine Wheel

Health practitioners trained in any field of medicine that touches upon mental health are qualified to practice Medicine Wheel with their patients. Here I use the term *Medicine Wheel* in its broadest sense—to denote any ritual, mental, or spiritual practice that revolves around (pun intended) circles or spheres. Medicine Wheel is a creative practice, applicable in psychotherapy that encompasses imaginal cosmologies spanning the history of humankind. This breadth of practice is due to the fact that the idea or image of circle-sphere-wheel is a universal archetype for unity or wholeness—it is, in one word, holistic. The Lakota say, "I am standing at the Earth's center. In a sacred manner I see the tribe gathered around me. Behold me. I AM" (Padilla, 1995, p. 12). Indigenous shamans were the first practitioners of Medicine Wheel, but one need not be a shaman to utilize its basic principles and processes.

Among mainstream psychologies taught today, I have found transpersonal psychology, humanistic psychology, archetypal depth and Jungian psychology, and spiritually-oriented psychology particularly open to and nurturing of Medicine Wheel practices. Transpersonal psychology encompasses them all, in the terminological sense that *trans* embodies omni-directionality beyond the *personal* human, and extends throughout the cosmos. Humans, then, "stand in" as the hub or center of their personal Medicine Wheel, whose spokes emanate equally in all directions to the cosmic sphere that surrounds them. In this way, the realm of psychology can be envisioned as the holistic web of life itself, woven by the archetypal patient-practitioners, who are personified according to their own mythic traditions. Grandmother Spider Woman, for instance, fits the mythic narrative of a female Native American patient-practitioner. In this shamanic practice, it is important to note that the patients also stand in as their own psychologist—practitioners, where psychotherapy and life are interwoven in the same web—the patient-practitioners' Medicine Wheel that is in continual transformation or rebirth. Thus, this essay fully empowers patients to co-create their own best-practices manual out of the physical, mental, and spiritual materials available to them in life—nature as experienced through all of their faculties in real time. It is that simple.

Credentials or Licenses Required to Practice Medicine Wheel

There are no licensing requirements to practice Medicine Wheel. However, the following universities and institutes teach disciplines that circumnavigate the practice of Medicine Wheel: transpersonal psychology at Sofia University in Palo Alto, California; existential, humanistic, and transpersonal psychology at Saybrook University in Pasadena, California; existential-humanistic psychotherapy at The Chicago School of Professional Psychology; archetypal depth and Jungian psychology at Pacifica Graduate Institute near Santa Barbara, California; and spiritually-oriented psychology at the California Institute of Integral Studies in San Francisco. While no credentials or licenses are required to practice Medicine Wheel on ourselves or with patients, it may be more effective when the patient-practitioner has been trained in some form of transcendent therapy; some form of visual therapy; and some form of movement therapy. Transcendence, vision, and motion correspond to our three realms of practice: spiritual, mental, and physical. Again, the prefix *trans* indicates an all-pervading, all-encompassing practice, where its name embodies its action of transcendence through all three of the spiritual, mental, and physical realms. In this constellation, *vision* is the image of an idea or mental construct, and *motion* is the ritual acting out of image and idea in the physical world. Transcendence is the fundamental transformative act, inclusive and accessible.

Examples of transcendent therapy are meditation techniques, prayer, and hypnosis; examples of visual therapy are guided visualization techniques, affirmations, and mandala-drawing therapies; examples of movement therapy are dance, yoga, and simply walking. The movement therapies are all centered around (pun intended) balance—the hub or still center within the human body, riveted to the still center of the outer world or cosmic sphere. Thus, balance engenders a holistic sense of "my place in space" in three dimensions—the personal Medicine Wheel.

Yet in practicing the physical, ritual Medicine Wheel, the ability of patient-practitioners to balance in the still center is the specific result, not the prerequisite. Whether the patient-practitioners are physically, mentally, or spiritually broken open, they can still practice Medicine Wheel perfectly. Ritual movements and objects, mental exercises, and transcendent techniques are virtually arbitrary. Trust that the right healing tool will exist, will come. Be available—it is that simple; include yourself in the web of life. We come into balance with nature through practicing our own nature, which some have described simply as *love*. Choosing from among the healing tools of my own received traditions, here is an exemplary quote from *Pantacle* by an 18th-century Rosicrucian practitioner and founder of The Martinist Order, de Saint-Martin (2013). His words describe a chain of Medicine Wheels linked together:

> Thus, from the first divine contract and the pure region where truth abides, a continuous chain of mercies and light extends to humanity, through every epoch, and will be prolonged to the end of time, until it returns to the abode from which it descends, taking with it all the peaceful souls it shall have collected in its course; that we may know that it was Love which opened, directed, and closed the circle of all things [p. 25].

While humans express spiritual experiences according to the religious traditions with which they are familiar, that is not a limitation, but rather a spherical container that transcends its own boundaries because of the universal nature of spiritual experiences. Sharing a received teaching, the Indian avatar Sathya Sai Baba offered: "There is only one religion—the religion of love" (Baba, personal communication, June 1985). "Sai Baba" means "Mother Father," so this adornment was received from an ancestor. Practicing Medicine Wheel brings healing from one's ancestors and animal guides through surrender to love. Nature spirituality, an expression of love, is perhaps the most universal form of religion; and nature, or the web of life, as the object of scientific disciplines like psychology, is thus the medium through which the patient-practitioner transcends from science to spirituality and vice versa. This inborn, transcendent capacity is that of nature's healer, the shaman. Nature spirituality is inborn in humans. We are shaman.

Additional Training Medicine Wheel Practitioners Seek

Some Medicine Wheel practitioners will be fortunate to find indigenous practitioners, or shamans, with whom they can study in person. Other practitioners will find shamanic courses of various quality and authenticity offered online, virtually. Reputable shamanic programs that offer in-person and online components, and that are readily accessible online include: The Foundation for Shamanic Studies; the Society for Shamanic Practice; the Four Winds Foundation; and Dance of the Deer Foundation.

Medicine Wheel practice is most effective when transmitted person-to-person, or when received by the visionary shaman in the dreamtime (Hummingbird, personal communication, November 1989). Additional training in practicing Medicine Wheel is shaman-specific, according to such factors as geographical location, cultural milieu or cultural choice, and genetic lineage. In terms of physical, mental, and spiritual realms, shamans living in the mountains may be more inclined to use a mountain as their place for physical ritual, with items from mountains as the objects in their ritual; or they may use a mountain as viewed from above as the subject of visualizations and mandala drawings, and transcend more effortlessly while meditating on a mountain, as opposed to on a riverbank or an ocean shoreline.

Repetition of the names of god-goddess is one form of meditation. An example of invoking a Native American god, Yahowah, is provided in a later section. Depending on the shamans' genetic lineage, they may prefer to invoke different gods, such as Shiva or Buddha. Names of gods used as mantras can be researched online, where you will find invocations such as Om Namah Shivaya and Om Mani Padme Hum. If the shaman is of multicultural lineage, it may be beneficial to invoke a variety of gods in turn, appropriate to the required healing.

Mandala-drawing therapies transfer the circle-sphere-wheel idea of wholeness, or unity, from inside the shaman's mind to the outside world in two dimensions. This mental transcendence from inner to outer world comes to fruition as the shaman's Medicine Wheel rug—a two-dimensional pattern created on the ground, or floor of the therapy room—in the center of which the shaman balances. If the shamans' geographical location is mountainous, they may create a stepped pattern out of square, multi-colored fabric layers to stand on. If they live in the desert, they may prefer a neutral solid-colored fabric. When the shaman trusts that the desired healing is available through their own life experiences, practicing Medicine Wheel becomes a delight. They may receive news of an appropriate Medicine Wheel rug coming their way as a gift, or by simply purchasing it for themselves. All of these are examples of receiving shamanic adornments (Irwin, 1994).

The shamans' cultural milieu or cultural choice may determine what movement therapies are available to them, and what ritual movements and items are appropriate for them to use. For instance, a healer living in San Francisco who self-identifies as Pagan may seek additional training in Wiccan ritual. Because Wiccan ritual objects are readily accessible in specialty stores, the shaman can choose whether to purchase or make a wooden magical wand—a traditional Wiccan tool for casting a magic circle. Shamans will bring their ritual wands to the therapy session, for the purpose of casting a healing circle around themselves, tailored to their current psychological imbalance. Holistic healing practitioners will act as spirit guide on the shamans' journey of transformation, providing a safe environment for their shamanic vision quest together. Specifics of the Wiccan Medicine Wheel may be similar to or coincide with specifics of the Native American Medicine Wheel, or they may not. Pagans might use candles of prescribed colors for each of the four cardinal directions, set up on the floor at four equidistant points on the circle surrounding the practitioner. In Wicca, the direction candles may be brown at North, blue at West, red at South, and yellow at East. One configuration of Native American Medicine Wheel practice uses colored-in quadrants, with black between North and West, red between West and South, yellow between South and East, and white between East and North. Other shamans situate the cardinal directions of their Medicine Wheel in the mid-points of each of the colored quadrants. Wiccans or shamans sometimes just use an inner visualization, or a small altar-sized version, of the Medicine Wheel. Here we are working towards a three-dimensional practice of Medicine Wheel, for therapy room, home, or outdoors.

The Medicine Wheel rug can be circular, square, or rectangular—centered in an imaginal circle-sphere-wheel. Alternatively, the Medicine Wheel can be demarcated using small stones positioned in a circle around a larger shaman stone. Shamans might also place smaller stones demarcating the spokes of the Medicine Wheel, emanating to the outer circumference stones. As in all Medicine Wheels that are laid out on the mountain, ground, or floor for practice, the shaman stands in the center, with the shaman stone at their feet. As the shaman's personal Medicine Wheel develops, it will become more and more three-dimensional with each adornment received. Whether the shamans construct their Medicine Wheels out of physical stones in a permanent outdoor circle on the ground, or out of an imaginal indoor circle demarcated by the corners of a rug at Earth's cardinal directions, they are equally effective due to the archetypal nature of Medicine Wheels. All of nature is the shaman's sphere.

Evidence-Based Research on Effectiveness of Medicine Wheel

The subtitle of the *Journal of Indigenous Research* (JIR), *Full Circle; Returning Native Research to the People,* is itself a testament to the effectiveness of Native practices in healing Native communities. In *JIR*'s first Issue, T. Thomason (2011) offers a succinct article entitled, "Best Practices in Counseling Native Americans." Therein, he addresses the question, "Are Native American counselors more effective with Native clients than non–Native counselors, or is there no difference?" (Thomason, 2011). His research found that half (50 percent) of respondents said that Native American counselors are more effective than non–Natives; 20 percent said there is no difference; 18 percent said it depends on the cultural competence of the counselor; and 12 percent said it depends on how traditional the client is. Another of his research questions asks, "How important is it to incorporate spirituality into counseling with Native American clients?" (Thomason, 2011). A majority (55 percent) of respondents said that it is very important; 41 percent said it depends on whether spirituality is important to the client; and only 4 percent said it is not important (Thomason, 2011).

The National Indian Health Board (NIHB, n.d.), has a Behavioral Health webpage that describes Native prevention and treatment practices. The section entitled, "Evidence-based Practices, Practiced-based Evidence, and Best, Promising, and Common Practices that may be of interest to MSPI projects or others working to address methamphetamine use or suicide," hosts an article on the "Red Road Approach to Wellness and Healing" (NIHB, n.d.). That approach integrates Native American healing methodologies, philosophy, and values with contemporary methods of chemical awareness, education, and chemical addiction therapy. The article finds that Medicine Wheel practice has grown to be a globally diversified approach to recovery, health, and healing. It also recommends the website, http://www.crcaih.org/medicine-wheel-inc.html. "Red Road" discusses the company, Medicine Wheel Inc., owned by Thin Elk, who has worked with over 400 tribes in North America. The Red Road Approach, a system of practice originated by Thin Elk, has been presented worldwide by a diverse sampling of indigenous cultures, organizations, and government entities (NIHB, n.d.).

Another article in the National Indian Health Board's (NIHB, 2014) "Evidence-based" section comes under the subsection, "Common Practices for Methamphetamine and Suicide Prevention Programming." The article, "Methamphetamine and Suicide Prevention Initiative (MSPI): Tribal partners' common and shared practices brief," describes how the initiative integrates and teaches cultural activities within more structured prevention programming. (NIHB, 2014). The research initiative found that successful components include dancing, drumming, traditional camps, and ceremonial practices. Significantly, these cultural activities were the most valued by MSPI participants, and were the activities that MSPI staff most enjoyed conducting (NIHB, 2014).

The Great Lakes Inter-Tribal Council (GLITC, n.d.) hosts an online report, "Inter-Tribal Prevention Strategic Plan Dissemination Materials." These materials include an overview of the Strategic Prevention Enhancement (SPE), which lays out a framework in which behavioral health, alcohol, tobacco, other drug abuse including prescription drugs, and suicide can be addressed within the cultural context of the tribes. The GLITC's (n.d.) evidence-based prevention is culturally-based, and culturally responsive. The SPE plan is based on evidence, from nationally-based prevention science, that "Culture is

Prevention" (GLITC, n.d.). Three essential aspects of the programs are: credible program practitioners; culturally-based prevention activities that include participation in traditional ceremonies, rituals, sharing stories, oral instruction, and modeling; and materials that include culturally relevant setting, dress, ornamentation, symbols, graphics, and sensory substances. The GLITC (n.d.) finds specifically that a process of change and growth comes about when using the Medicine Wheel, which is currently recognized as an inter-tribal symbol across Indian Country. Though different tribes draw, interpret, and practice the Medicine Wheel in different ways, it is a shared approach to life and the world. The GLITC (n.d.) further reports that it functions as a holistic model for many tribes. Stemming from the Native belief that all things in life and on Earth must be in balance in order to grow in a healthy way, each quadrant of the Medicine Wheel, while unique, is equal to the other quadrants. Natives ascribe unique developmental aspects to each direction of the Medicine Wheel, so that following the circle will allow one to grow in an effective and culturally responsive way (GLITC, n.d.).

Medicine Wheel Is Effective for Psychiatric Disorders

Native American mental health programs cover the full range of psychological problems and psychiatric disorders. Medicine Wheel has been shown to be effective within the microcosm of Native American mental health programs. Whether you are a Native American patient-practitioner, or a counselor from another indigenous genetic lineage, practicing Medicine Wheel will be beneficial. Because it is archetypal, it can be an integral part of treatment for any disorder, ranging from mild depression, to addiction, to schizophrenia. It is a creative, transformative practice that can be utilized to augment any other mental health practice over a limited, or an indefinite, period of time. While Medicine Wheel is grounded in the person's specific "my place in space," it extends beyond—transcends—the boundaries of physical, mental, and spiritual existence. Because Medicine Wheel is a timeless archetypal practice, it opens depth upon depth of the shaman's soul, and is therefore ideally taken on as a lifetime practice for self-transformation.

There is a well-known saying in holistic healing traditions: "When the student is ready, the master appears" (Maharishi Mahesh Yogi, personal communication, 1977–1978). But we don't acknowledge how often that master appears in the form of an image (Hillman, 1981/2004). Shamanic images are often regarded as a negative symptom of mental illness, when perhaps we should first honor them as master shamans themselves. I was drawn into the depths of my own soul, through Medicine Wheel shamans received over the decade just prior to teaching a course on Jung's *Red Book* (2009) at Pacifica Graduate Institute. In 2002, as I began work on a master's degree, I began to receive the Medicine Wheel shamans, first, in the form of a circle with simply a dot in the center—an archetypal Sun God image—the dot representing the firm anchor I was to need for the arduous work ahead. Second, as I struggled to make sense of Literary Theory, two dots appeared, marking opposite positions on the circumference of the circle, connected by a line across the circle. That depicted the technique into which I was being initiated: the Renaissance natural magician's art of opposites. Through reading the Inquisitional tortures of my genetic past, the European aspect of my soul was reborn.

After some time, with two more dots and a line intersecting the circle at right angles to the previous line—forming the cross and quadrants of the traditional Medicine

Wheel—I braved the vision quest of Critical Race Theory, reading crucifying novels by Native American authors who had suffered greatly. Then a new circle, with the rebirth of my Native American soul—with two equilateral triangles inscribed therein to form a hexagram—completed the circle of reintegration between my European Sun God soul and Native American Moon Goddess soul. I wrestled with writing my thesis on Renaissance natural magic for another year, graduating with a master's degree in Literature and Writing Studies in 2006.

Later, I needed a way to bring what had been a four-year spiritual and mental vision quest into the physical realm: my disembodied soul needed feet. I received the adornment of a Navajo rug on which to stand, woven in the "storm" design. By and by, this Medicine Wheel rug taught me about the four houses of the wind in the cardinal directions, and the lightning bolts that connected them to the center *hogan* or home. Still out of balance, I needed a shaman stone to anchor my feet to the center of Earth. So, after some time, I received a large Shiva Lingam stone to be my *hogan's* shaman stone. That completed a three-dimensional embodiment of the first Medicine Wheel circle I had drawn, with the simple dot in the middle: I was in balance on the Earth, as the Great Mother orbited the Sun.

In time, I received my Native name, Three Eagles, and her ritual invocation, while walking footstep-by-footstep up a Sierra mountain trail. A year later, I needed a ritual garment to embody that Sun God spirit guide of the East. After some time, I received the shamanic adornment of a buckskin coat with long fringe along the arms, delightfully similar to the ritual buckskin coat my Uncle Henry wore in a portrait painted by my grandmother. With that long fringe along my outstretched arms, it was clear that the ancestors had given Three Eagles her wings. After Golden Eagle, other animal guides began to come as shamanic adornments: Two-Horned Bison of the North, Harbor Seal of the West, Lynx Bobcat of the South. The next year I received a Lakota Sioux war club from a Native whom I met in the Sierras. I would come to surrender that to peace, to love, in the *hogan*. The next year brought an Apache storyteller's rattle, from another Native at a powwow, which I would use to invoke my animal guides of the four directions. And later, I received a Chickasaw shell gorget [pendant] Medicine Wheel during a visit with my own tribe—a personal adornment from Te Ata's grandson, H. Thompson.

In the Sierras, I climbed the great boulder mountain we called Indian Rock, where I grounded that shaman stone in the sphere of my heart, with Sky above and Earth below. The cosmic Medicine Wheel ritual was complete enough in 2010 for me to begin giving guest lectures at Pacifica. Then in 2012, after a 10-year Medicine Wheel vision quest, I began to teach my course on Carl Jung's *Red Book* (2009) at Pacifica, and to teach Medicine-Wheel-Vision-Quest™ courses at Ojai venues, in my home, and online. So you see that, as our masters, Medicine Wheel shamans are also patient. Our entire life is a vision quest. We are shaman. The Medicine Wheels come for us.

Sample Session in a Clinical Setting; Excerpts from Medicine-Wheel-Vision-Quest™ Techniques, Printed with Permission ©IAWHE (n.d.)

Directions from the practitioner to the patient are in quotation marks. Three Eagles' directions to the practitioner are not. K.L. Evans, Three Eagles, drew the figures in Coso petroglyph style.

"Together we'll practice Three Eagles' Medicine-Wheel-Vision-Quest™. Later, as you begin to create your own personal Medicine Wheel at home, we'll practice that together here also. Sit comfortably on a chair or floor cushion, at the foot of our Medicine Wheel rug, facing me. I'll face East, practicing Medicine-Wheel-Vision-Quest™ rituals and techniques as your shamanic spirit guide. Towards the end, I'll indicate when you're to perform the ritual movements and invocations with me. As you progress through our transformational sessions, we'll perform Medicine-Wheel-Vision-Quest™ together."

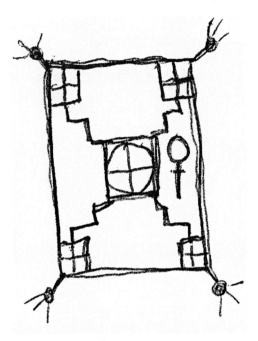

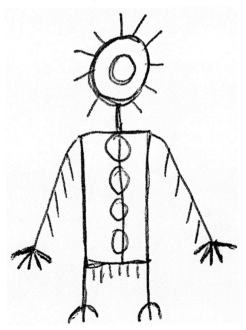

Medicine-Wheel-Vision-Quest™ Music

Meditation stills the mind in the soul.

"With eyes closed, meditate in silence to the transcendent music of IAWHE 3 (2015), from their CD *Medicine Wheel Vision Quest*" (available through www.iawhe.bandcamp.com).

Turn on the CD and play track 4, "Yahowah Chant."

Turn off the CD.

Medicine-Wheel-Vision-Quest™ Invocations, Visualizations and Shamanic Adornments

Invocation centers the body on Earth circling the Sun.

Medicine Wheel of the four seasons.

Stand at the foot of the central shaman stone, arms at your sides, palms open towards the shaman stone and the East.

Receive inner balance through the outer world.

Medicine Wheel of the seven directions.

Continue that ritual stance, with palms open towards shaman stone and the East.

Thunderbird Invocation

"I stand on the Stone
in the navel of the storm.
The lightening rod binds Earth to Sky."

Slowly raise your Thunderbird arms out to the sides, palms up, as you recite.

Top: Medicine Wheel storm rug, with shaman stone and storyteller's rattle. *Bottom:* "Summer … Fall … Winter … Spring…" *Following pages:* Figures for the Medicine-Wheel-Vision-Quest™ ritual (drawings by the author in Coso petroglyph style).

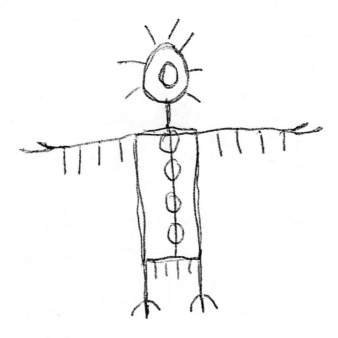

"Before me is the East
behind me is the West
on my left hand is the North"

Turn just the right palm down.

"On my right hand is the South."

Bend the right elbow, palm vertical, facing forwards.

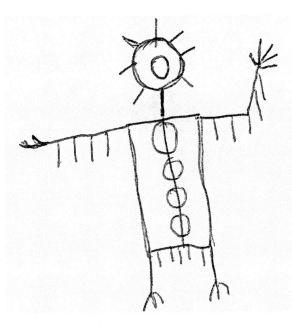

"Above me is the womb of Sky"

Lower the left arm, palm facing forwards.

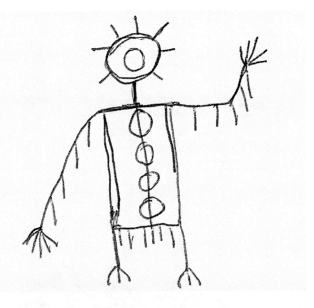

"Below me is the navel of Earth.
Love is the lightning bolt
calling ancestors and animal guides."

Medicine-Wheel-Vision-Quest™ Music

"Next, sit still in a relaxed meditation position, on a chair or floor cushion. With eyes closed, we'll continue vocalizing the IAWHE Embodied Invocation to music, while visualizing the descending and ascending Medicine Wheels."

Turn on the CD *Medicine Wheel Vision Quest* by IAWHE 3 (2015), and play track 3, "IAWHE Mantra" (available through www.iawhe.bandcamp.com). Proceed with vocalized meditation.

Turn off the CD.

"Now, drawing the attention inwards, continue this practice of IAWHE Embodied Invocation silently, enlivening the Medicine Wheel with your soul's gaze. Envision your body within a translucent sphere, as you repeat the invocation silently. And when you feel centered in your Medicine Wheel sphere, slowly open the eyes, balancing the soul's inner vision with the body's outward vision. For meditations with eyes open, you can repeat the IAWHE Embodied Invocation aloud or silently, as you go about your day. IAWHE can be invoked while sitting, standing, or walking."

Medicine-Wheel-Vision-Quest™ Practice, Assignments and Assessments

Ours is a transformative rebirth, wherein the shamanic practitioners' own souls constellate gods-goddesses, ancestors, and animal guides within their personal Medicine Wheel.

Week 1: Balance the shamans' footsteps on the Earth Medicine Wheel

"Please stand with eyes open, to practice the 'IAWHE EMBODIED INVOCATION' as a walking meditation. Follow me as we circumnavigate our Medicine Wheel, invoking IAWHE aloud as we perform the arm motions." … proceed…

"Next, we'll circumnavigate our Medicine Wheel, invoking IAWHE aloud, but without the arm motions." … proceed…

"Last, we'll circumnavigate our Medicine Wheel, invoking IAWHE silently within the soul, embodying IAWHE with our footsteps on Earth Medicine Wheel." … proceed…

Assignment

Always ask the shamanic practitioner to write down the assignment in their journals.

"In going about your daily life this week, invoke IAWHE whenever the practice comes to mind: aloud or silently; sitting, standing, or walking."

Assessment

The following week, after you have performed all the Medicine-Wheel-Vision-Quest™ ritual invocations for your patients, ask the shamanic practitioners to:

"Please share the results of your vision quest this week."

"Describe the kinds of balance your soul received during your vision quest this week."

"What physical, mental, and spiritual qualities or aspects came into balance through everyday Earthly life?"

In this way, grounding their bodies in Earth shaman stone, the shamanic practitioners deepen their trust that life will provide the required healings naturally. After you have discussed the shamanic practitioners' feelings of self-confidence and balance, ask them if they have any further self-reflective assessments. The shamanic practitioners invariably learn both good and bad things about themselves each week, so remind them that opposite footsteps are life's way of maintaining balance.

Continue *Weeks 2–4* sessions from Medicine-Wheel-Vision-Quest™ Techniques (available at https://www.threeeagles.net/medicine-wheel-techniques/).

WEEK 5: EMBODY NATURE'S FOUR ELEMENTS
AS THE SHAMAN STONE

"Please stand, in preparation for practicing a new transcendent ritual of the four directions. This time, as we call out the four directions in turn, we invoke their respective elements: North—Earth…. West—Water…. South—Air…. East—Fire. All the while we are standing, centered as the human shaman stone, hub of our personal Medicine Wheel. Let's perform 'INVOCATION OF THE ELEMENTS' together." … proceed…

ASSIGNMENT

Always ask the shamanic practitioner to write down the assignment in their journals.

"Practice 'INVOCATION OF THE ELEMENTS' daily. In the dreamtime, gather the four elements from Earth's distant directions, and ground them inside your human shaman stone, bringing them to life as adornments, to share with others as healing powers."

ASSESSMENT

The following week, after you have performed all the Medicine-Wheel-Vision-Quest™ ritual invocations for your patients, ask the shamanic practitioners to:

"Please share the results of your vision quest this week."

"Describe how you felt as human shaman stone."

"After gathering the four elements from the four directions, and bringing those shamanic powers down into life, in what ways did you share the adornments?"

In this way, we include ourselves in the circle of life. We are shamanic practitioners. The Medicine Wheels come for us (©IAWHE, n.d.).

REFERENCES

Great Lakes Inter-Tribal Council (GLITC). (n.d.). *Intertribal prevention strategic plan: Dissemination materials.* Retrieved from http://www.glitc.org/forms/epi/SPE%20Dissemination%20Materials%20%207-30-12.pdf

Hillman, J. (1981/2004). *Archetypal psychology.* In *James Hillman Uniform Edition* (Vol. I). Putnam, CT: Spring Publications.

IAWHE. (n.d.). Medicine-wheel-vision-quest™ techniques. In *Three Eagles Medicine-Wheel-Vision-Quest™*. Retrieved from https://www.threeeagles.net/medicine-wheel-techniques/

IAWHE 3. (2015). C. M. Evans (Producer). Yahowah chant & IAWHE mantra. On *Medicine wheel vision quest* [CD]. Ojai, CA: IAWHE.

Irwin, L. (1994). *The dream seekers: Native American visionary traditions of the Great Plains.* Norman, OK: University of Oklahoma Press.

Jung, C. G. (2009). *The red book: Liber Novus.* (S. Shamdasani, Ed.). New York, NY: W.W. Norton.

National Indian Health Board (NIHB). (n.d.). *Practice-based evidence and promising practices for suicide and substance abuse, specifically for American Indians/Alaska Natives: Red road approach to wellness and healing.* Retrieved from http://www.nihb.org/behavioral_health/prevention_treatment_practices_mspi.php

National Indian Health Board (NIHB). (2014). *Methamphetamine and Suicide Prevention Initiative (MSPI): Tribal partners common and shared practices brief.* Retrieved from http://www.nihb.org/docs/04292014/mspi_common_practices_brief_2014.pdf

Padilla, S. (1995). *Chants and prayers: A Native American circle of beauty.* Summertown, TN: The Book Publishing Company.

Saint-Martin, L.C. de (2013). It was love. *Pantacle.* San José, CA: Grand Heptad of the Traditional Martinist Order.

Thomason, T. (2011). Best practices in counseling Native Americans. *Journal of Indigenous Research: Full Circle; Returning Native Research to the People.* 1(1), article 3.

About the Contributors

Nitin **Anand** is an assistant professor in the department of clinical psychology at the National Institute of Mental Health and Neuro-Sciences (NIMHANS), Bangalore, India, where he attained his doctoral degree and clinical training. He has extensive experience in conducting psychological assessments and in providing counseling and psychotherapy for anxiety disorders, obsessive-compulsive disorders, and personality disorders. In addition to psychotherapy, his research interests include development of psychological assessments and mindfulness-based community interventions.

Priya Kayastha **Anand** is a consultant clinical psychologist at a private mental health setting in Bangalore, India. She attained her clinical training (MPhil) and doctoral degree (Ph.D.) from NIMHANS, Bangalore. She works in a private mental health clinic providing cognitive-behavioral and mindfulness-based interventions for adolescents and adults suffering from anxiety disorders, depression, obsessive-compulsive disorders, personality disorders, and relationship difficulties. She provides psychological interventions for school problems, parenting issues, learning disabilities, personality enhancement, and interpersonal difficulties in children and adolescents.

Nick **Atlas** is an author, artist, and transformative educator exploring the intersection of waking, sleeping, dreaming and being. The director of Evolutionary Education® and author of *The Light Travelers*, which details his own decade-long mystical journey, he facilitates a variety of personal and professional development courses both internationally and online. He serves as an adjunct professor of transpersonal psychology at Atlantic University and conducts pioneering research on lucid dreaming. For more info, visit evolutionaryeducation.org.

Christopher N. **Cross** is an internationally trained scientist and engineer with a range of expertise in the STEM fields as well as policy and non-profit development. He served as the program manager for the Grand Canyon National Park historic diversity research in coordination with a Healthy Parks Healthy People program grant.

Debbie Joffe **Ellis** is a licensed psychologist (Australia), a licensed mental health counselor (New York), and an adjunct professor at Columbia University, New York City. For many years she worked with her late husband, the pioneer of modern cognitive therapies, Dr. Albert Ellis, giving public presentations and professional trainings in Rational Emotive Behavior Therapy (REBT), as well as collaborating with him on writing and research projects until his death in 2007.

Renée **Emunah** is the founder/director of the drama therapy program at the California Institute of Integral Studies, author of *Acting for Real*, and coeditor of *Current Approaches in Drama Therapy* and *The Self in Performance*. She is an international trainer and recipient of the Schattner Distinguished Award for Outstanding Contribution to the Field of Drama Therapy.

Kathryn LaFevers **Evans**, Three Eagles holds a BA in comparative literature and research in consciousness, and an MA in literature and writing studies. She is retired adjunct faculty at Pacifica Graduate Institute, a member of APA Division 32, humanistic psychology; and of IAJS. A Chickasaw shaman and longtime practitioner of esoteric techniques and rituals, she teaches

Medicine-Wheel-Vision-Quest™ and natural magic through her company, IAWHE, www.three eagles.net.

Lillian **Eyre** is an associate professor and the chair of graduate music therapy at Immaculata University in Pennsylvania. She graduated from the University of Quebec then earned a Ph.D. in music therapy from Temple University. Her research interests include music therapy and narrative practices. She has worked in psychiatric clinics and in community mental health, and has a private practice specializing in adults with trauma. She was an editor and contributing author to *Guidelines to Music Therapy Practice in Mental Health* (2013).

Cheryl L. **Fracasso**, Ph.D., LMHC, is a licensed mental health counselor and certified clinical trauma intervention specialist. She served as a psychologist with the state of Washington for over five years, in addition to owning ShangriLa Wellness Center, a holistic healthcare center that focuses on a holistic approach to treating trauma. She also served as a faculty member for over nine years at the University of Phoenix, and has written and published extensively in the fields of energy medicine, near-death experiences, and holistic approaches to healing.

Harris L. **Friedman**, Ph.D., is an associated distinguished consulting professor at the California Institute of Integral Studies, an associated professor at the Salomons Institute for Applied Psychology at Canterbury Christ Church University (UK), and a visiting scholar at Harvard University. He retired as a research professor of psychology at the University of Florida, and has over 200 professional publications. He is a fellow of both the Association for Psychological Science and the American Psychological Association, and practices both clinical and organizational psychology part-time.

Susan Turner **Gabrielle** works for the state of Washington as a career coach and university instructor. She completed her doctorate (Ph.D.) and Integrative Wellness Coaching (IWC) certification through Saybrook University and is a member of the International Coach Federation, where she earned her Associate Coach certification.

Jules P. **Harrell** is a professor of psychology at Howard University. He is author of the book *Manichean Psychology: Racism and the Minds of People of African Descent* and has published numerous journal articles related to psychophysiological processes. Forty students have completed doctoral studies under his direction.

Sue Ann **Herron** is the executive director of Expressive Arts for Healing and Social Change: A Person-Centered Approach (PCEAT). As Natalie Rogers's biographer, her goal is to chronicle and elevate Dr. Rogers's work through a scholarly biography and to promote Rogers's legacy and PCEAT teachings around the world.

Fatimah L.C. **Jackson** has conducted research on human-plant co-evolution, health disparities, and population substructure in peoples of African descent. She is the chairperson of the Natural Sciences Division, the interim chairperson of the Department of Biology, and a professor of Biology at Howard University, where she was awarded 2017 STEM Woman Researcher of the Year.

Amanpreet **Kaur** is a doctoral scholar at the Department of Clinical Psychology, National Institute of Mental Health & Neuro Sciences (NIMHANS), Bangalore, India. Her doctoral research work is focused on development and evaluation of mindfulness-integrated cognitive behavioral intervention programs for professional caregivers working at palliative care centers.

J. Ryan **Kennedy** is the founder and executive director of Noeticus Counseling Center and Training Institute in Denver, Colorado. He is a licensed addiction counselor, licensed marriage and family therapist, licensed professional counselor, and board-certified dance/movement therapist. His professional background includes extensive work with graduate and post-graduate education particularly in the areas of experiential learning, contemplative education, spiritual emergence, diversity and multiculturalism, social and restorative justice, creative process work, expressive arts therapies, and body-centered psychotherapy.

Stanley **Krippner**, Ph.D., former director of the Maimonides Medical Center Dream Research Laboratory, was a professor of psychology at Saybrook University for 47 years. He is a fellow in the American Psychological Association (APA) and the Association for Psychological Science. He has received the APA Award for Distinguished Contributions to the International Development of Psychology, and lifetime achievement awards from the International Association for the Study of Dreams, the International Network on Personal Meaning, the Society for Humanistic Psychology, and the Parapsychological Association.

Joseph **Madigan** received his master's degree in art therapy from Long Island University and his doctoral degree in psychology from Saybrook University. His dissertation research investigated how making art sustains recovery from addictive disorders. He is a licensed mental health counselor and board-certified registered art therapist.

Kanika A.M. **Magee** is an assistant dean in the Howard University School of Business. She is a member of the Management Department faculty, teaching a course in leadership and spirituality. She also works with interfaith programs through the university's Chapel and has convened international gatherings around spirituality and service.

Michael **Mayer** is a licensed psychologist, a certified master Tai Chi instructor, and a pioneer in the integration of Tai Chi/Qigong and psychotherapy. He presents his Bodymind Healing Psychotherapy trainings at conferences and workshops nationally and internationally and has authored 20 publications, including six books and journal articles on mind-body healing. A co-founding faculty member of John F. Kennedy University's transpersonal psychology program, he co-founded an integrative medical clinic, and is the director of the Bodymind Healing Center (www.body mindhealing.com).

David S.B. **Mitchell** is a member of the psychology faculty at the University of West Georgia; his interests include cognition, culture, and contemplation. He teaches a number of undergraduate and graduate-level courses including classes on human growth and development, social psychology, culture and psychology, and introduction to general psychology.

Sal **Núñez** is a licensed psychologist, tenured professor, and director of the Community Mental Health Certificate Program at City College of San Francisco, Health Education Department. He is the president of Crossing Edge Consulting, an organizational psychology firm. His interests lie in community mental health, indigenous medicine, and medicinal drumming as a therapeutic approach.

Gary **Raucher** is a professor in the drama therapy program at California Institute of Integral Studies, San Francisco. He is certified as a teacher of meditation and Authentic Reiki®, and his interests include exploring synergies between contemplative practices, energy healing, diversity/inclusion work, and experiential psychotherapies. His clinical work spans age groups and diverse populations.

Grant J. **Rich** is the senior editor of five books: *Massage Therapy* (2002), *Pathfinders in International Psychology* (2015), *Internationalizing the Teaching of Psychology* (2017), *Human Strengths and Resilience* (2018), and *Teaching Psychology Around the World* (2018). He served as an NCBTMB national board member (2018–2019) and serves on the Walden University faculty.

Doug **Ronning** is a drama therapist in the San Francisco Bay Area specializing in the treatment of anxiety and compulsive disorders. He is an adjunct lecturer at the California Institute of Integral Studies, and creator of the event series Monster Movie Salon (http://monstermoviesalon.com), which combines drama therapy with film and cultural studies.

Ilene A. **Serlin** is the founder and director of Union Street Health Associates in San Francisco, California. She is a licensed clinical psychologist and board-certified dance/movement therapist. She has taught at the University of California, Los Angeles; Saybrook; and Lesley University in the United States and abroad. She is on the editorial board of *Journal of Humanistic Psychology* and *American Journal of Dance/Movement Therapy* and is in private practice in San Francisco.

Mahendra Prakash **Sharma** is a professor and department head, Department of Clinical Psychology, NIMHANS, Bangalore. He has offered cognitive-behavioral interventions and mindfulness-based interventions for a wide variety of mental health conditions which include anxiety disorders, obsessive-compulsive disorders, depression, and somatoform and personality disorders. Most significantly, he has pioneered work in India on mindfulness meditation in individuals suffering with medical and mental health conditions.

Marina A. **Smirnova** is a native of Russia. She serves as a core psychology faculty and as the Consciousness, Spirituality, and Integrative Health Specialization Coordinator at Saybrook University (Department of Humanistic and Clinical Psychology). She is an approved consultant in clinical hypnosis (through the American Society of Clinical Hypnosis); a certified Holotropic Breathwork facilitator (through Grof Transpersonal Training, Inc.); and a transpersonal consultant, facilitator, and mentor.

Christopher **Sowton** is a naturopath and psychotherapist based in Toronto, where his private practice focuses on dreamwork. Since 2003, he has been training healthcare practitioners eager to integrate dreamwork into their practice. He is a member of the International Association for the Study of Dreams and is the author of *Dreamworking—How to Listen to the Inner Guidance of Your Dreams* (2017), and *The Dreamworking Manual—A Guide to Using Dreams in Health Care* (2013).

Peta **Stapleton** is a registered clinical and health psychologist and is an associate professor of psychology at Bond University (Queensland, Australia). Prior to her position at Bond University, she spent 14 years as an academic for Griffith University. She is a world leader and researcher in Emotional Freedom Techniques and has been awarded many honors for her work.

Rosemary **Sword** along with her husband, the late Richard Sword, developed Time Perspective Therapy to assist their clients in overcoming PTSD. She is coauthor of *The Time Cure* (2012), *The Time Cure Therapist Guidebook, Living & Loving Better* (2017), and *Time Perspective Therapy: Transforming Zimbardo's Temporal Theory into Clinical Practice, Time Perspective Theory* (2015). She is the developer of *Aetas: Mind Balancing Apps* (which creates apps for iOS-based devices on TPT).

Caifang **Zhu** is the founder and director of the Beijing Clear-Orientation Center for Counseling and Meditation, and the deputy secretary of the International Transpersonal Association. He is a seasoned scholar and practitioner of Chan/Zen meditation and Tai Chi. He holds an MA from Harvard University and a Ph.D. from the California Institute of Integral Studies.

Philip **Zimbardo** is a world-renowned scholar, educator, researcher, and media personality. A professor emeritus at Stanford University, he is best known for his landmark Stanford prison study. Among his more than 500 publications is the bestseller *The Lucifer Effect* as well as many psychology textbooks including *Psychology: Core Concepts*, 8th edition (2017) and *Psychology and Life*, 20th edition (2019). He is the founder and president of the Heroic Imagination Project (www.heroicimagination.org), a world-wide nonprofit organization.

Index